Cold War Berlin

Cold War Berlin

Confrontations, Cultures, and Identities

Edited by
Konrad H. Jarausch
Stefanie Eisenhuth
Scott H. Krause

BLOOMSBURY ACADEMIC
LONDON • NEW YORK • OXFORD • NEW DELHI • SYDNEY

BLOOMSBURY ACADEMIC
Bloomsbury Publishing Plc
50 Bedford Square, London WC1B 3DP, UK
1385 Broadway, New York, NY 10018, USA
29 Earlsfort Terrace, Dublin 2, Ireland

BLOOMSBURY, BLOOMSBURY ACADEMIC and the Diana logo
are trademarks of Bloomsbury Publishing Plc

First published in Great Britain 2021
This paperback edition published 2022

Cover design: Adriana Brioso
Cover image © Bettmann/Getty Images

A catalogue record for this book is available from the British Library.

A catalog record for this book is available from the Library of Congress.

ISBN: HB: 978-1-7883-1071-0
          PB: 978-0-7556-3923-6
          ePDF: 978-0-7556-0278-0
          eBook: 978-0-7556-0277-3

Typeset by Integra Software Services Pvt. Ltd.

To find out more about our authors and books visit www.bloomsbury.com
and sign up for our newsletters.

Contents

Figures

Introducing Cold War Berlin

Konrad H. Jarausch, Scott H. Krause and Stefanie Eisenhuth

Three decades after the fall of the Wall, Cold War Berlin remains an extraordinary magnet for tourists who are searching for tangible signs of the East–West conflict. Each year hordes of local, national, and international travelers come to look for traces of the infamous barrier that divided the city for twenty-eight years between 1961 and 1989. Since the anger and relief of Berlin's citizens have rapidly obliterated the ugly edifice, tourists have to go to the Wall Memorial at Bernauer Strasse in order to get a partial sense of what it might have been like. Hundreds of thousands of visitors annually crowd at Checkpoint Charlie to photograph students in Soviet and American uniforms at the control hut's little replica, reenacting the border-crossing point. In addition to the obligatory *Döner* and souvenir stands, they can choose between a painted panorama that visualizes the scene in the divided city, a commercial museum of flight instruments, and a black box that suggests the global reach of the Cold War.[1] Somewhat disappointed by the disappearance of the actual Wall and confused by its spotty memorialization, many tourists wonder what the East–West confrontation might really have all been about.

This book attempts to address the question of the peculiar character of divided Berlin during the years of the Cold War. Why Berlin? Because history literally took place there. Thomas Lindenberger has pointed out that the experience of the Cold War "varied greatly" depending on time and place: "There were periods and places in which the Cold War was 'lived' in an acute and existential manner, in contrast to others in which it was only present as something rather remote, in the background rather than the foreground. Cold War experience is not a homogeneous quality to be encountered in similar consistency in all places affected by the Cold War."[2] The conflict shaped the city of Berlin and the city with its different milieus in turn shaped the conflict. Berlin was not an exchangeable background against which politicians acted and wrote world history. The heterogeneous urban society pursued its own interests. These interests changed over the decades, sometimes they came into conflict with one another, and often they were linked to what was happening on the other side of the Wall. In Berlin, the Cold War was a daily experience and something that could not be ignored. On the one hand, global developments were bundled here as if into a burning glass. On the other hand, due to its status in the world, Berlin was a special case in many respects and can only be compared to Munich or Dresden to a limited extent. Nevertheless, we can examine Berlin as an example—among other things, it helps us to understand how different actors at the local level behaved in relation to the global conflict.

The following chapters of this book thus focus on three dimensions that connect the history of this embattled city with the overall East–West conflict: the first section considers the city to be a particularly contested place and addresses Berlin as a global focal point of the Cold War, since control of the former German capital had both practical and symbolic importance. The second section then intends to "normalize" the city. The contributions investigate how the local population experienced the geopolitical peculiarity of the city and dealt with it in everyday life. They explore not only the implications of division, but also the continuing entanglements and mutual perceptions that resulted from Berlin's unique status. The third section then asks how these experiences were relayed and how now they are still being told: what identities did the division create, what narratives did it produce, and how do they shape today's debates? Has the city managed to forge a common memory culture out of a divided past?

The choice of these topics represents a post-Cold War perspective that is no longer doing intellectual battle *within* the conflict but rather seeks to reflect *about* it. A new generation of scholarship looks at the two halves of the city without necessarily praising the Eastern "socialist metropolis" as the wave of the future or defending the Western "outpost of freedom" in a red communist sea.[3] The growing emotional distance makes it possible to analyze local consequences of the ideological hostility, continued entanglements that challenged the European division and contested legacies of the Eastern and Western parts of the city more dispassionately.

Integrating Divided Historiographies

Cold War Berlin enjoys a curious blend of prominence and neglect in the literature. Since the conflict's conclusion, fresh work has expanded our perspective on successive crises, efforts at coexistence, renewed confrontations, and final détente from Europe to the globe. Access to communist government, party, and Stasi documents has made it possible to understand the interconnections between anti-imperialist struggles and the dynamics of the nuclear arms race on different continents.[4] Although once a central object and symbol of the East–West conflict, Berlin is gradually being reduced to a cipher, "an essentially empty space in which by chance as it were, a Cold War battle took place."[5] Academic interest has shifted away from Europe.[6] This global perspective has marginalized the contribution of local actors to the development, persistence, and eventual erosion of the conflict. Moreover, it tends to ignore that they experienced it on a daily basis on the ground. This is surprising given how contemporaries were keenly aware of Berliners' agency. At the height of the conflict, the US High Commissioner of Germany (HICOG) advised the incoming Allied commander bluntly on their relevance: "Our position here rests squarely on the support of this population. If we should ever lose its confidence, our position would become untenable."[7] General Maxwell Taylor received orders for a cultural competition over the hearts and minds of locals.[8]

Cold War Berlin presented a confluence of the global and local from the start. The ruins that the Nazis left behind had barely stopped smoldering when Social Democrats and communists reignited their rivalry over the city's dominant working-class demographics. Urban histories have documented this confrontation in meticulous detail, but only hinted at its larger relevance.[9] The 1945/46 Soviet-backed KPD ploy to absorb the SPD into the Socialist Unity Party (SED) hardened Americans' attitude. US Military Governor Lucius D. Clay's political advisor fumed: "Don't we care whether the real democrats have a chance here or not? Why did we fight this war?"[10] The internecine warfare across the Left predated the development of global Cold War strategies in Washington and Moscow. But the local feud anticipated a Manichean outlook that would mark the policies of both superpowers.

The opening skirmish of the global conflict in Berlin's ruins highlights the potential of *integrating* perspectives. Bringing compartmentalized literatures on East and West, on politics and culture into conversation offers the chance to illustrate not only entanglements across the wall but also links between the global and local that this unique urban space spanned.[11] Distinct political narratives, social milieus, and subcultures vied for discursive power in the quadripartite city. Integrating those various perspectives of local and global, both in East and West, brings into view how Berlin actors not only endured the global conflict, but also sought to exploit the bipolar world order for individual aims.

This collection builds on a new sensitivity to the East–West conflict's transnational reach and cultural dimension. The term "Cold War cultures" refers to the "diverse experiences, mentalities, and practices connected to the forty-year standoff" and to the contrary interpretations of those experiences in East and West.[12] It also highlights the ideological competition that sought to undermine the enemy camp while shoring up support for its own followers through slogans such as the "free world" or "camp of peace." Moreover, this concept also suggests that the contest between capitalism and communism had an impact on people's lives in a variety of ways—their definition of "good" and "evil," their individual mental maps, consumer culture, religiosity, media productions, and much more. In addition, this new perspective implies the need to look at the mental traces of forms of representation and memorialization after the end of the East–West conflict.[13] Hence this volume aims to explore Berlin as a site of contestation, interaction, and memorialization. It understands the Cold War not just as a time period but as a manmade conflict that shaped people's perception and worldview and that can be analyzed as a process of "doing the Cold War."

Cold War Battleground

Berlin has become a focal point for research on Cold War cultures because it is considered an exemplary battleground of ideological confrontations. Three signature crises of the East–West conflict revolved around the control of the defeated Nazi capital—the Soviet blockade and Allied airlift of 1948/49, the Khrushchev ultimatum and building of the Wall in 1958/61, and communism's surprising collapse in 1989/91.[14] In contrast to cities such as Paris or Warsaw, both safely located on opposite sides of the Iron Curtain, four-power-controlled Berlin lay in the middle of one part of a divided country, i.e., the Soviet zone or GDR, while simultaneously containing Western-controlled territory. That made the competition for the allegiance of its citizens particularly intense, with both sides using their half as a showcase for the superiority of their socialist egalitarianism or consumer democracy. As a result of this symbolic importance, the repercussions of the global conflicts in Asia, Africa, and Latin America were intensely felt on a local level in the divided city. For instance, during the Vietnam War, the West Berlin city government took the part of the Americans and the South Vietnamese, whereas the East Berlin regime and Western youths endorsed the North Vietnamese "liberation struggle."[15] For lengthy stretches of time, Berlin served not only as a haven for spies but also as a popular stage for Cold War politicians, making it an accurate barometer of East–West relations in general. In the late 1960s, however, the divided city "moved out of the spotlight of global attention" and had to face "the problems most modern cities were facing" at the time: "the myth of Berlin and the reality of the city had begun to drift apart."[16] While West Berlin was grappling with negative headlines ranging from corruption to the waste of public funds, East Berlin was further developed into a socialist metropolis. This contemporary comparison, which seems to contradict today's dominant narrative of the glittering and prosperous West Berlin and the grey and ailing East Berlin, culminated on the occasion of the city's double anniversary in 1987. The magazine *Der Spiegel* complained about the celebrations being "an absurd show-fight of systems" that West Berlin could probably lose due to endless discussions over the program, further bribery scandals, and a still unfinished International Building Exhibition. The author's cynical conclusion: Only the preference for "pomposity" would still connect the two halves as it was cultivated on both sides of the wall.[17]

The first set of chapters probes Cold War Berlin as a political and cultural battleground between East and West. Since postwar reconstruction was an effort to reject the poisonous Nazi legacy, the book begins with a presentation of the transformation of the city in the Third Reich. Christoph Kreutzmüller explores the staging of Berlin as the NS capital that sought to press a diverse metropolis into a racist mold, only to be reduced to rubble through bombing of its arms production and street fighting in the final battles of World War Two.[18] Carrying the story forward into the later 1940s, David Barclay looks at Berlin "as symbol and prize for the global conflict" among the four occupation powers. Competition over the defeated capital of the Third Reich triggered the Berlin blockade, the airlift, and the contested choice of the East Berliners for the Soviet model and of the West Berliners for the American Way. Since it implied control over Central Europe, Berlin became the key focal point of the Cold War in the heart of Europe, returning a degree of agency to the inhabitants of the city who were now called on to choose sides.[19]

After the GDR regime sought to make this choice for the local population by constructing the Berlin Wall in 1961, Gerhard Sälter analyzes how the East German population adapted to the existence of the barrier that constricted its everyday choices. By creating a special security zone behind the Wall, the SED restricted access to the territory behind it with intensive surveillance in order to reduce efforts at flight. But, ironically, this created a "certain obduracy" in a populace that resented being cooped up.[20] With an original combination of political leaders and rock stars, Andreas Etges examines the visits of prominent personalities who sought to reaffirm "Soviet Berlin" or "American Berlin" during the decades marked by the Wall. While the Kennedy visit in 1963 was an attempt to demonstrate continuing US commitment, Khrushchev's surprise stop a few days later was an effort to counterbalance the popular outpouring for JFK. Due to his "freedom message," it was more difficult to instrumentalize Martin Luther King during his visit to both halves of the city, since he criticized both US racism and Soviet repression. Concerts by David Bowie and Bruce Springsteen in West and East Berlin, respectively, appealed to a youthful public tired of the East–West confrontation by the end of the 1980s.[21] These chapters therefore show the (pop) cultural dimension of the power-political struggle, with ever more Berliners hoping to break out of the bipolar logic of the Cold War.

Local Entanglements

The study of a single divided city also makes the contradictory impulses of demarcation from and continued entanglement with the other half of the city more transparent. On the one hand, a closer look at the border regime reveals the extent of the division that cut across the cityscape, separating even different sides of a single street, ripping apart entire neighborhoods, and cutting "Westberlin" off from its hinterland.[22] The inner and outer city border not only divided families, but also constituted different worlds of everyday experience, the extent of which only became apparent after reunification. On the other hand, the city retained considerable dimensions of continued cross-Wall connections.[23] Borderlines "separate distinct polities spatially" but at the same time they also define "border zones" where "the same polities are closest to each other." Within these border zones interactions happen on a daily basis and may eventually "undermine or at least counterbalance the state of separateness itself."[24] In Berlin, cross-border encounters were a regular experience. West German school classes visited East Berlin, East German retirees visited their relatives in West Berlin, diplomats and members of the Allied forces could criss-cross the border almost unchecked. Since the 1970s, cross-border contacts in Berlin increased steadily. Hundreds of thousands of people visited the other side of their city each year. Karl Schlögel thus speaks of a specific generational experience "that was: border crossing and border control, gateway and rite de passage, a specific smell of coal dust and disinfectants, utmost concentration and fear upon entering a corridor whose end could hardly be reached without inner tension, a rendezvous of everyday life with the world of great politics and world history." According to Schlögel, the border checkpoints were "machine(s) of consciousness and identity," because here the border between over here and over there, between us and them, was "rehearsed and internalized"—despite or maybe even because of the cross-wall encounters they enabled.[25]

One result of this unusual historic situation was the parallel development of countercultures in Kreuzberg and Prenzlauer Berg. Young people sought to escape the polarizing pressures of the Cold War by creating public counterspheres that would allow them to criticize their respective system from within. The divided city held a magic attraction for youths who did not want to fit into the opposing ideological camps but sought to experiment with unconventional lifestyles, multicultural encounters, and sexual liberation.[26]

The second set of chapters therefore looks at the extent of the actual division as well as at the degree to which connections were maintained in spite of the Wall. In her study of urban planning and housing construction, Clara Oberle makes it clear that physically reconstructing the city was a daunting task that both sides faced. In the years of hunger, cold, and disease, the population was likely to embrace the political model that afforded it a better chance for survival rather than following either communism or capitalism as ideology.[27]

The evidence of continued and renewed entanglements across the divide is nonetheless also substantial. Hanno Hochmuth delves into the cross-border ties of everyday entertainment, in which Eastern visits to Kreuzberg movie houses were, after 1961, replaced by television watching in order to have access to international popular culture. Based on teacher interviews undertaken in 2004, he shows that the consumption of Western media, albeit directed toward private diversion, indirectly challenged SED control by presenting a more attractive lifestyle.[28] Timothy Brown argues that subculture in Berlin was more than a tribal youth rebellion of styles and mores, since it also included an avant-garde group of artists, seeking a novel fusion of art and politics. Cold War Berlin provided an almost ideal biotope for generational rebellion due to its lack of military draft, subsidized culture, global connections, and ideologized politics. While an anarchist protest culture developed initially in boroughs such as Kreuzberg in the West, the anti-authoritarian impulse also spilled over into Prenzlauer Berg in the East.[29]

The Wall also prompted companies such as Siemens to recruit guest workers from abroad since the GDR constructed the Wall to cut off the mass migration of workers to the West. As a result, a Turkish community collected in its shadow, turning the working-class neighborhoods along its path into "little Istanbul." Sarah Vierra explores the development of this unintentional multiculturalism in West Berlin boroughs, in which housing scarcity and work discrimination against the newcomers hardly lived up to the rhetoric of freedom, thereby subverting the liberal self-image of the West.[30] In diametrically opposed ways, these chapters show the impact of division on the life of the split city. Moreover, they illuminate the diversity of milieus and subcultures as well as the internal conflicts within each camp.

As Briana Smith shows, private art galleries including EP or the FRG's Permanent Mission also played an important role in creating East–West contacts by connecting action artists on both sides of the Wall with one another. By the 1980s, the border had become porous enough to allow some Westerners such as Josef Beuys to cross over and share their experiments with their Eastern colleagues in unofficial spaces, creating experimental networks and exhibitions that undercut the SED's insistence on socialist realism.[31] In a similar vein, Teresa Tammer discusses the struggle of LGBT people for social acceptance in East Germany. While East Berlin's gay community benefitted from the close proximity to the bourgeoning gay subculture culture across the divide, contacts to Western activists threatened to antagonize the GDR regime. Yet, after the Wall's collapse, these contacts proved instrumental in mobilizing the community quickly to finally abolish the infamous paragraph 175 of the civil code.[32] While rather restricted and asymmetrical, these multiple cross-border connections were an essential aspect of popular and artistic life in the divided city.

Memory Cultures

The continuous boom of memory studies suggests that the distinctive experiences of division have created conflicting recollections at the end of the Cold War.[33] The staging of major exhibitions, signature concerts, or other cultural events attempted to inspire a sense of "socialist metropolis" in contrast to a "democratic *Frontstadt*" narrative, justifying distinctive communist or capitalist identities. The doubling of institutions such as universities, opera houses, zoos, and bureaucracies was not just a windfall for united Berlin, but created also a fierce competition for their survival after the fall of the Wall. In the East, there was a widespread sense of loss when the peaceful revolution ended its function as capital of an independent country, called the German Democratic Republic, not only because many of its leading cadres found themselves unemployed.[34] But surprisingly, in the West, unification also led to a similar regret over the disappearance of the particular "island identity" of West Berliners who could take pride in being on the winning anti communist side.[35] The conflict between *Ostalgie*[36] and Western triumphalism was particularly sharp in the reunited city, because it also revolved around hegemony of memory cultures. The demolition of the Palace of the Republic and the decision to rebuild the Berlin Palace in its place marked the culmination of an extremely emotional debate on how to deal with Berlin's communist legacy.

Competing memory cultures have a long tradition in Berlin. Andreas Ludwig explores the changing self-representations of old Berlin in the socialist-inflected Märkische Museum during the GDR, the creation of a western rival Berlin Museum, and a bevy of borough collections, trying to recapture the local history of the city in its parts. During the 1980s, Western exhibitions got more complex and started to reflect its many tensions as well, while, in the East, a more official and self-affirmative view prevailed.[37] On the cusp of unification, memorialization began to extend into the postwar period, already anticipating some of the patterns of post-1990 memory conflicts.

Ironically, the clash of memorialization had already begun, as Krijn Thijs shows, before unification in 1987 with the celebration of the 750th anniversary of the founding of Berlin. Unwilling to launch common events, both city governments staged separate performances in order to legitimize the identity of the communist "capital of the GDR" or the cosmopolitan metropolis on either side of the Wall. While the Eastern festivities culminated in a gigantic parade of 291 floats with 40,000 marchers to show that history culminated in the GDR, the West had more difficulty in designing a decentralized approach with an exhibition and ship parade, signaling democracy.[38]

The last chapters look back on the Cold War in Berlin, trying to sum up its many paradoxical features three decades after the peaceful revolution. Stefanie Eisenhuth points out that the city was divided into two contrasting spaces of experience. While the Western identity was split generationally into the anti communist elders and the countercultural youths, Eastern memories were similarly divided into a recollection of socialist dictatorship and a dissident narrative in which the other side served as counterpoint.[39] By challenging the popular perception of the Wall as a single smooth surface, Paul Steege deconstructs the simplified bipolar divide of the East–West conflict. Instead of denouncing it as a GDR monstrosity, he interprets the barrier as an East–West coproduction in which both sides were complicit and explores Keith Haring's artistic efforts to overcome it by painting on it. For the period after unification, he ponders the multilayered disappearance of the Wall, calling for attention to its everyday experience in order to lay bare the violence contained in the building of barriers in general.[40] This perspective destabilizes the master narrative of Cold War Berlin, by stressing the features that it elides such as the abnormal normalcy of division and the presence of allied troops. The debate about how to recall the history of a divided city is therefore only just beginning.

Conclusion

This new research highlights the anomalous situation of a divided Berlin that fits squarely neither into the GDR nor into the FRG. No other city experienced such an astonishing succession of identities from Prussian residence via the seat of Weimar's vibrant cultural scene to destroyed Nazi center, GDR capital, and Western "outpost of freedom" to restored national capital within the span of one century.[41] Moreover, during moments of heightened crisis, the members of the divided city symbolically embraced their respective camps of the Cold War. But, in everyday life, East German citizens often griped at the privileged position of their Berlin capital in building resources, available food items, consumer goods, and the like. In West Germany, the subsidized Berliners were also outsiders, since their four-power status prevented their complete integration, attracting instead draftdodgers and artists, experimenting with alternative lifestyles and trying to break out of the bipolar logic of East–West confrontation. This complex double legacy might also help explain the contradiction between cosmopolitan openness to newcomers and stubborn provincialism in local politics. The transfer of most of the national government in 1999 was grafted onto a recovering metropolis that remained uncertain about its identity and therefore unable to develop a coherent master narrative as guide for the future.[42]

The recent work presented in this volume both reinforces and challenges traditional understandings of the Cold War. The crises of the blockade and the building of the Wall recall the danger of the military confrontation, arms race, and nuclear annihilation, since the superpowers confronted one another directly in the ruins of the defeated enemy capital. The victims who were killed trying to flee across the Wall are reminders of the repressiveness of the SED dictatorship that was only somewhat attenuated toward its final decade. In short, this violence is a record of needless human suffering due to superpower rivalry and misplaced social engineering. But the Berlin story also has a more encouraging side. Even during the high points of confrontation individuals still wanted to build bridges between East and West Berlin or simply overcame the division by visiting the other half of their city. On the political level, the second Cold War produced a "community of responsibility" between the Eastern and Western politicians who tried to keep the leaders of their respective blocs in check.[43] And, finally, the peaceful revolution, fall of the Wall, and unification not only reunited a partitioned city, but a divided country and an entire split continent.

And yet new challenges for the united city cloud this message of hope. On the one hand, legacies of the Cold War division continue to complicate the local politics of the new old capital. Election results show that the city is still divided between East and West. On the other hand, unforeseen problems such as the arrival of refugees confront urban life in some neighborhoods. In several Eastern districts, right-wing populism is met with as much enthusiasm as in other regions of Eastern Germany. A history of reunited Berlin that integrates both the divided past and the problematic present has yet to be written.

Notes

1   Uwe Aulich, "Neues Museum und Hard Rock Hotel im Zentrum," *Berliner Zeitung*, December 8, 2015.
2   Thomas Lindenberger, "'Divided but Not Disconnected. Germany as a Border Region of the Cold War," in: Tobias Hochseher, Christoph Laucht, and Andrew Plowman (eds.), *Divided but Not Disconnected. German Experiences of the Cold War* (New York/Oxford, 2010), pp. 11–33, p. 12.
3   Stefanie Eisenhuth and Scott H. Krause, "Inventing the 'Outpost of Freedom.' Transatlantic Narratives and the Historical Actors Crafting West Berlin's Postwar Political Culture," *Zeithistorische Forschungen/Studies in Contemporary History* 11 (2014) 2, pp. 188–211, www.zeithistorische-forschungen.de/2-2014/id=5093.
4   Odd Arne Westad, *The Cold War: A World History* (New York, 2018); idem, *The Global Cold War: Third World Interventions and the Making of Our Times* (Cambridge, 2005).
5   Paul Steege, "Finding the There, There. Local Space, Global Ritual, and Early Cold War Berlin," in: Gary Backhaus and John Murungi (eds.), *Earth Ways. Framing Geographical Meanings* (Lanham, 2004), pp. 155–72, p. 160.
6   John Lewis Gaddis, *The Cold War. A New History* (New York, 2005); Bernd Stöver, *Der Kalte Krieg 1947–1991: Geschichte eines radikalen Zeitalters* (Munich, 2007).
7   HICOG Berlin, *Briefing on Current Berlin Problems*, May 2, 1950, RG 466, US High Commissioner for Germany (HICOG), Berlin Element, Office of the Director, Classified General Records, 1949–55, E-162, Box 10, Folder Berlin, National Archives, College Park.
8   Scott H. Krause, *Bringing Cold War Democracy to West Berlin: A Shared German-American Project* (London, 2019), pp. 90–112.
9   Harold Hurwitz, *Demokratie und Antikommunismus in Berlin nach 1945*, 4 vols. (Cologne, 1983–90).
10 Edgar N. Johnson, *Fünf Monate in Berlin: Briefe von Edgar N. Johnson aus dem Jahre 1946*, (ed.), Werner Breunig (Munich, 2014), p. 192.
11 See Konrad H. Jarausch and Michael Geyer, *Shattered Past: Reconstructing German Histories* (Princeton, 2003); Konrad H. Jarausch, "Die Teile als Ganzes erkennen.

Zur Integration der beiden deutschen Nachkriegsgeschichten," *Zeithistorische Forschungen/Studies in Contemporary History* 1 (2004) 1, https://zeithistorische-forschungen.de/1-2004/4538; Frank Bösch (ed.), *A History Shared and Divided. East and West Germany since the 1970* (Oxford, 2018).

12   Thomas Lindenberger, Marcus M. Payk, and Annette Vowinckel (eds.), *Cold War Cultures: Perspectives on Eastern and Western European Societies* (New York, 2012), p. 1.

13   Konrad H. Jarausch, Christian F. Ostermann, and Andreas Etges (eds.), *The Cold War: Historiography, Memory, Representation* (Berlin, 2017).

14   Katharina Hochmuth (ed.), *Krieg der Welten: Zur Geschichte des Kalten Krieges* (Berlin, 2017).

15   Martin Klimke, *The Other Alliance. Student Protest in West Germany & the United States in the Global Sixties* (Princeton, 2010); Maria Höhn and Martin Klimke, *A Breath of Freedom. The Civil Rights Struggle, African-American GIs, and Germany* (Basingstoke, 2010).

16   Andreas W. Daum, *Kennedy in Berlin. Politics and Culture in the Cold War* (Buffalo, 2008), p. 204.

17   "Wat de kriegen kannst, det nimmste," *Der Spiegel* 41 (1987), pp. 55–66.

18   Christoph Kreutzmüller, *Final Sale in Berlin: The Destruction of Jewish Commercial Activity, 1930–1945* (New York, 2015).

19   David Barclay, *Schaut auf diese Stadt: Der unbekannte Ernst Reuter* (Berlin, 2000).

20   Gerhard Sälter, *Grenzpolizisten: Konformität, Verweigerung und Repression in der Grenzpolizei und den Grenztruppen der DDR 1952–1965* (Berlin, 2009).

21   Andreas Etges (ed.), *Europa trifft Amerika: Vergleichende und Transnationale Perspektiven* (Berlin, 2008).

22   Hans-Hermann Hertle, *Die Berliner Mauer: Monument des Kalten Krieges* (Bonn, 2007).

23   Edith Sheffer, *Burned Bridge. How East and West Germans made the Iron Curtain* (New York, 2011).

24   Lindenberger, *Divided, But not Disconnected*, p. 14.

25   Karl Schlögel, "Generation Marienborn—Essay," *Aus Politik und Zeitgeschichte*, 59 (2009) 21–2, pp. 3–6 (trans. Stefanie Eisenhuth).

26   Carla MacDougall, "'We Too Are Berliners.' Protest, Symbolism, and the City in Cold War Germany," in: Belinda Davis, Wilfried Mausbach, Martin Klimke, and Carla MacDougall (eds.), *Changing The World, Changing Oneself. Political Protest and Collective Identities in West Germany and the U.S. in the 1960s and 1970s* (New York/Oxford, 2012), pp. 83–101; Belinda Davis, "The City as Theater of Protest. West Berlin and West Germany, 1962–1983," in: Gyan Prakash and Kevin M. Kruse (eds.), *The Spaces of the Modern City. Imaginaries, Politics, and Everyday Life* (Princeton, 2008), pp. 247–74; Wilfried Rott, *Die Insel: Eine Geschichte West-Berlins, 1948–1990* (Munich, 2009).

27   Clara Oberle, *City in Transit: Ruins, Railways, and the Search for Order in Postwar Berlin (1945–1948)* (Diss., Princeton, 2006).

28   Hanno Hochmuth, *Kiezgeschichte: Friedrichshain und Kreuzberg im geteilten Berlin* (Göttingen, 2017).

29   Timothy Scott Brown, *West Germany and the Global Sixties: The Anti-authoritarian Revolt, 1962–1978* (New York, 2015).

30   Sarah Vierra, *At Home in Almanya? Turkish-German Spaces of Belonging in the Federal Republic of Germany, 1961–1990* (Diss., Chapel Hill, 2011).

31   Briana Smith's dissertation on East–West artistic networks at the University of Iowa will soon be accessible online at http://ir.uiowa.edu/etd/5854/.

32   Teresa Tammer, "Coming out in die deutsche Einheit. Vom Aufbruch und Abschied der DDR-Schwulenbewegung," in: Thomas Großbölting and Christoph Lorke (eds.), *Deutschland seit 1990. Wege in die Vereinigungsgesellschaft* (Stuttgart, 2017), pp. 313–33.

33   Aleida Assmann, *Das neue Unbehagen an der Erinnerungskultur: Eine Intervention* (Munich, 2013).

34   Marija Nikolaeva Todorova, *Post-communist Nostalgia* (New York, 2010).

35   Stefanie Eisenhuth and Martin Sabrow, "Westberlin. Eine historiographische Herausforderung," *Zeithistorische Forschungen/Studies in Contemporary History* 11 (2014) 2, pp. 165–87, www.zeithistorische-forschungen.de/2-2014/id=5090.

36   The term "Ostalgie" is a composite of nostalgia and the German word for "east." See Daphne Berdahl, "'(N)ostalgie' for the Present. Memory, Longing and East German Things', *Ethnos* 64 (1999) 2, pp. 192–211.

37   Andreas Ludwig, "Museen als Forschungsgegenstand anderer Wissenschaften," in: Markus Waltz (ed.), *Handbuch Museum. Geschichte—Aufgaben—Perspektiven* (Stuttgart, 2016), pp. 375–81.

38   Krijn Thijs, *Drei Geschichten, eine Stadt: Die Berliner Stadtjubiläen von 1937 und 1987* (Cologne, 2017).

39   Stefanie Eisenhuth, *Die Schutzmacht. Die Amerikaner in Berlin, 1945–1994* (Göttingen, 2018); idem and Scott Krause, "Negotiating Cold War Legacies. The Discursive Ambiguity of Berlin's Memory Sites," in: Karin Bauer and Jennifer Hosek (eds.), *Cultural Topographies of the New Berlin* (Oxford, 2018), pp. 130–54.

40   Paul Steege, *Black Market, Cold War: Everyday Life in Berlin, 1946–1949* (New York, 2007).

41   Brian Ladd, *The Ghosts of Berlin: Confronting Germany History in the Urban Landscape* (Chicago, 1997); Andreas Huyssen, *Present Pasts: Urban Palimpsests and the Politics of Memory* (Stanford, 2003); idem, "The Voids of Berlin," *Critical Inquiry* 24 (1997), pp. 57–81; Janet Ward, *Post-Wall Berlin. Borders, Space and Identity* (New York, 2011).

42   Michael Gehler, *Three Germanies: West Germany, East Germany and the Berlin Republic* (London, 2011).

43   Konrad H. Jarausch (ed.), *United Germany: Debating Processes and Prospects* (New York, 2013).

Part One

Locating Berlin in the Cold War

1

From Heart of Darkness to Heap of Rubble: Berlin as Nazi Capital

Christoph Kreutzmüller
Translated by Michelle Eley and Corinna Kahnke

Ciphers, Sceneries, and Analyses

Of course it had to be the Brandenburg Gate. Hastily summoned local SA units marched through this gate with great fanfare as soon as night had fallen on the day of Adolph Hitler's appointment as Reich Chancellor heading a "Cabinet of National Unity." The NSDAP apparently held special license for their march as the gate had been declared off limits for political demonstrations in the wake of the 1918/1919 Revolution. Whereas the media showed much interest in the novel spectacle, the reactions of passersby and residents were anything but uniform. While Jewish painter Max Liebermann colorfully denounced the columns passing his house, other witnesses appeared more curious than excited.

The SA men—drunk on more than just victory—had to weave their way through the onlookers, while the billowing torches obscured visibility. January 30, 1933, must have been a typical Berlin winter day. Gloomy and cold. Anything but ideal conditions for the press photographers. Accordingly, the few pictures that were taken are hardly impressive. For this reason, the SA reenacted the torch march the following summer in order to create better images of an event that, at this point, had already been elevated to the status of national revolution—and celebrated as a public holiday.[1]

These staged celebrations illustrate the significance of Berlin as a symbolically charged site of politics and power. Even though Munich remained the "capital of the movement," Nuremberg was being developed into the "city of the Reich party rallies," and Adolph Hitler often resided at the Berghof in Berchtesgaden as well as—after 1941—at the Wolf's Lair outside Rastenburg in East Prussia, Berlin proudly stood as an initiative of the party and subsequently transformed substantially. In 1945, Hitler deliberately chose to end his life here, but not before ensuring the city's destruction. Accordingly, studies on national socialism have referenced "Berlin" more frequently than they have any other German city in their indexes of places. However, the city has often been viewed as a cipher: from this perspective, the capital has stood (and stands) not only as a site of macro-political decisions, but also

Image 1 Photograph by Georg Pahl.

for the heart of darkness. Day-to-day developments in Berlin—especially before the war—have long been neglected.

By contrast, this chapter aims to sketch a more differentiated image of the local developments, amid the tension between outward perceptions and inward changes, and to shed light on select facets of Berlin's history.[2] Without claiming completeness, this chapter outlines the role of the capital of the Reich (*Reichshauptstadt*) as a symbolical locale and seat of government. In spite of all propaganda, the city was by no means a uniform structure. This tension will be highlighted in the second section of the chapter. Because of the Nazi era's significant impact on the postwar cityscape, this chapter will likewise investigate the role of Berlin as one of the most important armories of the Wehrmacht and shine a spotlight on the war within the city. A final section will sketch the city on the brink of the abyss that turned it "into the heap of rubble near Potsdam," as the writer Berthold Brecht famously quipped once.

A Staged Capital

Not only was Berlin by far the largest city of the Reich, and the capital of what was by far the largest state within the Reich—Prussia—it also had been the capital of the German Reich since 1871. While the city only received the honorific "Reich capital (*Reichshauptstadt*)" moniker in 1933, both Reich and Prussian bureaucracies had long established their headquarters there. Numerous foreign embassies, missions, special interest groups, organizations, and unions had followed suit. Not surprisingly, Reichswehr and later Wehrmacht and SS also showed their presence, particularly in the political center. There were and are thousands of streets named Wilhelmstraße in Germany, but only in Berlin was Wilhelmstraße much more than a postal address: "It has happened. We are seated in the Wilhelmstraße," noted Joseph Goebbels in his diary on January 31, 1933.[3] Until 1945, Wilhelmstraße was used as a matter of course as a metonym for the Reich's government. For this reason, the legal proceedings against twenty-one high-ranking officials of the German ministries in Nuremberg in 1947/49 were known as the Wilhelmstraße Trial.[4] After parliament in Tiergarten had demoted itself to an organ of acclamation in the wake of the Reichstag burning in 1933, Wilhelmstraße served as the nerve center for the national socialist regime. The most important ministries of the Reich, from the office of the Reich Chancellor and the Reich President's palace, to the Ministry of Foreign Affairs, were located on this street. In 1936, the national socialists added Göring's Reich Ministry of Aviation, which notably had emerged in part on the grounds of the former Prussian Ministry of War. Likewise, when the political—and racist—persecution apparatus was centralized in the form of the Reich Security Head Office of the SS (RSHA) in 1939, it was established just down the street.[5]

In 1943, author Ernst Friedrich Werner-Rades summarized the meaning of the "capital of the Reich" in a richly illustrated volume with the pathos so typical of the Nazis: "Berlin has, according to the Führer's will, the duty and the calling to be example and epitome of the Reich, illustration and inspiration of the greater German life, not a gargantuan assembly of people in the Brandenburg March, but the appointed capital of Greater Germany, worthy of its calling."[6] However, Werner-Rades continues, only "after the end of the war, will representative buildings herald that Berlin has become […] within and without, the true capital of the Third Reich."[7] Indeed, the widespread architectural development of the city was, above all, a promise for the future. Very little was realized, if one does not take into account the area-wide demolition of a whole city district for the planned north–south axis and the entailed compulsory relocation of Berlin Jews, an act that paved the way for their deportations from October 1941 on.[8]

Wilhelmstraße served not only as the site of political decisions and their bureaucratic implementation, it was also a workplace and meeting point for the ministries' staff. An analysis of the biographies of the Wannsee Conference participants shows very clearly, for example, that they already had encountered one another to some extent long before January 20, 1942. Nearly all of them lived in the genteel southwest of Berlin, and some were also members of those gentlemen's clubs that also served as "nodes" for the networks of the higher office functionaries of Wilhelmstraße. Others knew one another through the Prussian State Council and the Council of Ministers for the Defense of the Reich, and had met in the Academy for German Law or in the lobbies of the Reichstag.[9]

Cultural life might have been quickly reduced to NS standards after the ousting of detested, defiant, and/or Jewish artists. But Berlin remained a tourist attraction thanks to its cultural infrastructure, numerous PR campaigns, fairs, and large-scale events.[10] In 1938, the year of the annexation of Austria and the pogrom, visitors to Berlin already numbered more than 1.9 million, among them over 260,000 foreigners.[11] New localities of national socialist stagings of power complemented the old attractions for these visitors. They might have even cheered on the Changing of the Guards, a goose-stepping ceremony reinstated after 1933.[12] Berlin kept a peaceful front well into the war, while cities in the West of the Reich already experienced aerial bombardments. The regime's entertainment movies vetted by Joseph Goebbels cannily presented the capital as a place of longing, as "*Zwei in einer grossen Stadt*" ("two in a big city") of 1942 attests.[13] Likewise, the *Deutsche Wochenschau* newsreel showcased Berlin time and again. Thus, even though Western allied air power had long smashed German air defenses, a summer 1944 episode on the "5th German Soccer War Cup" finals sought to demonstrate that urban life went on in spite of blackouts and bombings.[14]

Goebbels played a key role in staging and marketing the capital. Since 1926, Goebbels had not only been Gauleiter, or district leader, of Berlin, i.e., the highest local representative of the NS movement, but was also appointed Reich Minister for Public Enlightenment and Propaganda in mid-March 1933. Although an affair in the late 1930s would cause his star to temporarily wane with Hitler, and even though the office of General Building Inspector broadened Albert Speer's power in the city, the small man from the Rhineland could command the entire party and propaganda machine at any time. In Berlin, Goebbels was master of the *Blockwarte* or block wardens, and the storm troopers and city government, and had furthermore requested, and received, as a contemporary comment emphasizes, in the "Statute of the Constitution and Administration of the Reich Capital Berlin" "considerably further reaching authority than usual."[15] Even before a legal process had been established in April 1933, the national socialist city commissioner (and later city president) Julius Lippert, appointed by Goebbels, started a large political and racist reshuffling of personnel. Accordingly, far more employees were dismissed in Berlin than in most of the other cities in the Reich—and frequently replaced by national socialists.[16] Very quickly, the cronyism got out of hand, so that even Goebbels had to admit in his diary that he was presiding over the "Berlin district's stables of corruption."[17]

This notwithstanding, Goebbels staged the Labor Day parades (beginning in 1933) as well as the Olympic Summer Games (1936), the visit of Benito Mussolini (1937), and the celebrations for Hitler's fiftieth birthday (1939), during which a whole boulevard—today's Strasse des 17. Juni bisecting Tiergarten—was dedicated to the man being celebrated.[18] Naturally, the parade of the Berlin garrison, as depicted in the *Wochenschau*, led through the Brandenburg Gate after the campaign against France in July 1940, and was accordingly received as *the* German victory parade.[19] In this spirit, Goebbels orchestrated his speech in the Berlin Sportpalast on February 18, 1943, to declare "'total war.'" As a matter of fact, the *Gauleiter* spoke at a district event in front of hand-picked guests. That he spoke in Berlin, however, gave him claim to a more extensive prominence across the Reich—and the capacity to conceal the fact that Hitler could not be convinced to speak in public following the defeat of Stalingrad.[20]

Stagings of that kind were, of course, always intended to appeal to both the Germans not living in the capital, and to foreign nations. Berlin was, after all, the focus of the world. Contrary to the German reporters, foreign journalists were not bound by the orders of the Ministry for Propaganda, but they suffered from lack of information and were punished directly as well, for example, by revoking their accreditations.[21] Yet, the anonymity of the metropolis shielded informal conversations with state and party functionaries, as well as meetings with German journalists and other informants. In the bars on the Kurfürstendamm or at the Zoo Gardens, in clubs, organizations, and at receptions, they were able to get their hands on further intelligence in addition to any official announcements, albeit in restricted fashion. If, for instance, there were any accounts at all of actions taken against the Jewish population, they usually came out of Berlin—or at least had been acquired in Berlin.[22]

While Goebbels was still moving into his new Propaganda Ministry office on Wilhelmstraße, the French magazine *Vu* published two photographs that had been taken two weeks before in a concentration camp located at Friedrichstrasse 234.[23] The two images, shot by press photographer Georg Pahl, who, incidentally, had also captured the picture of the torch march at the Brandenburg Gate, depicted the committal of ten men into the camp. It was also known as "Blood Castle" (*Blutburg*), located not far from what later became Checkpoint Charlie. One can assume that he took those photographs with the approval of the SA *Sturmbann*, which had erected the camp. Posing in the foreground of the photographs is an SA man with his rifle, which identifies him as an auxiliary police officer. In the absence of other images, these two shots rapidly became a symbol for the early terrors of the NS regime.[24]

Since the images and their forceful message could stand in for any national socialist persecution, captions describing a variety of offenses soon accompanied

Image 2 Photo by Georg Pahl, 01/30 1933 (DHM).

them. On March 22, New York's *Daily Mirror* published the second photo of the series with the general caption that "nazi police" were frisking captured opponents.[25] The *Winnipeg Free Press* commented that the photograph depicted "security police," who had captured and imprisoned "expelled communists in an underground labyrinth" in Berlin and were searching them for weapons before interrogation.[26] In Budapest, the political weekly paper *Társadalmunk* printed a version of the same shot on March 25, cut off on the upper edge with the caption: "Original shot of the court at Citadel Spandau. 'Hands up,' yells the SA man and aims his rifle at the detained men. Who knows if they are still alive."[27] In Shanghai, the *North China Daily News* published the photograph on April 17 with a note about communists who were arrested in basements, while the Chinese press referred to "fleeing Jews" who were being searched for money.[28] When a Manila newspaper printed the photo in June of 1933 with a similar caption, the local German envoy doubted its authenticity but was corrected by the Ministry of Propaganda that the image was "real." The description was, clarified the Ministry, "however quite hyperbolic."[29] The brochure of the *World Alliance for Combating Antisemitism*, published in London in June 1933, printed a much clipped and retouched version of the photo simply with the title: "Terror! Prisoners in Nazi barracks tortured for hours."[30]

In reaction to such negative publicity, Goebbels, Hitler, and Reich Minister of the Interior, Wilhelm Frick, attempted to steer the violent anti-Semitic pressure into a quasi-orderly direction. They decided to implement a "boycott" of Jewish businesses and to prepare a law on the exclusion of Jews from civil service.[31] One day *after* the publication of the proclamation, on March 28, Hitler informed his cabinet of those plans. He brushed aside concerns of the national-conservative members; however, he conceded to organize the campaign as an initiative of the party. Furthermore, the racist exclusion of Jews was to be passed off as justified reaction to the negative news coverage in the foreign press. Accordingly, the campaign in Berlin was also staged for the foreign press photographers with bilingual German–English posters.[32] With this course of action, the international "*Lügenpresse*" (Press of Lies), as it was called at the time, was to be taken into a would-be hostage situation. Following that, a de facto ban on photography, excluding propaganda events, was implemented in the capital to prevent further undesirable images from making their way abroad. Thus, no pictures can be found in the international press on the violent assaults against the Jewish population during the summer of 1935 and in June 1938. During the pogrom in November 1938, the Associated Press was at least able to send a wirephoto via London, and a few days later three additional photographs by airmail.[33] These photos continue to shape our image of the "Crystal Night" to this day.[34] In part hasty snapshots, they show, of course, only a very limited view: the perpetrators, the fearsome magnitude of violence, and the struggle for resistance of those attacked were not pictured.[35] It is even more remarkable that the international newspapers actually reported—in relative detail—on the scale of deportations, yet did not publish a single photo thereof. Public archives hold no images of the more than 55,000 Jews deported from Berlin as part of 184 individual transports between October 1941 and March 1945.[36]

An Amorphous Capital

Already in 1927, Walther Ruttmann had choreographed the hustle of the metropolis and its transportation system in the film *Berlin—The Symphony of a Metropolis (Berlin—Die Sinfonie einer Großstadt)*. Even if Russian Orthodox Christians and liberal Jews, garden plot owners and inhabitants of villas, artists, clerks, and workers all waited for someone at the famous "Standard Time Clock" at Zoo Station, they otherwise had few things in common. Berlin was not a monolithic city but a diverse metropolis that broke down into parallel worlds and habitats—the proverbial *Kieze*. In 1920, the formation of Greater Berlin had amalgamated eight cities, fifty-nine rural municipalities, and twenty-seven manor districts into one municipality of twenty districts. With a population of almost 4 million residents, Berlin had the third largest urban population in the world. By 1939, the number of residents had increased to nearly 4.4 million—almost 800,000 more than today.

And yet social stratification divided the city starkly. Friedrichshain or Lichtenberg in the East had very little in common with the bourgeois districts of Wilmersdorf, Charlottenburg, or Steglitz in West and southwest Berlin. Spandau on the Western edge led as much its own life as did Köpenick on the far side. The size of the city halls for these areas, built shortly before the compulsory merger of 1920, speaks of their desire for independence to this very day. In this sense, the swanky Kurfürstendamm may have seemed for many Berliners as far away as the Champs-Élysées or Piccadilly Circus. Even the residents of a typical apartment building often shared only the same postal address. The occupants of the desirable ground floor in the front house did not care to be acquainted with the tenants in the rear building, or with the inhabitants of the humble dwellings right next to them, known as *Belvedere*, which had been formed when suspended ceilings were installed in the high archways. In spite of the national socialists' claim of bringing about a unified people's community and enforced new rituals such as Sunday stews, living as neighbors did not necessarily mean a closer connection; it still often meant daily segregation.

When it came to characterizing Berlin, opinions differed sharply. Some perceived it as the beating heart of modernity, the locale of the cultural avant-garde, the city of lights, where life unfolded at night in cafes and cabarets, a metropolis measuring up to Paris, London, or New York.[37] Intellectuals, writers, and artists were fascinated by Berlin and attempted to express the city's rhythm, the speed, and the glamor of the metropolis. For others, among them the national socialists, Berlin embodied the abhorred modernity, the urban Moloch, devouring and destroying culture, a modern Babel, in which Christian values would drown and young people, especially, would fall prey to the temptations of the big city. It was not artistic sublimation but the trivialization of mass society that conservatives and nationalists thought to recognize in Berlin. In his diary, Goebbels wrote time and again—presumably as a play on Joe May's film, which was successfully produced in Berlin—of an "Asphalt Desert." "Sat for a long time with friends at Café Wilhelma," he wrote in September 1926, a few weeks before he would take over the leadership of the NSDAP in the city as the new *Gauleiter*. "Then we strolled through the streets. Berlin at night. A hotbed of sin! And

I am supposed to throw myself into that?"[38] These competing perceptions inspired literary representations that formed the basis for romanticized master narratives of the "Golden Twenties" only after World War Two and inspired the TV series *Babylon Berlin* even more recently.

Looking at it from the outside, the capital of the Reich before 1933 may have seemed not only a hotbed of sin but also a "red stronghold." Indeed, in the city council elections of 1919, workers' parties had been able to secure two-thirds of the votes, with the leftist-socialist USPD clearly in the lead. And even in the year 1932, when the national socialists claimed their great election successes, the left-wing parties held their lead in Berlin. During the Reichstag elections in November 1932, the communists even secured the highest number of votes and were able to stand their ground once more in the Wedding district during the anything but free elections in March 1933. Nevertheless, the majority of voters in the districts of Schöneberg, Steglitz, Wilmersdorf, and Zehlendorf had voted German nationalist between 1918 and 1932. Even in those districts popularly referred to as workers' districts, fissures fracture the seemingly homogenous image. In specific areas and *Kiezen*, the national socialists had already taken root long before 1933, with *Sturmlokale* serving as their strongholds. A Berlin invention, *Sturmlokale* were pubs that served as makeshift barracks for SA units. Payment was usually arranged in form of a guaranteed tab. This primitive but highly effective organizational structure kept the fighting spirits of the SA up. The party's forceful power, as Daniel Siemens has pointed out recently, resulted from a calculated political strategy of provocation, violence, and "propaganda of beatings."[39] Goebbels stylized the "Battle for Berlin" (among other things in his book of the same title) into a myth, which he invoked once more during the street fights with the Red Army in April 1945.[40]

Starting in 1933, the NSDAP experienced a large influx in Berlin, too. Everywhere, newly appointed *Blockwarte*—and secretly spying neighbors—kept watch for those who hung their flag out of the window and those who did not. In bars, too, the surveillance became increasingly consistent. When Hermann Fricke, a butler, left a beer bar in Düsseldorf Street on December 23, 1936, late at night, he finally lost it. He responded to what had become the nearly mandatory "Hail Hitler" with the battle cry "Red Front." Immediately, the fifty year old—a former KPF member, as it turned out later—was pursued by the other guests and seized at the next bar.[41] Dozens of similar incidents can be found in Berlin police reports. *Gestapo* and ordinary police mercilessly took action against presumed and actual political opponents. This enforcement of power and striving for total control, the terror in the streets, and administrative fright lead to an exodus. Thousands of Berliners persecuted for political or racial motives—among them workers, white-collar workers, large- and small-scale manufacturers, as well as internationally renowned artists and scientists—were fleeing from their home city.[42] Tens of thousands of others were deported and murdered. Among the victims of the racist, murderous politics was the former colonial soldier Bayume Mohamed Husen,[43] as was Rudolf Langen, who, together with four other boys who had been labeled Jewish half-breeds, was seized from a city welfare center, taken to Hadamar, where he was murdered—as "mentally disabled."[44]

A Capital as Armory

Since the Treaty of Versailles had halted important industries, such as the manufacturing of weapons and uniforms, Berlin had been suffering since the 1920s from high structural unemployment.[45] Berlin's economy, dependent on exports, took especially hard hits with the collapse of international trade from the late 1920s, so that the unemployment figures increased to 636,000 by the end of 1932, i.e., about 33 percent of the working population. Thus Berlin suffered—alongside the Silesian metropolis of Breslau—the highest unemployment rate of any major city in Germany.[46] Whereas the city was involved in the armament from day one, the unemployment rate did not decrease perceptibly until 1935.[47] However, the first signs of an economic overheating—shortage of basic materials—became noticeable as early as 1937. Furthermore, activity level and employment experienced a clear shift toward armaments-related industries in large-scale manufacting.[48] Soon, skilled workers in particular became a "scarce commodity." All prosperous large companies in the processing sectors reacted with rationalizations, and, more importantly, the introduction of conveyor belts, as these allowed for the replacement of specialized workers with unqualified ones. In parallel, the percentage of women in the workforce grew. For the first time, foreign workers were also recruited for industry—and with that, the groundwork for the kidnapping of hundreds of thousands of forced laborers was laid.[49]

At the same time, the capital was a node of commercial activity for Jews in the German Reich. By conservative estimation, every fifth Berlin company was run by or in cooperation with entrepreneurs who considered themselves Jewish or were persecuted for being Jewish. Consequently, about half of all Jewish businesses in Germany were located Berlin.[50] They were able to resist the destruction of Jewish commercial activity for a remarkably long time. Because the anonymity of the city promised possibilities for economic perseverance, it had already become a harbor for Jewish entrepreneurs long before 1933. After 1933, this trend increased—among other reasons because Berlin was the seat of the largest Jewish congregation and of the places that offered the promise of lifesaving documents. In the end, however, the result of their resilience was that the Nazis, their aides, and their claqueurs annihilated Jewish commercial activity especially violently.

While Jewish companies were liquidated or sold, Berlin's economy prospered. At the beginning of the war, companies located in Berlin made up not even 40 percent of the arms industry of what had become known as the Old Reich, or Germany, in its borders of 1937. In certain high-tech sectors, the city's importance for armaments was even greater.[51] The beginning of the war changed very little in the structure of businesses since distribution and steering systems were already established. The draft of male employees, however, had drastic effects. In replacement of those conscripted, women and former retirees, as well as concentration camp inmates and forced laborers were employed and exploited, respectively. "Memories of the Camp City," one Czech forced laborer labeled a photograph from Berlin. Camps of all sorts could be found everywhere:

At that time, Berlin was virtually plastered with high-rise barracks. In every gap of the giant city, be it ever so small, flights of brown building blocks, made from spruce wood and covered with tar paper, had settled in. Greater Berlin forms one single camp that crumbles apart between the solid buildings, the memorials, the office buildings, the train stations, the factories.[52]

In the end there were roughly 3,000 camps of various sizes and forms in Berlin.

Especially after the conquest of Belgium, Luxembourg, the Netherlands, and France, the *Reichswirtschaftsministerium* entertained deliberations that Berlin could take over both London's and New York's role as the center of world commerce and finance. De facto foreign trade, however, had come to a standstill, and banking business trickled to a halt. Excess liquidity led to an inflation of financial balances. The *Sparkasse* of Berlin City tripled its deposits during the course of the first four war years from about 825 million *Reichsmark* (1939) to 2.7 billion *Reichsmark* (1943) and thus finally reached the level of the then so-called major banks of Berlin, the Commerzbank, Dresdner-, and Deutsche Bank, the financial balances of which also nearly tripled between 1939 and 1944.[53] This flood of liquidity resulted from the strict rationing of consumer goods. Subsequently, the retail sector came to a halt. Even in the main shopping areas such as Leipziger Strasse or Kurfürstendamm, shops, coffee houses, and restaurants stood empty, as far as they had not already been destroyed during air strikes. More and more, commerce took place in the illegality of the black market.[54] Although food rations had to be cut for the first time in April 1942, the majority of the city's German population could still be provided for—at the expense of occupied areas—at a relatively high level until the end of 1944.[55]

The increase in air raids also played a role in the trend to concentrate arms production in larger factories. Since the smaller factories were often located in inner city areas, which were most at risk for air raids, it was suggested that they be closed so that the workers could be transferred to large-scale plants, where their work performance could be supervised more efficiently. Starting in 1942, numerous factories moved their operations into areas under less threat of air raids. At the end of 1944, Siemens alone was running approximately 140 "war relocation sites," which were spread across the whole Reich and those areas (still) occupied by the Reich.[56] At the end of 1944, a wave of site relocations by firms into the Western parts of Germany was underway as the last Jewish businesses were deleted from the Commercial Registry.[57]

Abyss

The Berliners who were part of what the national socialists promoted as *Volksgemeinschaft*, and who were not conscripted into the Wehrmacht, experienced the war first hand only with a time lag. After the German air force had destroyed Warsaw, Rotterdam, Coventry, and Belgrade, and knowingly condoned the deaths of civilians, the war returned virtually to its point of origin only in 1943. Although other cities were destroyed more comprehensively, no other city endured as many air raids as Berlin. Between November 1943 and March 1944, the allies launched seventeen major offensives that cost the lives of nearly 10,000 people. Berliners experienced the two largest attacks on February 3 and March 28, 1945, during which the old city center was reduced to rubble and ash.[58]

In order to reach the German capital first, the Red Army initiated an offensive that overran the German defenses along the Oder River in February 1945—at a very high cost. This bloodshed set the frontlines for the extremely violent urban combat that began on the morning of April 16, 1945. Thousands of civilians perished while the fighting raged in the streets and houses until Soviet commandos hoisted the red banner atop the shot-riddled Reichstag on May 2, 1945. The number of the Battle of Berlin's civilian and military victims remains unknown even today.[59] Neither can a final statement be made about the devastation that the war had inflicted on the psyche of the survivors. Essays assigned in the first postwar school year to schoolchildren living in the Prenzlauer Berg district offer but a small glimpse. The carnage at Schönhauser Allee boulevard on May 2 had seared itself into the memory of the boys:

> This attempted escape [by German troops] … began on May 2 at 3:30 in the morning, and it ended with a horrid catastrophe at 11:30 mid-day of the same day with a provisional cease-fire, shortly thereafter followed by the capitulation of Berlin … At that moment, no one would have thought of the dreadful blood bath that just occurred, if he had not had the gruesome sight before his eyes. Because in my cautious estimation, about 200 fallen and 500 wounded German soldiers were lying from *Wichertstrasse* to *Schönhauser Allee* [S-Bahn] station, next to countless quantities of weapons and equipment. Rocket launchers, guns, canons, tanks, vehicles, and humans were lying in an unimaginable chaotic entanglement. This was the most dreadful sight of my life, which I will never forget.[60]

In addition to the dead, who were hastily buried in mass graves, millions of cubic meters of debris remained. For its removal, reusable supplies were painstakingly recovered while the rest was piled up into mountains of rubble. This gargantuan effort created Berlin's second highest elevation, *Teufelsberg* or Devil's Mountain, which covers the first stages of another Nazi large-scale building project, Alfred Speer's School of Defense Technology. Unexploded ordinance constitutes another lasting legacy. To this day, thousands of unexploded bombs and grenades litter Berlin's subsoil. Nearly five decades after the conclusion of World War Two, in 1994, three construction workers lost their lives in Friedrichshain district when they hit an American bomb while laying the foundations for a new building.[61] Even though the deaths continued, the end of the Battle of Berlin was for many—for Jews who had gone underground as much as for forced and slave laborers—a liberation. However, the Berlin Senate finally decided only in 2008 that—in spite of the surrounding circumstances, especially the mass rapes— the whole city actually was liberated.

Summary

Of course, it had to be Berlin. Officially the first meeting of the Big Three after Germany's unconditional surrender was called "Berlin Conference of the Three Heads of Government of the U.S.S.R., U.S.A., and U.K." But, as the capital had been reduced to a heap of rubble, the allies decided to meet in Potsdam across the Havel River to try to finalize their strategy on how to administer Germany. Taking a cue from the plans the Allies advocated at Potsdam, the results of national socialist rule in and over Berlin can be summarized in three "Ds". Between 1933 and 1945 Berlin was, first, depopulated by political and racist persecution, aerial warfare, and street battles. The number of people living in the city sank from nearly 4.5 million people in 1942 to under 3 million in 1949. Second and simultaneously, the city was deindustrialized. This was partly due to racist prosecution—the destruction of Jewish commercial activity, and the result of the bombing and dismantling after the war. But it was also owed to the strategic considerations of companies that no longer saw a future in the divided city. Just like many others, Siemens moved its headquarters to Munich. In October 1948, only about 20,000 companies were listed in the Commercial Register. In 1930, there had still been nearly 50,000.[62] Third, the defeated city was demilitarized—albeit only of German military. West Berlin even became a refuge from mandatory military service. The former Wehrmacht and SS barracks were—until 1994—mainly used by the former allies.

But, the city was never demystified. While West Berlin tried to present itself as heir to the "Golden Twenties'" culture, East Berlin's SED tried to draw on the myth of a "red" Berlin, highlighting "workers" resistance against the Nazis. Even though the Wilhelmstraße became insignificant, Berlin was still the former German capital. To lose ground there was losing face. And, of course, it had to be the Brandenburg Gate. In its vicinity—and ironically in the future British sector of West Berlin— the Red Army erected a first victory monument. Just like its big brother, the huge monument the Soviets built in East Berlin's Treptower park, it still stands there today, explicitly protected by the 1990 Four-Plus-Two Treaty, that ended World War Two after the Cold War.

Notes

1   Michael Wildt and Christoph Kreutzmüller, *Berlin 1933–1945* (Munich, 2013), p. 17; Sven Felix Kellerhoff, *Hitlers Berlin: Geschichte einer Hassliebe* (Berlin, 2005), p. 89.

2   For a detailed overview of these developments, see Michael Wildt and Christoph Kreutzmüller, "Berlin 1933–1945: Stadt und Gesellschaft im Nationalsozialismus," in: Michael Wildt and Christoph Kreutzmüller (eds.), *Berlin 1933–1945* (Munich, 2013), pp. 7–16.

3   Entry 01/31/1933, in Elke Fröhlich and Angela Hermann (eds.), *Die Tagebücher von Joseph Goebbels*, Teil I, Aufzeichnungen 1923–1941, vol. 2/III (Munich, 2007), p. 85.

4   Das Urteil im Wilhelmstraßen-Prozess. Der amtliche Wortlaut der Entscheidung im Fall Nr. 11 des Nürnberger Militärtribunals gegen von Weizsäcker und andere, Schwäbisch Gmünd, 1950.

5   Laurenz Demps, *Die Wilhelmstraße: Eine Topografie preußisch-deutscher Macht* (Berlin, 1994).

6   Ernst Friedrich Werner-Rades, *Reichshauptstadt Berlin* (Berlin, 1943), p. 247. Cf. Werner-Rades, *München Hauptstadt der Bewegung: Im Auftrage des Reichsleiters Oberbürgermeister Karl Fiehler* (Munich, 1937).

7   Ibid.

8   Wolfgang Schäche and Hans J. Reichhart (eds.), *Von Berlin nach Germania. Über die Zerstörungen der Reichshauptstadt durch Albert Speers Neugestaltungsplanungen* (Berlin, 1990). Cf. Dagmar Thorau and Gernot Schaulinski (eds.), *Mythos Germania. Vision und Verbrechen* (Berlin, 2014).

9   Hans-Christian Jasch and Christoph Kreutzmüller, "The Participants. The Men of the Wannsee Conference," in: Hans-Christian Jasch and Christoph Kreutzmüller (eds.), *The Participants. The Men of the Wannsee Conference* (New York/Oxford, 2017), pp. 1–20, pp. 3–5.

10 Bjoern Weigel, "Inszenieren und zerstören. Kultur und Medien am Standort Berlin," in: Wildt and Kreutzmüller (eds.), *Berlin 1933–1945*, pp. 229–44.

11 Statistisches Amt der Stadt Berlin (ed.), *Berlin in Zahlen 1945* (Berlin, 1947), p. 247.

12 Julek Karl von Engelbrechten and Hans Volz (eds.), *Wir wandern durch das nationalsozialistische Berlin: Ein Führer durch die Gedenkstätten des Kampfes um die Reichshauptstadt* (Munich, 1937).

13 Elissa Mailänder, "Schlacht in den Wolken," in: Rainer Rother and Vera Thomas (eds.), *Linientreu und populär. Das Ufa-Imperium 1933–1945* (Berlin, 2017).

14 Deutsche Wochenschau, 720/27/1944. The match between the Dresden Sport Club and the Hamburg Airforce Sport Club ended 4:0.

15 Rudolf Suthoff-Groß and Ernst Luther, *Verfassung und Verwaltung der Reichshauptstadt Berlin auf der Grundlage des Gesetzes über die Verfassung und Verwaltung der Reichshauptstadt Berlin vom 1. Dezember 1936* (Berlin, 1938), p. 40.

16 "Fünf Wochen Berliner Kommunalpolitik," *Berliner Lokal-Anzeiger*, April 22, 1933.

17 Sabine Mecking and Andreas Wirsching, "Stadtverwaltung als Systemstabilisierung? Tätigkeitsfelder und Handlungsspielräume kommunaler Herrschaft im Nationalsozialismus," in: Sabine Mecking and Andreas Wirsching (eds.), *Stadtverwaltung im Nationalsozialismus: Systemstabilisierende Dimensionen kommunaler Herrschaft* (Paderborn, 2005), pp. 1–22, p. 9f. Cf. also Bezirksamt Wilmersdorf (ed.), *Kommunalverwaltung unterm Hakenkreuz: Berlin-Wilmersdorf 1933–1945* (Berlin, 1992).

18 Entry 08/11/1935, in *Die Tagebücher von Joseph Goebbels*, 1. Teil, vol. 3/1, 274. Cf. Frank Bajor, *Parvenüs und Profiteure. Korruption in der NS-Zeit* (Frankfurt am Main, 2004), p. 137f.

19 Christoph Kreutzmüller, "Die Verfassung und Verwaltung der Reichshauptstadt," in Wildt and Kreutzmüller, *Berlin 1933–1945*, pp. 51–68. Cf. Paul Spies and Gernot Schaulinski (eds.), *Berlin 1937: Im Schatten von morgen* (Berlin, 2017); Krijn Thijs, *Party, Pomp und Propaganda. Die Berliner Stadtjubiläen 1937 und 1987* (Berlin, 2012).

20 *Deutsche Wochenschau* Nr. 516, July 22, 1940.

21 Peter Longerich, *Joseph Goebbels* (Munich, 2010) pp. 551–5; Roger Moorhouse, *Berlin at War: Life and Death in Hitler's Capital 1939–1945* (London, 2010), pp. 336–41.

22 Martin Herzer, Auslandskorrespondenten und auswärtige Pressepolitik im Dritten Reich (Cologne, 2012), p. 93.

23 Bjoern Weigel, "Inszenieren und Zerstören: Kultur und Medien am Standort Berlin," in Wildt and Kreutzmüller, *Berlin 1933–1945*, pp. 245–60, p. 256f.

24 Tumultes, *VU*, 03/15/1933, Nr. 261, p. 384.

25 Irene von Götz and Christoph Kreutzmüller, "Spiegel des frühen NS-Terrors: Zwei Foto-Ikonen und ihre Geschichte," in *Fotogeschichte, Beiträge zur Geschichte und Ästhetik der Fotografie*, 131 (2014), pp. 73–5.

26 "I Shall Destroy," *Daily Mirror*, March 22, 1933.

27 "Make Arrests after Reichstag fire," *Winnipeg Free Press*, March 21, 1933.

28 "Rettenetes Adolf véres birodalma," *Társadalmunk*, March 25, 1933.

29 Letter from the German Embassy Shanghai to the Ministry of Foreign Affairs, September 4, 1933, Politisches Archiv des Auswärtigen Amts (PArch AA), R. 121121.

30 Letter from the Ministry of Information to the Ministry of Foreign Affairs, July 10, 1933, in: PArch AA, R. 121219.

31 World Alliance for Combating Anti-Semitism, *J'accuse* (London, 1933), p. 15.

32 Frank Bajohr, *Arisierung in Hamburg: Die Verdrängung der jüdischen Unternehmer 1933-1945* (Hamburg, 1997), pp. 44–54.

33 Christoph Kreutzmüller, *Final Sale in Berlin: The Destruction of Jewish Commercial Activity 1930-1945* (New York, 2017), pp. 105–10.

34 Three additional photographs from the Associated Press were also published in the *New York Times* on November 18, 1938. Norman Domeier recently pointed out that the AP cooperated with the NS regime starting in 1942; cf. Norman Domeier, "Geheime Fotos. Die Kooperation von Associated Press und NS-Regime (1942–1945)," in *Zeithistorische Forschungen/Studies in Contemporary History*, 14 (2017) 2, pp. 199–230, www.zeithistorische-forschungen.de/2-2017/id=5484.

35 Christoph Kreutzmüller and Bjoern Weigel, *Kristallnacht? Bilder der Novemberpogrome 1938 in Berlin* (Berlin, 2013).

36 Akim Jah, *Die Deportationen der Juden aus Berlin. Die nationalsozialistische Vernichtungspolitik und das Sammellager Große Hamburger Straße* (Berlin, 2013), p. 619.

37 Cf. Hans Ostwald, *Das galante Berlin* (Berlin, 1928).

38 Entry, September 17, 1926, *Tagebücher Goebbels*, Teil I, vol. 1/II, 132. Cf. Martin Broszat, 'Die Anfänge der Berliner NSDAP 1926/27', *Vierteljahrshefte für Zeitgeschichte* 8 (1960) 1, pp. 85–119.

39 Daniel Siemens, "Prügelpropaganda. Die SA und der nationalsozialistische Mythos vom Kampf um Berlin," in Wildt and Kreutzmüller (eds.), *Berlin 1933–1945*, pp. 33–48.

40 "Der längere Atem," *Der Panzerbär*, April 29, 1945.

41 Report of the 152th Police Precinct, December 23, 1936, Landesarchiv Berlin (LAB), A Rep. Pr. Br. 030, 21618. The police turned Fricke (born 02/16/1896) over to the Gestapo on December 24 1936. Fricke was transported to the Sachsenhausen concentration camp on January 17, 1940 where he died under unknown circumstances on July 29, 1944. Cf. Zugangsliste January 17, 1940, Archive Museum Sachsenhausen, D1, A/1196; Veränderungsmeldung, July 31, 1944, Archive Museum Sachsenhausen, JSU, 1/100.

42 Christine Fischer-Defoy, "Berlin im Exil. Eine tour d'horizon," in Wildt and Kreutzmüller, *Berlin 1933–1945*, pp. 211–27.

43 Marianne Bechhaus-Gerst, *Treu bis in den Tod. Von Deutsch-Ostafrika nach Sachsenhausen. Eine Lebensgeschichte* (Berlin, 2007), pp. 141–50.

44 Annegret Ehmann and Christoph Kreutzmüller, "Die fünf Jungen aus dem 'Haus Kinderschutz'," *Zeitschrift für Geschichtswissenschaft* 12 (2015), pp. 1057–76.

45 Ausschuss zur Untersuchung der Erzeugungs- und Absatzbedingungen der deutschen Wirtschaft (ed.), *Das Wirtschaftsleben der Städte, Landkreise und Landgemeinden. Verhandlungen und Berichte des Unterausschusses für allgemeine Wirtschaftsstruktur*, vol. 1 (Berlin, 1930), pp. 151f.

46   Ingo Materna and Wolfgang Ribbe, *Geschichte in Daten* (Berlin/Wiesbaden, 2003), p. 169.

47   Adam Tooze, *Wages of Destruction. The Making and Breaking of the Nazi Economy* (London, 2007), pp. 87f.

48   Johannes Bähr, *Industrie im geteilten Berlin (1945–1990): Die elektrotechnische Industrie und der Maschinenbau im Ost-West-Vergleich—Branchenentwicklung, Technologien und Handlungsstrukturen* (Munich, 2001), p. 40.

49   Cord Pagenstecher and Marc Buggeln, "Zwangsarbeit," in Wildt and Kreutzmüller, *Berlin 1933–1945*, pp. 127–42.

50   Kreutzmüller, *Final Sale*, pp. 78–80.

51   Cf. Kilian Steiner, *Ortsempfänger, Volksfernseher und Optaphon: Die Entwicklung der deutschen Radio- und Fernsehindustrie und das Unternehmen Loewe 1923–1962* (Essen, 2005), pp. 249f.

52   François Cavanna, *Das Lied der Baba* (Berlin/Weimar, 1988) (orig.: *Les Russkoffs*, Paris 1979). Cf. Buggeln and Pagenstecher, "Zwangsarbeit."

53   Statistisches Amt, Berlin, p. 187. Nicolai Zimmermann, *Die veröffentlichten Bilanzen der Commerzbank 1870–1944* (Berlin, 2005), p. 182.

54   Malte Zierenberg, *Stadt der Schieber: Der Berliner Schwarzmarkt 1939–1950* (Göttingen, 2008), pp. 85–162.

55   Michael Wildt, *Der Traum vom Sattwerden. Hunger und Protest, Schwarzmarkt und Selbsthilfe in Hamburg 1945–1948* (Hamburg, 1986), pp. 17–20.

56   Wilfried Feldenkirchen, *Siemens 1918–1945* (Munich/Zurich, 1995), pp. 154–6.

57   Bähr, *Industrie*, p. 44 and pp. 71f; Kreutzmüller, *Final Sale*, pp. 319–33.

58   Laurenz Demps, "Berlin im Bombenkrieg," in Wildt and Kreutzmüller, *Berlin 1933–1945*, pp. 357–71.

59   Sven Felix Kellerhoff, *Berlin im Krieg: Eine Generation erinnert sich* (Berlin, 2011), p. 7. Cf. Anthony Beevor, *Berlin the Downfall 1945* (London, 2002). Cf. Moritz van Dülmen and Bjoern Weigel (eds.), *May '45: Spring in Berlin—Everyday Life between War and Peace* (Berlin, 2015).

60   Essay from Werner W., o. D. (1945/46), LAB, C Rep.134–13, "Ich schlug meiner Mutter die brennenden Funken ab," in Annett Gröschner (ed.), *Berliner Schulaufsätze aus dem Jahr 1946* (Berlin, 1996).

61   "Ganz Berlin sitzt auf der Bombe," *Berliner Morgenpost*, August 4, 2004.

62   Deutsches Handelsadressbuch, *Reichsadressbuch für Wirtschaft und Verkehr* (Berlin, 1949), III.

2

Division of the Spoils: Berlin as Symbol and as Prize

David E. Barclay

Few Cold War symbols could have been more significant, or more threatening to both sides in that conflict, than Berlin.[1] Indeed, at the Vienna summit in June 1961, Nikita Sergeyevich Khrushchev described Berlin as "the most dangerous place in the world."[2] At no time, perhaps, was that danger more apparent than during the 1962 Cuban Missile Crisis, thousands of kilometers removed from Central Europe. The diplomatic historian, Ernest R. May, once pointedly observed that for John F. Kennedy, the missile crisis was in many ways more about the once and future German capital than about the island of Cuba itself:

> Kennedy interpreted the installation of missiles in Cuba as a move preparatory to a showdown on Berlin. For him, such a showdown would create a horrible dilemma. The United States had promised to protect the million and a half West Berliners from Soviet takeover, but had no means whatever for physically preventing the thousands of East German and Soviet troops that surrounded Berlin from taking control of the city if they chose to do so. The only protection for West Berlin was the US threat to respond to an attack by using nuclear weapons against the Soviet Union .... "A Soviet move on Berlin," Kennedy said to the joint chiefs of staff, "leaves me only one alternative, which is to fire nuclear weapons—which is a hell of an alternative."[3]

For much of the Cold War, Berlin was both an indispensable symbol *and* a very expensive prize, a "showcase of competing systems" (*Schaufenster der Systemkonkurrenz*).[4] As Martin Luther King, Jr., put it on his visit to Berlin in September 1964: "Here in Berlin, one cannot help being aware that you are the hub around which turns the wheel of history."[5] Around the same time, the American author and essayist, Wallace Stegner, proclaimed that the story of post-1945 Berlin was Homeric in its epic dimensions: "The *great* book on Berlin is going to be a sort of Iliad, a story that dramatizes a power struggle in terms of the men who waged it."[6]

But within a few years after King and Stegner had made these remarks, Berlin had lost much of its salience both as contested prize and disputed symbol, at least for the four occupation powers, if not for the two German states themselves. Indeed, the perceived worth of the prize and the importance and nature of the symbol—or, rather, symbols—varied significantly during the course of the Cold War. From the symbolism of the "classic" age of pre-Wall ideological and geopolitical competition to the Wall itself, from the so-called "heroic" period of "America's Berlin" as "outpost of freedom" in the 1950s and early 1960s to the age of American forgetfulness in the 1970s and 1980s, from the symbolism of the Stalinallee to the symbolism of Kreuzberg's "alternative" cultural scenes to the symbolism of the 750th anniversary celebrations in 1987 that Krijn Thijs has described so effectively in this book and elsewhere, Cold War Berlin as prize and symbol was every bit as protean and shifting as the larger city itself throughout its entire modern history.[7] Berlin has long been a place that has constantly reinvented and remade itself. To that extent, at least, Cold War Berlin—although a peculiar and unique place—did not represent a complete or total historical anomaly, as Brian Ladd, among others, reminded us some years ago. Berlin has long been a city of "startling incongruities," he writes, and this was as true before 1945 and after 1990 as it was during the years of Cold War division.[8]

In this chapter, we will consider six central arguments. Most focus on the relationship between the United States and West Berlin. Other contributions to this volume will deal in greater detail with the other occupation powers, especially the Soviet Union:

- At first, the United States was eager to continue cooperation with the Soviets in Berlin and elsewhere in Germany.
- "America's Berlin" began to emerge in late 1947, but only became part of the American national consciousness with the Airlift in 1948–9.
- After reaching its apogee in the early 1960s, the symbolic significance of Berlin for the United States declined drastically, especially with the completion of the Quadripartite Agreement of September 1971.
- The political leaders of West Berlin were worried about Americans' lack of attention to West Berlin, and consciously tried to create powerful symbols that, among other things, could remind American leaders that Berlin was a worthwhile prize.
- Soviet and East German attempts to transform East Berlin into a symbol of the superiority of socialism were numerous and generally consistent but not entirely successful.
- As the symbolic salience of Berlin as Cold War symbol declined, after the late 1960s the Western half of the divided city became a site of competing symbols and cultural resonances.

Let us deal with each of these points in turn.

Initial Allied Cooperation

Although effective four-power and local administration of Berlin faltered quickly after 1945, the Americans, and especially Lucius D. Clay, military governor of the US zone of occupation in Germany after 1947, remained eager to cooperate with the Soviets in what Dwight D. Eisenhower had originally called "an experimental laboratory" of postwar collaboration for peace.[9] One important example: As late as the summer of 1947, Clay raised no objections when the Soviet Union vetoed the selection of Ernst Reuter as lord mayor (*Oberbürgermeister*) of Berlin. In December 1946, the increasingly anti-communist Social Democratic Party (SPD) had emerged as the big winner in elections that had taken place in all four occupied sectors of the former capital city, and had selected the veteran SPD politician Otto Ostrowski as mayor. But when, in the spring of 1947, Ostrowski had met without authorization with representatives of the pro-Soviet Socialist Unity Party (SED), leading Berlin social democrats had objected vehemently, had ousted Ostrowski, and had named Ernst Reuter in his place. A veteran local politician who had held a number of important posts in Berlin and Magdeburg before 1933, Reuter had been persecuted by the Nazis and had returned to Berlin in late 1946 after eleven years in Turkish exile. From 1918 to 1922, Reuter had also been a member of the Communist Party, and indeed had served briefly as its general secretary before breaking with communism, returning to the SPD, and becoming a vehement anti-communist in later years. His selection as mayor in the spring of 1947 clearly represented a challenge to Soviet authority in the city, and to the position of the SED itself; in the summer, the Soviets simply vetoed his election. Just as significantly, Lucius Clay did not challenge the Soviet veto.[10]

In 1947 Berlin was obviously an important prize for the Americans, but not yet a symbol of democratic resistance to communism and Soviet expansionism. As the Reuter case showed, such feelings were stronger among Berlin social democrats— including people such as Franz Neumann—than among American occupation officials or for that matter some Berlin Christian Democrats including Ferdinand Friedensburg, who continued for years to advocate efforts to cooperate with Soviet occupation authorities.[11] Writing in English, Ernst Reuter put it this way in commenting on the unwillingness of the Americans to resist the Soviet veto:

> Shortly before my election General Clay accepted in the Control Council, the instance superior to Allied Kommandatura, the principle of previous approval of the Oberbürgermeister's election as demanded by the Russians. Thus it was obvious from the very first that a well-functioning administration of the city could not be established. This sudden decision of General Clay, the motives of which nobody could explain to us so far, was in our opinion the zero-point in the development of affairs in Berlin, id est, the point of the utmost compliance towards the Russian claims for dominancy, if you like, a sort of "Munich" for Berlin. Thus the Russians had, to my knowledge, already substantially won the battle about Berlin.[12]

For non-communist politicians like Reuter, the "Battle for Berlin" was potentially a life-and-death struggle. Thus anti-communist political leaders in Berlin emphasized not only the strategic significance but also the symbolic importance of the city well before the Western powers did so, out of fear that the Western powers might abandon both them and the city itself. In the words of US Ambassador Robert Murphy, State Department representative in Germany, in July 1947:

In their view, Germany stands before the fatal decision of the Great Powers and the extent of their apprehension concerning an unfavorable outcome is reflected in their outspoken fear that the western allies may withdraw from Berlin. They feel this would not only entail disaster for the non-Communist parties, but would also mean the abandonment of Berlin as a source of information and influence in the heart of the Soviet zone, that it would be capitalized by the Soviets as a sign of weakness on the part of the Western nations and might encourage them to set up a separate and highly integrated eastern German Bolshevist state with reconstructed armament industries based on Silesian coal.[13]

The Western powers, and especially the United States, would thus have to be reminded constantly of the importance of the city. Writing again in English, Reuter noted in December 1947 that:

Our heads will be on the line; and this struggle will be harder for us because, as a result of some bitter experiences, we cannot be confident that the Western powers will always and in every situation support us. The feeling of uncertainty is too great, and the terrible pressure that again and again weighs down on people is often too great. ... This war of nerves will soon get worse, and we cannot see where it will lead us.[14]

America's Berlin of the Airlift

As it turns out, Reuter and his allies were extraordinarily effective at projecting an image of heroic resistance, and, in this respect, the Soviet blockade and Allied airlift were almost made to order for them. This is not to imply that the threat was not real, only to suggest that the non-communist leaders of Berlin politics made very effective use of it in helping to create a new symbol of Berlin as beleaguered citadel of democracy. Neither was their concern entirely unjustified. In the spring of 1948, as Daniel Harrington has convincingly shown, "the Pentagon's first impulse was to evacuate" Berlin, especially after Lucius Clay's dire warnings to Washington about Soviet intentions; the ever-cautious General Omar Bradley, head of the US Joint Chiefs of Staff, was deeply skeptical about the viability of a Western presence in Berlin.[15]

But the Airlift succeeded far beyond even Clay's expectations. What Andreas Daum, Dominik Geppert, Scott Krause, Stefanie Eisenhuth, and others have described as "America's Berlin" emerged in the context of the airlift and the years immediately thereafter. Indeed, Eisenhuth argues convincingly that the blockade and airlift constituted the "foundational myth" of West Berlin and its special relationship to the United States. It was the joint creation of American occupation authorities on the ground, of the American media, and of an emerging anti-communist and democratic consensus in both the Western sectors of Berlin and in the United States.[16] It was consciously developed and sustained by Ernst Reuter and supporters such as his publicist and adviser Hans Hirschfeld, who wanted to ensure that the Western Allies would never be tempted to leave the city or forget their obligations to it. Symbolism was vital to the project of creating what Eisenhuth, drawing on Benedict Anderson, has called an "imagined community" of values between the United States and a democratic West Berlin.[17] Its physical expressions are mostly still with us and represent a major aspect of Berlin's landscape of architectural postwar modernism: the Free University of Berlin and the activities of the Ford Foundation there; the Steglitz Clinic that later became the Benjamin Franklin Clinic, the America Memorial Library (*Amerika-Gedenkbibliothek*), the airlift memorial at Tempelhof airport; the Amerika-Haus; or the Congress Hall (*Kongresshalle*), to mention several well-known examples. Or there was the huge public relations campaign in the United States around the "Freedom Bell" (*Freiheitsglocke*) for West Berlin's Schöneberg City Hall in 1950, and the sustained engagement of well-placed and influential Americans including Lucius Clay, Eleanor Lansing Dulles, or Shepard Stone for Berlin.[18] Scott Krause has written compellingly on what might be called the "American Berlin lobby," comparable in influence to the better-known (or at least more notorious) "China lobby."[19] Not to be overlooked, of course, was the continuing American military presence in West Berlin. The British and the French were also ubiquitous in their respective sectors—the annual British Military Tattoo was always a big event in West Berlin—but, given Cold War realities, until their departure in 1994 the Americans played an especially important role not only as "protective power" or *Schutzmacht* but also as a powerful cultural factor in the city, both as bearers and as mediators of US pop culture. Even the growing anti-Americanism of Berlin students and of the city's assorted "alternative" communities after the mid-1960s did not seriously lessen the impact of that cultural influence.[20]

Four-Power Berlin Agreement

Despite ambivalent feelings about West Berlin in West Germany, especially during the Adenauer years between 1949 and 1963, the federal government in Bonn regularly attempted to assert its presence in the divided former capital of the country, most significantly perhaps in the form of sustained West German financial subvention for West Berlin's artificial economy.[21] Such attempts, of course, whether they involved the official election of the West German president or the establishment of a Federal Environmental Office in West Berlin, invariably resulted in vehement protests from the Soviet side. In 1975, for example, the Soviets even objected when West German officials participated in the investigation of the terrorist kidnapping of Peter Lorenz, head of the West Berlin Christian Democratic Union (CDU).[22] For their part, of course, the Soviets and their allies insisted that East Berlin was the capital of the GDR, a contention that met with various responses from the three Western powers, from rejection to a sort of muddled acceptance, especially after the signing of the Quadripartite Agreement in 1971.[23] Of particular importance to the Western Allies, of course, was the maintenance of the four-power occupation status for Berlin as a whole.[24]

The project of ensuring continued Western support for West Berlin quickly assumed certain standardized and even ritualized forms, and these continued until the very end of the Cold War. Thus it became de rigueur for the governing mayor of West Berlin—who functioned, in the words of the *New York Times*, as a kind of prime minister and foreign minister of a small country—to visit the capital cities of the three Western powers, especially shortly after assuming office.[25] Ernst Reuter himself pioneered these trips, visiting the United States on three separate and really quite triumphal occasions between 1949 and 1953. Reuter's US visits were elaborate multicity occasions, by no means perfunctory affairs limited to Washington, DC. In the new television age, and with his remarkable language skills, Reuter was exceptionally telegenic, as was his protégé and successor Willy Brandt, who shared Reuter's capacity to express himself passionately and in colloquial American English.[26] Of course, not all governing mayors of West Berlin could muster such skills; individuals such as Walther Schreiber, Otto Suhr, Heinrich Albertz, Dietrich Stobbe, Hans-Jochen Vogel, or Eberhard Diepgen might have been worthy and capable officeholders, but they were the very opposite of charismatic. (Indeed, Richard von Weizsäcker was the only governing mayor of West Berlin after 1966 who could remotely claim to wear the mantle of charisma.) But all the way down to Walter Momper in the spring of 1989, the Cold War-era governing mayors of West Berlin continued this tradition, even if the American media and the American public paid less and less attention to them. And, of course, there were the reciprocal visits by major Western leaders. One hardly need mention the Kennedy visit in June 1963, or the visits of Lyndon Johnson in 1961, Robert F. Kennedy and Martin Luther King, Jr., in 1964, Queen Elizabeth II in 1965 and 1978, Richard Nixon and Valéry Giscard d'Estaing in 1969, Prince Charles in 1973, Jimmy Carter in 1978, François Mitterrand in 1985 and 1987, or Ronald Reagan on three separate occasions, most notably in 1987 when he called on Mikhail Gorbachev to "tear down this wall."[27] Increasingly, however, such visits became routine, obligatory affairs, suggesting that the city's significance both as showcase and as flashpoint shifted considerably over the course of the Cold War.

For Americans its significance, as prize and as symbol, was at its height during the so-called "heroic phase" between 1948 and the mid-1960s, culminating with the building of the Wall after August 1961 and John F. Kennedy's visit in June 1963. Thereafter the symbolic significance of the divided city for the "West" and especially for the United States dwindled almost to the point of irrelevance by the 1980s. The ultimate symbol of Berlin's Cold War division was, obviously, the Wall itself, but especially after the four-power agreement of 1971—arguably the turning point in the history of Cold War Berlin—the Wall became part of the landscape of what Ann Tusa originally called the "abnormal normality" of those years.[28] Reuter's original fears about American attention deficits and American forgetfulness were, in fact, quite justified. By the early 1980s, to at least some American leaders, it was not entirely clear that the originary four-power rights in Berlin mattered very much.

To be sure, military contingency plans by the West for the defense of Berlin, embodied in the well-known Live Oak organization—based in Belgium, and jointly administered by the USA, UK, France, and West Germany—with its regular military exercises, continued throughout all these years. Live Oak remained the ultimate expression of the determination by the three Western powers to assert their continued rights in Berlin, involving measured responses up to and including the possible use of nuclear weapons. In 1962 an incident on the transit *Autobahn* between West Germany and West Berlin came close to triggering a Live Oak response, the only time that such a thing ever happened; but even after the conclusion of the Quadripartite Agreement in 1971, the three Western Allies and West Germany continued to maintain the Live Oak organization and its military exercises until 1990.[29]

Symbolic Reassertion

Still, by the late 1970s and 1980s, Berlin had lost much of its value as a prize and much of its luster as a symbol, except perhaps in travel guides, for example, the famous Arthur Frommer *Europe on Five Dollars a Day* series, consumed by hundreds of thousands of American tourists. Frommer had begun his travel guides as a GI stationed in West Berlin in the 1950s, and subsequent editions of his much celebrated book glamorized and popularized Berlin as an edgy city full of spies and Cold War intrigue. This served to invest the city with a scintillating quality at the very time that, in the years after the mid-1970s, West Berlin's local politics had become increasingly provincial and squalid. The Wall itself had become a tourist attraction, increasingly ignored or sublimated by the population of Berlin itself. To American and British policymakers, however, West Berlin was increasingly something of a backwater, as their reports from about 1973 to the late 1980s frequently suggest. Indeed, so serious had the situation become as early as 1973, that John Kornblum, then a member of the US Mission in West Berlin and later Ambassador to Germany, felt obliged to write a formal memorandum on "Why Are We in Berlin?" for a seminar of major US foreign police decisionmakers. One of these was John Sherman Cooper, designated as first US Ambassador to the GDR, who openly questioned why the USA and its allies were still in Berlin three decades after the end of World War Two. Official American interest in Berlin continued to decline throughout the 1980s; and Kornblum is convinced that, had 1989 not intervened, the USA would have left Berlin by the mid-1990s.[30]

Confronted by the shifting realities of American interest in the divided city, the political leaders of West Berlin consciously tried to create their own symbols, to advance their own political interests and to ensure continued Allied support, all of course in the context of systemic competition with the East. (See the chapter by Clara M. Oberle in this volume about Berlin as a housing and urban planning laboratory.) Some examples are quite well known: in the 1950s, the Stalinallee in the East versus the Hansaviertel housing project in the West; or, three decades later, in 1987, the International Building Exhibition (IBA) in the West.[31] Housing projects in the West, such as the Ernst-Reuter-Siedlung, were built as close as possible to the sector boundary to East Berlin, a conscious strategy that West Berlin social democrats in particular strongly supported. Thus, for example, in 1955 Governing Mayor Otto Suhr had stated: "The reconstruction of destroyed city centers must be encouraged above all along the sector boundaries, both to eliminate the impression that the border areas consist of stone deserts and to give expression to our own genuine, future-oriented attitude about building and about life in general, in contrast to the façade culture of the eastern sector." His successor, Willy Brandt, noted similarly in 1959: "It is our responsibility to use the construction of buildings on the sector boundary in order to build out toward the other part of the city. Here we have to give creative expression to our determination that this city must still be regarded as one."[32] At the dedication of the Ernst-Reuter-Siedlung in Wedding, Senator Paul Hertz asserted that the settlement proved "that with it we are laying a cornerstone for a free and better future, for the unity of Berlin and of Germany."[33]

Ideological Contestation

Interesting and typical in this context was the long dispute in the late 1950s and early 1960s over the location of the new Philharmonie, and the role of music as political and cultural symbol. There is no question that, for West Berlin political leaders as various as the Christian democrat Joachim Tiburtius or the social democrat Willy Brandt, the Berlin Philharmonic Orchestra was a significant cultural and political advertisement for the city, especially as it began its frequent overseas tours under the aegis of Herbert von Karajan and orchestra intendant Wolfgang Stresemann, son of the Weimar foreign minister and himself an extraordinarily effective cultural diplomat. In 1973 Governing Mayor Klaus Schütz described the orchestra as an especially "effective ambassador" for the city, a sentiment that was echoed by virtually every other governing mayor of West Berlin.[34]

Thus the debate after 1956 over the location of the new Philharmonie, designed by Hans Scharoun, became a heated contest about cultural symbolism between the CDU and the SPD in West Berlin. The CDU, apparently resigned to the city's division, favored the construction of a new building in the Bundesallee, in the heart of West Berlin behind the façade of the old Joachimsthalsches Gymnasium. The SPD favored an entirely new structure on the Kemperplatz, very close to the sectoral boundary between East and West, where it could serve as a focus for what it imagined would once again be a new city center, and in the meantime draw attention to the city's division. Ultimately the SPD carried the argument, and Brandt put it this way at the *Richtfest* for the new building in 1961:

> When we laid the cornerstone about a year ago, no one could have imagined that the new Philharmonie would become so frightfully disconnected from our fellow citizens in the other part of our city. On that side they have built a wall, and in fact behind it a second wall, bristling with barbed wire and so strongly guarded that no East Berliner can escape from that great prison. On this side, we are working busily to construct a place of inspiration for everyone. Over there, tanks and machine guns ensure that nobody can escape their economy of coercion.[35]

And on October 15, 1963, when the Philharmonie was officially opened, Brandt emphasized that it had been built specifically to reach out to the citizens of the East.[36] It was thus a symbol of ideological contestation, at least in part, and represented another implicit challenge to the Soviet Union and the GDR.

How did the leadership of the Soviet Union and the GDR see Berlin, both as prize and as symbol?[37] Without becoming derailed in a resuscitated debate over the causes and reasons for the division of Germany (see the works of Melvyn Leffler, Carolyn Eisenberg, Wilfried Loth, Norman Naimark, and others), it is clear that the Soviets understood from the outset that there was indeed a battle for Germany and for Berlin.[38] They understood the value of the prize, which they had taken at such a high price in the spring of 1945. It was important, and was worth taking some risks for, as Stalin noted in his famous remarks to Wilhelm Pieck in the spring of 1948 about "kicking out" the Western powers.[39] But it was not worth risking real war in 1948–9, although thirteen years later the danger was indeed quite real and quite grave, more dangerous even than was perhaps realized at the time. Thus the main argument under this fifth heading is again more summary than original: rather obviously, the meaning of Berlin, both as prize and as symbol, was shifting and variable both for the Soviets and their uncomfortable allies in the GDR. A world of difference separates the conquest of Berlin by Soviet armed forces in 1945 from Mikhail Gorbachev's famous remarks about the forces of history on the occasion of the GDR's fortieth anniversary in October 1989. Of course the Soviets, like their Western counterparts, left a physical mark on Berlin, from the war memorials in Treptow Park and the Tiergarten to the Soviet Embassy on Unter den Linden (completed between 1950 and 1953) and beyond. For the GDR itself, of course, East Berlin was also a "showcase," a place of shifting meanings, discourses, and symbolism, from the Stalinallee to the Television Tower (*Fernsehturm*) to the Palace of the Republic (*Palast der Republik*) and, of course, the Wall itself. Here Martin Sabrow's important book on GDR memory culture is an essential reference.[40]

Subcultural Differentiation

By the 1960s and 1970s, that is, after the so-called "heroic" period, Cold War West Berlin had become a place with a dizzying array of cultural resonances and cultural symbols, often antagonistic and countervailing. When and how did it begin, at least symbolically? With the Rolling Stones concert at the Waldbühne in 1965? With the ratcheting up of Vietnam protests in 1966? With the emergence of the Extraparliamentary Opposition or "APO"? With the shooting of Benno Ohnesorg during demonstrations against the visiting Shah of Iran on June 2, 1967? With the shooting of Rudi Dutschke in April 1968? Although cultural phenomena can never be dated precisely, West Berlin had become a very different kind of symbol after the 1960s and especially after the "abnormal normalization" of 1971, a strange combination of unique cultural *Biotop*, radical social and cultural experimentation, open city, global city, and seedy, provincial backwater with an artificially skewed demography and a subsidized economy. Olaf Leitner's wonderful collection of interviews and memoirs regarding the West Berlin scene in the 1970s and 1980s is essential reading in this regard.[41] So too are the recollections of the British disc jockey Mark Reeder, a long-time resident of West Berlin, as well as accounts by Wolfgang Müller, founder of the legendary post-punk band *Die tödliche Doris*, and the American observer Paul Hockenos.[42] It was a city symbolized by squatters, alternative lifestyles, and cutting-edge music from David Bowie, Iggy Pop, and Brian Eno to industrial rock à la Blixa Bargeld and *Einstürzende Neubauten*. And for many young people, and not just Germans, West Berlin in particular became an almost imaginary place, a fantasy island of alternative lifestyles. For example, the politically and socially satirical comic strip *Doonesbury* has long been a kind of cultural documentary for American baby boomers. Its eponymous main character, Mike Doonesbury, had a younger brother named Benjy on the family farm in Oklahoma. In the early 1980s Benjy decided to become a punk, and renamed himself Saliva Putrid, or "Sal." When, in one strip in March 1982, Mike asks "Sal" what he intends to do with his life, he replies: "I want to go over to Berlin and work the punk clubs and live in a squatters house with German skinheads until I get a record contract."[43]

But it was also a city full of old-aged pensioners, traditional urban villages (symbolized by the German word *Kiez*), significant numbers of former foreign "guest workers" and their families (especially from Turkey), the constant presence of Allied military forces, and the continued reality of four-power occupation status. Certainly the best-known *Kiez*—or, perhaps, assemblage of *Kieze*—was the district of Kreuzberg, itself directly on the Berlin Wall and known for its alternative lifestyles.[44] But Kreuzberg was just one of lots of neighborhoods, many of them separated not by physical walls but by invisible walls of experience, generation, psychology, and social class. Moreover, both Berlins were geographically quite large, and many Berliners lived far removed from the center of things, whether in the East Berlin housing developments of Marzahn or the West Berlin developments of Gropiusstadt and the Märkisches Viertel. For some native West Berliners who grew up in neighborhoods far removed from Kreuzberg, the isolated city was an "island of the fortunate," a place of happy childhood memories utterly disconnected from alternative lifestyles.[45] And even for many nonnatives the divided city, although physically unappealing, was a kind of "paradise."[46]

All these communities occupied unique niches, a condition ultimately made possible by the Allied occupation regime and by the city's physical isolation. These niche societies rarely intersected or overlapped with each other. In fact, as Paul Hockenos has rightly noted, the alternative communities of West Berlin in the 1980s were often suspicious of outsiders:

> [I]n stark contrast to the post-Wall years of anarchy in eastern Berlin, where everybody was welcome, the subcultural niches in West Berlin were deep and narrow. Outsiders weren't coddled, they were barked at. You might get past the doorway of trendy bars such as Risiko or Kumpelnest, but you'd have to sport just the right coiffeur to get a drink.

> The house squatters were a breed unto themselves, who would bite your head off for daring to glance at their buildings, which were adorned with banners, flags and graffiti, presumably to be read. The scene's ill-humour fused perfectly with native Berliners' raw Berliner Schnauze, or Berliner insolence, ensuring that you'd likely get snapped at on all but lucky days.[47]

By the 1970s and 1980s, then, it increasingly seemed that the erstwhile "island city" of the 1950s and early 1960s had dissolved into an archipelago of little islands or atolls, culturally and politically quite distinctive, but all still surrounded by a communist sea that lots of islanders tried to ignore. East Berlin continued to occupy a privileged position in the GDR, which often aroused both envy and resentment in the rest of the country. When significant resources were drained from elsewhere to support the city's 750th anniversary celebrations in 1987, car stickers sometimes showed up in Leipzig with the slogan "821 Jahre Leipzig" or in Dresden with "781 Jahre Dresden" as a form of satirical protest against the special position of the *Hauptstadt der DDR*.[48] And then the Wall fell, and both the archipelago and the GDR disappeared into history.

The remaining chapters in this book explore in greater detail the disjointedness and resilience of Berlin, across and on both sides of the Cold War divide, while discussing and dissecting Cold War Berlin's assorted memory cultures and symbolic discourses. They remind us again that Berlin has long been a restless place that, as noted at the outset, has reinvented and rediscovered itself in myriad ways.

Notes

1   On Berlin as "complex of symbols," see the important article by Simone Derix, "Der Symbolkomplex Berlin. Berlin-Diskurs und Berlin-Praktiken nach 1945," in: Michael C. Bienert, Uwe Schaper, and Hermann Wentker (eds.), *Hauptstadtanspruch und symbolische Politik. Die Bundespräsenz im geteilten Berlin* (Berlin, 2012), pp. 183–208.

2   Quoted in Frederick Kempe, *Berlin 1961: Kennedy, Khrushchev, and the Most Dangerous Place on Earth* (New York, 2011), p. xv.

3   Ernest R. May, *John F. Kennedy and the Cuban Missile Crisis*, November 18, 2013 (updated), www.bbc.co.uk/history/worldwars/coldwar/kennedy_cuban_missile_01. shtml. See the frequent references to the Cuba-Berlin linkage in Ernest R. May and Philip D. Zelikow (eds.), *The Kennedy Tapes: Inside the White House during the Cuban Missile Crisis* (New York, 2002).

4   Michael Lemke (ed.), *Schaufenster der Systemkonkurrenz. Die Region Berlin-Brandenburg im Kalten Krieg* (Cologne, 2006); idem, *Vor der Mauer. Berlin in der Ost-West Konkurrenz 1948 bis 1961* (Cologne, 2011), pp. 37–40.

5   www.buzzfeed.com/germanyinusa/2014-marks-the-50th-anniversary-of-martin-luther-k-fr91#.oclOXoZ6za.

6   Wallace Stegner, "On the Writing of History," in *The Sound of Mountain Water* (New York, 1997), p. 203.

7   Krijn Thijs, *Drei Geschichten, eine Stadt: Die Berliner Stadtjubiläen von 1937 und 1987* (Cologne, 2008); idem, *Party, Pomp und Propaganda: Die Berliner Stadtjubiläen 1937 und 1987* (Berlin, 2012).

8   Brian Ladd, *The Ghosts of Berlin: Confronting German History in the Urban Landscape* (Chicago, 1997), p. 3, p. 171.

9   Daniel F. Harrington, *Berlin on the Brink: The Blockade, the Airlift, and the Early Cold War* (Lexington, 2012), p. 75.

10   On all these matters, see David E. Barclay, *Schaut auf diese Stadt. Der unbekannte Ernst Reuter* (Berlin, 2000), esp. pp. 211–40.

11   On Friedensburg, see his memoirs, *Lebenserinnerungen* (Frankfurt am Main, 1969), and the sympathetic account by Gerhard Keiderling, *Um Deutschlands Einheit: Ferdinand Friedensburg und der Kalte Krieg in Berlin 1945–1952* (Cologne, 2009).

12   Ernst Reuter to A. L. Barber, April 27, 1948, in Ernst Reuter, *Schriften—Reden*, vol. 3, Artikel—Briefe—Reden, (eds.) Hans E. Hirschfeld and Hans J. Reichhardt (Berlin, 1974), p. 375.

13 Robert Murphy to Secretary of State, July 12, 1947, National Archives, College Park, Maryland, Record Group (RG) 59, 740.00119 Control (Germany)/7-1247; Murphy to Secretary of State, July 16, 1947, ibid., 862.00/7-1647.

14 Reuter to Elizabeth Fox Howard, December 27, 1947, in Reuter, Schriften—Reden, 3: 325–7. See also Reuter to Karl Reuter, December 26, 1947, in ibid., 3: 323–4; Reuter to Gustav Oelsner, December 28, 1947, in ibid., 3: 327–9; Reuter to Konrad Engelmann, January 4, 1948, in ibid., 3: 333–4.

15 Harrington, *Berlin on the Brink*, p. 75.

16 Andreas W. Daum, "America's Berlin, 1945–2000: Between Myths and Visions," in:, Frank Trampler (ed.), *Berlin: The New Capital in the West. A Transatlantic Appraisal* (Washington, 2000), 49–73; Dominik Geppert, "'Proclaim Liberty Throughout All the Land': Berlin and the Symbolism of the Cold War," in: Dominik Geppert (ed.), *The Postwar Challenge. Cultural, Social, and Political Change in Western Europe, 1945–1958* (Oxford, 2003), pp. 339–63; Scott H. Krause, 'Neue Westpolitik: The Clandestine Campaign to Westernize the SPD in Cold War Berlin, 1948–1958', *Central European History*, 48 (March 2015) 1, pp. 79–99; Stefanie Eisenhuth, *Die Schutzmacht: Die Amerikaner in Berlin 1945–1994* (Göttingen, 2018), pp. 182–96. For general histories of West Berlin, see Wilfried Rott, *Die Insel: Eine Geschichte West-Berlins 1948–1990* (Munich, 2009); Elke Kimmel, *West-Berlin: Biografie einer Halbstadt* (Berlin, 2018). A scholarly history of West Berlin has yet to appear. For a recent general history of the entire city, see Jens Bisky, *Berlin: Biographie einer großen Stadt* (Berlin, 2019).

17 Eisenhuth, *Schutzmacht*, pp. 189–291.

18 For example, see Jean Edward Smith, *Lucius D. Clay: An American Life* (New York, 1990); Leonard Mosley, *Dulles: A Biography of Eleanor, Allen, and John Foster Dulles and Their Family Network* (New York, 1978); Volker R. Berghahn, *America and the Intellectual Cold Wars in Europe* (Princeton, 1991). On the Freedom Bell, see Veronika Liebau and Andreas W. Daum, *Die Freiheitsglocke in Berlin/The Freedom Bell in Berlin* (Berlin, 2000).

19 Scott H. Krause, *Bringing Cold War Democracy to West Berlin: A Shared German-American Project, 1940–1972* (Abingdon, 2018).

20 On the US military presence in Berlin, see, above all, Eisenhuth, *Schutzmacht*. See also Udo Wetzlaugk, *Die Alliierten in Berlin* (Berlin, 1988); Robert P. Grathwol and Donita M. Moorhus, *American Forces in Berlin: Cold War Outpost, 1945–1994* (Washington, 1994); idem, *Berlin and the American Military: A Cold War Chronicle* (New York, 1999); Gabriele Heidenfelder, *From Duppel to Truman Plaza: Die Berlin American Community in den Jahren 1965 bis 1989* (Hamburg, 1998); Friedrich Jeschonnek, Dieter Riedel, and William Durie, *Alliierte in Berlin 1945–1994. Ein Handbuch zur Geschichte der militärischen Präsenz der Westmächte*, 2nd ed. (Berlin, 2007); Michael Bienert, Uwe Schaper, and Andrea Theissen (eds.), *Die Vier Mächte in Berlin. Beiträge zur Politik der Alliierten in der besetzten Stadt* (Berlin, 2007); and the publications of the Alliierten Museum.

21 See the essays in Bienert et al. (eds.), *Hauptstadtanspruch*, especially Frank E. W. Zschauer, "Bundeshilfen für Berlin," pp. 209–20.

22 Foreign and Commonwealth Office, memorandum, July 9, 1975, The National Archives, Kew (hereafter: TNA), FCO 33/2742.

23 Michael Lemke, "Ost-Berlin als Hauptstadt der DDR 1959–1990," in: Bienert et al. (eds.), *Hauptstadtanspruch*, pp. 263–82.

24 For example, see "Bonn Group Paper on Western Legal and Political Positions on Berlin for Use with Third Countries," March 22, 1977, TNA, FCO 33/3249.

25   Walter Sullivan, "Ernst Reuter Dies; Mayor of Berlin," *New York Times*, September 30, 1953.

26   Björn Grötzner, *Outpost of Freedom. Ernst Reuters Amerikareisen 1949 bis 1953* (Berlin, 2014).

27   For example, see Andreas W. Daum, *Kennedy in Berlin* (Cambridge, 2007); Jens Schöne, *Ronald Reagan in Berlin. Der Präsident, die Staatssicherheit und die geteilte Stadt* (Berlin, 2016).

28   Ann Tusa, *The Last Division: Berlin and the Wall* (London, 1996), chap. 2.

29   On Live Oak, see, for example, Gregory W. Pedlow, "Allied Crisis Management for Berlin: The LIVE OAK Organization, 1959–1963," in: William W. Epley (ed.), *International Cold War Military Records and History* (Washington, DC, 1996), pp. 87–116; Sean M. Maloney, "Berlin Contingency Planning: Prelude to Flexible Response, 1958–63," *Journal of Strategic Studies*, 25(2002), pp. 99–134. See also the documents in "Berlin. Live Oak/Sea Spray," TNA, DEFE 11/872, including detailed descriptions of Live Oak exercises such as "Steadfast I" in 1976, and S. J. Lambert, "Background Note on Live Oak," June 25, 1975, TNA, DEFE 24/881.

30   On the above, see David E. Barclay, "A 'Complicated Contrivance': West Berlin behind the Wall, 1971–1989," in: Marc Silberman, Karen E. Till, and Janet Ward (eds.), *Walls, Borders, Boundaries: Spatial and Cultural Practices in Europe* (New York, 2012), pp. 118–22. See also idem, "On the Back Burner—Die USA und West-Berlin 1948–1994," in: Tilman Mayer (ed.), *Deutschland aus internationaler Sicht* (Berlin, 2009), pp. 25–36; idem, "Kein neuer Mythos. Das letzte Jahrzehnt West-Berlins," *Aus Politik und Zeitgeschichte* 65 (2015) 46, pp. 37–42.

31   There is a large literature on postwar planning, architecture, and the "Systemkonkurrenz" between the two parts of the divided city, but see especially Emily Pugh, *Architecture, Politics, and Identity in Divided Berlin* (Pittsburgh, 2014); Jörg Haspel and Thomas Flierl (eds.), *Karl-Marx-Allee und Interbau 1957. Konfrontation, Konkurrenz und Koevolution der Moderne in Berlin* (Berlin, 2017); Adrian von Buttlar, Kerstin Wittmann-Englert, and Gabi Dolf-Bonekämper (eds.), *Baukunst der Nachkriegsmoderne. Architekturführer Berlin 1949–1979* (Berlin, 2013).

32   Cited in Dieter Hanauske, *"Bauen, bauen, bauen … !" Die Wohnungspolitik in Berlin (West) 1945–1961* (Berlin, 1995), p. 354.

33   Cited in Wolfgang Bohleber, "'Kein Bauwerk haben wir bisher errichtet, das an Bedeutung dem heutigen gleicht'. Die Ernst-Reuter-Siedlung in der Ackerstraße," in: Berliner Geschichtswerkstatt (ed.), *Der Wedding—hart an der Grenze. Weiterleben in Berlin nach dem Krieg* (Berlin, 1987), p. 219.

34   "Herbert von Karajan hat das Ansehen Berlins vermehrt," Landespressedienst Berlin, November 23, 1973; "Botschafter Berlins? Zur Japan-Tournee des Berliner Philharmonischen Orchesters," April 27, 1988.

35   Quoted in Susanne Stähr, "Die Kunst der Verwandlung. Epochenwechsel mit Herbert von Karajan," in: Stiftung Berliner Philharmoniker (ed.), *Variationen mit Orchester. 125 Jahre Berliner Philharmoniker*, vol. 1, Orchestergeschichte (Berlin, 2007), p. 248.

36   Quoted in Herbert Haffner, *Die Berliner Philharmoniker. Eine Biografie* (Mainz, 2007), p. 207.

37   Most of these remarks so far have focused on the West in general and the USA in particular, and for reasons of space—plus the fact that other contributions in this volume add a great deal of understanding to these matters—we will have little to say here on Soviet and East German views of Berlin.

38   Among many titles, see Melvyn P. Leffler and David S. Painter (eds.), *Origins of the Cold War: An International History*, 2nd ed. (New York, 2005); Melvyn P. Leffler and Odd Arne Westad (eds.), *The Cambridge History of the Cold War*, vol. 1, Origins, 1945–1962 (Cambridge, 2012); Norman M. Naimark, *The Russians in Germany: A History of the Soviet Zone of Occupation, 1945–1949* (Cambridge, 1997); Carolyn Eisenberg, *Drawing the Line: The American Decision to Divide Germany, 1944–1949* (Cambridge, 1998); Wilfried Loth, *Die Teilung der Welt. Geschichte des Kalten Krieges 1941–1955* (Munich, 2000); John Lewis Gaddis, *The United States and the Origins of the Cold War, 1941–1947*, rev. ed. (New York, 2000); Vladislav M. Zubok, *A Failed Empire: The Soviet Union in the Cold War from Stalin to Gorbachev*, 2nd ed. (Chapel Hill, 2009); Bernd Stöver, *Der Kalte Krieg: 1947–1991* (Munich, 2017).

39   Vladislav Zubok and Constantine Pleshakov, *Inside the Kremlin's Cold War: From Stalin to Khrushchev* (Cambridge, 1997), p. 52.

40   Martin Sabrow (ed.), *Erinnerungsorte der DDR* (Munich, 2009).

41   Olaf Leitner, *West-Berlin! Westberlin! Berlin (West)! Die Kultur—die Szene—die Politik. Erinnerungen an eine Teilstadt der 70er und 80er Jahre* (Berlin, 2002).

42   Mark Reeder, *B Book. Lust und Sound in West-Berlin 1979–1989*, transcribed by Hollow Skai and edited by Jörg A. Hoppe (Hamburg, 2015), to accompany the film *B Movie*; Wolfgang Müller, *Subkultur West-Berlin 1979–1989. Freizeit* (Hamburg, 2013); Paul Hockenos, *Berlin Calling: A Story of Anarchy, Music, the Wall, and the Birth of the New Berlin* (New York, 2017). Hockenos deals tellingly as well with alternative cultures in East Berlin. See also Barclay, "Kein neuer Mythos." On West Berlin politics during the 1980s, see Detlef Stronk, *Berlin in den achtziger Jahren. Im Brennpunkt der deutsch-deutschen Geschichte* (Berlin, 2009).

43   *Doonesbury*, March 4, 1982, http://doonesbury.washingtonpost.com/strip/set/91.

44   See, above all, Hanno Hochmuth, *Kiezgeschichte. Friedrichshain und Kreuzberg im geteilten Berlin* (Göttingen, 2017), esp. his chapter on Kreuzberg's "counter-publics" (*Gegenöffentlichkeiten*), pp. 146–68.

45   Kerstin Schilling, *Insel der Glücklichen. Generation West-Berlin*, 2nd ed. (Berlin, 2005).

46   For example, see Rudolf Lorenzen, *Paradies zwischen den Fronten. Reportagen und Glossen aus Berlin (West)* (Berlin, 2009); Ulrike Sterblich, *Die halbe Stadt, die es nicht mehr gibt. Eine Kindheit in Berlin (West)* (Reinbek, 2012); Horst Bosetzky, *West-Berlin: Erinnerungen eines Inselkindes* (Berlin, 2013). Peter Schneider, *Berlin Now: The City after the Wall*, trans. Sophie Schlondorff (New York, 2014), esp. pp. 63–82; Tanja Dückers, *Mein altes West-Berlin. Berliner Orte*, 2nd ed. (Berlin, 2016).

47   Paul Hockenos, "In Cold and Claustrophobic 1980s' West Berlin, You Paid a High Price for Freedom," January 19, 2018, www.thelocal.de/20180119/confessions-of-a-west-berliner-the-walled-city-was-for-those-who-could-hack-it-which-wasnt-everyone. See also Hockenos's important book, *Berlin Calling: A Story of Anarchy, Music, the Wall, and the Birth of the New Berlin* (New York, 2017), esp. parts I and II.

48   Adelheid von Saldern, "Einleitung," in: idem (ed.), *Inszenierte Einigkeit: Herrschaftsrepräsentationen in DDR-Städten* (Stuttgart, 2003), p. 9.

3

Policing the Border Area in East Berlin: Rules, Conflicts, and Negotiations, 1961–89

Gerhard Sälter
Translated by Michelle Eley & Corinna Kahnke

The historical narrative of the Berlin Wall has been dominated by the actions of the powerful and the suffering of others.[1] We know who built the Wall and why, how the Western powers reacted, and how the ruling Communist Party of the GDR (the SED) used these facts to stabilize its power.[2] Less attention has been paid, however, to how the population of the GDR and East Berlin dealt with this Wall that further restricted its already limited mobility.[3] Reactions in the fall of 1961 included spontaneous protest as well as declarations of loyalty and hopes for the future—not all of which were expressed voluntarily—that were founded on a growing equanimity within the state party.[4] However, after the new ruling conditions were firmly established, the Wall meant first and foremost a restriction in people's everyday life.

This chapter discusses several reactions to the restrictions on everyday life that were produced by the border regime. It looks at the spaces close to the Berlin Wall as an example of negotiation processes in the East German dictatorship.[5] Analyzing the conflicts between state agencies and populations in the border area behind the Berlin Wall helps us to understand how the GDR dictatorship functioned on an everyday level. This example primarily exposes existing differences and discussions that took place between state agencies that developed different attitudes and generated conflicting interests regarding the shaping, implementation, and coordination of state security measures. This approach may help to change the pervading image of SED rule as a monolithic state apparatus that could be directed by central orders.[6] The second point is to show ambiguities in the relationship between state and party agencies and the population. Norms were to a point open to negotiation—even where the border regime was concerned—and transgressions in everyday life were tolerated to a certain degree. This casts a new light on the strategies available to the population to handle with state agencies and their impositions in the GDR dictatorship on an everyday level.

Space/Rules

In the GDR, leaving the country without authorization had been criminally prosecuted as desertion of the Republic since the end of the 1940s.[7] In order to curb the escape movement to West Germany—and for additional reasons[8]—the leadership of the SED under Walter Ulbricht and Erich Honecker had a Wall erected in 1961. In terms of a drastic reduction in the number of escapes, it was a success. However, by cutting the remaining social ties between the two halves of the city, the barrier created new motives for the residents of East Berlin and the GDR to flee. This development, together with persisting economic and political problems, made it difficult for the SED to achieve its self-appointed goal of putting a complete halt to the escape movement. For the SED, each refugee who made it to the West in spite of the Wall and gained the attention of Western media felt like a defeat in the battle of ideologies and a reflection of an underlying rebellion.[9]

By constructing the Wall, the SED transformed a political conflict about social regulation that had stemmed from a lack of consensus between the state leadership and the people into a police matter at the Berlin Wall. Preventing the criminalized act of state desertion was the job of the police, and the decision to instead deploy the military at the border without restricting the authorized use of firearms to exceptional situations is proof of the importance the SED assigned to the issue.[10] Because these measures proved insufficient to stop those fleeing in spite of intensive control of the Wall, the SED expanded its approach. Access to the Wall was to be preempted, and those fleeing were to be arrested as they approached the border.

As part of this strategy, a special zone was to be established along the Wall requiring a special permit for access. A model for this zone already existed at the internal German border where a restricted area with graduated access had been in place since 1952. Numerous restrictions on access and authorized activities were implemented in the border area.[11] A similar security zone was to be established at the Wall. To this end, in September and October of 1961, many border residents were removed from this border area. The SED had thousands of residents resettled. The abandoned buildings were then walled up in order to restrict flight and to transform the houses themselves into obstacles to escape attempts. In order to successfully establish the SED's ever-expanding security requirements for the border area, this action was followed later by resettlements in smaller numbers from around 1965 until 1967 and in 1985.[12]

The planning for the border area proceeded quickly. After a draft was laid out in September 1961, the party apparatus presented its plan for an order to the Ministry of the Interior.[13] The proposal had been accepted in January by the National Defense Council of the GDR, a de facto committee of the SED Party leadership and the SED Politburo. In March, the proposal was approved by the commander of the Soviet Forces Group in Germany, Marshal Ivan S. Konev, who had assumed the role of a Soviet military governor.[14] On the basis of Soviet Ambassador Mikhail G. Pervukhin's intervention, a final decision was postponed, and the SED attempted to obtain Moscow's approval from the head of the Communist Party of the Soviet Union (CPSU).[15]

This satisfied neither the local officers of the border police (transformed in 1962 into border troops under the command of the Ministry of Defense), who were held personally responsible for each successful escape, nor the political leaders of the GDR. In anticipation of the decision from Moscow, local border commanders at some sectors of the Wall, in collaboration with local officials, had already issued directives for the creation of the border area—as did the city commander General Helmut Poppe, head of the border troops in East Berlin, in September 1962. It was only with special passes issued by the commanders of the local units that entry into a few buildings, complexes, and streets near the border was permitted. The city commander's report does not indicate exactly when these restrictions, described as "measures for order," were first put in place; they likely date from November 1961.[16]

Border troops and the secret police (the *Stasi* or MfS) considered the absence of a barrier in the military hinterlands of the Wall and the deficient surveillance to be a significant cause of the relatively high number of successful escape attempts. The city commander therefore encouraged Defense Minister Heinz Hoffmann in 1962 to improve surveillance there. Demolishing buildings and resettling additional residents would create the prerequisites for a deep array of control posts in the border area and enable the detection of potential escape preparations.[17] The Ministry for State Security (MfS), of which the secret police of the GDR was a part, identified the absence of border regulations in Berlin as the cause of the high number of escapes.[18]

Meanwhile, the National Defense Council addressed the topic again on May 30, 1962. It resolved to establish a border area, consisting of a ten- to 100-meter-wide strip behind the Wall, according to local conditions. The traffic in the immediate vicinity of the Wall was to be restricted and unauthorized people were to be denied access. The area was to be closed to traffic with additional fencing to keep passersby away. To supplement the monitoring of local residents and pedestrians, residential buildings, factories, and arcades were to be demolished to form an open terrain.[19] With that, the creation of a distinct, especially guarded space at the Wall began independent of opinions being voiced in Moscow.

The Council of Ministers of the GDR and an order of the Minister of Defense, both of which came into effect on June 22, 1963, legalized the special regulations in the border area after Soviet reservations had been dispelled.[20] On July 18, the city commander demanded additional signage and blockades and ordered that the border area be cartographically defined. Access roads were to be secured with permanent barricades (barbed wire fencing, painted lines, earth walls, etc.). Further access roads were to have checkpoints with tollgates. The Ministry of Defense ordered the border troops to complete the marking of the border area by noon on June 23.[21]

The provisions of the June 1963 decree entered the Border Regulation of the GDR in March 1964, making them permanent.[22] On the GDR side of the Wall—in some instances, in the middle of Berlin's city center—an area was established in which life was regulated by a special security concept. In the beginning, fences blocked the border area at many points, and police guarded the entrance points, but in the early 1970s barriers began to disappear. Afterwards it was possible to enter the entire border area without restriction, although it continued to be prohibited. The size of the area continued to change until 1989. In the 1970s and 80s, after the border barrier constructions were removed and surveillance throughout the GDR was intensified, the area was scaled down.

Policing/Prevention

The border area had been established so that escapees could be identified and arrested before they reached the border fortifications. Therefore, defining and marking the area as restricted was not enough; the area required additional police surveillance, which was aimed at two groups in particular: residents who were generally already under suspicion of planning an escape, and foreigners. The border area was heavily patrolled by border police and the East German Police (*Volkspolizei*).[23] Violations of the border regulations, in particular of regulatory restrictions on everyday life, as well as violations of the reporting obligations and the evasion of those reports, were each punishable by up to 2,000 marks and imprisonment of up to two years.[24] Entry and residence without explicit authorization were prohibited.

The population living in the border area was registered by July 25, 1963, after which the police began conducting identification checks at the entrances to the border area and patrolling inside the area.[25] Residents had to register with the civil authorities in order to be allowed to continue living in the border area. Moving into the area also required a permit. So-called district committees determined, with considerable input from the *Volkspolizei* and the secret police, who would be permitted to move into the area. Residents had to appeal to the *Volkspolizei* to receive passes for their visitors, and these were initially only granted in the case of the death of an immediate family member. Cultural or political events were strictly forbidden. Restaurants, cinemas, and boarding houses had to close. Employees of businesses in the border area also required special passes, which were limited to six months. This also applied to doctors and craftsmen, which had a considerably adverse impact on the everyday lives of the local population. In 1963, some 16,000 residents in East Berlin and 16,000 employees of 120 companies were affected by these restrictions. To minimize the demands of monitoring, additional people were moved out of the restricted area, businesses were relocated and buildings demolished.[26]

Monitoring access to the restricted area was the task of the *Volkspolizei*. The purpose of time-restricted and especially limited permits for residents and employees that had to be renewed regularly was to screen people who had access to the Wall vicinity. Specific groups, immigrants from West Germany or returned escapees, were generally not granted passes. The same was true for stateless persons and Western foreigners. "Work-shy or asocial elements" and "promiscuous persons" were also deemed high-risk groups. Immigrants from the West and foreigners who already worked or lived there were to be monitored. Passes for private visitors were only issued in urgent cases.[27]

The authorities of the GDR could expel people from the border area with a simple order, regardless of how long they had resided there. Such orders were issued by the Department of Internal Affairs of the Municipal Administration in collaboration with the secret police, border troops, and *Volkspolizei*. People were constantly being expelled until 1989. From December 1979 to May 1982, twenty-five applications for expulsion were filed by the border troops alone, two of them in Berlin.[28] Compared with the rest of the GDR, the pressure to conform socially grew considerably in the border area as a result of the latent threat of expulsion. This affected not only political dissidence but also lifestyles that were classified as "asocial" or nonconformist.

Such decisions could not be contested legally, but they were subject to revision by appeal. In the 1980s, it was possible in some individual cases to acquire a permit authorizing a move into the border area by petition—mostly in cases where the Municipal Residence Commission had been sloppy, allowing people to move into residences without verifying the status of their permit beforehand. In one case, a man who had been found guilty of a political offense, who had attracted attention for "provocative behavior towards the *Volkspolizei*" on several occasions and who lived with a friend in the border zone without registering with the police, was even able, at least temporarily, to stay by petitioning Erich Honecker, threatening to quit his job and applying to leave the country.[29]

Over time, the border area became subject to surveillance by border troops, the *Volkspolizei*, and the secret police, a level of control that was intense, even by GDR standards. The border guards surveyed the hinterland of the Wall from their watchtowers in the border strip and set up patrols in the border area. In the police stations along the Wall, half of the personnel was employed exclusively for this purpose.[30] They checked IDs and passes and during foot patrols collected information from residents that they could follow up onsite. The buildings were also inspected regularly. Cellars and attics had to be fitted with locks that met specific security standards, but that could readily be unlocked by the border troops.[31] Measures to monitor the border area worked quite well to prevent escapes; in the early 1980s approximately 80 percent of all potential escapees were arrested before reaching the first obstacle at the border strip.[32] However, this monitoring also had adverse effects: the residents felt they were being continuously watched.

Security authorities were supported by a number of honorary assistants and informers.[33] Border troops and the *Volkspolizei* employed so-called volunteer assistants who were brought in for additional support in the evenings. In contrast to the informants of the secret police who remained invisible, these people were employed in the border area primarily for patrolling. Gatekeepers were charged with checking residence permits at building entrances. In the 1980s, additional support groups recruited from the local population of the border area were added. In allotment gardens, nursery schools, schools, and other public establishments, "border security groups" (*Grenzsicherheitsaktive*) had to be on the lookout for foreigners and help prevent escape attempts. In the border area of Berlin's Treptow district, in which 1,367 people resided in 1984, the *Volkspolizei* had at its disposal more than 178 volunteer assistants; the number of border troop assistants is not known, but was likely about fifty. Furthermore, there were twenty-three "committees for order and safety in the border area," forty-six "border safety groups," and 279 "associates of the social border notification reporting system."[34] Moreover, civil authorities and additional persons were also involved in the surveillance system.[35] The border area was thus covered by a tight system of surveillance. These volunteer assistants did not always work according to guidelines, but their existence alone strengthened the enormous pressure to conform.

Transgression/Conflicts

The residents in the border area were required to submit applications to the *Volkspolizei* for private visits weeks in advance so that an investigation could be conducted by the secret police. Permits were approved only restrictively, and applicants had to provide detailed justification. Because of the mandatory authorization process, many activities that were in themselves quite ordinary, such as having visitors or bringing home a girlfriend in the evening, were connected with a disproportionate amount of bureaucratic effort, had to be aborted, or became illegal. To comply with border regulations, a significant part of social life had to take place outside the border area, and therefore outside the domestic setting.

The numerous inspections and the intense monitoring resulted in a large number of temporary arrests, which tied up a considerable amount of the *Volkspolizei* forces, who had to investigate whether it was a simple misdemeanor punishable by fine, or a case of preparing an escape or even an actual flight attempt. In the border area of the Potsdam district, the *Volkspolizei* detected 60 percent of the 1,392 prosecuted cases of violations of the border regulations in 1982 and 1983; the others were reported by different authorities.[36] Many of the people who were arrested had not understood the significance of the restricted area. In other cases, everyday logic had led them to ignore the prohibitions. In 1984, two pupils from Teltow were arrested in the border area because they wanted to pick up a school friend. They were taken to the police station and intensely interrogated and finally handed over to their parents who were lectured by the *Volkspolizei* about the border regulations. Another pupil was arrested because he had helped his mother, a postal worker, carry the mail. A man was arrested while visiting family friends because he had stepped two meters into the border area. For this, he had to pay a fine of ten marks.[37] Numerous such examples exist: again and again, people ended up, purposely or unintentionally, in the border area.[38]

The implementation of the access restrictions was already causing considerable problems in 1965/6. Many businesses in the border area did not comply because the efforts of controlling were too time consuming. During business deliveries, attention was not always paid as to whether the drivers had a border permit, and there was a reluctance to repeatedly send people without a permit away. To some extent, violations were an outgrowth of everyday necessities. Many people entered the border area for personal reasons, for example, to bring women home safely or to take a shortcut. Others overlooked the prohibition signs when they were under the influence of alcohol.[39] Neither did doctors let the lack of a pass keep them from visiting patients. There were visitors from both East and West Berlin who simply wanted to see the Wall. Numerous people were also confused, disregarded the warning signs, entered the border area to tell the border soldiers their opinions on the border regime, or to criticize the SED, or the political system of the GDR.[40] The implementation of the restrictions caused problems from the start, especially in places where security authorities had to rely on the cooperation and obedience of the people.

From the perspective of the authorities, the problem was exacerbated by border area residents who assisted escapees, as the alarmed SED leadership of the district Potsdam determined in 1965. There were examples of citizens using their knowledge of the area to provide "help and assistance" to escapees. The district leadership concluded that this security problem could only be resolved through the close collaboration of all security agencies and local party representatives with the residents at the border.[41]

But surveillance and close cooperation remained ineffective. The Berlin Criminal Investigation Department determined that, in 1976, people were no longer abiding by the border regulations and were entering the border area without authorization, justifying their actions offensively. According to their analysis, 90 percent of the border regulation violations were connected to visits from friends and family. In accounts from the *Volkspolizei*, border area residents abetted the misdemeanors by not exerting enough influence on their visitors and not urging them to obey the border regulations. A portion of the population was of the opinion that passes were no longer required.[42]

The obstinate disregard for the regulations irritated the *Volkspolizei* even more since they were not used to being publicly contradicted. Some residents were obviously fed up with the restrictions and had little fear of punishment. The longer the Wall stood, the less necessary seemed the special regulations to a growing proportion of the population. Having grown accustomed to the Wall, they found the restrictions increasingly anachronistic. Living space in East Berlin had grown scarce, making apartments in the border area more acceptable, but younger people in particular were less eager to tolerate the associated restrictions on their everyday lives.

The conflicts point to a fundamental problem that was related to security concepts for the border area. A portion of the border residents distanced itself from the state, which relied on residents' compliance and strove for their collaboration. It was not only the restrictions that created tension but also the increasingly visible distrust on the part of the regime. Evidently, the majority of those who had reluctantly, but successfully assimilated into the system felt especially annoyed. Citizens who had shown willingness to offer the cooperation expected of them at work and in their free time, as well as the ostentatious loyalty demanded, especially chalked this fundamental mistrust up to the state.[43] They saw it as a personal affront and insult, when they were denied passes for friends and family members. The secret police reported that those who were affected by the rules and the surveillance measures repeatedly criticized the lack of trust, and this information was spread in the state apparatus.

Repression/Negotiations

By implementing specific regulations in the border area behind the Wall to solve the problem of escapes, the SED created a new source of urban disorder. The restrictions were so severe and palpable that they considerably diminished the quality of life. Everyday tasks led to regulatory infractions whose connection to the border regime made them a matter of state security in the view of the SED. The party attempted to solve this self-created regulatory problem by intensifying surveillance.

The *Volkspolizei* responded to violations with temporary arrests. That enabled them, along with the secret police, to use interrogations and personal data searches to determine whether the person in question had been under suspicion of attempting an escape in the past. If that was not the case, the arrested person was released, usually after intensive instruction and paying a fine. However, detailed reports and accounts of such cases had to be submitted in writing. For the *Volkspolizei*, arresting people who were barely aware of having done something wrong took considerable effort, but did not appear to have a deterring effect.

The SED tried to strengthen public relations in an effort to change the attitudes of at least a part of the population. By 1965 "honorary military political advisory councils" had been formed at the daily papers, and, in 1964, the *Märkische Volksstimme*, the Potsdam district newspaper, published 139 articles about the border troops. This meant that Potsdamers could read about matters of border control and the successes of the border troops over breakfast every three days.[44] Strong pressure was placed on people to act as informants. When students at a school in Berlin's Köpenick district discovered an escapee in October 1965, they were already so well-conditioned that one of them informed the *Volkspolizei*, while the others kept an eye on the escapee. As a reward, the *Volkspolizei* awarded the young informer a new bicycle during the rollcall for the Young Pioneers, and the *BZ am Abend* published a laudatory article.[45]

But the propaganda was not sufficient. According to the criteria of the border troops, satisfactory integration of the border had not been achieved by the early 1970s. At a conference with the secret police, General Erich Peter, chief of the border troops, pointed out that over half of all escapees were residents of the border area. An officer of the secret police seconded him, stating that the statistics showed that the pressure on the Berlin Wall was stemming from the hinterlands near the border.[46] It remained so for the next several years, which seemed to be a problem especially because the residents in the Wall's vicinity were more successful in their escape attempts than those who lived further away in the GDR. The relatively high involvement of the border residents in the flight movement remained a problem for the SED until 1989.

One of the possibilities that was repeatedly discussed among the security agencies and the SED was to place greater restrictions on the allocation of passes. The use of passes to regulate access was the source of constant conflict between the residents and the *Volkspolizei* and SED. The last was cautious in this point, because it endangered the other goal of party officials, namely, to mobilize the border population's help in securing the border. Because the permits required verification from the *Volkspolizei* and secret police in coordination with other agencies, they involved relatively long processing times. The discontent produced by this and the denial of private applications concerned the party officials responsible for engaging the population's collaboration in different social and political efforts of the SED.[47]

The differing responsibilities generated conflict among the agencies involved in the procedures for authorization. The border troops, which were held responsible for any successful escape attempts, had the strongest interest in limiting access to the border area as much as possible. The fewer people let through, the simpler their surveillance and monitoring assignments in the border area, and the fewer potential escapees reached the Wall. The secret police defined escape prevention as their central concern in the mid-1970s. In their function as the overarching security authority, they sided with border troops. They repeatedly complained that the monitoring was sloppily managed and the stipulated consultation with their own responsible departments was often overlooked. The *Volkspolizei*, by way of contrast, saw the review of applicants chiefly as extra work that required additional personnel. They tried to minimize the demands on their everyday duties. Standing in direct contact with the applicants and moreover under pressure to provide explanations, they were willing to some extent make some concessions. Local party councils feared the resentment of the citizenry and attempted to live up to their own claims of socialist justice. Furthermore, the criticism from border troops and secret police called into question the supposed educational successes in the mobilization of border residents for the political and social order of the GDR. They therefore mostly followed a similar line to the *Volkspolizei* and argued for easing regulations.[48]

On the basis of these different interests and viewpoints, the involved institutions laid out differing criteria for the approval of passes, the permissions for moving into the border area and expulsion orders. This led to conflicts over the general guidelines that had to be dealt with in numerous exceptional cases and which led to pointing blame when an issued pass facilitated an escape.

Criticism often targeted the practice of the *Volkspolizei*, which was described as too liberal. As early as 1963, border officers criticized that passes were being granted without prior thorough personal investigation. Moreover, the number of passes and permits for West Germans was too high.[49] It was suggested that the *Volkspolizei* should use more intensive monitoring practices to limit illegal entry. In 1967 a high-ranking border officer complained that businesses in the border area, more specifically their police-like industrial security, gave out worker passes that were valid for one month to "allegedly verified persons." According to him, at some railway buildings, a permit signed by a manager granted access to the border area. In addition, other companies were not sufficiently controlling entry onto their company grounds. In fact, even the East Berlin Construction Ministry only kept one logbook in which visitors had to sign themselves in. Such negligence yielded unfettered border area access to a large number of people, which significantly heightened the threat of escape.[50]

This is the line of argumentation that the border troops followed in the succeeding years. In 1974 the chief of the border troops criticized that "untrustworthy elements" were still able to travel into the border area and would exploit this for the "reconnaissance, preparation and realization of a border breach." Apparently, the *Volkspolizei*'s investigation of the applicants was insufficient, and they issued too many permits.[51] Such criticisms, compounded by individual cases in which pass holders had managed to escape, successfully focused the attention of the secret police on the escape of pass holders, and this attested to the considerable deficiencies in the verification and issuing practices of the *Volkspolizei*. The secret police further expanded the screening of applicants for entry to the border area. In addition, their district offices acquired a veto right against an affirmative decision from the

Volkspolizei.[52] As a result, the secret police deepened their influence on the permit process in the last decades of the GDR. Whether they were successful in those efforts is not an issue for this chapter.

A second option to restrict illegal access entailed exerting direct pressure. Company managers who repeatedly sent craftsmen and other service personnel into the border area without a valid pass were summoned by the *Volkspolizei* or received a written warning. The same happened to residents who frequently received guests without passes: in the 1970s, they were summoned for a reprimand by the *Volkspolizei*. Because expulsion from the border area and the loss of one's residence was a real possibility, there were often "no further incidents" to record after such a summons.[53] In this way, specific successes were achieved, but they required a great deal of effort.

Third, to facilitate the inspection and be able to detect potential escapees, the secret police and the *Volkspolizei* established personalized und indexed border files that they would use to detect repeat offenders. After an arrest in the border area, the person was investigated at the next police station. If the individual did not have a permit, a fine was imposed. Furthermore, the *Volkspolizei*, together with the secret police, determined whether they were dealing with a case of attempted flight or scouting of the border fortifications. The personal data was recorded to make it possible to trace who had been found in the border area illegally at different locations or by different agencies. Should this be the case, or if the person was known to the authorities, the secret police either took him into custody or placed him under surveillance.

People held under suspicion included returnees and immigrants from West Germany. In Berlin, they were recorded in files that were kept by the *Volkspolizei* district offices (*Inspektion*). In 1965, it was possible to identify a person who was recorded in the files. On October 10, an employee of the secret police who had deserted was arrested in the city district of Köpenick. In the hearing, he admitted having talked in a restaurant about the possibility of fleeing to West Berlin with a man whose name he did not know. The only thing he knew about the man was his approximate age and that he had already fled to the West once before. Five days later the district office in Berlin-Mitte was able to present a list of fifty-three men living in the near vicinity of the restaurant, who were recorded returnees. The secret police arrested a man having identified him using photos included with the list.[54]

The Berlin criminal investigation department also kept files on people who had profited from an unauthorized visit to the border area. Because visitors could only be discouraged by draconian measures, pressure had to be put on those who were visited, who were more easily influenced by the threat of expulsion. In 1976, the Border Task Force of the Criminal Investigation Department began to create a file in the Mitte district on people who frequently had visitors without passes. In 1977, the file included fourteen people and served as the basis for the aforementioned police warnings. The *Volkspolizei* created a similar file for Prenzlauer Berg in 1973, with entries dating back to the year 1971.[55] A "file of border endangerer" of the Criminal Investigation Department is also mentioned in 1981, but it is unclear how long it was kept and what type of person was recorded in it.[56]

Because violations of the border regulation were generally handled by different authorities onsite and punished with a warning or a small fine, the accumulation of instances of illegal entry could not be assessed using locally managed files. In order to find out who was surveying border facilities and planning an escape and who had been caught multiple times doing so, the data needed to be compared. Therefore, the secret police centralized recordkeeping in May 1980. From then on, according to Instruction 1/80, all violations of border regulations had to be fed into a central database of persons (*Zentrale Personendatenbank*, ZPDB). The database included investigation results of the secret police as well as violations assessed by the *Volkspolizei*, their assistants, the border troops, the border assistants, and other authorities.[57]

The centralization of the data, however, did not completely solve the problem of local investigations. It soon became evident that neither the border troops nor the *Volkspolizei* had submitted thorough arrest reports. The other security authorities were not capable or willing to hand over detailed reports on relevant data quickly because the task required a comparatively high effort on their part.[58] In 1983, for example, only 35 percent of cases of the *Volkspolizei* in the district of Potsdam were reported to the secret police.[59] Neither continual criticism nor the increase of secret police agents working as police officers in the *Volkspolizei* had an impact on this deficit. In 1986, the suspicion was expressed that many border violations not only were not reported, but were not even punished "in order to spare someone from having to write a report."[60]

Conclusion

The SED built the Wall in an attempt to solve a problem: the majority of the GDR population did not agree with its ideas on social order, and therefore many wanted to leave the country. Feeling to stand in competition with the Federal Republic, the party perceived the growing escape movement as rejection by part of the population and a form of rebellion against its rule in the GDR. By establishing a restricted area behind the Wall as means to solve the persistant escape problem, the GDR rulers turned a political conflict into a long-term regulatory matter for the police. The restrictions connected with the regulations for the border area made common behavior patterns illegal. It was, in the end, the security concept for the border area, which produced violations of norms. The longer the Wall stood, the more anachronist the restrictions felt to a growing number of residents, who responded by simply disregarding them as bothersome.

With that, the SED in East Berlin created a new phenomenon of urban disorder. The context of the border regime turned everyday actions into potentially state-endangering offences. When the party reacted by casting a dense net of surveillance over the municipal territory, a permanent conflict between border residents and security authorities arose. The deployment of numerous informants and voluntary assistants in both open and secret surveillance created an extraordinary social pressure to conform. Nevertheless, the imposed administrative fines and the threatening gestures lost their ability to deter through fear. The state mistrust that was expressed through the surveillance only strengthened the conflicts of loyalty within a border population that was growing increasingly self-confident.

The violations of the border regulations were so frequent and their disregard so blatant that the *Volkspolizei*, which was tasked with enforcing them, refused to step in, in part to avoid further conflicts with the population but also to conserve their own resources. They were prepared to use legal measures in the border area to put selective pressure on residents. Although local councils of the SED, which were concerned about the loyalty and the mobilization potential of the population, followed a similar line. The *Volkspolizei* drew criticism from the border troops, who wanted to deflect the escape problem as far as possible from the realm of their responsibility and from the Wall. They were seconded by the secret police, the *Stasi*, and the central SED leadership, who perceived the escape problem as a severe threat to the existence of the GDR. Regulating access led to a long-lasting conflict among the involved agencies, a conflict they were unable to resolve. Due to a lack of cooperation, implementing central files also proved unsuccessful, in particular because the substantial curbing of violations and escape attempts by the border population remained the standard of measure.

Through a cautious defiance, as becomes visible in the breach of the border regulation, and against the background of sustained conflict between the authorities involved in the border regime, some residents were able to reclaim a degree of social freedom of movement in direct conflict with the state power. Such negotiation processes are especially visible at the border, as becomes apparent with the successive reduction of in the size of the border area. The relevance of the border regime for the SED leadership prompted a relatively heavy amount of reporting, and the conflicts connected to it vividly highlight stances, strategies, and processes. For a social history of the GDR that is interested in studying social conflicts, their conditions and results, as well as in the question of the legitimacy of the socialist social order, the border regime remains a central subject.

Notes

1   A first version of this chapter was presented in the section Geographies of Transgression in the History of the City at the 10th International Conference on Urban History, Ghent, September 2010.

2   Frederick Taylor, *The Berlin Wall. 13 August 1961–9 November 1989* (London, 1996); Klaus-Dietmar Henke (ed.), *Die Mauer. Errichtung, Überwindung, Erinnerung* (Munichen, 2011); Manfred Wilke, *Der Weg zur Mauer. Stationen der Teilungsgeschichte* (Berlin, 2011); Gerhard Sälter and Manfred Wilke, *Ultima Ratio: Der 13. August 1961. Der Mauerbau, die Blockkonfrontation und die Gesellschaft der DDR* (Berlin, 2011).

3   Thomas Lindenberger, "'Diktatur der Grenze(n). Die eingemauerte Gesellschaft und ihre Feinde," in: Hans-Hermann Hertle, Konrad H. Jarausch, and Christoph Kleßmann (eds.), *Mauerbau und Mauerfall. Ursachen, Verlauf, Auswirkungen* (Berlin, 2002), pp. 203–14; Thomas Lindenberger: "Das Land der begrenzten Möglichkeiten. Machträume und Eigen-Sinn der DDR-Gesellschaft," *Deutschland Archiv*, August 10, 2016, www.bpb.de/232099.

4   Patrick Major, "Vor und nach dem 13. August 1961: Reaktionen der DDR-Bevölkerung auf den Bau der Berliner Mauer," *Archiv für Sozialgeschichte* 39 (1999),

pp. 235–354; Gerhard Sälter, "Reaktionen auf den Mauerbau in Berlin und der DDR," *Deutschland Archiv*, June 24, 2011, www.bpb.de/geschichte/zeitgeschichte/deutschlandarchiv/53746/reaktionen-auf-den-mauerbau?p=all.

5   On the negotiation processes in the GDR, see Patrick Major, *Behind the Berlin Wall. East Germany and the Frontiers of Power* (Oxford, 2010).

6   See, conversely, Norbert Elias, "Über die Vorstellung, dass es einen Staat ohne strukturelle Konflikte geben könne," in: idem (ed.), *Die höfische Gesellschaft. Untersuchungen zur Soziogenese des Königtums und der höfischen Aristokratie* (Frankfurt, 1983), pp. 405–15.

7   Gerhard Sälter, *Grenzpolizisten. Konformität, Verweigerung und Repression in der Grenzpolizei und den Grenztruppen der DDR (1952–1965)* (Berlin, 2009), pp. 15–24.

8   Sälter and Wilke, *Ultima Ratio*, pp. 32–4.

9   Gerhard Sälter, "Fluchtverhinderung als gesamtgesellschaftlich Aufgabe," in: Klaus-Dietmar Henke (ed.), *Die Mauer. Errichtung, Überwindung, Erinnerung* (Munich, 2011), pp. 152–62.

10 Jochen Maurer and Gerhard Sälter, "The Double Task of the East German Border Guards: Policing the Border and Military Functions," *German Politics and Society* 29 (2011) 2, pp. 23–39.

11 Sälter, *Grenzpolizisten*, pp. 26–32.

12 Gerhard Sälter, "Zu den Zwangsräumungen in Berlin nach dem Mauerbau 1961," *Deutschland Archiv* 44 (2011) 4, pp. 546–51.

13 *Statement on the Securing of the State Border*, draft, undated [September 1961] and unsigned, BA-MA, VA-07, 8447, pp. 94–9; *Draft for an Order of the MdI*, undated [January 1962]; political grounds for this order; BA/SAPMO, DY 30, 3685, pp. 36–7.

14 National Defense Council [NVR], 9th Session, Minutes, TOP 4 and enclosure 10–12, January 11, 1962, BA-MA, DVM 1, 39466, p. 5, pp. 111–32. Additional drafts in BStU, SdM, 2615, pp. 237–62. Writing of Ulbricht's to Konjew, in which he requests approval and his response, January 17 and February 3, 1962, BA/SAPMO, DY 30, 3691, sheet 99, 129.

15 Letter from Ulbricht to Nikita S. Chruschtschow, May 30, 1962, in which he speaks of a misunderstanding of Perwuchin's; BA/SAPMO, DY 30, 3658, pp. 66–8. In December 1962, the secret police appointed to the absence of a border regulation for Berlin as the reason for the night flight numbers; February 12, 1962, BStU, ZAIG, 545, p. 36.

16 City commander to minister of defense, *border demarcation*, September 29, 1962, BA-MA, VA-07, 9057, pp. 247–54.

17 Ibid.

18 MfS, Development of Desertion of the Republic August 13, 1961– December 31, 1961, February 12, 1962, BStU, ZAIG, 545, p. 36.

19 NVR, 11th Session, minutes, May 30, 1962, TOP 2, BA-MA, DVW 1, 39468, pp. 1–3, 9–17. Ulbricht forwards the suggestion for the creation of a restricted area again on June 23, 1962, on October 19, 1962 the acting minister of defense Admiral Waldemar Verner informed him of approval of the new Soviet commander-in-chief, General Iwan I Jakubowski; ibid., p. 93, pp. 126–8.

20 *Regulation on Measures for the Protection of the State Border between the GDR and West-Berlin*, June 21, 1963, Law Gazette of the GDR II, 1963, pp. 381–3. On the reaction of the people, see an analysis of the secret police; BStU, ZAIG, 780.

21 City commander, *Order 34/63*, June 18, 1963; MfNV, Directive 48/63, June 21, 1963; BA-MA, DVM 1, 12916, pp. 114–17, pp. 111–13.

22 *Regulation on the Protection of the State Border*, March 19, 1964, Law Gazette of the GDR II, 1964, pp. 255–7; see Peter J. Lapp, *Gefechtdienst im Frieden. Das Grenzregime der DDR (1945–1990)* (Bonn, 1999), p. 126.

23 City commander, *Order 34/63*, June 18, 1963, BA-MA, DVW 1, 12916, pp. 114–17.

24 *Regulation on the Protection of the State Border*, June 21, 1963, in Law Gazette of the GDR, II (1963), pp. 381–3; see Lapp, *Gefechtdienst*, p. 126, pp. 132–3, 152–3.

25 City commander, *Implementation Report*, July 4, 1963, BA-MA, DVW 1, 12916, pp. 131–3.

26 *Ordinance on the Regulations in the Border Area*, June 21, 1963, in *Law Gazette of the GDR*, II (1963), pp. 382–4.

27 MdI, *Directive 30/61*, June 5, 1961, BA Berlin, DO 1, 2.2, 58332. National Defense Council (NVR), 7th conference, 8/28/1961, Resolution, TOP 2 and Annex (Anlage) 5, BA-MA, DVM 1.

28 *Overview of Resettlement out of the Border Area*, July 1982, BStU, MfS, Sec. Neiber, 113, pp. 256–8.

29 Ibid., pp. 222–9.

30 Volkspolizei, Information map [Auskunftskarte], 1984, LAB, C Rep. 303, Nr. 11 (2).

31 *Border Troops, Property and Site Inspection*, undated [1963], BA-MA, VA-07, 5807, pp. 27–8.

32 BStU, MfS, Abt. VII/2, Bericht.

33 Thomas Lindenberger, "Vaters kleine Helfer. Die Volkspolizei und ihre enge Verbindung zur Bevölkerung, 1952–1965," in: Gerhard Fürmetz, Herbert Reinke and Klaus Weinhauer (eds.), *Nachkriegspolizei. Sicherheit und Ordnung in Ost- und Westdeutschland 1945–1969* (Hamburg, 2000), pp. 229–54; Gerhard Sälter, "Loyalität und Denunziation in der ländlichen Gesellschaft der DDR. Die Freiwilligen Helfer der Grenzpolizei im Jahr 1952," in: Michael Schröter (ed.), *Der willkommene Verrat. Beiträge zur Denunziationsforschung* (Weilerswist, 2007), pp. 159–84.

34 Volkspolizei, Information map [Auskunftskarte], 1984, LAB, C Rep. 303, Nr. 11 (2).

35 Sälter, Fluchtverhinderung, pp. 158–61.

36 MfS, BV Potsdam, Abt. VII, Osl. Thoß, *Status Report [Lagebericht]*, January 23, 1984, BStU, BV Potsdam, Abt. VII, 1086, pp. 3–19 (according to this report, the *Volkspolizei* reported 707 violations in 1982 and 685 in 1983).

37 MfS, BV Potsdam, *Border Location Reports [Grenzlageberichte]*, January 24, 1984, BStU, BV Potsdam, Abt. VII, 1129, Bd. 1, pp. 11–12, 21, 49.

38 MfS, BV Potsdam, *Border Location Reports [Grenzlageberichte]*,1984, BStU, BV Potsdam, Abt. VII, p. 1129, 1130.

39 Volker Koop, "Den Gegner vernichten," *Die Grenzsicherung der DDR* (Bonn, 1996), pp. 129–34.

40 Border Troops [Grenztruppen], arrest log, 1961–1966, BA-MA, GT, 5130, 5131, 5132, 5133 and 5134.

41 Stadtkommandantur, Politverwaltung, Special Information [Sonderinformation] 6/65, February 19, 1965, BA-MA, VA-P-07, 638, pp. 21–6.

42 Border Command [Grenzkommando] Mitte, transcript, June 15, 1976, BA-MA, GT 6601, pp. 134–44.

43 See the contribution from Gitta Heinrich in: Jens Arndt (ed.), *Glienicke. Vom Schweizerdorf zum Sperrgebiet* (Berlin, 2009), pp. 148–55.

44 City Headquarters, Public Relations, July 17, 1965, BA-MA, VA-P-07, 638, pp. 132–48.

45 Gerhard Sälter, *Interne Repression. Die Verfolgung überlaufener MfS-Offiziere durch das MfS und die DDR-Justiz (1954–1966)* (Dresden, 2002), pp. 139–40.

46 Command of the Border Troops, transcript, May 12, 1970, BA-MA, GT 2129, pp. 1–10.

47 ZK der SED, Abt. Sicherheitsfragen, *Excerpt from the Report from August 1984*, BStU, BV Potsdam, Abt. VII, 640, pp. 2–8.

48 A dissertation project is being prepared on these conflicts at the Stiftung Berliner Mauer.

49 Ergebnisse der bewaffneten Organe des MdI bei der Sicherung des Sperrgebiets, March 1963, BA-MA, GT 1184.

50 *Bericht für eine Koordinierungberatung*, March 16, 1967, BA-MA, VA-07, 5811, pp. 14–17, pp. 44–5.

51 MfNV, Vorlage für die Kollegiumsitzung on July 26, 1974, BA-MA, DVW 1, 55585, pp. 21–43.

52 MfS, *Dienstausweisung 10/81*, July 4, 1981, BStU, BV Magdeburg, KD Halberstadt, 1268, pp. 3–60.

53 Grenzkommando Mitte, *Transcript*, June 15, 1976, BA-MA, GT 6601, pp. 134–44.

54 BStU, GH 111/79, pp. 100–11; see Sälter, *Interne Repression*, pp. 135–45.

55 VPI Mitte (traffic police inspectorate), *Bericht*, 143/77, LAB, C Rep. 903-01-04, Nr. 1265. Frontier command Mitte, *Transcript*, June 15, 1976, BA-MA, GT 6601, Folio 143–4.

56 MfS, BV Magdeburg, September 3, 1982, BStU, BV Magdeburg, KD Halberstadt, 1131, pp. 11–13.

57 MfS, BV Potsdam, Abt. VII, *Lagebericht*, October 9, 1985, BStU, BV Potsdam, Abt. VII, 1086, pp. 198–213.

58 Ibid., p. 217.

59 MfS, BV Potsdam, Abt. VII, Osl. Thoß, *Lagebericht*, January 23, 1984, BStU, BV Potsdam, Abt. VII, 1086, pp. 3–19.

60 MfS, BV Potsdam, Abt. VII, Osl. Thoß, *Assessment*, November 21, 1986, BStU, BV Potsdam, Abt. VII, 872, pp. 59–62.

4

Kennedy, Khrushchev, King, and Springsteen: Staging Visits in a Divided City

Andreas Etges

In the summer of 1988, Berlin was the pop and rock 'n' roll capital of the world.[1] Among others, Joe Cocker, James Brown, and Bryan Adams performed at the outdoor bicycle racetrack in Berlin Weißensee in East Germany. On July 19, "The Boss" himself, Bruce Springsteen, and the E-Street Band played in front of a crowd of 160,000 ticket holders as well as many, many more who had entered the grounds after the state youth organizers had caved in to popular demand and opened all the gates. Officially, it had been declared a "Konzert für Nikaragua," celebrating the ninth anniversary of the Sandinista Revolution. The series of concerts had been organized as a reaction to the three-day "Concert for Berlin," held at the Reichstag the year before, when David Bowie, Genesis, and other international bands had rocked West Berlin on the occasion of the 750th anniversary of the city. Fans in the East who had tried to get close enough to hear the music, some of them shouting "down with the Wall" and celebrating the reformist Soviet leader Mikhail Gorbachev, had been driven away by the police and the *Stasi*, the GDR's secret police. In 1988, there was another series of concerts held at the Reichstag, but this time the East German government was prepared, and its youth organization FDJ brought some Western superstars including James Brown to the GDR. The "Godfather of Soul" sang in one part of the city while, at the same time, Pink Floyd played in the other. On June 19, 1988, Michael Jackson was scheduled to perform at the Reichstag. The *Stasi* was now placed on alert, fearing confrontations with East German Jackson fans this time.[2]

At first, the possibility of a diversionary concert (*Ablenkkonzert*) was discussed. The idea was to show Jackson's performance on video screens in a stadium with a brief tape delay so that—should an undesirable political statement be made—the broadcast could be interrupted and video of an earlier Jackson concert shown. Instead, as part of the three-day *Friedenswoche der Berliner Jugend* (Berlin Youth Peace Week) in Weißensee, Canadian Bryan Adams, introduced by East Germany's figure skating star and Olympic champion Katarina Witt, brought "'The Summer of '69" to the East in a virtual song contest with Michael Jackson. Still, thousands of young East Germans instead went to the Brandenburg Gate to hear the "King of Pop's" first concert in Berlin and this time West German TV crews trying to report on this were harassed by the *Stasi*.[3]

During the Cold War, the international credibility of both the United States and the Soviet Union was in part tied to their credibility in a divided Germany and a divided Berlin. If there was "America's Berlin," as Ernest May has convincingly argued, then there surely was "Russia's Berlin" as well.[4] East and West Berlin were of special symbolic significance. They were showcases to prove the superiority of the respective systems they represented and were competing politically, ideologically, economically, and culturally. That also made the divided city especially attractive for international visitors, politicians, artists, and others. And, in the summer of 1988, it provided music fans on both sides of the Wall with a spectacular lineup of stars.

At other times during the Cold War, it was political "stars" competing for attention in Berlin, sometimes in close temporal proximity with one another. On June 26, 1963, President John F. Kennedy came to West Berlin. Only two days later, his Soviet counterpart, Nikita Khrushchev, arrived in East Berlin. Both were actors on a global stage and in late June of 1963, the city became their platform for carefully choreographed performances featuring multiple directors. Andreas Daum, in his major study on "Kennedy in Berlin," has emphasized "the dynamics of the public sphere and the performative quality of politics."[5] Regarding Cold War Berlin, this involved ensuring a certain level of visibility, not just of military forces, but also of prominent representatives. The visits by Kennedy and Khrushchev to Berlin, the latter planned as a direct response to that of Kennedy, were staged for many different audiences. In order to understand their importance, meaning, and symbolism, they need to be put into the larger historical context of the Second Berlin Crisis. The latter also provided the backdrop for another visit to Berlin, in this case to both parts of the divided city, by the American civil rights leader, Martin Luther King, Jr. from September 12–14, 1964. With few exceptions, those who have written about the visits of King, Khrushchev, and Kennedy to Berlin—the last of which garnered the most attention—have used Western sources. For this chapter, the East German press, especially the official party daily, *Neues Deutschland*, was analyzed.

Credibility and the Second Berlin Crisis

For the United States, the Berlin Airlift—a reaction to the blockade of the Western part of the city that Stalin had imposed on June 24, 1948—had long-term consequences. US security interests became even more closely tied to those of Western Europe than before, the goal of defending the freedom of West Berliners became crucial to American credibility in the Cold War and was also invoked during the Cuban Missile Crisis or in American justifications for escalating its military engagement in Vietnam.[6] Partly as a consequence of that, for a couple of decades the governing mayor of Berlin assumed a symbolic and political role that was at least as important as that of the German chancellor. As the top representative of Berlin, Willy Brandt was welcomed to the White House by Kennedy as early as mid-March 1961. Chancellor

Konrad Adenauer, in stark contrast, did not meet the president in Washington until November 1962.[7]

Kennedy's visit to the divided city in June 1963 has to be seen in the context of the Second Berlin Crisis. In November 1958, during Eisenhower's second term, Khrushchev had issued an ultimatum to the other three occupying powers—France, the United Kingdom, and the United States—demanding a new status for East Germany and West Berlin.[8] Khrushchev wanted Berlin to become a "free" and demilitarized city. He also threatened to sign a separate peace treaty with the GDR. The goal was to drive the Western powers out of the city. His ultimatum eventually expired, but the Soviet leader renewed it soon after the Vienna summit meeting with Kennedy in early June 1961. This put even more pressure on the American president, who many felt had not stood up to Khrushchev in Vienna. What was at stake was what Robert McMahon described as one of "the most critical of all U.S. foreign policy objectives," namely, credibility. McMahon rightly emphasized its "double meaning." In addition to credibility vis-à-vis its "enemies," America's credibility with its allies was equally important. They should not doubt that the US would be ready to use military force to defend their freedom and territorial integrity.[9] This was as much about capabilities as about beliefs and perceptions which "could be as important as the real thing," as John Lewis Gaddis argued.[10]

Kennedy needed to reaffirm and restore American credibility on Berlin twice in the summer of 1961, the first time with the Soviet leadership. The stakes were high, and the outcome of the Berlin conflict, as former Secretary of State Dean Acheson argued after the Vienna summit, "will go far to determine the confidence of Europe—indeed, of the world—in the United States. It is not too much to say that the whole position of the United States is in the balance." The consensus was that Kennedy had to send a clear message to counter the perception of weakness. He did so in a TV and radio address on the Berlin Crisis on July 25, 1961. The American president warned the Soviets that an attack on West Berlin "will be regarded as an attack upon us all." The security and freedom of West Berlin was inseparable from that of America. In his so-called "three essentials," Kennedy made clear where no compromise would be possible: 1. the occupation rights of the Allies in West Berlin; 2. free access to West Berlin; 3. the freedom of the West Berliners. Kennedy talked about Berlin's political significance at length:

> For West Berlin lying exposed 110 miles inside East Germany, surrounded by Soviet troops and close to Soviet supply lines, has many roles. It is more than a showcase of liberty, a symbol, an island of freedom in a Communist sea. It is even more than a link with the Free World, a beacon of hope behind the Iron Curtain, an escape hatch for refugees. West Berlin is all of that. But above all it has now become—as never before—the great testing place of Western courage and will, a focal point where our solemn commitments stretching back over the years since 1945, and Soviet ambitions now meet in basic confrontation.[11]

In his speech, Kennedy also asked Congress for even more defense spending and requested money for civil defense. According to public opinion polls at the time, a majority of the American public supported him on this and was ready to go to war for the freedom of West Berlin.[12] In Moscow, reactions were strong. According to John McCloy, the chairman of the Council on Foreign Relations and former US High Commissioner in Germany, Khrushchev stated that the president had "in effect declared preliminary war" on the Soviets.[13]

The speech had an additional, unintended effect. The fact that Kennedy had repeatedly and deliberately spoken only about West Berlin had also been registered in East Germany, so that the stream of people leaving the country via West Berlin actually grew, putting additional pressure on the SED and on Khrushchev, whose own credibility—not least because of the two ultimatums—was also closely tied to the city. He finally agreed to the request by the East German leadership to close the border between East and West Berlin. The process began on August 13, 1961. Robert Dallek fittingly described the American reaction to what became "the Wall" as "studied caution."[14] The State Department sent out a strong protest, but that was it for a couple of days. There was even a sense of relief within the Kennedy administration that a war to defend the freedom of West Berlin had become very unlikely now. Kennedy's adviser Kenneth O'Donnell described the president's view of the situation:

> Actually he saw the wall as the turning point that would lead to the end of the Berlin crisis. He said to me: "Why would Khrushchev put up a wall if he really intended to seize Berlin? There wouldn't be any need of a wall if he occupied the whole city. This is his way out of the predicament. It's not a very nice solution, but a wall is a hell of a lot better than a war."[15]

But Kennedy had underestimated the psychological effect of the events in Berlin that would lead to a second crisis of credibility that summer, this time with America's allies. According to Edward R. Murrow, who had arrived in West Berlin on August 12, the USA was now facing "a crisis of confidence which endangers quite seriously our position." Kennedy's speech on July 25, the director of the United States Information Service (USIA) argued, had been viewed as a firm public confirmation of the United States' commitment to Berlin. In contrast to that, the American reaction to the border closing had led to "disillusionment," a "feeling of letdown."[16] This is reflected in the August 16, 1961 edition of West Germany's largest daily tabloid *Bild-Zeitung*, which in characteristically large letters ran the front page headline:

> The East is Acting—What Is the West Doing?
> The West Is Doing NOTHING.
> President Kennedy Remains Silent …
> Macmillan Is Hunting …
> and Adenauer Is Complaining about Willy Brandt.[17]

The main message of the paper's editorial on the left-hand side of the front page read: "We are disappointed": disappointed in the Western alliance, which claimed that Allied rights had not been touched and which seemed to leave the Germans, and especially the West Berliners, alone in one of their darkest hours. Partly moved by public pressure, Berlin's Governing Mayor Willy Brandt had already sent a letter to Kennedy with a similar message the day before. In it, he criticized the weak reaction of the Western Allies, and while he did not doubt Allied guarantees of the freedom of West Berlin, he warned of "political psychological dangers in two respects": a growing confidence of the Eastern powers and "a crisis of confidence in Western powers." West Berlin, instead of being the place people flee to, could now become the place that people flee from, Brandt warned.[18]

While Kennedy was angry about the rather undiplomatic letter from Germany, he quickly understood that something needed to be done to restore America's credibility. Murrow, mostly worried about the "psychological climate," had recommended to "take a number of steps which need not necessarily affect the substance of our position but which if sufficiently well publicized would evidence the interest and support which we have so often pledged."[19] Kennedy did just that by sending Vice President Lyndon B. Johnson and General Lucius D. Clay, the hero of the airlift, as his personal emissaries to Berlin. Furthermore, 1,500 additional American soldiers were ordered to West Berlin to restore confidence. In a letter to Brandt, Kennedy called the latter "symbolic—but not symbolic only." That was also true of his decision to send Johnson and Clay. "This was not shallow show business," Andreas Daum wrote, "but performed crisis management in the service of *realpolitik*."[20]

On August 20, 1961, Ambassador Walter C. Dowling cabled to Washington that Johnson and Clay had brought a "record-breaking one million" people to the streets. Johnson, who at first had not been happy about his mission to Berlin, literally mingled with the crowds and even happily drank from open bottles of wine handed to him. The visit was an "overwhelming success in restoring Berlin morale […] the most significant event in Berlin history since lifting of blockade," Dowling reported. Like Clay and Johnson, the 1,500 American soldiers who had been sent from West Germany to West Berlin to demonstrate one of the three essentials—access—were cheered by large crowds: "Battle group commander said only comparable welcome 'was when we liberated France.'"[21] The *Washington Sunday Star* on August 20, 1961 called it "a good deal of play acting. And yet, at this time and in this place, the most absurdly theatrical gestures can be of the greatest importance."[22] Two years later, the president himself would receive an even more triumphant welcome in West Berlin.[23]

Kennedy in Berlin

The year 1963 proved a difficult time in transatlantic relations. The Kennedy administration had concerns about the Franco-German treaty of friendship (Elysée Treaty), which French President Charles de Gaulle and West German Chancellor Konrad Adenauer had signed in January 1963. The Americans saw the treaty as signaling a possible Franco-German axis that could even lead to a separate settlement with the Soviet Union. One of the main purposes of Kennedy's visit to Western Europe and especially to West Germany in June 1963 was therefore to reassert the importance of the Western alliance under American leadership, especially against French attempts to reduce US influence in Europe. Again, that involved much more than a traditional power play and also meant outperforming de Gaulle. The

French president had visited Germany in early September of the previous year and received a warm welcome from hundreds of thousands of people in the streets. On September 4, 1962 at Bonn City Hall, the former leader of the French resistance against Nazi occupation spoke of his admiration for "the great German people" (*das große deutsche Volk*)—in German! Another goal of Kennedy's trip was to renew American credibility in Europe, which had suffered during the height of the Second Berlin Crisis in 1961. The Berlin visit would be the highlight of that trip—together with Kennedy's stop in Ireland, which had a special personal meaning for the descendant of poor Irish immigrants.[24]

Once Kennedy's plans to visit Western Europe had become known in early 1963, Adenauer invited him to add Germany to his itinerary. Willy Brandt quickly followed with his own invitation to the president. By the second half of March, Kennedy had committed to visiting West Berlin. It would be the final destination in Germany after Cologne, Bonn, Frankfurt, and Wiesbaden. Kennedy would be the first American president to come to the city since 1945. There was some debate at home as to whether the president should go to Europe at this point in time. Some thought he should focus instead on the major civil rights conflicts being played out in places such as Birmingham, Alabama. Others doubted that anything could be achieved. The trip was, however, carefully planned, especially the day Kennedy would spend in the Western part of divided Berlin.[25]

On that day, the focus would not be on political discussions or meetings, but on making an impression. A telegram from the Berlin Mission to the State Department sent on May 1, 1961, discussed the preliminary planning and the goals of the president's visit. These included "to demonstrate anew and unmistakably breadth and depth of US-Berlin solidarity [...] in impressive and personalized form." Kennedy's visit should "produce advantageous political impression internationally" as well as give Berliners "helpful (albeit at moment not essential) psychological lift." To reach these goals and to get "maximum (preferably record) public attendance," several suggestions were made. Instead of Kennedy spending hours inside City Hall, the tour of the city in an open limousine should be extended. The telegram also called for "additional crowd capacity areas [...] for supplemental mass appearances" as well as "increase[d] exposure of important target groups to the president."[26] Most of those recommendations were taken up.

President Kennedy spent only eight hours in the city, much of that time being driven through the streets.[27] The carefully planned fifty-three-kilometer-long route passed along Kurfürstendamm and the Gedächtniskirche as well as some of the new housing developments. More than 1 million cheering people lined the streets. For the afternoon, another speech at Freie Universität Berlin had been added. The university, founded with American support in 1948, had become an important symbol of the close relationship between the USA and Berlin. And here the president would be exposed to one of the most important target groups: German students.

Kennedy did not plan to visit the Eastern part of the city and had said so again in a press conference in Bonn on June 24. But he did insist on a stop at Checkpoint Charlie, where, in October 1961, the famous tank confrontation had taken place. Not doing so might have been interpreted as a show of weakness. Brandt had instead wanted him to visit the monument for the victims of the Wall. Kennedy also stopped at the Brandenburg Gate.[28]

His visit was met with much interest, and not only in Berlin. German TV and radio provided complete live coverage. In addition, there was partial live coverage in the USA and in other places around the world. In part because de Gaulle's visit loomed large, many people wondered whether the American president would say a few words in German. Some statements had been prepared for him in "German" or rather in something that would sound German when read:

ish FROYA mish
im FRY-en bear-LEAN tsu zine.
dee SHTAT ist ine LOISH-tendes zim-bowl
fear oy-RO-pah oont dee GANTSA VELT.
ear MOOT
oont ee-ra OUSE-dow-ar
habn dee VORTA
ish bin ine bear-LEAN-ar
tsu inem shtolt-sen be-KENT-niss
VAIR-den lassn.[29]

Kennedy possibly felt somewhat uncomfortable reading this strange "German" and he decided not use most of the lines. Seeing the Wall in a number of places, Kennedy was touched and also decided that the draft for his main speech at City Hall in Schöneberg, which had gone through many revisions, did not feel appropriate anymore. Instead, he decided mostly to improvise what would become one of his most famous speeches. He did use a couple of lines in German, including the now iconic *Ich bin ein Berliner*, written down on a notecard a few minutes before.[30] But he added a strong criticism of communism and the Wall, calling it "the most obvious and vivid demonstration of the failures of the communist system, for all the world to see, […] an offense not only against history but an offense against humanity, separating families, dividing husbands and wives and brothers and sisters, and dividing a people who wish to be joined together." Kennedy also argued that cooperation with the Soviets would not be possible.[31] That, however, was in sharp contrast to the content and spirit of another one of his famous speeches, delivered at the American University in Washington, DC, just a couple of weeks before. In it, Kennedy had powerfully questioned the Cold War logic, emphasized what both sides had in common, and shown his readiness to negotiate.[32] Indeed, the tone of his speech at Berlin's City Hall shocked some of his advisers. A few hours later, Kennedy used his speech at Freie Universität Berlin to reaffirm his commitment to working together with the Soviets.[33]

Overall, Kennedy's trip was a tremendous success, its impact going beyond West Berlin and West Germany. After only his first day in the country, Universal Newsreels could happily tell viewers back home that he had "won friends by the millions." And, even more importantly, in Cologne, "twice the number" of people had welcomed the American president than had greeted the French president the year before, "when he was here to woo Adenauer into the French camp." Narrator Ed Herlihy made it sound as if that made the United States twice as important as France.[34] That part of the mission seemed to have been accomplished with ease. In addition, the cheers of "Ken-ne-dy" from millions of people in the streets could also be regarded as signs of thankfulness by the German people and the West Berliners for the help and support the United States had given them for so many years. While Kennedy had been celebrated like a pop star in several Latin American countries before, the proximity to the communist bloc in divided Berlin ensured that his triumphant day in the city sent a much bigger political message to both East and West. Some of that was due to the careful planning that had gone into every detail of his Berlin visit. But, ironically, the trip is best remembered for the speech at City Hall where Kennedy had disregarded the script. In what, as his widow Jackie wrote, might be her husband's most remembered words, Kennedy had strongly and emotionally connected Western ideas of freedom to the city: "All free men, wherever they may live, are citizens of Berlin, and, therefore, as a free man, I take pride in the words 'Ich bin ein Berliner!'"[35]

East Germany and the Kennedy visit

On the other side of the Wall, Kennedy's visit had been regarded with much concern. After his plans had become known, the East German authorities even considered denying him overflight rights. But that position did not find support in Moscow, partly because the Americans had the right to use an air corridor. Instead, measures focused on publicly attacking Kennedy and the West German government, including the support of peace demonstrations in the Federal Republic and the distribution of a newspaper and leaflets in West Berlin on the day of Kennedy's visit criticizing America's policy toward Cuba and—in the spirit of Khrushchev's ultimatum—demanding a normalization of the relationship between West Berlin and the GDR. In addition, the president was told: "Ami go home!"[36] The space between the pillars of the Brandenburg Gate was covered with red cloth and the East German flag. This made it impossible for Kennedy to look through it. When he had reached an elevated platform near the Brandenburg Gate, a large sign in English was driven in front of the gate, reminding the president of the Yalta and Potsdam Agreements as well as warning him of German militarists and "Nazism."[37]

Weeks in advance of Kennedy's visit, East German media had launched an anti-American propaganda campaign. It was directed by the "agitation committee" of the Central Committee of the SED, the GDR's ruling party. The *Agitationskommission*, whose main job was to control and guide mass media to win public support for government policy, had asked East German media not to overrate Kennedy's visit. Instead, they should focus on the denial of civil rights to African Americans, on the influence of revanchists in Bonn who did not recognize the new German borders, and on the Nazi past of German politicians.[38] And so they did.

In May and June 1963, *Neues Deutschland* published dozens of articles on Kennedy, American politics, and the president's planned trip to Germany. A major focus was on racial segregation and the civil rights movement in the United States. Describing protests and police violence in places such as Birmingham, Alabama, the newspaper in late May criticized that while Kennedy saw the USA as a model democracy, African Americans were still living without rights like slaves and suffering the "inhuman terror of malicious white rabble-rousers."[39] In an editorial, Kennedy, the "crusader for democracy," was criticized for not doing enough to support black Americans.[40] Repeatedly, the *New York Times* columnist Walter Lippmann and others were quoted as saying that Kennedy should stay at home and take care of important domestic issues. That seemed to make even more sense if one took the view that little could be achieved in Western Europe. There were political crises caused by scandals in Britain and Italy. In the Federal Republic, Adenauer had announced that Ludwig Erhard would soon replace him. And the successor for the recently deceased Pope John III would have been crowned only a few days before Kennedy's arrival.[41]

The negative reporting was briefly muted after Kennedy had given his "Peace Speech" at the American University on June 10, especially since it had received a positive response from Khrushchev. And while it was criticized that Kennedy's rhetoric was partly contradicted by his actions, the focus shifted to the revanchists in West Germany.[42] Several articles dealt with their strong criticism of Kennedy and accused Adenauer of supporting them. In a lengthy article, Foreign Minister Lothar Bolz warned the American president of these warmongers who wanted to draw the United States into a nuclear war. A cartoon depicted four representatives of militaristic *Landsmannschaften* (Germans born in the former Eastern territories of the Reich) demanding *Lebensraum* in the East, the reintegration of the former German territories in the East that were lost after World War Two, and the nuclear bomb. Adenauer asked for Kennedy's help in achieving these goals.[43] Another cartoon showed the president shaking hands with Hans Globke. Adenauer's chief of staff was depicted as a Nazi with a bloody hand that signified that, as one of the official commentators of the Nuremberg Laws, he bore responsibility for the death of millions of people. For the East German government, people such as Globke were proof that the Adenauer government had not broken with the German Nazi past. Since Kennedy did not listen to the many warnings, he was guilty by association.[44]

When the day of Kennedy's arrival in Germany drew closer, *Neues Deutschland* once again focused on America's domestic problems such as social injustice, high crime rates as well as racial segregation and violence against African Americans. A couple of cartoons showed Kennedy getting ready to preach order and human rights abroad instead of putting his own house in order. America's military involvement in Vietnam was also criticized.[45]

A few days before Kennedy was scheduled to arrive, *Neues Deutschland* made fun of the security precautions for his visit to West Berlin.[46] But there was comparatively little coverage of his actual trip and none on the enthusiastic welcome he received in places including Bonn and Cologne. His speech in the historic Paulskirche in Frankfurt was criticized because he had not discussed a German peace treaty.[47] The same was true for his day in Berlin. Again, there was no mention of the public response, but now the comments on what Kennedy had said became vicious. They were aimed especially at the president's speech in front of City Hall. For *Neues Deutschland*, it had included "vile anti-communist attacks," which provided direct support to West German revanchists. It was—rightly—pointed out that this was "the language of the Cold War" and that it contradicted Kennedy's speech at the American University on June 10. And while Kennedy had previously been accused of associating with former Nazis, an editorial now drew a direct comparison between his speech and those of Nazi leaders: "Weren't these the anti-Communist tirades of Hitler and Goebbels that poured through the loudspeakers?" But the Wall had shown Kennedy the limits of his power. And there was special satisfaction that the sign that was driven in front of the Brandenburg Gate had supposedly disturbed Kennedy so much that he had left the Gate much sooner than originally planned, and that the message had had an impact on him for the rest of the day. The fact that the *New York Times*—seen as the official US paper—showed a photo of the sign on its front page with a translation the next day was also celebrated.[48] That some international press outlets had remained critical of Kennedy's visit was duly noted.[49] The *Aktuelle Kamera*, East Germany's main TV news program, quoted *I.F. Stone's Bi-Weekly* in its evening edition on June 26:

> There's a Wall Nearer Home than Berlin. Mr. Kennedy, like the rest of us, has much to learn in the racial crisis. It will not be solved by fitful leadership. He cannot make one good TV talk and then rush off to be photographed at the Wall in Berlin. He'd better stay home and concern himself with the no less real wall between white and black at home.[50]

The East German authorities had not been able to completely hide undesirable information from their own public, however. By listening to the live coverage by West Berlin radio stations, East Germans had witnessed the enormous impression Kennedy had made. Some East Germans held up a sign at Checkpoint Charlie welcoming Kennedy, and East German construction workers successfully smuggled a bouquet of flowers to Kennedy.[51] But, overall, they felt that they had done well, controlling the impact and to some degree even disrupting the president's plans. But the most spectacular reaction to the Kennedy visit came two days after he had left the city.

Khrushchev in Berlin

In early June, the CIA had reported rumors in SED circles that Nikita Khrushchev might come to East Berlin around the time of Kennedy's visit to the Western part of the city, possibly "in order to confer with President Kennedy." While there was no hard information, the CIA quite correctly regarded these rumors as "perhaps an indication of the party members' concern over the possible impact of the presidential visit and the need to counter it."[52] Officially, the Soviet leader was still planning to visit Yugoslavia. But on June 24, one day after Kennedy had arrived in Germany, it was announced that Khrushchev would visit East Berlin and East Germany, beginning on June 28. The official reason was the seventieth birthday of East Germany's leader, Walter Ulbricht, but *Neues Deutschland* admitted that it was a surprise visit, indirectly indicating that it had been planned not long in advance.[53] Communist Party leaders from Hungary, Poland, Czechoslovakia, and Bulgaria would come to Berlin as well.

In contrast to Kennedy, whose visit to the city marked the first by a US president after 1945, it was Khrushchev's seventh time in Berlin.[54] But this visit was supposed to be special, precisely because it was designed as a direct response to Kennedy's triumph. And not only was it triggered by it, Kennedy's visit also served as a model for how to stage such an event. The West German *UFA-Wochenschau* newsreel correctly stated that Khrushchev's visit was meant to "counterbalance" Kennedy's.[55]

To build up emotions in the East German public, there was a lot of positive press coverage in advance of Khrushchev's arrival. Daily front page headlines informed the readers about the upcoming visit. Day by day, even *Neues Deutschland* more and more resembled the tabloid press on its front page, with headlines getting larger and turning red and the text losing its formal tone. While on June 25 the newspaper at the top of the front page somewhat formally announced the "Visit of Comrade N.S. Khrushchev to the GDR," the next day—again at the top of the front page—the headline read "Berlin Expecting Nikita." And it quoted international media confirming that this was a sign of the unlimited support of the Soviet Union for East Germany.[56]

At the same time, GDR newspapers were still critically discussing Kennedy's visit to West Berlin. The evening paper *BZ am Abend* announced Khrushchev's visit in a small red box on the front page next to the large black headline: "Waves of Protest in the USA," claiming that 20 million African Americans were demanding civil rights and the end of segregation. The article neither mentioned an existing petition signed by millions of people nor listed demonstrations whose number could have come close to 20 million, but the point was abundantly clear: Kennedy had left his country during a major crisis. In a similar way, the Berlin daily *Berliner Zeitung* printed both the announcement of Khrushchev's visit and an article on racial violence and protest in the USA on its front page.[57]

Many articles in East German newspapers focused on the growing anticipation. "Ordinary citizens" described how much they were looking forward to be part of the crowds welcoming the Soviet leader. *Neues Deutschland* predicted a "triumphant welcome." Berliners were officially asked to decorate the city and put up thousands of flags.[58] The *BZ* described the visitor as a statesman who stood for peace, and on June 28, *Neues Deutschland* announced on its front page in large red letters: "Welcome, Germany's Best Friend" next to a welcome poem written by Willi Layh.[59] That same day, the main headline of *Berliner Zeitung* was also printed in large red letters, welcoming Nikita Khrushchev in both Russian and German.[60] As had been the case during Kennedy's visit to West Berlin, schools and factories would be closed so that hundreds of thousands of people could line the streets to see and cheer the special international guest (not all of them happily or voluntarily), many shouting "Ni-ki-ta" the same way Berliners on the other side of the Wall had shouted "Ken-ne-dy" a few days before. Just like Kennedy, the Soviet leader would be driven through the city in an open car, led by the police motorcycle squad. Newspapers printed the route in advance on their front pages.[61] And just like Kennedy, Khrushchev would give a speech at City Hall, in this case, the Red City Hall in East Berlin.

At the beginning of his speech, he said that recently other international visitors had been in Berlin, "some travel to West Berlin—others to East Berlin." Next he discussed why they all came to the city: "Some say that they visit West Berlin with the goal of normalizing the situation and ending the 'Cold War,' even though their actions actually show the opposite." Khrushchev did not mention Kennedy explicitly, but everyone knew to whom he was alluding and whom he was criticizing. The main part of his speech, however, was about the achievements of socialism and in praise of the brotherhood and cooperation between the socialist countries.[62] That Khrushchev, as a reaction to Kennedy's strong criticism of the Wall, said "I love the Wall" in that speech is wrong. But a day later he told workers at a machine tool factory in Berlin-Marzahn:

> I have read that the president of the United States of America looked at the Wall with great discontent. He did not like it at all.
> But I like it extraordinarily! [Applause] The working class of the GDR built a wall. The hole was blocked so that no wolf could break into the German Democratic Republic anymore. Is that bad? That is good! [Applause].[63]

Beginning with the *BZ am Abend*, which, in its edition of June 28, was already celebrating Khrushchev's visit, as well as the *Aktuelle Kamera*, which described his tour though the city as "incredibly triumphant," the East German press tried to find headlines that would match those of Western newspapers that had covered the Kennedy visit. The *BZ am Abend* repeatedly spoke of embracing "Nikita" in large black headlines underlined in red.[64] On the front page of the *Berliner Zeitung*, large red letters read: "He was welcomed by the hearts of the citizens of Berlin." The newspaper covered the visit on several pages in text and pictures, calling it a "great national event." That was probably a deliberate allusion to how Willy Brandt, just a few days before, had characterized Kennedy's visit as: "A great day in the history of our city."[65] *Neues Deutschland*—in large red letters on the front page—emphasized that half a million people had cheered the Soviet leader, giving him an "unparalleled welcome." It also showed a picture of his literal embrace with Walter Ulbricht at Schönefeld Airport.[66] The fact that international news media reported on the Khrushchev visit was cited as additional proof that it had been an "event of importance in world politics."[67]

The competition did not end with the actual visits. On both sides, official documentaries were produced to commemorate the two "historic" visits: *Germany Greets Kennedy—Four Historic Days* in West Germany[68] and *Thanks to the Friend* by East Germany's state-owned film production company DEFA.[69] The Liga für Völkerfreundschaft (League for Friendship among Nations) in East Berlin published a multilingual brochure, partially in color, about the Khrushchev visit.[70] In the West, several publishing houses sold special editions of their newspapers or magazines devoted to Kennedy's trip to Germany. The Press and Information Office of the West Berlin state government published a special color brochure.[71] Record producer Deutsche Grammophon Gesellschaft produced a vinyl LP record with Kennedy's speeches on it.[72]

In contrast to Kennedy, who had only spent eight hours in Berlin, Khrushchev stayed for three days. And while Kennedy's visit was the only one of his presidency, the Soviet leader had been to Berlin several times before. Ignoring the triumphant welcome Kennedy had received wherever he had stopped in Europe, in East Germany, the divisions inside the Western alliance and inside Germany itself were emphasized even after the president had left. With other communist leaders joining Khrushchev in East Berlin, the message here, in contrast, was one of unity and cooperation.[73] As a direct response, the West German *UFA-Wochenschau* explicitly mentioned frictions inside the Eastern bloc. Citing international media, it called the "opportunistic fraternization" in East Berlin a "fiasco."[74]

Given the official endorsement of the American civil rights movement by the East German government, the visit by Martin Luther King, Jr. to Berlin the following year might also have been used to celebrate "unity" and "cooperation." But the GDR had trouble endorsing King's message of "freedom."[75]

King in Berlin

On a visit to the United States in May 1964, Willy Brandt met Martin Luther King, Jr. for the first time and invited him to Berlin. Together with Ralph Abernathy, his vice president at the Southern Christian Leadership Conference, the civil rights leader came to the divided city from September 12 to 14 that same year.[76] King, who would receive the Nobel Peace Prize in December 1964, was celebrated in both Germanys for his activities fighting racial segregation in the United States. As Maria Höhn and Martin Klimke write in their seminal study on the civil rights struggle and Germany, King and others like him seemed to especially fit the GDR's "ideological commitment to combat imperialism, colonialism, and racism."[77]

King had a full schedule on September 13. He signed the golden book at Rathaus Schöneberg, spoke at a memorial service for John F. Kennedy at the Berlin Philharmonic Hall, and then took part in a reception at the Berlin Academy of Arts.

In his comments on John F. Kennedy at the Berlin Philharmonic Hall, King praised the dead president for his commitment to civil rights and his willingness to use federal power to enforce it as well as for his new thinking on the Cold War. His violent death, King said, had led to a "period of profound soul searching." He also spoke of Kennedy's dream, which in parts resembled the dream King himself had so powerfully spoken of during the March on Washington. And he quoted Kennedy's "Ich bin ein Berliner."[78] Afterwards he addressed more than 20,000 people at the *Waldbühne*, an open air stage, about the civil rights movement, its Christian roots, and how much still needed to be achieved. King also talked about the Cold War divisions that were so dramatically visible in Berlin.[79]

Next, King went to see the section of the Berlin Wall where early in the morning Michael Meyer had been shot while trying to flee East Germany. The twenty-one-year-old had been rescued by a US soldier after shots had been fired from both sides. King also inspected where the bullets had hit a building. Later that day, King received an honorary doctoral degree of the Theological School of the West Berlin Protestant Church in the home of Bishop Dr. Otto Dibelius. In the early evening, he arrived at Checkpoint Charlie in order to cross the border into East Berlin and give a sermon at Marienkirche (St. Mary's Church). It was followed by another church service at Sophienkirche (Sophia Church) and a meeting with representatives of the Protestant Church Berlin Brandenburg. King had been invited to East Berlin by Provost Heinrich Grüber, a former pastor at Marienkirche, who after the building of the Wall had not been allowed to return to East Germany and now lived in West Berlin.[80]

That he planned to visit East Berlin and talk there had been reported both in the US press and announced by West Berlin radio as well as in at least one East German paper. The *BZ am Abend* put a short announcement about King's planned sermon in its "In a Nutshell" section on September 12.[81] So it should not have come as a complete surprise to the East German border guards when, according to the border guards' report, the prominent civil rights leader arrived at the border crossing on September 13 at around 7:40 pm. However, they did not immediately recognize him and King did not have his passport with him. Members of the State Department had taken it away, most likely to prevent him from getting into East Berlin, possibly because of the incident earlier in the day. King himself told his driver Ralph Zorn that it had been done for "security reasons." Zorn, an American-born priest who lived and worked in West Berlin, and Alcyone Scott of the Lutheran World Foundation tried to get King across anyway, convinced that, because of his fame, he would be recognized. According to the report of the East German border guards, the two claimed that the man with them had forgotten his passport in West Berlin. But without identification, they did not want to let the "negro theologian" into "democratic Berlin." Finally, one of the border guards did recognize the civil rights leader. In the end, after superiors had given their OK, King's American Express card was accepted as identification and around 7:52 pm he could continue his trip to Marienkirche, where more than 2,000 people were already waiting for him. In order to accommodate everyone who had come out, it was decided that King would speak also at Sophienkirche, which meant that King would be giving effectively the same speech three times that day.[82]

King's appearance in East Germany was met with mixed feelings by the government. Racial segregation and the civil rights movement with King as its most prominent leader had received quite a lot of coverage in East German media, partly because it offered an opportunity to criticize the United States. But while in the end King had been allowed to enter the country even without a passport, he was not granted an official welcome and there were no meetings with East German officials. His visit had not been advertised or used for propaganda purposes, and there were no interviews with him. Very likely, King would have rejected any attempt to be used for anti-American propaganda purposes by the East German regime, not the least because of charges by some of his critics in the United States that he was already cooperating with communists.[83]

King's brief visit to East Berlin did not make it onto the front page of every major newspaper. *Neues Deutschland*, using a short news article by East Germany's news agency ADN, hid a small news item on King's sermon in Marienkirche on page 2, calling him "a well-known negro clergyman." The *Berliner Zeitung* printed only a slightly longer version of the same report on page 8, adding a sentence on King's speech at Waldbühne. Neither newspaper seems to have sent a reporter to cover the event.[84]

Other papers did report about King on their front page. The *BZ am Abend* printed a photo of King and Zorn on the pulpit of Marienkirche. The text was similar to the one in the other papers, but mentioned that the service had started with the choir performing a song "in which the American negroes express their longing for freedom."[85] The *Neue Zeit* published by far the longest article. The daily of East Germany's CDU, a block party supporting the ruling SED, showed a picture of King and black African students from Humboldt University on its front page. The main headline quoted the last sentence of King's speech: "We will be free one day." The remainder of the headline as well as the main text then focused on the racial situation and the civil rights struggle in America.

While "We will be free one day" could indeed have been read as a comment on human rights in East Germany, none of the articles in the East German press elaborated on what else King had said at Waldbühne and in both churches. His "freedom" message and his comments about the East–West division explain the unease which his visit had provoked among the East German authorities and media. King, who had witnessed the cruelties connected to the Wall earlier that day, spoke about Berlin "as a symbol of the divisions of men on the face of the earth." He also said that "God's children" lived on both sides of the "wall" and that "no man-made barrier can obliterate that fact," emphasizing that "in Christ there is no East or West, no North or South." Later in the speech he again came back to the theme that with Jesus Christ's "victory [...] over the world, whether it be an Eastern world or a Western World," even political division could be overcome. King refrained from openly taking sides, but his message could also be interpreted as a rejection of East German-style socialism.[86] King's final words could have come straight out of one of his speeches to an audience of Americans fighting for civil rights: "With this [Christian] faith we will be able to work together, to pray together, to struggle together, to suffer together, to stand up for freedom together, knowing that we will be free one day." But to many in the audience this was a message of hope that their own freedom could be achieved. That sentiment is also expressed in the gospel song the choir had sung as a welcome to King. "Go down Moses" includes the line "Let my people go."[87]

King, in pointing out and attacking some of the ugly sides of the United States, could be useful to East German propaganda. He and others were praised "as the heroes of the 'other America'—the America of the oppressed."[88] Accordingly, a few days after King had left Berlin, the *Neue Zeit* strongly defended King against an attack in the obscure right-wing weekly *Wochen-Echo*, which among other things had accused him of being a communist.[89] But at the same time, King's rhetoric, which had also been vilified as "Communist" by some of his opponents in the United States, called into question the legitimacy of the East German regime. The FBI, which considered King to be one of the most dangerous men in America, regularly wiretapped him. On September 14, the *Stasi* had his speech at Marienkirche taped.

Conclusion

The building of the Wall meant a stabilization of the situation in Berlin. There was no more threat of immediate war. After the peaceful and somewhat lucky ending of the Cuban Missile Crisis in October 1962, Kennedy and Khrushchev began some attempts at détente with the Limited Nuclear Test Ban Treaty and the Hot Line Agreement. Kennedy's speech at the American University was another important step to real understanding and cooperation. Nevertheless, that did not mean an end to Cold War rivalries, as Kennedy's and Khrushchev's respective visits to Berlin prove that Berlin still mattered, also in world politics. But since the superpowers had shown that they did not want to go to war over Berlin, the competition moved to a different and far less dangerous level; it often took place in a highly charged public sphere, with prominent "actors" and on different "stages"; not buttressed by tanks, but amplified by loudspeakers. And while King was praised on both sides, over the years things started to change in each "camp."

When in 1987 President Ronald Reagan visited West Berlin on the occasion of the 750th anniversary of the city's founding and delivered his famous demand: "Mr. Gorbachev, tear down this wall," Germans saw the United States and especially its president much more critically than they had in the early 1960s. While many Berliners cheered Reagan, there were also mass demonstrations against him. On the other side of the Wall, things were also not quite the same anymore: Mikhail Gorbachev, who had become the leader of the Soviet Union in 1985, was still "embraced" on his arrival. But he was not welcomed as the best friend of the GDR by the East German leadership in 1989 or cheered as "Gorbi" in the East German media like he was in the West. There were open disagreements about the future course of East Germany, and the Soviet Union had turned from a model country into a problematic ally. At the same time, Gorbachev became increasingly popular in the West. After Reagan and Gorbachev had signed the INF Treaty in December 1987, eliminating medium-range nuclear missiles, the Cold War became less of a military contest. Finally, the summer of 1988 was marked not by a competition of political figures in the still divided city, but by a battle of the bands.[90] The latter turned out to be a logistical challenge for East Germany, where concerts on such a large scale had never taken place. The stage was built with material needed to construct highway bridges. The long cables from the mixer to the stage were covered with conveyor belts from bucket-wheel excavators used in large surface mining. It was even more difficult to control the ideological message. In 1987, David Bowie had greeted those listening on the other side of the Wall in German. When in the following year the stage in West Berlin was again built next to the Reichstag, medical concerns served as a pretext for preventing the concert from crossing the border: Loud music ostensibly posed a health risk for those in the nearby university clinic Charité and noise limits were imposed on Pink Floyd. Neither the band nor music promoter Peter Schwenkow was ready to follow this order, however, and Schwenkow later had to pay a large fine.

There were also difficulties with Springsteen. The artist and his managers had not been informed that his concert was advertised as a solidarity concert for Nicaragua. When he found out a few hours before the concert, the show was nearly canceled. His management was not ready to accept the argument that "Nicaragua" should be seen as just another sponsor like Coca-Cola or Pepsi. In the end, the political banners were taken down from the stage—yet posters and the tickets still read "Concert for Nicaragua" and "Nicaragua in the heart," respectively.

Whether out of anger about how the East German concert organizers had tried to instrumentalize him or whether he would have done it anyway, Springsteen did comment on the East–West division. Introducing *Chimes of Freedom*, he said that he had not come in order to support or oppose a government, but to play his music for the East Berliners "in the hope that one day all barriers will be torn down."[91] Springsteen had originally wanted to say "walls," but when his fearful West German concert organizers intervened, he agreed to speak of "barriers" instead. That most likely did not make much of a difference to many in the audience. The Springsteen concert surely did not start a movement that led to the fall of the Wall, as Erik Kirschbaum has implied. But it showed to what extremes the East German regime was prepared to go in order to pacify its youth. It paid in hard currency for Western stars to counter those playing in the West. And up to 300,000 East Germans—some waving home-made flags of the class enemy—joined Bruce Springsteen on July 19, 1988 during the largest concert in the history of the country in singing *Born in the USA!*[92]

Notes

1   The author would like to thank Silvia Gerlsbeck for her excellent job proofreading this article.
2   Cf. the film *Mein Sommer '88—Wie die Stars die DDR rockten*, Germany 2013.
3   Jörg Wagner, "Die Musik überwindet die Mauer," *Deutschlandfunk*, June 6, 2012, URL: www.deutschlandfunk.de/die-musik-ueberwindet-die-mauer.871. de.html?dram:article_id=207770; Hans-W. Saure, "Toter Michael Jackson. Stasi-Akte aufgetaucht!," *Bild*, August 18, 2009, www.bild.de/unterhaltung/leute/stasi-akte-aufgetaucht-9196136.bild.html (accessed February 16, 2016).
4   Ernest R. May, "America's Berlin: Heart of the Cold War," *Foreign Affairs* 77 (1998) 4, pp. 148–60.
5   Andreas W. Daum, "'Atlantic Partnership' or Simply 'A Mess'? Performance Politics and Social Communication in the Western Alliance during the Kennedy Presidency," in: Manfred Berg and Andreas Etges (eds.), *John F. Kennedy and the "Thousand Days": New Perspectives on the Foreign and Domestic Policies of the Kennedy Administration* (Heidelberg, 2007), pp. 17–37, p. 19. Cf. idem, *Kennedy in Berlin: Politik, Kultur und Emotionen im Kalten Krieg* (Paderborn, 2003).
6   Andreas Etges, "Western Europe," in: Petra Goedde and Richard Immerman (eds.), *Oxford Handbook on the Cold War* (Oxford, 2013), pp. 158–73, p. 161. Cf. John F. Kennedy, "Radio and Television Report to the American People on the Soviet Arms Buildup in Cuba, October 22, 1962," www.jfklibrary.org/Asset-Viewer/sUVmCh-sB0moLfrBcaHaSg.aspx; "President Lyndon B. Johnson's Address at Johns Hopkins University: Peace Without Conquest," April 7, 1965, www.lbjlibrary.net/collections/selected-speeches/1965/04-07-1965.html (both accessed September 24, 2020).
7   A major reason for Brandt's visit was the urgency of the Berlin problems. The fact that Adenauer came much later surely also had to do with German federal elections in September 1961 and Kennedy's somewhat difficult relationship with the German chancellor, who was nearly twice his age.
8   On this, the Vienna summit and its aftermath, see Michael R. Beschloss, *The Crisis Years: Kennedy and Khrushchev, 1960–1963* (New York, 1991).
9   Robert J. McMahon, "Credibility and World Power: Exploring the Psychological Dimension in Postwar American Diplomacy," *Diplomatic History* 15 (1991), pp. 455–72, p. 455. Cf. Jonathan Schell, *The Time of Illusion* (New York, 1976), esp. pp. 343–55; Daryl Grayson Press, *Calculating Credibility: How Leaders Assess Military Threats* (Ithaca, 2005), p. 1. Press used three test cases: appeasement policy, the Berlin crises, and the Cuban Missile Crisis.

10 John Lewis Gaddis, *Strategies of Containment: A Critical Appraisal of American National Security Policy during the Cold War* (Oxford, 2005), p. 90, quote on p. 212.

11 John F. Kennedy, Radio and Television Report to the American People on the Berlin Crisis, July 25, 1961, www.jfklibrary.org/archives/other-resources/john-f-kennedy-speeches/berlin-crisis-19610725 (accessed March 8, 2020).

12 Asked whether in case of East Germany completely closing access to the city "the United States and its Allies should or should not fight their way into Berlin," 71 percent answered "'should fight." Only 15 percent were opposed. The Gallup Poll, *Public Opinion, 1935–1971*, vol. III: 1959–1971 (New York, 1972), p. 1729.

13 Telegram from the Embassy in the Soviet Union to the Department of State, Moscow, July 28, 1961, in *Foreign Relations of the United States* (FRUS), 1961–1963, vol. XIV, Berlin Crisis, 1961–1962. (Washington, 1993), pp. 231–4, 233.

14 Robert Dallek, *An Unfinished Life: John F. Kennedy, 1917–1963* (Boston, 2003), p. 426.

15 Kenneth P. O'Donnell and David F. Powers, *"Johnny, We Hardly Knew Ye": Memories of John Fitzgerald Kennedy* (Boston, 1972), p. 303.

16 Telegram from the Mission at Berlin to the Department of State, Berlin, August 16, 1961, in *FRUS*, 1961–1963, vol. XIV, pp. 339–41, p. 340.

17 "Der Osten handelt—was tut der Westen? Der Westen tut NICHTS! Präsident Kennedy schweigt … Macmillan geht auf die Jagd … und Adenauer schimpft auf Willy Brandt," *Bild*, August 16, 1961.

18 Brandt to Kennedy, August 16, 1961. A translation of the letter is included in Telegram from the Mission at Berlin to the Department of State, Berlin, August 16, 1961, in *FRUS*, 1961–1963, vol. XIV, pp. 345–6.

19 Telegram from the Mission at Berlin to the Department of State, Berlin, August 16, 1961, in *FRUS*, 1961–1963, vol. XIV, p. 340.

20 Kennedy to Brandt, August 18, 1961, in *FRUS*, 1961–1963, vol. XIV, 352–3, 352. Daum, *Atlantic Partnership*, p. 25.

21 Telegram from the Mission in Berlin to the Department of State, Berlin, August 20, 1961, in Vice-Presidential Security File, Box 2: Vice-Presidential Travel File, Berlin, Germany. Folder 3: Report and Related Papers re Vice President Johnson's Trip to Germany August 19–20, 1961, LBJ Presidential Library.

22 Quoted in Daum, *Kennedy in Berlin*, p. 217, fn 122.

23 The visit by another special envoy sent by the president will not be covered in this chapter. But the fact that his brother, Attorney General Robert F. Kennedy, came to West Berlin in February 1962 is another indication of the city's prominence in American foreign policy at the time.

24 Cf. Andreas Etges, *John F. Kennedy*, exhibition catalogue (Wolfratshausen, 2003), pp. 134–5; Daum, *Kennedy in Berlin*, pp. 56–9.

25 Cf. ibid., pp. 60–74.

26 Telegram from the US Mission in Berlin to the Department of State, May 1, 1963, National Security Files (NSF), Box 241 Trips and Conferences: President's Trip. Europe 6/63-7/63. Germany 1/17/63-6/10/63 [Folder 1 of 2], John F. Kennedy Presidential Library (JFKL).

27 Brandt and Adenauer had argued about who would ride in the car with Kennedy and who would sit where. In the end, both would join the president, who, because of his back problems, sat on the right side of the car in order to be able to lean on the back door. Brandt sat next to him.

28 John F. Kennedy, The President's News Conference at the Foreign Ministry in Bonn, June 24, 1963, www.jfklibrary.org/asset-viewer/archives/JFKWHA/1963/JFKWHA-197/JFKWHA-197 (accessed February 6, 2019).

29 "I am proud to be in free Berlin. This city is a shining symbol for Europe and the whole world. Your courage and your perseverance have made the words 'I am a Berliner' a proud declaration." A similar document to "Arrival in Berlin" with German phonetic phrases and official English translation was also prepared for his arrival in Germany. Both can be found here: President's Office Files. Countries. Germany: JFK visit, June 1963, www.jfklibrary.org/asset-viewer/archives/ JFKPOF/117a/JFKPOF-117a-007 (accessed February 23, 2016).

30 Actually, Kennedy said this line twice. The first time, the reaction of the crowd was much stronger after the translator had repeated the words. Kennedy noticed this and self-ironically proclaimed: "I appreciate my interpreter translating my German!" John F. Kennedy, Remarks at the Rudolph-Wilde-Platz, Berlin, June 26, 1963, www.jfklibrary.org/Asset-Viewer/oEX2uqSQGEGIdTYgd_JL_Q.aspx (accessed February 2, 2019).

31 Ibid.

32 John F. Kennedy, Commencement Address at American University, Washington, DC, June 10, 1963, www.jfklibrary.org/archives/other-resources/john-f-kennedy-speeches/american-university-19630610 (accessed February 2, 2019).

33 Andreas Etges, *John F. Kennedy* (Munich, 2003), pp. 86–7.

34 Universal Newsreels, Kennedy in Europe, June 23, 1963, www.jfklibrary.org/learn/ about-jfk/media-galleries/universal-newsreels-1963 (accessed March 8, 2020).

35 Jackie Kennedy to Willy Brandt, January 3, 1964, in Willy-Brandt-Archiv im Archiv der sozialen Demokratie der Friedrich-Ebert-Stiftung. Kennedy, Remarks at the Rudolph-Wilde-Platz.

36 See the pictures of the leaflets in Etges, *Kennedy* (exhibition catalogue), p. 141; SED-Westberlin an Kennedy, *BZ*, June 26, 1963.

37 Photos and a transcription of the text can be found at www.jfklibrary.org/Asset-Viewer/Archives/JFKWHP-1963-06-26-B.aspx (accessed February 2, 2019).

38 Agitationskommission beim ZK der SED on June 7 and 14, quoted in *Reaktionen in der DDR auf den Kennedy-Besuch*, www.dhm.de/archiv/ausstellungen/kennedy/ berlinbesuch/ddr/medien.html (accessed February 2, 2019).

39 "So sehen Freiheit und Menschenwürde in den USA aus!," *Neues Deutschland* (ND), May 25, 1963.

40 "Aufgabe für Kennedy," *ND*, May 27, 1963.

41 "'New York Times': Kennedy sollte Reise verschieben" *ND*, June 6, 1963; "Kennedy-Reise umstritten," *ND*, June 7, 1963; Also "'New York Herald Tribune': Kennedy soll Europa-Reise absagen," *ND*, June 9, 1963; "DPA zur Kennedy-Reise: Unter einem unglücklichen Stern," *ND*, June 11, 1963; "Kennedy-Reise umstritten," *ND*, June 12, 1963; "Kennedy gehört nach Birmingham," *ND*, June 17, 1963; "Meinung des Auslands zur Reise Kennedys," *ND*, June 25, 1963.

42 "Gemeinsames Interesse Vereinigte Staaten-Sowjetunion," *ND*, June 12, 1963; "Zwiespältig," *ND*, June 12, 1963; "Von großem Interesse. Moskauer Rundfunk zur jüngsten Rede des USA-Präsidenten Kennedy," *ND*, June 13, 1963; "Das heißt deutlich: Die Bonner Ultras wollen die USA in einen Atomkrieg hineinziehen!" *ND*, June 15, 1963; "Nikita Chruschtschow zur Rede jüngsten Rede des US-Präsidenten: 'Das Wort vom Frieden muß durch praktische Taten bekräftigt werden'," *ND*, June 16, 1963.

43 "Dr. Bolz: Lassen Sie sich nicht von den Bonner Kriegstreibern mißbrauchen, Präsident Kennedy!," *ND*, June 15, 1963. Cartoon, *ND*, June 25, 1963. Cf. "USA-Präsident von Revanchisten beschimpft," *ND*, June 17, 1963; "Ziele der Revanchehetze," *ND*, June 18, 1963; "Schlammflut des Revanchismus überschwemmt

Westdeutschland," *ND*, June 18, 1963; "Handschrift der Ultras," *ND*, June 19, 1963; "Revanchisten wollen Kennedy einspannen," *ND*, June 20, 1963; "Wozu die Bonner Militaristen Kennedy mißbrauchen wollen," *ND*, June 23, 1963; "Kennedy und die Revanchisten," *ND*, June 25, 1963.

44   Cartoon Globke, *ND*, June 25, 1963. An earlier article had made a comparison between Nazi Germany and racists in the American South. Cf. "Aufgabe für Kennedy," *ND*, May 27, 1963.

45   "'Schreien Sie laut um Hilfe!' Menschenunwürdige Zustände vor Kennedys Haustür," *ND*, June 22, 1963; "So leben die Neger im 'freiesten Land der Welt'," *ND*, June 21, 1963; "Neuer Rassenmord in den USA," *ND*, June 26, 1963; "39 Negerkinder eingekerkert," *ND*, June 26, 1963. Cf. other articles in the international section of *ND*, on June 25 and 26, 1963. Cartoons, *ND*, June 22 and 26, 1963.

46   "Kennedy kommt! Versiegelt sämtliche Mülltonnen!," *ND*, June 21, 1963.

47   "Kennedy-Rede in der Frankfurter Paulskirche: Kein Wort über Abrüstung und deutsche Friedensregelung," *ND*, June 26, 1963.

48   "Kennedy stieß in das Hörn der Revanchisten"; Editorial: "Die Sprache des Kalten Krieges"; "Blick auf die Wahrheit raubte Kennedy den Überblick über die Lage": all *ND*, June 27, 1963; "Das schweißtreibende Wort," *ND*, June 29, 1963. See also "Gestern Sprecher der Ultras," *BZ am Abend* (BZ), June 27, 1963; "Wahrheit von Potsdam schockte Kennedy," *Berliner Zeitung* (BLZ), June 27, 1963. That the speech at Free Universitity Berlin a few hours later included different statements about peaceful coexistence and cooperation was noted as well.

49   "Kennedy-Besuch im Feuer der Kritik," *ND*, June 29, 1963.

50   Links to the script can be found here: Reaktionen in der DDR auf den Kennedy-Besuch, www.dhm.de/archiv/ausstellungen/kennedy/berlinbesuch/ddr/medien.html

51   Cf. Reaktionen in der DDR auf den Kennedy-Besuch.

52   CIA Telegram, *Reactions in the SED District Potsdam to the Forthcoming Presidential Visit to West Berlin*, June 4, 1963, in National Security Files, Box 241 Trips and Conferences: President's Trip. Europe 6/63-7/63. Germany 1/17/63-6/10/63 [Folder 2 of 2], JFKL.

53   "Besuch des Genossen N.S. Chruschtschow in der DDR," *ND*, June 25, 1963; "Berlin erwartet Nikita," *ND*, June 26, 1963.

54   See the list in "Zum siebenten Mal in der DDR," *ND*, June 27, 1963; "Heute zum 7. Male," *BZ*, June 28, 1961.

55   UFA-Wochenschau 362, July 5, 1963, www.filmothek.bundesarchiv.de/video/584552 (accessed February 2, 2019).

56   "Besuch des Genossen N.S. Chruschtschow in der DDR," *ND*, June 25, 1963; "Hochstimmung: Morgen kommt Chruschtschow," *ND*, June 28, 1963; "Thema in der ganzen Welt," *BLZ*, June 26, 1963.

57   "Nikita Chruschtschow kommt zu Besuch" and "Protestwelle in den USA," both in *BZ*, June 25, 1963. "Nikita Chruschtschow besucht die DDR" and "Blut fließt in den USA," both in *BLZ*, June 25, 1963.

58   "Hochstimmung: Morgen kommt Chruschtschow," *ND*, June 28, 1963; "Bürger der Hauptstadt!," *BZ*, June 26, 1963; "Unsere Hauptstadt erwartet Nikita Chruschtschow," *BLZ*, June 26, 1963. Similar demands were printed in the following days as well. See citizens' statements in *ND*, June 26, 1963.

59   "Staatsmann des Friedens kommt," *BZ*, June 26, 1963; "Willkommen, bester Freund der Deutschen"; "Nikita Chruschtschow," poem by Willi Nayh, both *ND*, June 28, 1963. See also "Ein Freund kommt!," *BLZ*, June 26, 1963.

60 "Herzlich willkommen!," front page, *BLZ*, June 28, 1963.

61 *BZ* and *BLZ*, June 27, 1961.

62 See transcripts of the speech in *ND* and *BZ*, both June 29, 1963.

63 See the identical transcripts of the speech: "[D]ann sprach Nikita Chruschtschow," *BLZ*, June 30, 1963; "Wölfen wurde das Loch verstopft," *ND*, June 30, 1963.

64 "Sei umarmt Nikita," *BZ*, June 28, 1963. Transcript of *Aktuelle Kamera*, June 18, 1963, in *Reaktionen in der DDR auf den Kennedy-Besuch*, www.dhm.de/archiv/ausstellungen/kennedy/berlinbesuch/ddr/gegenbesuch.htm (accessed February 2, 2019). "So schloß Berlin Nikita in die Arme," *BZ*, June 29, 1963.

65 "Die Herzen der Berliner schlugen ihm entgegen," *BLZ*, June 29, 1963.

66 "Empfang ohne Gleichen," *ND*, June 29, 1963.

67 "Schlagzeilen über Chruschtschow und Ulbricht beherrschen die Weltpresse," *ND*, June 30, 1963. Cf. "Weltagenturen berichten über Chruschtschow-Besuch" and "20 Fernsehstationen übertrugen Empfang Chruschtschows," both in *ND*, June 29, 1963.

68 *Deutschland grüßt Kennedy—Vier geschichtliche Tage*, produced by Deutsche Wochenschau GmbH, 1963 (fifty-nine minutes) for the Adenauer government, www.filmothek.bundesarchiv.de/video/590218 (accessed February 2, 2019).

69 *Dank dem Freunde*, DEFA, July 12, 1963, twenty-five minutes.

70 Sonderdruck zum Besuch von Nikita S. Chruschtschow in der DDR (Berlin, 1963).

71 *Ein großer Tag in der Geschichte unserer Stadt—26. Juni 1963: John F. Kennedy in Berlin* (Berlin, 1963). Cf. Berliner Illustrierte, Special Print: *Präsident Kennedy in Deutschland* (Berlin, 1963).

72 Deutsche Grammophon Gesellschaft, *Kennedy in Deutschland: Im Zeichen der Freundschaft*, 1963.

73 Cf. "Lord Sandwich: 'Westberlin fehlt Satzzeichen? Dinosaurier ohne Hoffnung auf weitere Existenz'"; "De Gaulle greift Kennedy an"; "'Westeuropa-Gebäude' erschüttert," all in *ND*, June 29,1963.

74 UFA-Wochenschau 362, July 5, 1963.

75 Cf. the comprehensive new study on East Germany and the civil rights movement: Maria Schubert, *"We Shall Overcome": Die DDR und die amerikanische Bürgerrechtsbewegung* (Paderborn, 2018).

76 Willy Brandt, *Begegnungen und Einsichten: Die Jahre 1960–1975* (Hamburg, 1976), p. 87. Cf. Maria Höhn and Martin Klimke, *A Breath of Freedom: The Civil Rights Struggle, African American GIs, and Germany* (New York, 2010), p. 91.

77 Höhn and Klimke, *A Breath of Freedom*, p. 4. Their chapter entitled "Bringing Civil Rights to East and West: Dr. Martin Luther King in Cold War Berlin" is the best analysis of King's visit to Berlin. Ibid., pp. 89–105.

78 But in the Berlin speech, he added some remarks, including the ones about Kennedy's dream. On the first page of the manuscript, he also wrote "Ich bin ein Berliner" in German. For the speech manuscript, see id., *Comments on John F. Kennedy at the Berlin Festival*, West Berlin, September 13, 1964, web.archive.org/web/20181010052237/http://www.thekingcenter.org/archive/document/comments-john-f-kennedy-mlk-berlin-festival (accessed September 24, 2020). It was published without the handwritten remarks in *Transition* 15 (1964), pp. 27–8.

79 The speeches King gave at Waldbühne and later at Marienkirche and Sophienkirche are pretty much identical. The content will be discussed in more detail in the context of his visit to East Berlin.

80 Höhn and Klimke, *A Breath of Freedom*, pp. 97–8. Cf. Tracing an Untold Story: Dr. Martin Luther King's Visit to Cold War Berlin, in web.archive.org/web/20170621113527/http://www.aacvr-germany.org/index.php/images-7/dr-martin-luther-kings-visit-to-cold-war-berlin (accessed March 8, 2020).

81 "Martin Luther King kommt," *BZ*, September 12, 1964. Cf. "Dr. King Foresees 'Social Disruption' If Goldwater Wins," *New York Times*, September 13, 1964, p. 66; "2 Berlins to Hear King," *Washington Post*, September 12, 1964.

82 Höhn and Klimke, *A Breath of Freedom*, pp. 99–100; Schubert, *"We Shall Overcome,"* pp. 211–22; Georg Meuselm, *Das Wunder vom Checkpoint Charlie. Kollege Martin Luther King—der Mann, der durch die Mauer ging*, www.lebenshaus-alb.de/magazin/008756.html (accessed March 8, 2020). Andreas Malessa, "Ein Prophet der Einheit. Wie Martin Luther King vor 50 Jahren unter heiklen Bedingungen nach Ost-Berlin einreiste," *Deutschlandradio Kultur*, September 14, 2009, www.deutschlandradiokultur.de/kalter-krieg-ein-prophet-der-einheit.1278.de.html?dram:article_id=297485 (accessed February 2, 2019). All texts include quotes from the border guard report. A translated excerpt can be found at web.archive.org/web/20170621113527/ and http://www.aacvr-germany.org/index.php/images-7/dr-martin-luther-kings-visit-to-cold-war-berlin#3 (accessed March 8, 2020). The account by Stefan Appelius, "Martin Luther King in Ost-Berlin: 'My dear Christian friends in East Berlin,'" in: *Chrismon*, September 2009, includes several factual errors regarding King's border crossing. Appelius also writes that there had been no announcements in the East German press.

83 Schubert, *"We Shall Overcome,"* pp. 212–13.

84 "Martin Luther King in der Marienkirche," *ND*, September 14, 1964; "Gottesdienst mit Dr. King," *BLZ*, September 14, 1964. The term "Negro" was not intended to be derogatory. At the time, it was still commonly used, even by people like King.

85 "Dr. Martin Luther King in der DDR-Hauptstadt," *BZ*, September 14, 1964.

86 King had surely had not felt that his "dream" had already become reality in the GDR, as Werner Rümpel, the general secretary of the Friedensrat claimed in a speech in 1989. Quoted in Schubert, *"We Shall Overcome,"* p. 263. As Schubert states, King never explicitly discussed the GDR.

87 Martin Luther King, Jr., Sermon Held at St. Mary's Church, September 13, 1964, at www.aacvr-germany.org/GenSys/DVD/publishing/XML-Files/XML/S_10003_LS.xml (accessed March 8, 2020).

88 Höhn and Klimke, *A Breath of Freedom*, p. 4.

89 "Westberliner Unbehagen," *NZ*, September 17, 1964.

90 Cf. *Mein Sommer '88*.

91 He spoke in German: "In der Hoffnung, dass eines Tages alle Barrieren abgerissen werden." Cf. *Mein Sommer '88*; Michael Pilz, "Wie Springsteen die Mauer zum Wackeln brachte," *Die Welt*, July 19, 2013, www.welt.de/kultur/musik/article118180430/Wie-Springsteen-die-Mauer-zum-Wackeln-brachte.html (accessed February 2, 2019).

92 Erik Kirschbaum, *Rocking the Wall: Bruce Springsteen. The Berlin Concert That Changed the World* (New York, 2013).

Part Two

Disjointed and Resilient Local Entanglements in the Cold War

5

From Old War to Cold War: Berlin as Urban Planning Laboratory in the First Postwar Years

Clara M. Oberle

This chapter seeks to contribute to the wider discussion of Berlin and its place in the Cold War by turning to the immediate postwar, Allied-occupied city. An area well-suited for critical "locating" of the Cold War may be that of housing; by its very nature, location matters. The situation in rubble-strewn Berlin entailed an urgent housing crisis, with a million residents and thus about one-third of the city rendered homeless by 1945.[1] In this setting, a very engaged Allied–German network of professionals concerned with urban planning and housing—the so-called International Committee for Building and Housing [abbr. International Committee]—emerged and operated. While Allied Housing Subcommittee and International Committee records are incomplete and dispersed across archives in the USA, France, Britain, Russia, and Germany, they deserve investigation for they may contribute to our understanding of Cold War agency and even the way we think about the nascent Cold War itself.

This International Committee for Building and Housing had been created by the Allied Control Council's Subcommittee on Housing within weeks of the July 4 arrival of the Western Allies in Berlin, following Soviet initiative. Next to Berlin-stationed Allied urban planners, architects, economists, and lawmakers who were all members of the military administrations, it also included their German counterparts. As of October 1945, for two and a half years, this quadrilingual urban experts' think-tank met once a week in Berlin-Dahlem, under alternating Allied chairmanship. Members of the Berlin Magistrate Housing Department were always present as this was mandatory for them—often it was the department head, Hans Scharoun himself, who appeared—but many more people seemed to have participated voluntarily. In the course of the first postwar year alone, members of the group, qua committee, organized a formal archive and research network, the so-called International Research Council on Housing, presented lectures (for instance on Igelit houses), exhibitions (such as Berlin Plant), and excursions (for instance, to Warsaw), invited guest speakers (Gropius came, New York City counsel members were invited), created an architecture library (mainly taken from Technische Hochschule and former Bauakademie holdings), discussed ways to conceptualize the problems of the modern metropolis, experimented with designs and policies, and helped draft housing policies for Berlin and Germany. Their urban laboratory was rubble-strewn Berlin.

In conditions of scarcity and competition over limited resources such as housing in the aftermath of war, one might expect divides to become pronounced. As this study of the Allied Housing officers' and the International Committee's response to the housing crisis suggests, however, a more complex dynamic emerges: just when in other arenas the Cold War was evolving as apparent conflict, not least over resources, here we have a story of convergence. Open conflict in transportation matters was already apparent in 1945, ranging from disputes over dismantling of tracks, confiscation of trains and locomotives, police authority over stations, to control over Reichsbahn and BVG operations.[2] In the area of food supply, differences between East and Western Allies—e.g., with both Soviet *pajoks* and US CARE package food supplies bypassing magistrate central distribution and accompanied by political messages, or with the Soviet refusal to deliver produce from their occupation zone to Berlin's Western sectors from July 19, 1946 on—likewise indicated East–West Allied conflicts could translate to conflicting policies.[3] The sources of the International Committee meanwhile suggest that competition for authority and common scarcity might also lead to a convergence of policies. Thus, if we look at the realm of housing, the emerging Cold War appeared as one in which—in light of Allied competition—we see joint experimentation, collaboration, leading even to a joint law, Control Council Law 18, the housing law for all of Germany.

An overarching question of the chapter is thus how we might think of the nascent Cold War. What motivations or experiences helped determine its shape in the realm of housing? What agency and room for maneuver was there for the actors involved? And related to this, which housing ideas and practices gained particular prominence among the members of the Allied International Committee on Building and Housing and the International Research Council? As the chapter traces these, it asks how Cold War, old war, and the specificities of the place—Berlin—factor into this story. Finally, what insights might a study that focuses on mid-level professionals provide? In a conclusion, the chapter thus considers implications for our understanding of place and of Berlin in the early Cold War, for our overall concept of "Cold War" and the agency of the actors in it.

The Berlin Setting and the Challenge of Governability

One key motivation in the creation and collaborative work of the International Committee lay in the very conditions on the ground, experienced by all four Allies in similar fashion: a gravely disorienting, rubbled urban landscape which the members of the military administrations struggled to navigate, and a housing, homelessness and refugee crisis in Berlin that they perceived as urgent and dangerous.

Indeed, Berlin's housing structure, although not as destroyed as often depicted, was affected by the war and the more than 50,000 tons of shells dropped over the city.[4] The districts of Mitte, Friedrichshain, Tiergarten, and Kreuzberg, densely populated areas, sites of commercial and political power, industry, and, perhaps most importantly, the districts in which Berlin's main railway stations stood, had borne the brunt of the attacks.[5] By April 1945, more than 500,000 apartments were completely destroyed, and while we don't have entirely reliable figures, an estimated 1 million people were rendered homeless.[6] Compared to housing in 1943, the loss amounted to about one-third of all apartments. Of the remaining dwellings, some were in disrepair. Of course, all in all, 70 percent of all housing structures were only mildly damaged or even entirely intact; compared to many other European cities (Rotterdam, Minsk, Warsaw), the damage was very small, and average housing space per person was still greater than in most other European cities.[7] Yet even to the European Allies, the destruction was serious, keenly noticeable. At the same time, again much like in large parts of Europe in a period spanning war and first postwar years, there were substantial population movements.[8] In Berlin, there was mainly an influx of people into the city, fewer leaving. Thousands of evacuated Berlin children were returning, as were released German POWs. Then there were ethnic Germans arriving from places further east and south; by February 1946 half a million people were entering Berlin every month. Added to this were large numbers of so-called displaced persons, critically eyed by local populations. All of this—in the setting of a broken city, one perceived as more destroyed than it was—amounted to the perception of overcrowding and chaos in the eyes of Allies.

When reading the records of American and German descriptions of the Berlin cityscape, one is struck by actors' preoccupation with the debris, chaos, and destruction. As T.J. Kent, an urban planner assigned by OMGUS to Berlin in September 1945, reported, "looking down on the pocked city from the air, one sees block after block of white rubble heaps and thousands of black, roofless, honeycombed shells that once were five-story apartments."[9] The effect of this sight was "so awful and created such gruesome mental images that it was not possible to think in constructive terms" at first.[10] On the ground, Soviet Red Army members in particular, but Western Allied forces as well, repeatedly got lost in the "urban jungle" or "sea of debris" that represented Berlin. Street signs were often absent, renamed illegally by local grassroots antifascist groups, and, even if present, not always helpful. Berliners were quick to notice "strange detouring" and Allied disorientation.[11] Indeed, once on location and amid the rubble, members of the occupation forces likened the appearance of fragmented houses, homeless people, and rubbled streets to "a surrealist painting," and British, French, Soviet, and American forces alike feared spreading disease, guerilla war, and uprisings.[12] A less lyrical observer described Berlin as simply "a mess."[13]

Amid the debris, with streets no longer recognizable, and a population very much in flux and unaccounted for, the Allies thus deemed orientation, and therefore also control over Germans extremely difficult. Memories of uprisings in other postwar scenarios, not least of Petrograd in 1917 (as far as western Allies were concerned), or Berlin and Munich in 1919, were present in the Allies' minds, as situations to be avoided. Even before they entered Berlin, they had been part of abstract discussions for postwar Berlin and Germany. Winning and maintaining a peace would involve serious planning.[14] Indeed, despite Allied military leaders' and various military government branches' hesitation to allow for Berlin urban planning, such planning was embraced in order "to retain control in the interest of the occupying forces."[15] The Berlin experiences on the ground made the need for "keeping the peace" through planning even more urgent to the Allied housing officers and even colleagues of other departments.[16] In this manner, they, of course, connected to much of modern urban planning, concerned first and foremost with governability and control.[17]

Furthermore, next to concern about potential German aggression in the immediate postwar, the members of the Allied occupation also feared, rightly so, the detrimental health effects of inadequate and lacking housing. Especially during the winter months, even for Germans a minimum of habitable space of "hygienic weatherproofness" was to be made available.[18] Deaths related to excessive exposure to cold and precipitation could significantly increase in the winter months. The numbers of pneumonia, influenza, and tuberculosis patients were repeatedly becoming so high that hospitals could no longer take them in.[19] The Allies were thus most interested in fighting a war against the cold. Even more threatening, in the first postwar months, outbreaks of cholera, typhoid fever, and dysentery were threatening to take on pandemic dimensions, posing a threat to Berliners and Allies alike.[20] Again, similarly to the urban planning response of earlier centuries, one motivation thus also came from the threat of epidemics spreading. Not only were they spreading, they were also transgressing boundaries. Thus distinctions between occupiers and occupied, refugees, DPs, and other inhabitants, or divides between political systems and any Cold War sides would simply be permeable, the problem of epidemics a shared one. These conditions of coexistence necessitated practical cooperation beyond ideological divisions in other realms.

It is against this background of Allied experiences in Berlin on the ground with disorientation, health, and governability concerns that we can come to understand the creation of the International Committee. What followed then was a highly involved joint effort by Allied housing officers to acquire local knowledge and to find solutions aimed at greater control of place, plagues, and people. As the founding documents indicate, a main reason for the establishment of the International Committee on Building and Housing was thus access to such resources as to operate effectively in Berlin. Allied planners working for the Allied military occupation were far away from their home libraries and lacked the most basic reference works. More importantly, planning and housing professionals on all Allied sides lacked information on Berlin. Blueprints, maps, and statistics of a wide variety, whether on the hygiene or traffic infrastructure, the location of hospitals in the various *Bezirke*, the social composition, the health of the population, housing stock of different neighborhoods, or the layout of apartment complexes and neighborhoods, first and foremost, would help orient themselves and then to formulate responses on location.[21] A center of urban, metropolitan studies, these urban experts argued, and a central information center for knowledge of Berlin itself would thus be key.[22] In order to create this library, archive, and network, the help of Germans was necessary. Berlin's architects and planners knew the literature and could locate many of the necessary materials. Moreover, men like Martin Mächler, Karl Böttcher, or Hans Scharoun and their staff of the Berlin housing administration were also a living archive and resource.[23] As the growing scholarship on Berlin architects' biographies has shown, the largest part of the Magistrate Planning Department members had already worked in the planning and building departments of Berlin itself in the previous decades, some spanning all regimes.[24]

A Global Housing Question

The Berlin housing crisis, disorientation, and the need for a reference center, while pressing, was however not the only motivation for joining. Besides practical concerns for Berlin, the founders of the International Committee and its Research Council had also made it their mission to study "the new problems as they pose themselves to metropolitan cities such as Moscow, Berlin, and Paris" (US, Polish, and British cities are later also invoked).[25] Architecture, urban planning, and housing featured prominently in the activities of the Committee. They would hear talks and learn about housing plans in the Netherlands, in Poland, in the Soviet Union, in Britain.[26] In particular, they wanted to learn from their peers about different solutions to the problem of overcrowding and homelessness and the possibility of adopting "new building technologies" for cheap and quick new buildings.[27] Although large-scale, long-term planning schemes were of initial interest and the International Committee even hosted an exhibition and oversaw a Berlin planning competition, the challenge of providing mass housing quickly and cheaply for a range of constituents proved to be at the center of conversations.

The housing crisis was, after all, not limited to Berlin: all of Europe suffered from a severe housing crisis, and much of the world seemed to be engaged in discussing it. The 1945 and 1946 volumes of practically all architectural and urban planning journals from Germany, Britain, France, the USA and, to some extent, the Soviet Union are indicative of this.[28] And there was public interest in the housing question. Countless popular publications on the problem of housing "Europe's Homeless Millions" were published in the mid-1940s. The discourse on housing included a large public on all Allied sides.[29] France, after all, had lost more than 1 million homes in the war. And in Britain and the Soviet Union, the figures were dramatically higher, as the Allies were keenly aware, as is evident even in the Potsdam agreements themselves.[30] But also beyond Europe, in the USA, Canada, or Australia, in Brazil, South Africa and Japan, governments and architects were concerned with affordable, mass-produced housing. Not least as, in the US case, they had to accommodate returning soldiers and meet the growing expectations of those on the home front, such that by May 22, 1946, US Congress would declare a "national housing emergency."[31] Labor migration during the war had added to the housing problems. In the Soviet Union, large-scale destruction in the war, migrations of industry and laboring populations (forced) and war-related massive population shifts, had led to a most severe housing crisis and an interest in finding affordable, mobile solutions. Even in cases where they had been abroad for several years, Allied personnel stationed in Berlin were aware of dire housing needs in their home countries and communities.[32]

Furthermore, a worldwide shortage of building materials such as wood, cement, steel, and brick had aggravated the situation and motivated participation in the Committee. Innovative techniques and materials might help solve the crises at home and help domestic industry. The postwar years (just as the last wartime years) were marked by a veritable race for new building patents that would allow the cheap mass production of housing, both in the interest of housing the homeless cheaply and quickly, but also in the interest of economic profit. Thus, President Truman, as Europeans keenly noted at the time, had proclaimed that "housing must be transformed into a new industry, more important even than the automobile industry."[33] Given both economic interest and housing shortage, the top US housing officer, Wilson Wyatt, noted that new building technologies were receiving "a flurry of attention" from politicians, industry, and the general public alike.[34] Similar attention is evident in French, British, and Soviet records.

The world was interested in developing and testing new housing technology, and the housing debates in Berlin were informed by this greater discourse. It comes as little surprise then that recycled and synthetic materials (e.g., polyethylene, igelit, plexiglass, fake wood, and asbestos) were the most frequently discussed technical topic in the earlier meetings at the Berlin International Committee on Building and Housing, as were the processes and technologies such as the Brom patent that enabled prefabricated building.[35]

All sides hoped that after a period of only limited international intellectual exchange during the war, much could be learnt from the other. While the British and French members of the Committee occasionally voiced concern about intellectual property rights, industrial espionage, and the problem of sharing insights with Germans, the interest to *learn* from fellow Allies and Germans themselves appeared to dominate. Of course, much of Bauhaus research on cheap, prefabricated housing had been received abroad already earlier,[36] but since 1933, the Nazis had poured considerable resources into further development in that area, as had German companies such as MAN, so the participants hoped that most recent German technological knowhow could be gained now.[37] Besides the aforementioned lectures, the members of this International Committee, Germans and Allies alike, organized excursions across Germany to learn more about the possibilities in this realm.

In the first months of its existence, into mid-1946, the Berlin-stationed urban experts thus most enthusiastically welcomed what they regarded as an opportunity to explore and develop architectural mass production and standardized housing, to be of use for their own country but also for the Berlin setting. They very likely also sought out collaboration with the newly reconstituted Technical University (April 1946) and its Institut für Städtebau, and through Scharoun to a variety of Berlin planners with ties to the Werkbund tradition.[38]

In turn, the International Committee presented a platform for Scharoun and colleagues to highlight their ideas and plans, push for funding, and present their work. They, too, used it as tool to not only hold on to existing Berlin architectural writing collections, but to even add to the collection and invite prominent architects from abroad. The Scharoun correspondence furthermore suggests that he and his German colleagues operated with great confidence, hoping their contributions and urban planning, as well as the Weimar-era planning traditions would help the German cause and that of making Berlin a *Weltstadt* again.[39]

Housing as Legitimacy and the Politics of Comparison

The collaborative activities of the members of the International Committee may be read as reaction to a shared context of a global postwar housing crisis and both professional and respective Allied interests expressed within these. Cooperation was not a given. Yet cooperation, and sharing libraries and technologies might ensure that not only *one* side would get a hold of valuable knowledge. But there is another story to be told. The Allied common attention to housing and planning also fit into a larger history of rule in the age of mass politics. Whether liberal democracy, authoritarian regime or dictatorship, by the twentieth century, housing quality, standards and welfare served as *the* chiffre for the legitimacy of a regime or aspiring political actor. Contemporaneous discourses on housing in the Allied home societies themselves show the prominence of expectations vis-à-vis housing; one that had grown especially in conjunction with war. Accelerated by the wartime sacrifices and heightened expectations concerning the postwar period—Nicole Rudolph, Norman Naimark, Mark Edele, Natalie Belsky, Amir Weimer and Bradley Abrahams have worked on this—state involvement in housing and planning had become the expected norm.[40] The increasingly vocal housing demands and expressions of entitlement threatened the legitimacy of regimes. This was evident in popular protests, petitions, lawsuits in all Allied states, but likewise in Berlin, Hamburg, and across Germany where they were closely monitored.[41] The main work for which the Committee on Building and Housing may still be known—Berlin Plant, a 1946 exhibition organized by members of the Allied Housing Committee, which showcased each of the Allies' best housing solutions in a "national style"—can indeed be read as motivated by common efforts to gain legitimacy on the ground.[42]

Cold War Comparisons

Berlin Plant, with its exhibition of differences in style, can also, however, be regarded as exemplar of Cold War competition and difference. It may already point toward the later Cold War exhibitions historian Paul Betts has examined in such detail, including the 1953 Besser Leben-Schöner Wohnen show in East Berlin, the So Wohnt Amerika exhibition in 1949 by OMGUS, the Marshall Plan model home exhibitions, publications such as "Rental Barracks of Capitalism, Living Palaces of Socialism," to culminate in the famous Khrushchev–Nixon kitchen debates.[43] As Greg Castillo likewise has shown in his study of "Peoples at an Exhibition" and of the US- and Soviet-sponsored training of German architects (in the former case, a program designed with UNC Chapel Hill), the Allies indeed used architecture and urban planning as arms in their systemic competition.[44] Architectural historians have suggested that architecture and urban planning lent itself well to this competition, thanks to the practical necessity for housing, the existing political divide on location, the potential for each of the competing regimes to find a base of support in the population, and the symbolic power of housing.[45]

The converging work of the International Committee and the Allied Housing Committee of the Control Council in this context, their embracing even of joint exhibitions, may thus be read as response to and even expression of the early stages of this competition. It is also visible in the discussions and press releases of members of the Housing Committee on minimum housing standards, in which, for example Soviet housing officers publicized their demands for absurdly high minimum housing standards compared to French and British demands.

Likewise, Berlin newspapers reflected this competition, one, *Berliner Zeitung*, for instance contrasting the role of the Soviet Military Administration in providing glass for winter repairs on Berlin housing, school, and hospitals, a *grosszügige Hilfsaktion*, with the limited help by the *nichtsowjetischen Besatzungssektoren*.[46] Such articles appeared precisely when Berliners, in this case, the Berlin guild of glass cutters had publicly criticized one particular Cold War side, likely much aware that such comparisons would be challenging legitimacy. The Cold War competition is likewise evident in Scharoun's even mentioning the production of a *Propagandafilm* on housing and reconstruction.[47] All of this points to the propagandistic value and the element of comparison. Allied opinion surveys and letters of Berliners to their district housing administration, to Mayor Louise Schroeder, or to Hans Scharoun's office, furthermore show that Berliners indeed made these comparisons between the Allies.

Comparisons with National Socialism

Without doubt, the work of the International Committee was motivated by nascent Cold War competition with housing as shorthand for legitimacy. It would moreover evolve into distinctive searches for a recognizable socialist versus Western-style urban modernism. But simultaneously, we can read the competition as part of a longer practice of states seeking legitimacy, across the dictatorship-democracy or the prewar–war–postwar divide. The sources on Allied housing work *also* suggest that conflict between Soviets and Western Allies in the emerging Cold War was not the only and possibly not even the most important motivation for common engagement with housing. Rather, earlier competition mattered. Not least, it was the competition with (or against) national socialism, one which all Allies in 1945 and 1946 shared. The Allied emphasis on housing, and eventually, their common approach should therefore also be read in the context of its competing against national socialist propaganda. The latter had proposed it was the state or system's responsibility to plan and provide adequate housing for the entire *Volk*. It is evident, for example, in early NS election campaigns, in later rhetoric from the *Volkswohnung* program, or in the messages of the *Sowjet Paradies* exhibition, which had furthermore fed into expectations of abysmal housing under the Soviets, Hitler's and Goebbels' verdict that "the peace would be terrible," the Allies brutish.[48]

Allied housing officers represented their respective state's interests for governability and control, and one motivation in their engagement and eventual convergence may have been systemic competition and winning over the populations. It was not only competition between Cold War rivals but just as much between the Allies and the ghosts of national socialist housing promises and propaganda. Yet one must be careful not to consider Allied housing officers as solely "seeing like a state" (to use James Scott's idiom), representing national interest, Allied governance concerns, or Cold War sides. They were also professionals, driven by common professional interests.

Professional Motivations and the Urban Laboratory

Shared professional interest guided much of the work of the members of the International Committee on Building and Housing. The exchange of ideas by the Committee's architects, planners, and their German counterparts was vivid and enthusiastic, not least because they were all in once place and eager to reconnect with an international community after the isolating years of war. Unfortunately, besides their names (Smith, Nuttall, Druwing, Dix, Henry, Thompson, Paddock, Rhodes, Woltschegorsky, Schnitke, Fayolle, Varroquier, the visiting Kent) and ranks (between lieutenant and major), there is little else we know about these housing officers and planners.[49] We know that some, Fayolle, and Nuttall, for instance, had worked in city planning offices before and during the war. Kent, not a permanent member, was famously the director of the urban planning office for the City of San Francisco. Yet as opposed to Hans Scharoun—Head of the Berlin Magistrate Building and Housing Department at the time—who had expertise in urban reconstruction from the aftermath of World War One, most of these men do not appear to have been published or well-known practitioners of the field. In their requests for Berlin planning literature and overall communications, they do, however, indicate a professional background in urban planning or architecture.

As urban planners and architects, they could advance their education, learning, and professional networks. The involvement in the International Committee—with its international guest lectures, Dahlem-based rich architectural library, access to Weimar- and Nazi-era patents and plans, and field trips—presented an opportunity to learn and share resources. Their interest, for example, in sharing knowledge of new serialized building techniques sometimes even went counter to the interests of high command, concerned with industrial espionage and the danger of letting German urbanists acquire more knowledge and power.[50] And while there was a clear state or national interest by each side in finding cheap building solutions and devising planning for the reconstruction of war-ravaged cities, these interests also were those of the architectural and urban planning profession. We see similar phenomena among professionals from other backgrounds, who likewise saw the particular postwar setting in Berlin as an opportunity to exchange. They could explore the new and catch up, expressing the sentiment—as Red Army officer Wladimir Gelfand did: "Now is the time […], to see, what one hasn't seen to date—the world abroad—and to learn about all those things of which one knew so little, of which one didn't have a clear idea."[51] To the Allied architects, likewise, Berlin was an opportunity. And Berlin would be their perfect urban laboratory. Here, Berlin planners were "bravely trying to educate themselves and adjust their thinking as they cope[d] with their problems so that both their emergency and long-range plans [would] be of practical value to Berlin and the world."[52] T.J. Kent, reporting back to his own professional association (the MIT-based American Institute of Urban Planners), thus enthusiastically reported that the thinking and work produced in Berlin, this urban laboratory, would educate and be "a challenge to our own planning skill." It was possible that here "the most advanced ideas of urban organization" would emerge. It was an "unprecedented opportunity."[53]

Thus, the Allied housing officers, as architectural professionals, very much welcomed partially destroyed Berlin as an urban laboratory in which new ideas and techniques could be tested. British Military Administration housing officers embarked, for example, in Spandau on "the experiment of constructing six new houses of an agreed design within the limits of the standards laid down by Control Commission."[54] The language of experimentation abounds. And all four Allies plus the Berlin-stationed German architects participated in the development of new prototypes of mass-producible new building that were to be exhibited as part of Berlin Plant.[55]

But the short-term outcome of all of these efforts was indicative of the biggest problem: lack of resources. Funds, skilled labor, and, once again, building materials were missing, and given Germany's role and given the housing shortages in every one of the Allied nations at that time, funds for reconstruction and building were not yet forthcoming by 1946. So rather than real houses, Berlin Plant showed miniature models of "national style." And the six houses built by the British in Spandau (they looked rather like Quonset huts) hardly solved the problem of making up for more than 500,000 missing dwellings in Berlin.[56]

In this very concrete situation of material scarcity in Berlin, experienced by all, the need for finding practical solutions may have led to very practical cooperation beyond ideological divides. Since their arrival in Berlin in 1945 and well into 1947, a top concern of Allied architects and urbanists was material and even manpower shortages.[57] During this period, collaboration, for example, in common tasks (generating statistics for all of Berlin, surveying housing across the city) and shared personnel, materials, patents, techniques, and libraries were all expressions of very practical solutions that transcended ideological difference.

From Reconstruction to Redistribution or from Architecture to Law

These practical efforts aside, Allied housing officers stationed in Berlin were keenly aware of continuously growing German discontent regarding the housing crisis for which "Allied bombing terror" and the Allied occupation were blamed.[58] While Berlin Magistrate architects and planners around Scharoun, Bonatz, and Mächler continued to work on massive urban planning and reconstruction schemes, Allied housing officers, from 1946 on, began to slowly spend less time in meetings of the International Committee on Building and Housing (which was dissolved in 1948) with its emphasis on intellectual exchange about new planning, new building, and new materials and technologies. The Research Council section of the International Committee, which from October 1945 until June 1946 had met every Thursday, by August 1946 had "ceased to function."[59] Discussions of polyethylene houses, skyscrapers, modular homes, or central "house robots" were left to the dreams of Berliners and German architects and urban planners for the time being.[60] Even Scharoun's opening speech of the jointly organized Berlin Plant exhibition indicated a turning away from the initially innovative emphasis: "At this moment, finding sufficient dwelling space appears more important than the sum of all technical innovations."[61]

Allied cooperation across the Cold War divide did not end here. These same Allied housing officers had turned their collective attention rather to finding immediately effective solutions that would house the estimated 1 million homeless Berliners. For German resentment had increased, as had the cases of highly contagious diseases. Information and surveys gathered of the city had made clear that despite its initial appearance, much of Berlin was still intact and Berlin was, overall, not as crowded as it looked. And thus not just the Soviets saw what some earlier thinkers about the urban housing question, including Engels and Lenin, had already noted for postwar settings: new construction did not have to be the solution. *Redistribution* would already solve the housing crisis.[62] Western Allies in Berlin agreed.[63] As one British housing inspector in Berlin noted: "[T]he problem seem[ed] less one of emergency repair than of redistribution of living space."[64]

Eventually, with the aid of the Berlin Magistrate, the Allies jointly wrote a new housing legislation for Berlin and all of Germany in March 1946, one that aimed to redistribute housing and entitled every Berliner to housing. Berliners and Germans, the law (Kontrollratsgesetz Nr. 18) ultimately provided, would have to make room for one another, if need be, through forced sharing and requisitioning. This would also distribute the population more evenly across the city. For the occupiers on the ground were concerned with the spread of disease and growing unrest in the densely inhabited areas. In other words, overcrowding was thus to be prevented. And, no less important: as Germans seemed rather resentful, providing housing for the largest number of people was important as well. The new housing law, with the promise to house everyone, at a minimum standard (at least seven square meters per person), was thus meant to assure everyone: we (the occupiers/authority/state) are taking care of you and are thus legitimate and worthy of approval.[65]

Within mere months after this law was put into effect (in August 1946), Berlin homelessness was thus drastically reduced.[66] All large-scale rebuilding plans and new technologies originally discussed in the International Committee for solving the crisis had been replaced by a practical policy of redistribution. This policy, by Allied standards, could be regarded as a success: it presented a solution to the urgent housing crisis, got the population off the street and into residences and thus more easily governed, and neither uprisings nor pandemics developed in the setting of the partially destroyed city. Moreover, precisely while Germans had become attuned to pick up on any divide between nascent Cold War sides, this was a policy that made delegitimizing comparisons difficult.

Implications of this Study

Does the story of the short life of the International Committee (1945–1948) and the Research Council (1945–1946) then represent a story of failure? And how might the brief history of intensive exchanges between Allies from all sides and Germans fit into our project of locating Berlin in the Cold War and the Cold War in Berlin? The following are some implications of this study.

Concerning the Specificity of Place and the Role of Berlin in the Cold War

This story of convergence of ideas and policies, and of changing approaches shows what a focus on the immediate setting can contribute. There is by now a large body of literature on different Allied ideas for Germany as they were expressed in the planning stages of the war. Yet, the case of the International Committee for Building and Housing and the emerging joint Allied housing policy after 1945 indicates that it did *not* follow a blueprint. Rather it came as reaction to the often (especially to the Western Allies) shocking conditions of scarcity on the ground, observable on a daily basis—in Berlin. Moreover, it was arguably precisely because of the impact of the shared space, one in which the problems encountered were common, and one in which the competition already by 1945 had become palpable, that the solutions also converged. A perspective on mid-level professionals thus shows that Cold War policies, in this story, were not produced only in Moscow or Washington.

Like Paul Steege, who in *Black Market-Cold War* has called for a "shift from the rarified space of international diplomacy and the halls of power to everyday battles to cope with scarcity," this study suggests that in order to understand Cold War politics in Berlin and beyond, a focus on the low- and mid-level actors operating on the ground is fruitful.[67] It indicates that the Allied urban planners' and architects' entanglements in everyday struggles on the ground also impacted policies, not least as their studies in the International Committee led them to the realization that redistribution was possible. That common ground for them was Berlin.

This study also points to the importance of practical considerations in the nascent Cold War. The very conditions of scarcity and health threats, not unique to Berlin but experienced there, can be a factor in understanding convergence and collaboration across the ideological divide. Thus, the greater the competition for scarce resources, the more joint activity and convergence of policy we see in the area of urban planning and housing. This fits with findings of some recent histories of later postwar architecture and urban planning work beyond Europe, in socialist countries of Africa, the Middle East, and Asia during the Cold War. Their authors have also emphasized the importance of place and scarcity. As Łukasz Stanek reminds us, this scarcity ensured that there emerged "multiple, pragmatic forms of collaboration between various actors on both sides of the Iron Curtain."[68] The Berlin setting of 1945–8 bears striking similarities to these findings: while some of the official rhetoric and self-presentation may have stressed Cold War difference, pragmatic approaches, and shared practical concerns onsite—in conditions of scarcity—led to collaborative efforts across the Iron Curtain divide.[69]

Proximity matters in many ways when we consider the Cold War in Berlin, in which the Allies literally were on common ground. With such physical proximity these mid-level members of the Allied occupation may have striven to accept this coexistence across ideological lines in search for a new and practical "normal."[70] Moreover, space mattered in other ways. The Allied housing officers were on location in Berlin, the furthest distance of travel between Allied sides was Karlshorst to Dahlem, less than twenty-five kilometers, so meetings of the International Research Council would have involved manageable commutes for any member travelling to it. Such proximity allowed also for a frequency and structure of exchange that made a convergence of ideas possible. Meeting in person weekly, sometimes for ten hours at a time, surveying the city on foot, together, and collecting urban planning resources as group, developing ideas jointly was thus possible.

Conflict and the Nascent Cold War Conversation

This study takes place during the nascent Cold War in Berlin, with marked differences and outright conflict already visible in many areas. It has asked about the convergence in approach and successful collaboration we see in the case of housing (compared to political, transportation, or economic branches). At first glance, this may appear as counter to common understandings of the Cold War as a story of difference and division. The case of housing shows that precisely because of the conflict and competition, approaches could be common. Given the presence of all Allies in the city, divergences in housing policies would be visible, tangible, and commented on by Berliners. The Berlin setting added weight to the politics of comparison. It is possible that precisely because of the centrality of housing for legitimacy—housing itself being a symbol (and Berlin, in turn a symbol in the Cold War, as David Barclay has shown)—finding a policy in which one did not lose out in the competition became so important. A joint Allied approach was thus at once a response to German practices of comparison and response to the growing competition.

In the planning and housing exhibitions that emerged in this period, precursors to the famous kitchen debates, we can read difference and ideological competition of the nascent Cold War. But we must also note that similar media and fora were embraced, that there was a common Allied interest in "branding" their mass housing solutions. Anthropologist Katherine Verderey has thus read the Cold War as not only a military confrontation but "a cognitive organization of the world," the search for a recognizable "socialist" or "Western aesthetic," a "socialist" or "US style."[71] The story of housing plans and exhibitions such as Berlin Plant can be placed in this Cold War cultural tradition. When it came to finding practical housing solutions, the discussion of redistributive models through new housing laws, we likewise see this. It was not only the story of competition or even entanglements. The Cold War was *one* conversation. Yet its direction was open and could fluctuate. The study suggests that in the years 1945–6 especially, the nascent Cold War was not a one-way street. There was room for cooperation and finding a common language, amid differences.

Narrating a History of Berlin and the Nascent Cold War

The Cold War as giving shape to the conversation (or *being* this conversation) in this Berlin setting is one prominent and important story we can tell with the records of the International Committee. But it is not the only one. Shifting perspective from high ranking to mid-level representatives of the Cold War sides can also be fruitful for another reason. For the mid-level members' work and motivations, operating in this

Cold War context must also be understood as part of the history of their professions. By nature, the work of housing and urban planning is collaborative, driven by aggregate actors.[72] The participants of the International Committee as practicing urban planners may have already been predisposed to operate in collaborative terms. Not only the time span, but also the object of study—in this case, a profession and group set up to work collaboratively—clearly has an impact on the story we tell of "Berlin in the Cold War, the Cold War in Berlin."

Moreover, one may read this case as part of a larger, international history of urban professionals, technocrats, and governments already embracing population management thinking. Geoff Eley has placed such population management approach in the "deep history" of Empire building and social engineering that "extends both back to the 1880s or even 1860s and forward to the end of the twentieth century."[73] Others have read them as spanning the 1930s and 1950s especially.[74] Such a management approach could involve the movement of populations within a city (moving unhoused Tiergarten, Kreuzberg, or Neukölln residents), and it could be applied to the "streams" of refugees, DPs, returnees whom the Allies tried to direct. The ultimate goal here was placement, even if temporary, control, and governability. This approach suited Western capitalist, emerging welfare-corporatist, and Stalinist systems alike. It could be applied to the movement and management of labor, and to the movement and management of so-called "displaced" populations (displaced by war, the movement of capital, ethnic, and political cleansing). Here, despite the postwar rhetoric of Cold War difference and new beginnings, the continuities with wartime and earlier approaches should not be overlooked. It was the experiences and practices of Civil War, the Great Depression, and especially World War Two—and the immensity of the postwar housing challenge—that gave prominence to such managerial approaches and allowed for a remarkable convergence across the political divides.[75]

Berlin's history in the immediate postwar has come to be associated with the emerging Cold War systemic competition, and rightly so. The evidence presented shows that this nascent Cold War competition was also present in the realm of housing, keenly felt as it related to claims to authority by each side. Yet longer spanning professional histories as well as records from the very postwar moment itself call for caution when reading the years of 1945 and 1946 as driven by Cold War considerations alone. Older population management and urban planning traditions can help explain the postwar convergence of approaches, and so can the shared challenges and common ground on which they found themselves in 1945. The records of the Allied housing officers working in Berlin during this period, and the joint German–Allied activities of the International Committee on Building and Housing capture an important moment then: it was one of an unstable, rubbled, potentially disease-ridden Berlin, one in which Allied urban planners could at once compete and collaborate, one in which neither the end of the Old War, nor the power of the Cold War was yet firmly cemented. It was undeniably there, but the form and expression it would take was still subject to experimentation and practical considerations. Motivations could thus coexist: from Old War to Cold War, to a simple war against the cold.

Notes

1   Hauptamt Für Statistik und Wahlen des Magistrats von Groß-Berlin (ed.), *Berlin in Zahlen, 1946-1947* (Berlin, 1949), pp. 185-9. The statistic includes figures for 1945.

2   Anthony James Nicholls, "Zusammenbruch und Wiederaufbau: Die Reichsbahn während der Besatzungszeit," in: Lothar Gall and Manfred Pohl (eds.), *Die Eisenbahn in Deutschland: Von den Anfängen bis zur Gegenwart* (München, 1999), pp. 245-79. LArch, C Rep 309, A 4990, Tätigkeitsbericht des Dezernats 47, August 3, 1945, pp. 1-2. LArch, C Rep 309 A 5021, Wiederaufbau und Demontagen, 1946-1948, correspondence between Reichsbahn Director Kreikemeyer and SMAD officers Petroff, Malowitzki, Jegunov and SMAD Transportation Director KvashninLArch, C Rep 309, A 4992. Letters of Magistrats Architekt Paschke, Reichsbahndirektion Berlin, SMAD, and OMGUS-Berlin district liaison office Kreuzberg, November 11, 1946, April 19, 1947, May 30, 1947, July 28, 1947.

3   Paul Steege, *Black Market, Cold War: Everyday Life in Berlin, 1946-1949* (New York, 2007), pp. 37-8, with reference to Arthur Schlegelmilch, *Hauptstadt im Zonendeutschland: Die Entstehung der Berliner Nachkriegsdemokratie 1945-1949* (Berlin, 1993), pp. 443ff.

4   Reinhard Rürup, *Berlin 1945: Eine Dokumentation* (Berlin, 1995), pp. 13-14; Laurenz Demps, "Die Luftangriffe auf Berlin: Ein dokumentarischer Bericht," in *Jahrbuch des Märkischen Museums* VIII (1982), pp. 21-2.

5   Ibid., p. 60, Doc. 71 and 72.

6   Statistik von Groß-Berlin, *Berlin in Zahlen*, pp. 185-9.

7   Ibid., pp. 185-95.

8   See Mark Mazower, "Displacement and Social Crisis," in: *Dark Continent: Europe's Twentieth Century* (London, 1998), pp. 214ff.; István Deák, Jan T. Gross, and Tony Judt (eds.), *The Politics of Retribution in Europe: World War II and Its Aftermath* (Princeton, 2000); Pieter Lagrou, *The Legacy of Nazi Occupation: Patriotic Memory and National Recovery in Western* Europe, *1945-1965* (New York, 2000), pp. 262-91.

9   T.J. Kent, "Report on Berlin, 1945," *Journal of the American Institute of Planners*, 12 (1946) 1, pp. 5-17, here p. 5.

10 Ibid., p. 5.

11 Margret Boveri, *Tage des Überlebens: Berlin 1945* (Munich, 1985), p. 83.

12 Public Records Office [PRO], Foreign Office Files [FO] 1012/516, Letter on "The German Housing Situation in the British Zone," October 15, 1946, p. 1.

13 National Archives and Record Administration [NARA], RG 260, AG 728.3. Letter Frank A. Keating to Col. Bryan L. Milburn, December 20, 1946.

14 The Universities Committee on Post-War International Problems, *Final Report on the Work of the Committee, 1942-1945* (Boston: Universities Committee on post-war international problems, 1945), "Treatment of Defeated Enemy Countries," v. III, p. 3, v.V, p. 9, 11-12. For Britain, see, e.g., *When We Build Again* (London, 1941), p. vii; Wolfgang Leonhard, *Die Revolution entläßt ihre Kinder* (Köln, 2000).

15 Bundesarchiv [BArch], Akten der Sowjetischen Militäradministration in Deutschland [SMAD], Z 47 10134, op. 10, d. 4 str. 83, Correspondence between Directorate for Labor/Manpower and Directorate of Economy on the work the Allied Control Commission Housing Subcommittee, April 30, 1946.

16 T.J. Kent, "Report on Berlin 1945," p. 6.

17 James C. Scott, *Seeing Like a State: How Certain Schemes to Improve the Human Condition Have Failed* (New Haven, 1998), esp. pp. 53-84 on urban planning.

18   BArch, SMAD, Z 47, 10134, op. 10, d. 3, str. 110–12, Allied Control Council,
      Working Group on Housing, of September 26, 1945 and Op. 8, d. 6, str. 3–7,
      Instruction of December 3, 1945. PRO, FO 1051/803, Housing Reports, Housing
      Branch, Housing Report September 29, 1945, p. 2, and PRO, FO 1051/803, Housing
      Reports, Housing Branch Fortnightly Report, October 3, 1945

19   NARA RG 260 OMGUS 1945–6 AG 720, Public Health, Berlin Report, December
      1945, January 1946, April 19, 1946, April 24, 1946.

20   In just June 1945, US health officials noted the number of persons registered as
      infected with dysentery in the Russian zone of Berlin had doubled from 1,100 cases
      to 2,380. See NARA, OMGUS RG 260, AG 720, Department of Public Health Berlin,
      July 12, 1945 Report. Berlin-stationed officials continuously reminded their superiors
      that "the problem of sanitation in Berlin was 'of paramount importance for all of us
      who live here.'" See also, e.g., January 1946 Report; April 19, 1946 Report.

21   Akademie der Künste, Archiv für Baukunst [AdK AB], Scharoun Nachlaß, Sch-01,
      Internationales Kommittee für Bau- und Wohnungswesen, October 1945. Re: "Die
      Notwendigkeit, unverzüglich in Berlin ein Zentrum für Studien und ein Archiv
      für die englischen, amerikanischen, französischen, russischen und deutschen
      Architekten und Städtebauer zu schaffen."

22   Ibid.

23   AdK AB, Sch-01, Internationales Kommittee für Bau- und Wohnungswesen, cf. e.g.,
      November 1945 lectures by Scharoun and Mächler on Berlin-City planning in the
      1920s.

24   Werner Durth, "Zwischenzeiten im Epochenwechsel," *Informationen zur
      Modernen Stadtgeschichte*, v. 2 (1994), or idem, *Deutsche Architekten: biographische
      Verflechtungen 1900–1970* (Braunschweig, 1986); Jeffrey Diefendorf, *In the Wake of
      War: The Reconstruction of German Cities after World War II* (Oxford, 1993).

25   AdK AB Scharoun Nachlaß, Sch-01, Intl. Kommittee für Bau- und Wohnungswesen,
      October 1945, point 2: "Studium der neuen Probleme, wie sie für die großen Städte,
      z.B. Moskau, Berlin, Paris gestellt werden."

26   Ibid.

27   Ibid., and fn. 21.

28   See especially the 1945 and 1946 issues of *Neues Bauen, Der Bauhelfer, L'Architecture
      d'Aujourd'hui, Journal of Land and Public Utility Economics, Architectural Record*, and
      Journal of the American Association of Planners, or the Marxist publication *The New
      Masses*, and *Arkhitektura i stroitel'stvo*.

29   See, e.g., Fred K. Koehler, on housing *Europe's Homeless Millions*. Headline Series,
      November–December 1945, n. 54; Republished by New York: Foreign Policy
      Association, 1946; but also the daily press, including Janet Flanner in *Time Magazine*,
      Margaret Bourke-White in *Life*, Henry Ries for the *New York Times*, and issues of *Le
      Monde, London Times*, or *Izvestia*.

30   "Potsdam Conference Protocol of the Proceedings," Art. 17, cited in Senate
      Committee on Foreign Relations and the Staff of the Committee and the Department
      of State (eds.), *A Decade of American Foreign Policy: Basic Documents, 1941–49*
      (Washington, 1950). See also Frédérique Boucher, "'Arbiter vaille que vaille, se loger
      coûte que coûte," in Danièle Voldman, *Images, Discours et Enjeux de la Reconstruction
      des villes françaises après 1945*, Cahiers de l'Institut d'histoire du temps présent 5
      (June 1987), p. 157.

31   Report by Wilson Wyatt, the Housing Expediter of the National Housing Agency
      and study by Richard D. McKinzie, "Oral History Interview with Lincoln Gordon,"

Washington, DC, July 17, 1975 on the work of the Committee on Demobilization of Controls after Victory, the Civilian Production Agency, on Truman, and Wilson Wyatt, Housing Expediter of the National Housing Agency.

32   E.g., Letter by mother in Dnjepopetrovsk to son stationed in Berlin, September 20, 1945, Wladimir Gelfand, *Deutschland Tagebuch 1945–1946: Aufzeichnungen eines Rotarmisten*, trans. Anja Lutter und Hartmut Schröder (Berlin, 2005), p. 132.

33   See, for example, French reporting in *L'Architecture d' Aujourd'hui*, no. 12, Juillet 1947, issue on "Techniques Américaines: Urbanisme et Habitation," p. 79.

34   Wilson Wyatt, *A Report to the President from the Housing Expediter*, February 7, 1946 (Washington, 1946).

35   AdK AB, Scharoun Nachlaß, Sch-01, Internationales Kommittee für Bau- und Wohnungswesen Records.

36   Eric Mumford, *The CIAM Discourse on Urbanism, 1928–1960* (Cambridge, 2000); Walter Prigge, 'Frankfurter Fordismus' in Rosemarie Höpfner (ed.), *Ernst May und das Neue Frankfurt, 1925–1930* (Berlin, 1986).

37   AdK AB, Scharoun Nachlaß Sch-01, Internationales Kommittee für Bau- und Wohnungswesen Records.

38   AdK AB, Scharoun Nachlaß, Sch-01-1502/16, no date. See also Sch-Korrespondenz und Vorträge, 1940er Jahre, M. Mächler Korrespondenz.

39   Ibid.

40   Nicole Rudolph, *At Home in Postwar France: Modern Mass Housing and the Right to Comfort* (New York, 2015); Amir Weiner (ed.), *Landscaping the Human Garden. Twentieth-Century Population Management in a Comparative Framework* (Stanford, 2004); Bradley Abrams, "The Second World War and the East European Revolution," *East European Politics and Societies* 16 (2002), pp. 623–64.

41   Mark Edele, "Soviet Veterans as an Entitlement Group, 1945–1955," *Slavic Review* 65 (2006) 1, pp. 111–37; Christine Varga-Harris, "Forging Citizenship on the Home Front: Reviving the Socialist Contract and Constructing Soviet Identity during the Thaw," in: Polly Jones (ed.), *The Dilemmas of De-Stalinization: Negotiating Cultural and Social Change in the Khrushchev Era* (London, 2006), pp. 101–16. See also, e.g., FO 1051/804, Housing Reports Berlin 1946.

42   AdK AB, Scharoun Nachlass, Mag 2, 3 File Number: Sch-01-1501, "Berlin Plant."

43   Paul Betts, "Building Socialism at Home: The Case of East German Interiors," in: Katherine Pence and Paul Betts (eds.), *Socialist Modern: East German Everyday Culture and Politics* (Ann Arbor, 2008), pp. 100–21, esp. pp. 104 and 108.

44   Greg Castillo, "Domesticating the Cold War: Household Consumption as Propaganda in Marshall Plan Germany," *Journal of Contemporary History* 40 (2005) 2, pp. 261–88; Greg Castillo, "Design Pedagogy Enters the Cold War: The Reeducation of Eleven West German Architects," *Journal of Architectural Education* 57 (2004) 4, pp. 10–18.

45   Emily Pugh, *Architecture, Politics and Identity in Divided Berlin* (Pittsburgh, 2014), p. 31. See also Klaus von Beyme and Werner Durth (eds.), *Neue Städte aus Ruinen: Deutscher Städtebau der Nachkriegszeit* (Munich, 1992).

46   "Berlin braucht 20 Millionen qm Glas," *Berliner Zeitung*, June 2, 1946.

47   AdK AB, Scharoun Nachlass, Korrespondenz 1945, Mag. 1/18.

48   Deutsche Informationsstelle der NSDAP, *Deutsches Leben,* issue "So wohnt der deutsche Mensch" (n.d.); Reichspropagandaleitung der NSDAP, *Das Sowjetparadies: Ausstellung der Reichspropagandaleitung der NSDAP: Ein Bericht in Wort und Bild* (Berlin, 1943). See also Hans-Erich Volkmann (ed.), *Das Russlandbild im Dritten Reich* (Cologne, 1994).

49   AdK AB, Scharoun Nachlass, Intl. Kommittee für Bau- und Wohnungswesen, Sch-01, 1945–146.

50   PRO, FO 1051/803. Housing Records I, H.H. Nuttall, Report on the International Research Council on Housing, June 21, 1946.

51   Wladimir Gelfand, *Deutschland Tagebuch 1945–1946. Aufzeichnungen eines Rotarmisten* (Berlin, 2015), p. 116.

52   T.J. Kent, "Report on Berlin 1945," Part II, *Journal of American Institute of Planners* 12 (1946) 1, pp. 14, 17.

53   Ibid., 14.

54   PRO, FO 1051/803. Housing Records I, July 1946 Housing Report, p. 21.

55   AdK AB, Scharoun Nachlass, Internationales Kommittee für Bau- und Wohnungswesen, Sch-01, 3. Treffen des Int. Kommittees, October 25, 1945.

56   PRO, FO 1051/803. Housing Records I, July 1946 Housing Report, p. 21.

57   PRO, FO 1051/803 Major HP Fielder, July 31, 1945.

58   See also April 18, 1945, Lt. Daniel Lerner report to PWD SHAEF on German civilian population, Doc. 1 in Ulrich Bordsdorf and Lutz Niethammer (eds.), *Zwischen Befreiung und Besatzung: Analysen des US-Geheimdienstes über Positionen und Strukturen deutscher Politik 1945* (Weinheim, 1995), pp. 38–9.

59   PRO, FO 1051–1160, International Research Council on Housing, Letter Nutall to Singleton, August 16, 1946.

60   AdK AB, Nachlass Scharoun, Intl. Kommittee für Bau- und Wohnungswesen, Sch-01-1503, Vorprüfungsberichte für die Arbeiten an dem Wettbewerb "Berlin Plant."

61   AdK AB, Nachlass Scharoun, Sch-01-1501, 'Zur Eröffnung der Ausstellung', August 22, 1946.

62   Friedrich Engels, *Zur Wohnungsfrage: Die grundlegende Schrift zur Wohnungsfrage im kapitalistischen Staat und in der Übergangszeit*, Sozialdemokratische Schriftenreihe (Hottingen-Zürich, 1872). "This much, however is certain: Already now the large cities have so much housing stock available, that, if rationally used, any real housing crisis can be resolved immediately." Engels' work on the housing question gained great relevance in immediate postwar Germany. It appeared in new editions in the French zone of occupation (Singen, 1947) and in the Soviet zone of occupation (Berlin, 1948). On redistributive housing, see, e.g., BArch, SMAD, Z 47, 10134, op. 10, d 3., str. 200–1, December 4, 1945.

63   PRO, FO 1051/803. Major Nuttall Report, September 10, 1945, pp. 1–2.

64   PRO, FO 1051/803, Housing Reports I, "Housing in Berlin," letter Brigadier Ryan to A. E. Joll, August 30, 1945, pp. 1–2; ibid., PRO, FO 1051/803, Housing Reports I, letter Mahor H. Nuttall to Lt. Col. J. D. Watt, September 6, 1945.

65   LArch, C Rep 309, A 5064, Auszug aus dem Verordnungsblatt der Stadt Berlin Nr. 13 vom 18. 3. 1946, "Kontrollbehörde, Kontrollrat Gesetz Nr. 18."

66   Statistik von Groß-Berlin, ed., *Berlin in Zahlen*.

67   Steege, *Black Market, Cold War*, 19.

68   Łukasz Stanek, "Introduction: The 'Second World's Architecture and Planning in the Third World,"—Special Edition of "Cold War Transfer: Architecture and Planning from socialist countries in the 'Third World,'" *Journal of Architecture* 17 (2012) 3, pp. 299–307, p. 299.

69   Ibid., p. 300.

70   For an examination of "normalcy" as category, see Sheila Fitzpatrick, "Postwar Soviet Society: The 'Return to Normalcy', 1945–1949," in: Susan J. Linz (ed.), *The Impact of World War II on the Soviet Union* (Princeton, 1985).

71   Katherine Verdery, *What Was Socialism, and What Comes Next* (Princeton, 1996), p. 4.

72   Stanek, Introduction, p. 299.

73   Geoff Eley, "A Disorder of Peoples: The Uncertain Ground of Reconstruction in 1945," in: Jessica Reinisch and Elizabeth White (eds.), *The Disentanglement of Populations: Migration, Expulsion and Displacement in Postwar Europe, 1944–1949* (London/New York, 2011), p. 297.

74   See Thomas Etzemüller (ed.), *Die Ordnung der Moderne: Social Engineering im 20. Jahrhundert* (Bielefeld, 2009), especially pp. 26ff.

75   Bradley Abrams, "The Second World War and the East European Revolution"; Philip Nord, *France's New Deal: From the Thirties to the Postwar Era* (Princeton, 2012).

6

Entangled Entertainment: Cinema and Television in Cold War Berlin

Hanno Hochmuth
Translated by David Burnett

East and West Berlin were entangled in a multitude of ways. In spite of competing systems, there were numerous connections both before and after the erection of the Wall between the two halves of this divided city. Modern entertainment culture was a very important one. It was a driving force of entanglement processes, as it overcame in equal measure social and spatial boundaries.[1] This is a key reason why popular entertainment was frequently politicized in spite of its being rooted in the simple need for entertainment.[2] This goes especially for the postwar period marked by system confrontation, in which audiovisual media in particular offered cross-border entertainment and therefore became the object of heated political conflicts.[3] Political and pedagogical elites in both East and West initially reacted with the same resentment toward the newfangled entertainment enjoyed by postwar youth, condemning it as "trash and filth" (*Schmutz und Schund*) merely because it didn't conform with traditional educated middle-class notions of high culture and serious entertainment. In the GDR, Western-oriented juvenile entertainment was branded as an "ideological diversion of the class enemy" and was hence doubly stigmatized.[4]

The entanglement and politicization of modern entertainment culture are particularly manifest in East and West Berlin, as will be shown in the following with respect to the Berlin neighborhoods of Friedrichshain (East) und Kreuzberg (West). These two districts shared a common border, on the fault line of the Cold War.[5] And yet this East–West entanglement in the form of a transborder culture of entertainment was subject to constant historical change, mirroring processes of media transformation from cinema to television. In this chapter, I will show, first, how before 1961 East Germans flocked to cinemas close to the border in Kreuzberg. Second, using interviews with contemporary witnesses in Friedrichshain, I will show how the practice of going to nearby Western cinemas was replaced in East Berlin with the widespread consumption of Western television after the construction of the Wall. Third, I will show that modern media entertainment in the divided urban community of Berlin was a particularly explosive issue, conflating as it did the ideological boundaries of the Cold War with traditional fears about the unbridled amusement of urban working-class youth. Cultural criticism and the Cold War often went hand in hand here, hard as this may be to imagine nowadays in the new "party capital" of Berlin.

The Kreuzberg Border Cinemas

Kreuzberg, like other West Berlin districts, had a total of ten so-called border cinemas (*Grenzkinos*) prior to 1961. These were located close to the sector border and mainly targeted visitors from East Berlin and elsewhere in the GDR. The real draw of border cinemas was the wide array of popular American entertainment films they offered at reduced prices.[6] East Berlin cinemas could not compete in this regard. Most were in poor condition with superannuated projection equipment dating largely from the prewar period. The East, moreover, did not produce enough feature films, and not enough circulating copies of the ones it did, to meet the city's considerable demand for entertainment. More importantly, however, was that most of the films running in East Berlin movie theaters had a distinctly didactic tone. A large proportion of contemporary East German films was set in the world of socialist manufacturing— precisely what the majority of moviegoers were trying to escape from during their hours off.[7] It is therefore no surprise that many of them chose to go to Western cinemas instead, which promised a temporary respite from the harsh realities of daily life under the SED regime.

For the operators of these West Berlin cinemas, the steady stream of East German moviegoers was a huge source of income. Although they paid only 50 pfennigs per show on presenting an East German ID—and often a mere 25 pfennigs for matinée screenings, less than half of the regular price—they nonetheless filled up the cinemas, even in the late 1950s when in many places the rise of television was leading to "cinema extinction." Moreover, at the behest of the American-occupying forces border cinemas were exempt from paying the usual entertainment tax to the Berlin Senate. This gave the operators of these cinemas a considerable competitive advantage over movie theaters in the Western hinterland.[8]

The successful West Berlin model met with harsh criticism in the Eastern half of the city. The daily "mental border crossing"[9] of the population of East Berlin and its interest in American productions were a political thorn in the side of the SED. The films being shown at these cinemas did not conform with the notions of good entertainment that the GDR had inherited from the Weimar Republic and its working-class culture. Non-purposeful pastimes that did not promote the education and edification of the public were not part of the concept of entertainment espoused by the SED well into the 1970s.[10] This turned out in the long term to be a big disadvantage for the East in the competition between a socialist and a capitalist model of Germany, a battle also being waged in the domain of popular media.[11] The West was eminently more attractive, not least in terms of its entertainment offerings.

But even in West Berlin, critics lamented the popular westerns and gangster movies being screened in the border cinemas. These hostile reactions were a culture-critical statement rooted in the paternalist "trash and filth" campaigns that began at the turn of the twentieth century.[12] Even in the 1950s, this sense of resentment was still widespread, often coupled with a deep-seated anti-Americanism among parts of the social elite.[13] The Berlin Senate fought a vicious battle with private cinema operators about the quality of movies being shown at border cinemas. The issue was mainly sexual licentiousness and graphic depictions of violence. The debate culminated in the so-called All-Berlin Cultural Plan (*Gesamtberliner Kulturplan*) of 1958, explicitly taking into account moviegoers from the East. Only quality films, so-called *Prädikatsfilme*, which were given the rating of "valuable" or "especially valuable" by the Film Evaluation Office in Wiesbaden were eligible for state subsidies. This was in no way detrimental to the appeal of West Berlin border cinemas, however. East Berliners were allowed to purchase their admission tickets using Eastern currency at a set exchange rate of 1:1, and the number of East German moviegoers in West Berlin border cinemas actually increased to 600,000 a month.[14]

The SED was suspicious of this stream of viewers and kept close tabs on them. Indeed, East Berlin functionaries were often among the best authorities on what was playing in West Berlin. Despite this sense of mistrust, there were occasional attempts to learn from the enemy,[15] allowing the East to gain some ground. Thus, for example, in 1956, during the brief political "thaw" in the GDR, East Berlin cinemas temporarily increased their popularity by pandering to public tastes and importing Western movies (albeit not American ones). Border cinemas were set up in the East, attempting to lure Western visitors by offering popular Western movies at lower prices. But even with reduced fees for the unemployed, these movie theaters failed to live up to expectations and, in the end, the cinema war was clearly decided in favor of the West.[16] It was only the erection of the Berlin Wall that succeeded in keeping East German moviegoers out of West Berlin cinemas for good. With that the economic basis of border cinemas vanished overnight, forcing five of the ten Kreuzberg border cinemas to close by the end of 1961.[17]

Michael Lemke talks about an "entangled society" in characterizing divided Berlin before the construction of the Wall.[18] The intense politicization in both halves of this city during the height of the Cold War notwithstanding, the societies of East and West Berlin remained closely intertwined prior to 1961. This was particularly true in day-to-day life. The inhabitants of this divided city crossed borders to shop for food, go to school, and earn their living, but especially for entertainment, which included going to the cinema. The entertainment offerings of this entangled "media public sphere" were appropriated in a private manner by consumers, who followed their personal entertainment preferences and flocked to *The Magnificent Seven* and *Ben Hur*. Thus, the Kreuzberg border cinemas linked not only East and West but also the public and the private sphere.

Western Television in East Berlin

With the construction of the Wall in 1961, electronic media overtook the role that border cinemas once occupied, becoming the most important link between East and West. This included Western radio programs, which were available on the airwaves throughout most of the GDR and had a formative influence on developments in the East. The popular broadcaster Radio in the American Sector (RIAS), for instance, played a crucial role in the national uprising of June 17, 1953.[19] The SED therefore sought to prevent its people from listening to the RIAS program by disturbing its frequencies. The jamming of radio signals, however, only affected medium and long wave, but not very high frequencies (UKW) that were most commonly used in Berlin. By the 1960s and 1970s, the number of jamming signals decreased. The SED no longer invested in jamming radio techniques.[20]

Western TV shows, too, were an important bridge between East and West.[21] With the exception of the so-called "valley of the clueless" in the region of Dresden and a few areas in the remote northeast corner of the GDR, most East Germans—about 80 percent—were able to tune into the two main West German national broadcasters, ARD and ZDF, in the 1970s and 1980s.[22] Western television became all the more important once it became a mass medium. In the course of the 1960s, the majority of households in the GDR gained access to a TV set.[23] Most could pick up Western channels, which subsequently took on the role of a surrogate public sphere in the GDR.

East Berlin had almost ideal conditions for receiving radio and television programs due to its close proximity to West Berlin broadcasting stations. And yet there was nothing free and easy about tuning in to Western stations, the act itself being highly politicized as it undermined the SED's media and information monopoly. Listening to or watching Western media was denounced by the SED as "ideological diversion of the class enemy." The culmination of this ideological struggle against Western German media was the "Lightning Contra NATO Stations" campaign in the fall of 1961, when the SED, having sealed the border, now cracked down on "mental border-crossers." Thousands of members of the Free German Youth (FDJ) were sent up on to rooftops across the country to check which way the antennas were facing and correct them if necessary.[24] The tenement blocks of Friedrichshain, built in quadrangle fashion, made this task even easier, allowing eager FDJ members to literally jump from roof to roof. What they failed to take into account, however, were the antennas some occupants had secretly installed under the roofs in the attics of their buildings and, hence, out of public view.[25]

Another strategy for disguising the consumption of Western media was restricting communication about it to a wholly private context. The distinction between public and private in the GDR was something people learned early on.[26] Schoolchildren were careful about what they said in public about the TV programs they watched at home. Under no circumstances were their teachers allowed to find out that they and their families were familiar with Western TV. Thus, many parents impressed on their children from a very young age that it was better to keep quiet in public about their evening viewing habits, because even a candid answer to seemingly harmless questions—what the "Little Sandman" character looked like in the East German bedtime show or the trademark East German clock ident—could serve as an indication to teachers which TV stations they watched at home and hence get parents or pupils into trouble.[27] As the chief agency of education in the GDR, the school system jealously guarded the SED's information monopoly. One of its major tasks was to educate the "new socialist individual," who was supposed to be free of all capitalist influences. But given the existence of a "dual television landscape,"[28] this was an all but hopeless endeavor, leading to countless conflicts between teachers and pupils.[29]

The consumption of Western television in the GDR can best be reconstructed by analyzing these conflicts. This task presents two primary difficulties, however. On the one hand, TV reception is fleeting by nature and hard to trace historically;

contemporary audience research on television in the GDR would only permit drawing indirect conclusions about East Germans' consumption of Western programming.[30] On the other hand, the fact that these audiovisual media were oriented toward a national audience and broadcast nationwide makes it hard to reach any specific conclusions about the local consumption of Western television in the capital of the GDR. Media-historical interviews, however, are one way to retrospectively reconstruct historical media behaviors. Seven interviews with former East German teachers at polytechnic high schools (POS) in Friedrichshain and Prenzlauer Berg will serve as a basis for the following investigation of Western television and its politicization in East Berlin.[31] Granted, these interviews are not a representative or objective reflection of past reality, but are merely an individual and limited approach to the topic. It was evident that the interviewees constructed their biographies as the interview progressed and were not immune to interpretive patterns acquired since the events transpired. A critical interpretation of these interviews with former teachers has to take into account the radical break in social relations, their personal, professional and material development, changes in the school system, as well as the transformation of the media landscape since 1989.

The teachers interviewed often had no time to watch television because of their heavy workload.[32] Added to this was the systematic convergence of curricular and extracurricular activities in the GDR. As propagandists of the state, teachers had to organize flag ceremonies or communist youth-group activities such as afternoon "Pioneer" meetings and a mandatory year-long civics class for FDJ members; they had to maintain contact with factory or farm brigades sponsoring children's groups, do military recruiting, and much, much more.[33] They were highly public individuals and had considerably less free time than their fellow citizens. Furthermore, television—in particular entertainment shows—contradicted in many respects the values and social prestige of the educated middle classes that many teachers in the GDR were trying to convey, in spite of the fact that they themselves rarely came from this social background. Thus, in spite of the wholesale replacement of educators and cultural elites in the GDR, conventional paradigms of the teaching profession had largely remained intact.[34] This included the widely shared conviction among teachers that reading a good book was always preferable to watching TV.

It is thus all the more remarkable that the majority of teachers surveyed indicated that they did, in fact, watch television on a regular basis. And almost all of them sooner or later had some experience with Western programming. Some came from functionary families that tended to toe the party line and refused to turn on ARD and ZDF for ideological reasons, or from regions where they couldn't get Western stations. And yet most of them began to watch both East and West German programming at the latest when they started their own families and began their careers. Western television, however, was more present in East Berlin than it was in other parts of the country. One of the teachers interviewed, who had come to Friedrichshain to work at a POS after teacher training in Neubrandenburg, experienced a kind of culture shock in Berlin:

> I'd sometimes meet up with colleagues from work. I was in Berlin now! And they'd say: "Hey, have you seen this?" Something completely idiotic to me nowadays:

Dallas. At 9:30 the whole street echoed with its theme song. And, well, you'd end
up watching it too, and actually thought it was pretty cool. It was a totally different
world. [...] Just seeing the whole Western lifestyle and how the people there
dressed, all fancy-schmancy, and then all the thrilling intrigues. It definitely had
something. [...] I think that was my introduction to Western television.[35]

These statements bespeak the ubiquity and allure of Western television. They also
show that it was not uncommon to talk with colleagues at school about the experience
of watching programs made by the class enemy. A teacher who wanted to be accepted
by other teaching staff had to take part in this kind of small talk. To be sure, this kind
of communication about Western TV was only possible in a more narrow, private
circle, in which there was a kind of tacit agreement—quite typical, incidentally, in a
"dictatorship of limits" like the GDR, where individuals had certain freedoms and a
scope of maneuver as long as they remained in their immediate social surroundings,
but quickly encountered limits the higher up they went.[36] There was certainly no
discussing Western programs with school directors or administrators, since the latter
had an unequivocal claim to political leadership and considerable powers of sanction.

And yet the remarkable thing is that none of the teachers interviewed could recall
any kind of official prohibition. Instead, they made repeated mention of it being a
"taboo" to watch Western television. This term would indicate that Western television
in the GDR existed in a legal gray zone. With the exception of the service regulations
for members of the armed forces, there was no law making it a punishable offense to
tune in to Western programs. That private television-watching habits were nonetheless
a taboo topic is probably attributable to the abovementioned campaigns from the early
1960s against using Western radio and television. The "antenna-storming" after the
construction of the Wall was accompanied by the demanding of written declarations
renouncing the use of Western media. "Voluntary" agreements of this sort were
expected especially of university students, and served in the case of violations as a
lever for possible expulsion. Several of the teachers interviewed recalled university
classmates being punished to set an example after they were caught using Western
media or admitted to having done so. One teacher, who began his teacher training in
East Berlin in the fall of 1961, told the following about a fellow student:

> He'd watched a soccer game with his study group—it's really quite ridiculous—
> in the Mitte district of Berlin, on a TV set with a tabletop antenna. As chance
> would have it, the picture was better on the Western channel. So they switched
> to the Western channel and turned off the sound, then listened to the game on
> the radio while following the picture on TV. And for fear of being denounced,
> this individual [...] said that he simply wanted to state for the record that he was
> watching Western television with his study group—about five or six people—and
> that, while he was sorry about it, he just wanted to get it out in the open so that
> everything would be fine.[37]

The student was lucky and was not expelled. Too many of his classmates were
involved in the affair and the demand for new teachers was simply too great to expel

them all from teachers' training college. And so the students got away with a warning and were allowed to continue their studies. Said teacher, however, had learned his lesson from the public disciplinary procedure that followed and refrained from using Western TV or radio after that. This applied to entertainment shows as well. After all, the student was not criticized for watching a political information program on Western TV but for tuning in to a sports event, and this just because of better picture quality. The authorities in this instance were not only interested in upholding the SED's monopoly on information; the reception of Western entertainment shows was actually considered a threat: the dreaded "ideological diversion of the imperialist mass media."[38]

This belief in the direct negative influencing of the East German population through Western media had two basic causes. First, the SED clung tenaciously to Lenin's understanding of the mass media as a propaganda tool, so that the entertainment function of television was long underestimated. East German television was conceived as a journalistic medium in which even cultural content was meant to reflect socialist convictions.[39] Entertainment was there to serve propaganda interests. The SED imputed this same intention to Western television—although, granted, with a different agenda. It suspected that the capitalist "consciousness industry" was lurking behind the enemy's entertainment shows and was out to manipulate unsuspecting East Germans.

The second cause for the rejection of Western entertainment programs was to be found in the generational conflict that emerged in the GDR in the 1950s. The old communist leaders, socialized in the Weimar labor movement and hence eager to spread education to the masses, as well as the functional elites of the immediate postwar generation, the so-called generation of reconstruction (*Aufbaugeneration*), which experienced tremendous upward mobility after the war, both had trouble understanding the generation that followed. Although the latter were the first generation of East German citizens supposedly raised in an atmosphere free of capitalist influences and hence fulfilling the ideal of the new socialist individual, many young people had other aims in life than building socialism, and generally seemed more interested in jeans and rock and roll. Hence the younger generation had become an "internal enemy."[40] Political and educational functionaries blamed this situation on Western entertainment and took vigorous measures to counteract it—antenna-storming, confiscation of TV and radio sets, making public examples of offenders.[41]

The consumption of Western television and radio was thus systematically politicized, even though the consumers of these programs rarely had political motivations and mostly did so for personal pleasure. The media habits of most East Germans were primarily an individual pursuit of happiness aimed at satisfying their personal needs.[42] In this respect, the GDR was no different from other modern societies.[43] This essentially unpolitical satisfaction of needs in the GDR took on a political character, however, in the context of the Cold War and given the existence of mass media spanning the Cold War divide. It was this that made the private consumption of Western television a form of cultural resistance and occasionally of silent protest. The thrill of doing something forbidden was sometimes just as important.

The fact that Western TV became a political taboo stood in stark contrast to the daily media habits of most East German citizens. As public propagandists and private consumers, the teachers interviewed found different ways of dealing with the conflict between political expectations and personal viewing behavior. By no means were they mere "transmission belts" of the SED dictatorship who implemented in a linear manner the claims to power of state and party and systematically opposed their students using Western media. In reality, they developed *eigensinnig* (self-willed) strategies of dealing with this problem.[44] Some teachers did, in fact, renounce Western television, demanding that their children and students do the same. This was probably done in the spirit of timeserving more than as a matter of conviction. While there were teachers who consistently rejected Western television on ideological grounds, pragmatic considerations were usually the deciding factor. As teachers and multipliers of state power, they imagined they were under particular scrutiny and abstained from watching Western TV at home in the interest of protecting themselves, so as not to be denounced by their own children. By willingly putting on ideological blinders and only tuning in to East German television, they also avoided uncomfortable truths and confrontations. For the very same reason, these teachers demanded that their students also toe the line and only use East German media. Some teachers found this was the easiest way to nip discordant voices in the bud.

Other teachers ignored the television-viewing habits of their students and regularly watched Western programs themselves. Remarkably, they did not feel conflicted; they simply repressed the dissonance between the authorities' demand for loyalty and their own media-consuming habits. The majority of interviews confirmed this finding. Political loyalty to the East and an orientation toward Western media were by no means mutually exclusive. Many teachers felt they had earned a loyalty bonus through their considerable social commitment in other, often conflict-ridden areas where accountability toward their superiors was greater—their efforts, for example, to get as many schoolchildren as possible to take part in the *Jugendweihe*, the state-sponsored communist coming-of-age ceremony. It was only natural, then, to minimize this claim to loyalty in their own private sphere. At least at home they deserved a break and should be able to tune in to whatever they wanted, *Dallas* or *Einer wird gewinnen*.[45] This tacit arrangement extended to the viewing habits of their students. Many teachers basically condoned what they themselves practiced.

Finally, some teachers adopted a third strategy with regard to Western television by openly repudiating the claim to renounce watching Western TV. These were no closet oppositionists, but self-assertive SED members whose fundamental convictions as socialists allowed them to deem certain demands of the party as fallacious and reinterpret them with reference to the founding fathers of socialism. This widespread form of *eigensinnig* behavior in the GDR found expression in the words of a teacher in Friedrichshain:

> At some point I told myself, it's a stupid demand, and I looked for arguments to back it up and said, for example: Karl Marx developed his theory of capitalism while living in the midst of capitalism. He experienced it as reality and was able to think critically and develop a theory out of it and judge for himself if what he

had seen was good or bad. We're constantly supposed to condemn a system that we actually know nothing about, except what they're generous enough to share with us. So I said to myself: This is nonsense, no way. I can't live in water and still stay dry.[46]

The teacher quoted here taught civics (*Staatsbürgerkunde*) and was therefore even more responsible for the political-ideological education of his pupils, and hence routinely ran into trouble when his students came with conflicting information they'd gleaned from Western programs. He had no choice but to watch these shows himself in order to reduce this cognitive dissonance. If he hadn't, his students would have "cooked his goose," he recalled in retrospect. Paradoxically, it was the restrictive information policy of the SED that forced him to be more open toward Western television. Like many other teachers, he felt let down by his own country's television programming, which doggedly remained silent about certain political events that Western TV reported on exhaustively:

There were a lot of things we had no information about. I remember once, for example, when a Korean airliner was shot down, causing the deaths of hundreds of people. And I remember it so clearly, because we asked: "Is it true or not, because Western TV reported on it and Eastern TV said nothing?" Then we made some inquiries at the district committee of the Party: "Is it true?"—"It's not true." Then, day by day, a little bit more of the truth came out, and in the end the story went: It was suspected of being a spy plane, that's why. Whatever the case may have been, we were totally left in the dark. And the dumbest comment was when they said: "If you have a class standpoint, you'll know what to say to your students." In other words: Ernst Thälmann was a wonderful person, so none of that can be true.[47]

Teachers were largely left to their own devices when it came to the topic of Western television. And their insecurity only increased in the last two decades of the GDR. This can be traced back to three new challenges that teachers faced with no clear instructions from the Ministry of Education on how to deal with them in the classroom. First, the party line on Western TV changed in 1971 when Erich Honecker came to power. The new head of state and party leader declared in 1973 that everyone could "turn on or off Western mass media as they pleased, especially West German radio and television."[48] The party leadership slowly began to accept the fact that Western TV was perceived by East German citizens as an increase in their quality of living and therefore had a stabilizing effect.[49] The school system was hardly affected, however, by this piecemeal liberalization. Teachers were not given an official "all clear" with regard to Western TV. Completely abandoning the bogeyman of "Western media" would have eroded the socialist self-image that schools were supposed to communicate. The result was that for many teachers their earlier experiences of conflict and prohibitions encountered in the 1960s remained a formative influence. Come 1989, the taboo of Western television had hardly been lifted in the GDR.

Second, East German television underwent a fundamental change in 1971 after a speech by Honecker at the Eighth Party Congress of the SED when he attested to a "certain tediousness" of their own television programming. Two great program reforms took the entertainment needs of East German viewers into consideration, evincing clear parallels to Honecker's economic and social policy, which aimed to win the population's loyalty by offering more consumer choices. This included the Saturday evening variety show *Ein Kessel Buntes* ("A Cauldron of Color"), which now featured original performances by stars from the West. Then, in 1982, "alternative programming" was introduced, moving all political magazine shows on East German television from primetime slots to later in the evening, giving way to entertainment shows increasingly imported from the West.[50] In their attempts to attract viewers, East German program directors had learned from the enemy. Hence television in the GDR became more and more like its counterpart in the West.[51] Teachers who for years had fought against the pernicious effects of Western entertainment shows were suddenly deeply irritated by the conformist nature of East German television and had a lot of explaining to do to their students. They felt like they'd been stabbed in the back by their own TV stations.

Third, television in West Germany also underwent a momentous change with the advent of private television stations in 1985, which, as of 1987, were freely available on the airwaves in East Berlin as well. The private broadcasters SAT 1 and RTL Plus offered mostly American series to begin with. Private TV also established entirely new formats like the morning edition—an unfamiliar challenge for many of the teachers interviewed.[52] One of the teachers from Friedrichshain recalled:

> I was astonished to find out that my students were even watching television *before* they came to school. I was pretty flabbergasted. I couldn't understand why anyone would watch TV before school. And it was obviously private stations they were watching. […] These students were usually the ones whose grades were not so good, and it was naturally hard not to comment: "You should sleep a little longer instead of watching TV." By the late 1980s, the situation was a little more relaxed, though. It was not about politics anymore, but the fact that they were simply spending too much time in front of the TV set. It was evident in their poor performance, their lack of concentration, in everything.[53]

Teachers were opposed to morning programs not so much in their function as the propagandists of the state and guardians of the SED's monopoly on the media but in their role as concerned educators. It was in their own professional interest that they struggled with private broadcasters for the attention of their students. By associating the American shows broadcasted on private stations with the notion of "trash and filth," they reactivated a deep-seated resentment characteristic of their profession, the loathing of American popular culture, thus calling to mind the postwar years in East and West when an educated middle-class elite was waging a hopeless battle against dime novels and jazz music.[54] The fear that private television was dumbing the population down was rooted in a long tradition of German cultural criticism on the part of concerned educators. In this regard, the politicization of entertainment in the GDR needs to be viewed not merely against the backdrop of the SED's desire to structure everyday life according to its own dictatorial interests, but also as part of a cross-system engagement with modern mass culture and the entertainment-oriented mass consumption it entailed.

Conclusion: Media History as Urban History

In East Berlin, this cultural struggle had an added element of controversy given that it was primarily working-class youth from older East Berlin neighborhoods whom the SED leadership considered especially susceptible to imported Western entertainment. Just like in the immediate postwar period, when juvenile delinquents such as the notorious Gladow gang on Schreinerstrasse in Friedrichshain were inspired by American gangster movies to carry out their own heists,[55] popular Western media were suspected of corrupting working-class youths. This was evident in the state's reaction to the massive numbers of East Germans going to Kreuzberg border cinemas prior to 1961, which after the construction of the Wall were replaced with the widespread reception of Western radio and television programs. Even though the SED's attitude toward "political-ideological diversion of the class enemy" did relax somewhat over the decades, the enjoyment of Western TV in the East remained politically charged.

The fact that interest in Western entertainment shows mostly sprang from an unpolitical desire for distraction tended to get short shrift. And yet, in a broader sense, Western media did convey alternative lifestyles different than the ones on offer in the GDR. They showed how different life was on the other side of the Wall—and how many ways there were to have fun. Thus, the Blattschuss Brothers singing their *Kreuzberg Nights* on the ZDF hit parade in 1978 conjured up images of the "Wild West" in the minds of East Berliners.[56] When Western popstars such as David Bowie performed on the immediate Western side of the Brandenburg Gate in 1987, during celebrations to mark the 750th anniversary of Berlin, East German fans flocked to the Eastern side before being dispersed by their own security forces. For the very first time, indignant fans reacted by publicly chanting "The Wall must go!" or singing "Kreuzberg nights are long …" with ambiguous reference to the West Berlin May Day riots.[57] Even though there was no direct link here to the fall of the Wall two years later, these events presaged the system-defeating power of a Western entertainment culture that had served as a central connector between East and West Berlin throughout the city's division.

Entertainment culture between East and West was not a one-way street, however. Countless West Berliners made pilgrimages to East Berlin in order to go to the opera or theater, or to buy cheap books, records, and alcohol. And yet there is no denying that this entanglement was largely asymmetric on account of the greater appeal of Western entertainment. Whereas Western movies, television series, and radio shows were eagerly followed in East Berlin, the West Berlin subculture of the 1980s more or less completely ignored the East.[58] The history of entertainment culture in East and West Berlin thus exemplifies the asymmetric histories, both parallel and entangled, of East–West German postwar history.[59]

At first glance, the entanglement of mass media between East and West Berlin may not seem all that different than that between the GDR and the Federal Republic overall. On closer examination, however, the special situation of Berlin reveals specific historical features with regard to entertainment culture. Personal entanglements between East and West Berlin were largely replaced by media entanglement after 1961. The comparison between the visits of the Western border cinemas and the consumption of the Western TV reveals that the entangled relations shifted after the erection of the Wall and a concomitant media transformation, but the phenomenon of a cross-border entertainment culture nonetheless remained in place.

This had very concrete effects on the history of East Berlin, where Western television played a special role for reasons other than optimal reception. The many prewar buildings in East Berlin with their antennas on and under the roof, but also the working-class social structure in many parts of East Berlin's inner-city districts made Western television a political issue, one that shifted over time, however, the fear among educated middle-class elites of "ideological diversion of the class enemy" gradually giving way to more traditional anxieties about the dangers of urban working-class youth and their unregulated consumption of Western entertainment. Urban history and media history therefore need to be viewed in tandem, as inextricably linked. In this regard, the history of entangled entertainment in East and West Berlin points to the methodological potential of an integrated German postwar history.[60]

Notes

1   Kaspar Maase, *Grenzenloses Vergnügen. Der Aufstieg der Massenkultur 1850–1970* (Frankfurt am Main, 1997).

2   Michael Meyen, *Hauptsache Unterhaltung. Mediennutzung und Medienbewertung in Deutschland in den 50er Jahren* (Münster, 2001).

3   See, especially, Uta G. Poiger, *Jazz, Rock, and Rebels: Cold War Politics and American Culture in a Divided Germany* (Berkeley, 2000).

4   Hanno Hochmuth, "Vergnügen in der Zeitgeschichte," *Aus Politik und Zeitgeschichte* 62 (2012), B 1–3, pp. 33–8.

5   Hanno Hochmuth, *Kiezgeschichte. Friedrichshain und Kreuzberg im geteilten Berlin* (Göttingen, 2017).

6   On the border cinemas of West Berlin, see, especially, Michael Lemke, *Vor der Mauer. Berlin in der Ost-West-Konkurrenz 1948 bis 1961* (Cologne et al., 2011) pp. 483–509; Andrea Gerischer and Kerstin Jablonka, *Geschichte von Orten im Wrangelkiez. Eine Ausstellung in Schaufenstern* (Berlin, 2008), pp. 33–5.

7   Lemke, *Vor der Mauer*, pp. 487–9.

8   Ibid., pp. 495–7.

9   Michael Meyen, "Geistige Grenzgänger. Medien und die deutsche Teilung. Ein Beitrag zur Kommunikationsgeschichte der ersten beiden Nachkriegsjahrzehnte," *Jahrbuch für Kommunikationsgeschichte* 1 (1999), pp. 192–231.

10   Wolfgang Mühl-Benninghaus, *Unterhaltung als Eigensinn. Eine ostdeutsche Mediengeschichte* (Frankfurt am Main, 2012).

11   Thomas Lindenberger (ed.), *Massenmedien im Kalten Krieg. Akteure, Bilder, Resonanzen* (Cologne, 2006).

12   Kaspar Maase, *Was macht Populärkultur politisch?* (Wiesbaden, 2010), pp. 79–111.

13   Poiger, *Jazz, Rock, and Rebels*.

14   Lemke, *Vor der Mauer*, pp. 501–4.

15   See the various contributions in Martin Aust and Daniel Schönpflug (eds.), *Vom Gegner lernen. Feindschaften und Kulturtransfers im Europa des 19. und 20. Jahrhunderts* (Frankfurt/New York, 2007).

16   Lemke, *Vor der Mauer*, pp. 497–501.

17   Archive of the FHXB Friedrichshain-Kreuzberg Museum: Materials on the border cinemas of Kreuzberg.

18   Michael Lemke points out that "until 1961, characteristics of a cross-system 'mixed' society had developed on account of historically rooted entanglements in Berlin and unique present-day relationships in culture and daily life. These characteristics came into existence thanks to a multidimensional exchange in the context of (and despite) the Cold War, against a backdrop of relative openness and the porousness of these systems." Lemke views the erection of the Wall in part as a reaction to the increasing daily entanglement of a politically divided Berlin. Lemke, *Vor der Mauer*, p. 20.

19   Bernd Stoever, "Radio mit kalkuliertem Risiko. Der RIAS als US-Sender für die DDR 1946–1961," in: Klaus Arnold and Christoph Classen (eds.), *Zwischen Pop und Propaganda. Radio in der DDR* (Berlin, 2004), pp. 209–28.

20   Franziska Kuschel, *Schwarzhörer, Schwarzseher und heimliche Leser. Die DDR und die Westmedien* (Göttingen, 2016), pp. 66–9.

21   Hanno Hochmuth, "Feindbild und Leitbild. Westfernsehen in der DDR," in: Martin Aust and Daniel Schönpflug (eds.), *Vom Gegner lernen. Feindschaften und Kulturtransfers im Europa des 19. und 20. Jahrhunderts* (Frankfurt/New York, 2007), pp. 271–92.

22   Michael Meyen, *Denver Clan und Neues Deutschland. Mediennutzung in der DDR* (Berlin, 2003), p. 19.

23   Axel Schildt, "Der Beginn des Fernsehzeitalters. Ein neues Massenmedium setzt sich durch," in: Axel Schildt and Arnold Sywottek (eds.), *Modernisierung im Wiederaufbau. Die westdeutsche Gesellschaft der 50er Jahre* (Bonn, 1993), pp. 477–92.

24   Marc-Dietrich Ohse, *Jugend nach dem Mauerbau. Anpassung, Protest und Eigensinn (DDR 1961–1974)* (Berlin, 2003); Kuschel, *Schwarzhörer, Schwarzseher und heimliche Leser*, pp. 124–36.

25   Ibid., p. 198.

26   Dorothee Wierling, *Geboren im Jahr Eins. Der Jahrgang 1949 in der DDR. Versuch einer Kollektivbiographie* (Berlin, 2002), pp. 148ff.

27   Kuschel, *Schwarzhörer, Schwarzseher und heimliche Leser*, p. 9.

28   Axel Schildt, "Zwei Staaten—eine Rundfunk- und Fernsehnation," in: Arnd Bauerkämper, Martin Sabrow, and Bernd Stöver (eds.), *Doppelte Zeitgeschichte. Deutsch-deutsche Beziehungen 1945–1990* (Bonn, 1998), pp. 58–71.

29   Hanno Hochmuth, "Politisiertes Vergnügen. Zum Konflikt um das Westfernsehen an Schulen in der DDR," in: Ulrike Häußer and Marcus Merkel (eds.), *Vergnügen in der DDR* (Berlin, 2009), pp. 287–303.

30   Michael Meyen estimated for the 1980s that 20 to 25 percent of viewers in the GDR were watching Western programs. Michael Meyen, "Kollektive Ausreise? Zur Reichweite ost- und westdeutscher Fernsehprogramme in der DDR," in *Publizistik* 47 (2002) 2, pp. 200–32.

31   I conducted the interviews in 2004 as part of my unpublished master's thesis: Hanno Hochmuth, *Der Klassenfeind im Klassenzimmer. Westfernsehen und sozialistische Erziehung in der DDR der Siebziger und Achtziger Jahre* (Free University Berlin, 2004).

32   On the occupational tendency of teachers to place excessive demands on themselves, see Peter Hübner, *Arbeitszeit und Arbeitsbelastung Berliner Lehrerinnen und Lehrer* (Berlin, 1996), pp. 7ff.

33   Sonja Kudella, Andreas Paetz, and Heinz-Elmar Tenorth, "Die Politisierung des Schulalltags," in: Ministerium für Bildung, Jugend und Sport des Landes Brandenburg (ed.), *Geschichte, Struktur und Funktionsweise der DDR-Volksbildung, vol. 2: In Linie angetreten. Die Volksbildung der DDR in ausgewählten Kapiteln* (Berlin, 1996), pp. 21–211, here pp. 54ff.

34   Sonja Häder, *Schülerkindheit in Ost-Berlin. Sozialisation unter den Bedingungen der Diktatur (1945–1958)* (Cologne, 1998), p. 337.

35   Interview with Frau A., February 2004.

36   Thomas Lindenberger, "Die Diktatur der Grenzen. Zur Einleitung," in Thomas Lindenberger (ed.), *Herrschaft und Eigen-Sinn in der Diktatur. Studien zur Gesellschaftsgeschichte der DDR* (Cologne et al., 1999), pp. 13–44.

37   Interview with Herr K., February 2004.

38   On the SED's concerns about "ideological diversion through imperialist mass media," see Gunther Holzweissig, *Die schärfste Waffe der Partei. Eine Mediengeschichte der DDR* (Cologne/Weimar/Vienna, 2002).

39   Simone Barck, Christoph Classen, and Thomas Heimann, "The Fettered Media. Controlling Public Debate," in: Konrad H. Jarausch (ed.), *Dictatorship as Experience* (New York, 1999), pp. 213–30, here p. 223.

40   Dorothee Wierling, "Die Jugend als innerer Feind. Konflikte in der Erziehungsdiktatur der sechziger Jahre," in: Hartmut Kaelble, Jürgen Kocka, and Hartmut Zwahr (eds.), *Sozialgeschichte der DDR* (Stuttgart, 1994), pp. 404–25.

41   Ohse, *Jugend nach dem Mauerbau.*

42   Michael Meyen, *Hauptsache Unterhaltung;* Mühl-Benninghaus, *Unterhaltung als Eigensinn.*

43   Thomas Lindenberger, "Geteilte Welt, geteilter Himmel? Der Kalte Krieg und die Massenmedien in gesellschaftsgeschichtlicher Perspektive," in: Klaus Arnold and Christoph Classen (eds.), *Zwischen Pop und Propaganda. Radio in der DDR* (Berlin, 2004), pp. 27–44, here p. 38.

44   *Eigensinn* (self-will, willfulness) is not to be confused with resistance and opposition. What is meant are the interpretive and meaning-producing aspects of individual and collective behavior in social relationships. These interpretive and behavioral patterns in dealing with the unreasonable demands of authority range from preemptive obedience to open protest. On the concept of *Eigensinn*, see Alf Lüdtke, *Eigen-Sinn. Fabrikalltag, Arbeitererfahrungen und Politik vom Kaiserreich bis in den Faschismus* (Münster), 2015 [1993]; Thomas Lindenberger applied the concept in a fruitful way to the history of the GDR: Lindenberger, "Die Diktatur der Grenzen."

45   The American series *Dallas*, that is, which ran from 1981 to 1991 on ARD in West Germany, as well as the popular Saturday night game show *Einer wird gewinnen* ("Someone Will Win"), which aired on ARD from 1964 to 1987 and was hosted by the legendary Joachim Kulenkampff (1921–98). Michael Reufsteck and Stefan Niggemeier, *Das Fernsehlexikon* (Munich, 2005), pp. 238–40, pp. 316–18.

46   Interview with Herr K., February 2004.

47   Ibid.

48   Quoted in Gunther Holzweissig, "Massenmedien in der DDR," in: Jürgen Wilke (ed.), *Mediengeschichte der Bundesrepublik Deutschland* (Bonn, 1999), pp. 573–601, here p. 589.

49 In 1985, the SED regional leadership in Dresden even allowed the founding of "interest groups for foreign TV," which, using homemade satellite dishes, finally brought reception of Western TV to the "valley of the clueless." By allowing this "mental emigration," they hoped to stem the wave of actual emigration, which was highest in the Dresden region. Stefan Wolle, "Der Traum vom Westen. Wahrnehmungen der bundesdeutschen Gesellschaft in der DDR," in: Konrad H. Jarausch and Martin Sabrow (eds.), *Weg in den Untergang. Der innere Zerfall der DDR* (Göttingen, 1999), pp. 195–212; Kuschel, *Schwarzhörer, Schwarzseher und heimliche Leser*, pp. 231–9.

50 Wolfgang Mühl-Benninghaus, "Medienpolitische Probleme," in: Heide Riedel (ed.), *"Mit uns zieht die neue Zeit ...." 40 Jahre DDR-Medien* (Berlin, 1993), pp. 9–20; Franca Wolff, *Glasnost erst kurz vor Sendeschluss. Die letzten Jahre des DDR-Fernsehens (1985-1989/90)* (Cologne, 2003), p. 118.

51 Hochmuth, "Feindbild und Leitbild," pp. 283ff.

52 Kuschel, *Schwarzhörer, Schwarzseher und heimliche Leser*, p. 242.

53 Interview with Frau G., March 2004.

54 Maase, *Grenzenloses Vergnügen*.

55 On the Gladow gang, see Annett Gröschner and Grischa Meyer, *Das Fallbeil. Gladows Gang. Eine Berliner Blockadezeitung*, special issue of "Theater der Zeit" (Berlin, 1999).

56 Hochmuth, *Kiezgeschichte*, pp. 280–4.

57 Krijn Thijs, *Drei Geschichten, eine Stadt. Die Berliner Stadtjubiläen von 1937 und 1987* (Cologne, 2008), p. 274.

58 Christian Semler, "1968 im Westen—was ging uns die DDR an?," *Aus Politik und Zeitgeschichte* 53 (2003) 45, pp. 3–5. The remark of West Berlin musician Blixa Bargeld in an interview from the 1980s was paradigmatic when he admitted he had never been to the Eastern half of the city. The interview is in the film *B-Movie: Lust & Sound in West-Berlin 1979–1989* (Germany, 2015), 92 min, written and directed by Jörg A. Hoppe, Klaus Maeck, Heiko Lange.

59 Christoph Kleßmann, "Konturen einer integrierten Nachkriegsgeschichte," *Aus Politik und Zeitgeschichte* 55 (2005) 18–19, pp. 3–11.

60 Konrad H. Jarausch, "'Die Teile als Ganzes erkennen.' Zur Integration der beiden deutschen Nachkriegsgeschichten," *Zeithistorische Forschungen/Studies in Contemporary History* 1 (2004) 1, pp. 10–30.

7

The Politics of Subculture in Both Berlins

Timothy Scott Brown

On the night of November 24, 1987, agents of the State Security (*Stasi*) raided the Zionskirche (Zion Church) in communist East Berlin. The church served as a haven for political and cultural nonconformism, in keeping with the Protestant Church's role as one of the few (limited) safe spaces for dissent under the communist regime. Pastor Hans Simon opened his doors to hippies, punks, and other young dissidents, making the Zionskirche a central institution of the alternative scene in East Berlin's Prenzlauer Berg district. The previous September, a group of activists had founded a so-called "Environmental Library" (*Umweltbibliothek*) in the church's basement offices. The group collected and made available hard-to-find books, staged exhibitions, and produced a newspaper, the *Environmental Pages* (*Umweltblätter*), which combined environmental themes with social criticism and political commentary. Alongside this nominally legal newspaper—ostensibly produced for "internal church use"—activists of the Umweltbibliothek helped print *Grenzfall*, the newspaper of the illegal citizens' group Initiative for Peace and Human Rights (*Initiative Frieden und Menschenrechte*—IFM). On the night of November 24, with the album *Keine Macht für Niemand* by radical West Berlin rock group Ton Steine Scherben blasting on a cassette player in the background, activists watched grimly as *Stasi* agents tore apart and photographed the premises.[1]

Stasi agents failed to catch *Umweltbibliothek* activists in the act of printing *Grenzfall*; indeed, even worse, from their perspective, the raid only spread the name of the *Umweltbibliothek* around the country, provoking some of the first open citizen protests in the GDR. The notoriety of the *Umweltbibliothek* inspired imitators around East Germany, while expressions of solidarity poured in from West Germany and beyond. Erich Honecker received a letter of protest signed by the American folk singer Joan Baez, the linguist and anarchist Noam Chomsky, alongside and representatives of groups such as the War Resisters' League, Peace Activists East West, Across Frontiers, Campaign for Peace and Democracy East West.[2] Small grassroots groups in the Federal Republic saw their own situation reflected in that of the *Umweltbibliothek*. "We ourselves have already been raided five times," wrote one; "The same thing happens to all sorts of groups in the BRD on a regular basis."[3]

Declarations like these astonished the activists of the *Umweltbibliothek*, in their relative isolation behind the Wall,[4] but need hardly surprise the historian—the 1980s were a high moment of border-crossing movements of solidarity across national and bloc boundaries, aimed against the twin dangers of environmental degradation and an ever-escalating Cold War. They were also part of a longer postwar trajectory in which *subculture* achieved an unparalleled importance in divided Berlin. The Beat Wave of the mid-1960s (on both sides of the Wall); the West Berlin anarchist scene of the 1970s; the Prenzlauer Berg underground of the 1980s of which the *Umweltbibliothek* was a part; the "Berlin Wonderland" of the early 1990s—these are the stations of insurrectionary youth's struggle with state power in postwar Germany. Subculture had its roots in loose, pre-political associations of youth organized around musical genre and personal style, as in the various rock and roll riots of the late-1950s and early-mid-1960s, and the Beat Wave and "Gammler" scenes from the mid-1960s on; but its characteristic feature from the mid-1960s on was a self-politicization that proceeded in step with the overall surge in leftwing student and countercultural politics of the 1960s and 1970s. Subculture in Cold War Berlin, in other words, was much more than a site of "resistance through rituals"—it was a site in which serious politics were formulated and practiced.[5]

The analysis of subculture has produced a voluminous literature, much of it emphasizing the status of subculture as a site of meaning developed through symbolic practices related to style and habitus. For scholars associated with the Center for Contemporary Cultural Studies (CCCS) in Birmingham, England (the "Birmingham School"), the spectacular youth subcultures of postwar Britain—Teddy Boys, Mods, Punks, Skinheads—represented cases of "class struggle by other means"; that is, they were understood as sublimated attempts to come to grips with the subordinate position of the working class at the level of style.[6] More recent work in cultural and communication studies has emphasized subculture's role in responding to or facilitating cultural transfer—especially in relationship to popular music—that, in turn, plays a role in the construction of youth identity and youth politics.[7]

In Berlin from the mid-1960s on, however, subculture was more than a phenomenon of tribal youth rebellion whose political meaning had to be adduced by scholars. It was a self-theorizing body of thought and practice that was widely understood to be a form of politics—sometimes because a form of radical politics was ascribed to it by anxious sociologists, as in the case of the so-called "Gammler," or Beatniks, who began to populate the centers of German metropoles around 1966–7—but more often because it itself openly practiced an explicit form of radical activism. Subculture in Cold War Berlin actually existed at the intersection of these two phenomena—youth in the street enacting a rebellion of lifestyle and mores, and avant-garde groups attempting to create a fusion of art and politics at the level of daily life.

The origins of this fusion can arguably be traced to the infamous Kommune I (First Commune) and its antecedent formations (Gruppe Spur, Anschlag, and Subversive Aktion). Founded in early 1967 as the culmination of several years of radical interventions, the commune was an explicit attempt to forge a marriage between updated Marxist and anarchist traditions, Reichian psychoanalysis and sexual experimentation, and Situationist theories of cultural provocation. West Berlin was chosen as a site for the commune precisely because of the explosive nature of the city's situation as a Cold War *Frontstadt* ("front line city"), and because of the concentration of Right-leaning media in the city.[8] As one of the founders put it, using the language of Situationism, West Berlin was "'ripe for a spectacle.'"[9] Launching a series of actions aimed at the intersection of consumerism and anticommunism, tweaking the sensibilities of the citizenry and obtaining outraged media coverage, the communards opened up a space for subculture in the city.

The Kommune I itself became a gathering space for cultural and political rebels, and its high media profile inspired the founding of other communes around West Germany, and also in East Berlin, where a copycat commune calling itself K1-Ost (Kommune I East) attempted to enact a similar mixture of psychoanalytical experimentation and oppositional political engagement.[10] In both cases, communal living was expressive of broader political commitments. The sixties' communards of the first hour did not merely "Turn on, tune in, drop out," as in the influential injunction of psychedelic guru Timothy Leary—rather, they sought to revolutionize private life while galvanizing the public sphere. Members of K1-Ost, having been punished already for attempting to do the latter in the wake of the crushing of the Prague Spring in Czechoslovakia, were forced to focus more on the former.[11] Practicing partner swapping and anti-authoritarian childrearing in their efforts to "destroy the 'bourgeois family'," the communards attempted to overcome their social programming through "group therapy" sessions on the West Berlin model.

With the rise of the leftwing student movement and counterculture of the 1960s, experiments such as these became an object of theoretical analysis as well as a self-conscious site of practice whose relative merit vis-à-vis more traditional forms of oppositional politics (e.g., student activism) was the object of fierce debate. At stake was the question of whether (sub)cultural activity in and of itself—defined as collective nonconformism at the level of style and habitus, combined, in the case of Kommune I, with a public politics of scandal—represented a form of political engagement, or whether, in fact, it represented a repudiation of politics. In historical hindsight, there is little doubt that cultural and political forms of radicalism reinforced one another, and must be examined together.

Subculture in Cold War Berlin: Nine Theses

On the basis of these initial observations it is possible to posit the first of a series of propositions pertaining to the role of subculture in Cold War Berlin:

1. Subculture in Cold War Berlin was a site of the intersection of culture and politics. As is well-known, the young avant-gardes who helped catalyze the West German "1968" drew as much from radical artistic traditions as from political ones. Inspired by French Situationism and Dutch Provo, a group such as Subversive Aktion fused artistic and political forms of radicalism into a potent new mixture. These initiatives unfolded against a backdrop of a rising youth culture that, as early as the 1950s, held the seeds of a wide-ranging youth politicization. The political radicalism with youth rebellion had been foreshadowed as early as 1962 in the so-called Schwabing Riots, was well-established by the time of a pair of infamous 1965 riots—one at a Rolling Stones concert in West Berlin's Waldbühne, the other by young Beat fans in the East German city of Leipzig—and fully matured by the end of the decade in radicalized subcultures like the proto-terrorist West Berlin "Blues." The political content of the subcultures that arose out of the politicization of the new youth culture—combined with a thoroughgoing politicization of the arts and artists—derived heavily from initiatives in the realm of cultural production, ranging from literature and publishing to music performance and production, to the visual arts to the underground press.

2. *Subculture in Cold War Berlin was simultaneously global and local.* A key feature of this explosion of creativity was the influence of the transnational. Subculture, with its strong connection to the arts and various kinds of cultural consumption, was particularly marked by the local adoption of globally circulating influences. Yet, subculture was also heavily conditioned by the topography, both concrete and imagined, of the local environment. Because subculture was typically the domain of small groups of protagonists operating within discrete spatial confines, the concept of *scenes* is particularly useful for understanding the workings of global/local interactions. These communities of affinity were based around one or more shared commitments— to cultural provocation, neo-Marxism, rock music, dope smoking, or any number of other more-or-less subversive activities—and rooted in shared spaces both semi-private (music venues, pubs, and bars) and public (the street). These localities were connected in turn to transnational communities of affinity—*publics*—organized around cultural consumption (reading books, listening to music, consuming images). These communities stretched far beyond the borders of the nation state to encompass distant sources of cultural production and international readerships/listenerships/viewerships.[12]

The existence of scenes and publics was by no means confined to the Western half of Germany and Berlin. On the contrary, in the GDR, *scenes* became a key locus of resistance to the communist regime. Membership in transnational publics, likewise— reading publics, listening publics, style publics—represented one of the chief means by which East German dissidents forged and enacted their connections to the broader world. Through publics, East and West Germany were connected abroad—to Anglo-American pop culture, to rock and roll, to the writings of Che and Marcuse—but also across the border to one another. Kommune I members Fritz Teufel and Ranier Langhans visited the communist half of the city on more than one occasion to mingle with its young dissident intelligentsia, and it was in part out of this trans-Wall interplay that the inspiration arose for the founding of K1-Ost.[13] Such connections picked up steam with the rise of the Alternative Scene in West Germany and the efforts of the Greens to forge connections with dissidents across the Wall. The smuggling of an Amiga 500 computer into East Berlin for the use of the *Umweltbibliothek* is only one of the most striking such examples of this sort of cooperation that, while the exception and not the rule, was nevertheless highly significant for the East German recipients of this kind of aid.[14]

3. *Subculture in Cold War Berlin was topographically determined.* As suggested earlier, the ground for subculture in Berlin was laid—literally—by the spatial arrangements created by the Wall. The building of the wall in August 1961 transformed

central districts such as Kreuzberg and Prenzlauer Berg into marginal ones. The former, bounded on three sides by the wall, became a major scene location in West Berlin by the end of the 1960s, later an epicenter of the squatting movement in West Germany. The latter, known as Kreuzberg was for its unrenovated buildings and low rents, became home to one of the main bohemian-artistic underground in the GDR in the 1970s and 1980s. Prenzlauer Berg was a site of alternative culture, first and foremost, because leftwing politics on the West German model was not permitted to enter the public sphere in the GDR. It is worth noting, however, that cultural circles in the West often dropped out in a way that was not dissimilar, and indeed, were criticized for doing so by more explicitly political militants.

After the fall of the Wall, Prenzlauer Berg, along with Mitte and Friedrichshain, became the locus of a second great wave of squatting, which, at its highpoint, saw some 130 buildings in various East Berlin districts occupied.[15] This post-Wall squatting scene became a site of continuity for activists, such as those of the *Umweltbibliothek*, who sought radical-democratic alternatives to both state socialism and capitalism, and who, in this way, had much in common with their Western counterparts. It is an irony of history that the cultural-political creativity central to subculture in West Germany—from 1968 to the squatting, autonomist, and techno music scenes that followed in the decades after 1968—was predicated precisely on destruction—the leveling wrought by the clash of competing totalitarianisms and total war on a previously unimaginable scale, written on the very topography of the city. It is in ruins, and on the margins of the ideological division stamped on the urban topography of Berlin, that leftwing radicalism and alternative culture flourished; and it is with questions of urban topography that an analysis of subculture in Berlin must inextricably be linked.

4. Subculture in Cold War Berlin was a key site of anarchist theory and practice. The history of subculture in Berlin from 1968 through *Die Wende* and its aftermath is also a history of anarchism. This was true not just because of the prominence in these scenes of methods of direct action, but because subcultural scenes from Kommune I on explicitly sought to recover the history of anarchism and to adapt it to current circumstances. It has often been overlooked, in the face of the West German student movement's fascination with the Marxist (and often Marxist-Leninist) traditions, that anarchism occupied a significant location among the Extra-Parliamentary Opposition's various historiographical-intellectual recovery projects. As early as 1966, with the publication of Rudi Dutschke's *Bibliography of Revolutionary Socialism*, the recovery of anarchism was on the table in student circles.[16] Anarchism placed its stamp on the formation of Kommune I via Situationism, which actively opposed Bolshevist state socialism and valorized great anarchist lost causes of history such as the Spanish Revolution and the Kronstadt Uprising. Similar preoccupations filtered into the Berlin anarchist scene centered on the Hash Rebels and periodicals like *Agit 883* and *Fizz*, which read Bakunin and flirted with—and sometimes practiced—revolutionary violence.[17]

Anarchism was ideologically suited to subculture in several ways. First, it resonated with the emphasis on "doing your own thing" characteristic of the sixties' counterculture generally—imported directly into Germany via the international underground press (although individualist approaches were, of course, only one of anarchism's historical manifestations). Equally important, anarchism arose out of, and helped to bolster, a characteristic orientation of New Left movements: a rejection of the Cold War binary. It is little wonder that portions of the '68er movement influenced by Marxist-Leninist and "workerist" positions had trouble understanding subculture as a form of politics. Subversive groups in both East and West had to interact with the ruling paradigm in the two zones of the city, either directly or conceptually. And precisely because anarchism rejected systems of power based on totalizing ideologies whether explicit (Marxism as deformed by Stalinist bureaucracy), or implicit (the market economy and parliamentary democracy as the best of all possible worlds), it made sense to many activists in Cold War Berlin both as ideology and as practice.[18]

Anarchism was particularly attractive wherever activists sought to contest the primacy of Marxism-Leninism. This was true in the so-called "undogmatic" or Sponti scene in West Germany/West Berlin, which conceived of itself as a counterweight to the rise of the more or less dogmatic "K-Gruppen" from the latter half of 1968 and, as is well-known, was a key early feature of the ideological standpoint of the French-German activist Daniel Cohn-Bendit, a leading protagonist not only of the French May but of the subsequent Sponti scene in Frankfurt.[19] In the GDR, similarly, anarchism represented a site of radical-left ideas free of the stain of Stalinism. The founder of the *Umweltbibliothek*, Wolfgang Rüddenklau, was an admirer of Gustav Landauer and Peter Kropotkin, and anarchism was a significant presence in Jena as well, a hotbed of opposition to the communist regime.[20] The anarchist emphasis on direct democracy, direct action, and the right of nonparty militants to drive radical change free of a controlling bureaucracy was tailor made for resistance against a regime that abrogated to itself the right to determine the course of society without input from below.

It is worth noting, as well, that the embrace in GDR opposition circles of the murdered German Communist Rosa Luxemburg—an inheritance of a broader valorization of nonconformist and non-Bolshevik Marxism in the international New Left—was similarly a manifestation of resistance to the narrative according to which Bolshevism's successors held the keys to the revolutionary kingdom. In the famous Luxemburg demonstration of January 1988, in which members of the *Umweltbibliothek* were arrested, Luxemburg's famous statement—"Freedom is always and exclusively freedom for the one who thinks differently"—provided a bridge from revolutionary communism to the impulse to "live in truth" so influential in the revolutions of 1989.

5. *Subculture in Cold War Berlin was DIY ("Do It Yourself")*. The post-Wende scene of "autonomous urbanism"[21] involving squats, underground clubs, and cultural workshops of all types had been foreshadowed already in the West Berlin of the late 1960s/early 1970s. There, the self-organizational principle inherited from the student movement and nascent underground milieu produced something like an alternative society in West Berlin. By the beginning of the 1970s, a map of "Berlin Collectives" in the underground newspaper *Hundert Blumen* could feature initiatives including squats and alternative cultural spaces such as the Georg von Rauch and Tommy Weissbecker houses; the leftwing rock group *Ton Steine Scherben* and the agit-prop collective "Rock Front"; Homosexual Action West Berlin; feminist groups such as Brot und

Rosen; the Wagenbach publishing collective; a number of underground newspapers; the "Sozialistisches Zentrum"; the "Rote Hilfe": leftwing lawyers collectives; street-theater, teachers', and children's' groups; and various technical collectives (film and audio-visual, etc.).[22]

This effort at establishing leftwing counterinstitutions was based on principles of self-organization which, as noted already, were often explicitly, and at all times at least implicitly, anarchist in orientation. Its guiding ethos was DIY or "Do It Yourself," a term associated primarily with the punk scene(s) of the 1970s and 80s—where it referred to efforts to bypass official and top-down means of production, distribution, and sales as a form of cultural activism from below—but present in principle already in the nascent alternative milieu of the 1960s, with its underground press, leftwing publishers and bookstores, bands, and venues.[23] With the rise of the squatting scenes in West Berlin (to a lesser extent also in East Berlin), and then after 1989 in the neglected former Eastern districts where the Wall had stood, DIY became *the* principle guiding attempts to remake the face of daily life outside bourgeois property relationship and legal norms. These scenes saw attempts to make concrete the direct-democratic, self-organizational implication of sixties' radicalism, with emphasis on daily life in the spaces of the city. They saw a continuation of 1968's anticapitalist politics, made concrete in struggles for individual buildings and neighborhoods, and sharpened after 1989 in concrete struggles against gangs of neo-Nazi skinheads and football hooligans.[24]

6. *Subculture in Cold War Berlin was a site of communicative practice.* A key focus of subculture's DIY orientation was communication. Communication was a central trope of the anti-authoritarian revolt of 1968. Both the student movement and the counterculture sought in different ways to foster the creation of an alternative society (*Gegengesellschaft*) in which new political and cultural values were to replace old ones. Communication was a crucial means through which this aim was to be accomplished. Communication was intimately linked to the politics of daily life that marked the rise of communal living from 1968 on, being one of the key goals of the late 1960s' founding of communes in West Berlin. As a piece in the *Subkultur Berlin* volume published by the editors of the underground newspaper *Linkeck* put it, communes were necessary precisely "because communication is impossible in our society."[25] Communes included not only the legendary Kommune I but, among others, the Potskommune, the Kommune 99, and the Linkeck commune associated with the eponymous journal. The association of alternative living arrangements with independent cultural production was the rule rather than the exception. An early characteristic activity of the Kommune I, indeed, was the production of bootleg texts of lost revolutionary classics. These included books by members of the Frankfurt School, especially Wilhelm Reich's *Function of the Orgasm*, as well as classic texts of Marxism and anarchism. Bootleg publishing not only subverted capitalist means of production and distribution, but facilitated one of the central projects of 1968: the recovery of older revolutionary traditions for use by a new generation of radicals.

The Rotaprint machine of the Kommune I later found its way into the hands of Gerd Möbius, founding member of the radical Rote Steine theater troupe, and brother to Ralf Möbius, singer of the agit-rock band Ton Steine Scherben. The Scherben themselves were early 1970s' pioneers in DIY practices like 'zine making and recording and releasing their own music, practices that from the end of the decade would be associated with the punk movement. Characteristically, they had their own communes, first in the Tempelhofer Ufer in West Berlin, later in the rural setting of Friesenhagen in Rhineland-Palatinate. They produced their own underground newspaper dealing with issues from women's and gay liberation to Black Power and the American Indian Movement, and reprinting their manifesto "Music is a Weapon," which laid out their rationale for the connection between art and politics. A product of the Kreuzberg anarchist milieu, their lyrics questioned authority in all its forms. It is not for nothing that the lyrics of the song *Keine Macht für Niemand* ("No Power for No One") from the eponymous LP playing in the *Umweltbibliothek* on the night of the *Stasi* raid challenged the totalizing ideologies of Cold War systems of power and called for the destruction of walls both literal and figurative.[26]

The goal of creating an alternative public sphere drove oppositional efforts in the GDR as well, in the development of an artistic-bohemian underground in Prenzlauer Berg, in the culture of salons in private apartments, and in the creation of samizdat or underground literary productions. The *Umweltbibliothek* was an explicit attempt at creating communication in a society in which it was discouraged. Inspired by the so-called "flying universities" in Poland—alternative education projects based in private apartments—the *Umweltbibliothek* also shared in ideas of "rank and file democracy" associated with the alternative movement in the Federal Republic. The communicative goals of the UB were expressed by collecting and disseminating texts and information, sponsoring exhibits, and providing space for reading and discussion. With the protests against the *Stasi* raid of November, 1987, they expanded to include open criticism of the communist police state.

Characteristically, underground cultural production was key, first in the form of the *Umweltblätter*, then from October 1989 in the form of *telegraph*. The latter paper continued the *Umweltblätter*'s goal of breaking the state's monopoly on information. The themes represented within offer a snapshot of a moment of transition in which activists from the Prenzlauer Berg dissident milieu took up new themes. With the death of the East German regime, the activists of the *Umweltbibliothek* stood at a liminal point in the history of underground Berlin. The collapse of authority represented by the fall of the Wall led to the takeover of numerous buildings, an unprecedented explosion of creativity at the intersection of art, politics, and daily life, and increasingly fierce struggles over the disposition of urban space as authority sought to reconstitute itself. It is characteristic that the legend on the masthead of *telegraph* read "unfriendly to the authorities and to developers."[27] The subcultural milieu in Berlin at *Jahreswende* 1989/90 mounted a fierce challenge to both.

7. Subculture in Cold War Berlin was a vessel for more than one kind of politics. The early 90s' liminal moment of "real existing anarchy" in the historic center of Berlin underlines a key fact about subculture: it was by no means solely or exclusively leftwing.[28] Early issues of *telegraph* are heavily stamped by the battle between the left and neo-Nazi skinheads and soccer hooligans, who used the collapse of authority in central Berlin to found their own squats, from which they harassed and attack anarchists and other leftists.[29] The phenomenon of rightwing skinheads was completely familiar to the editors of *telegraph*, who, as former members of the East Berlin dissident milieu, had had to contend with vicious attacks as early as October 1987, when neo-Nazis stormed a concert in the Zionskirche by the two punk bands Element of Crime (West Berlin) and Die Firma (East Berlin). Their continued engagement with the problem of neo-Nazi violence, which reached a crescendo in the early post-Wende years, underlines again the importance of subculture not just as a site of alternative lifestyle, but of principled political engagement.

8. Subculture in Cold War Berlin was self-historicizing and self-theorizing. Subculture was not just a site of active political engagement, but of theory. Indeed, the two were intimately bound together; for the political meaning of subculture was far from fixed. Sorting through partially contradictory and overlapping concepts such as "underground," "subculture," and "counterculture" was a major preoccupation of the underground press, where the question of what it actually meant to practice politics was heavily debated. The underground journal *Song* was an early and important player in these debates, which involved, in part, attempts to decide whether subculture was a site of undifferentiated hippy-like hedonism or whether it contained within itself a critical aesthetic and political stance. The Austrian theorist Rolf Schwendter, a key advocate of the value of subculture, argued against those who dismissed youth nonconformism as a distraction from urgent political tasks. Writing in *Song*, Schwendter cited Rudi Dutschke's deployment of the terms "subculture" and "oppositional milieu," arguing that subcultures represented a living example of Herbert Marcuse's "great refusal."[30] Following up on these ideas in his 1971 book *Theory of Subculture*, Schwendter argued that in order to be considered "progressive," subcultures must possess the potential to remake society. That is, they must be political.[31]

The chief threat to subculture's emancipatory potential lay not in the hedonism of some of its agents, however, but in the potential for capitalism to turn its rebellion into a commodity. The leading West Berlin radical paper *Agit 883* recognized that subcultural identity could play a role in freeing consciousness and strengthening resistance to capitalism's demands at the level of daily life; but it also criticized the role played by hippies in the commercialization of the underground.[32] By the end of the 1960s, many recoiled from the increasingly commercial overtones of terms such as "counterculture" and "underground." The editors of one underground newspaper worried about the increasing extent to which young people were "buying their lifestyle instead of creating it themselves."[33] A radical group dedicated to radicalizing school pupils[34] worried similarly about the effects of advertising, noting that young people were beginning to play a role created for them by the system itself.[35]

In the heart of West Berlin's militant anarchist subculture, loose associations of militants calling themselves "The Blues" or "Hash Rebels" practiced subculture as a form of direct action. Fighting to protect subcultural spaces and music venues from incursions by the police, they envisioned themselves as part of a broader struggle "against the slave-system of late-capitalism."[36] Even within the West Berlin anarchist scene, the Hash Rebels' upholding drug use as a revolutionary act met with skepticism; nevertheless, their own brand of direct action intervened in broader debates about commodification. In one infamous incident, members of the Blues scene attacked the

West Berlin premier of the musical *Hair*, arguing that it represented nothing more than capitalism's theft of authentic rebel culture. "*Hair*," they argued, "only appears in the guise of the subculture in order to gratify capitalist demands."[37]

On the other side of the Wall, in the absence of cooptation via consumption, the problems of subculture were of a different order. Here, the concept of political space is crucial. In the West, a debate about the efficacy of subculture as a means of political struggle could unfold precisely because of the open-ended vistas of capitalism's cultural landscape. To be sure, groups including the Blues faced and fought against state repression, such as the police raids on clubs like the Zodiak Arts Lab that formed part of the back story to the group's attack on the premier of *Hair*.[38] In the broader youth scene, however, the lines between *acting* the part and *looking* the part—in a scene based heavily on markers of visual identity made available in the first place by capitalism (e.g., blue jeans)—were thin indeed. Capitalism's "tolerance," in this context, could indeed be "repressive" from the standpoint of militants worried about recuperation. In the East, by contrast, the state waged an intermittent but durable war against youth nonconformism, basing its actions on the assumption that elements of subcultural habitus—e.g., long hair—were sufficient evidence of antistate views.

From the cultural crackdown after the Eleventh Plenum of the Central Committee of the Socialist Unity Party (ZK der SED) in December 1965 (targeting among other things rock groups and their fans), to the regime's attempts to police the after-effects of the Prague Spring,[39] to the intermittent crackdowns of the Honecker years, the East German regime could never make up its mind about whether allegiance to cultural forms originating in the West were consistent with loyal citizenship.[40] As a consequence, it jeopardized the very loyalty it sought to protect.[41] In contrast to the "repressive tolerance" adduced by Herbert Marcuse in the West, the communist regime in East Germany practiced a "repressive *repression*," inadvertently charging the symbols of subcultural belonging with rich political meaning. The resulting politics were often merely a politics of simple refusal, as opposed to a program of broader social revolution; nevertheless, the more totalizing the claims of the regime, the greater the explosive power of even small symbols of resistance to it.

Even if the state helped forge oppositional communities through its opposition to symbols of subcultural habitus, this does not mean that the GDR was immune to debates about the value of subculture like those in the West. The East bloc generally, as Robert Gildea and others have shown, was rich with such debates.[42] In K1-Ost, for example, there existed considerable tension between the needs of subculture and the needs of politics; or more precisely, between the desire to partake of the youth revolution in appearance, music, and mores, and the need to be politically active. In the later phase of the commune, the goal of establishing a "common political praxis" came to subsume all others, with the emphasis shifting to a study of classic texts of Marxism-Leninism and support for Third World liberation. The latter aspect of the "global" proved no solution to the problems of the local, when Fidel Castro's statement of support for the crushing of the Prague Spring exposed the limitations of the Third World revolution as a model for political action in the GDR. The search for political effectiveness eventually led some communards into the arms of the party, while others fled the country for new lives in the West.[43] To be sure, the pressure placed on the commune by the Stasi made its situation unique; but in another way, its travails represented merely another face of the dilemma experienced in the West, around what politics was, and whether subculture—in this case involving group-psychoanalytic explorations on the model of Kommune I—represented a legitimate form of politics, or a diversion from it.

9. *Subculture in Cold War Berlin had the power to shake the state.* We know from the scholarship on official responses to the new youth culture surrounding rock and roll in the late 1950s/early 1960s how much even the largely unpolitical subcultures challenged state power.[44] Regimes in both Germanies, but especially in the East, politicized music and subculture "from above," rendering them threats even when no threat was intended. As we have seen, subcultures were also capable of politicizing themselves "from below."[45] Sometimes this was with explicitly negative aims, as in the case of rightwing radical skinheads in both divided and in post-unification Germany. More often, it was with emancipatory aims, as in the groups fighting against the twin oppressions of communist dictatorship and Cold War anticommunism on both sides of the Wall. Even here, in West Berlin, the potential existed for violent extremism, as in the example of a subcultural-cum-terrorist group like the Movement 2nd June.[46]

In the case of a group such as the *Umweltbibliothek*, activists more or less forced into a subcultural role by the totalizing demands of the state exercised an outsized influence. The *Umweltbibliothek* was tiny compared to citizens' opposition groups such as Initiative for Peace and Human Rights and New Forum. It existed in an uneasy relationship with the Protestant Church in its dual role as protector and arbiter of opposition in the GDR. But it is precisely the *Umweltbibliothek*'s atypicalness that is the point: its activists were only one of a succession of small subcultural avant-garde groupings that helped shape postwar German politics and society over a period of crucial decades. Such groups acted alongside—or often, subversively within—larger mass movements, shaping and in turn being shaped by them. Operating mostly or entirely outside formal political institutions, they drew their strength from alternative cultural-political milieux out of which they sprang. Yet, as the case of the *Umweltbibliothek* suggests, they held the ability to shake the power of the state, or at a minimum, to place their stamp on the face of daily life in the urban environment in such a way as to challenge state power locally.

Conclusion

The story of subculture in Berlin does not come to a close with the end of the Cold War. Indeed, some of the most interesting developments occurred during the interregnum between the fall of the Wall in November 1989 and German reunification in October of the following year. The anarchic "Wonderland" created by squatters and artists in the ruins of central Berlin after the dismantling of the Wall, commemorated in recent exhibitions and publications, was in many ways a culmination of the politics of daily life that marked subcultural praxis on both sides of the wall over the previous three decades.[47] That scene, unfolding in now-legendary squats such as Im Eimer and Tacheles, was driven by many of the young artists and musicians who had been active on the margins of GDR society. Suddenly freed, if only for a brief moment, from the constraints of state authority, they erased the boundaries between art and daily life in a way that called to mind the Situationist-inspired slogan of May 1968 in Paris: "All Power to the Imagination." The swift reassertion of state authority and capitalist property relationships, marked by violent struggles with police over the clearing of squatted buildings and city blocks, brought the initial phase of this spontaneous utopia quickly to an end. Its after-effects lingered throughout the 1990s, however, and indeed, continue to the present day.

The techno scene that grew up in the ruins of post-*Wende* Berlin inherited many of the historical values and practices of subculture, even if it lacked the explicit politics that, as we have seen, characterized subculture from the mid-1960s on. A genuine mass movement, it became a vehicle for the intermixing of "Ossies" and "Wessies" in a sort of "reunification from below."[48] Spontaneous and ephemeral, it focused above all on autonomy, claiming freedom from all structures, including those of the totalizing ideological systems which had left their mark on the city in whose ruined districts they danced. Was the liberating subcultural experience of mass parties in refurbished buildings held together through hard work and creativity—hallmarks of the DIY spirit central to the active brand of subculture characteristic of Cold War Berlin—a form of politics? Certainly, the movement's challenge to capitalist property relations must be seen as at least implicitly political. Who in the second decade of the twenty-first century can imagine a scene that sought to occupy and use buildings without trying to own or sell them? The striking absence of a spirit of speculation in the scene suggests, at a minimum, a different mental world than today's, even if it reflected an exhaustion with ideology as much as an embrace of it. To be sure, as housing shortages and gentrification continue to be hot-button issues, the politics of urban space in Berlin is not going away. To what extent the conditions of neoliberal austerity might produce, in reunified Berlin, the active variety of subculture that reigned during the Cold War will be the subject of a future historian.

Notes

1   Wolfgang Rüddenklau, *Störenfried: DDR-Opposition 1986–1989* (Berlin, 1992).
2   Letter to Erich Honecker, undated, Robert Havemann Gesellschaft.
3   Umwälzzentrum, "An die Freunde und Freundinnen von der Umweltbibliothek," undated, Robert Havemann Gesellschaft.
4   Rüddenklau, *Störenfried*, p. 158.
5   See Thomas Hecken, *Gegenkultur und Avantgarde 1950–1970: Situationisten, Beatniks, 68er* (Tübingen, 2006); Detlef Siegfried, *Sound der Revolte: Studien zur Kulturrevolution um 1968* (Weinheim, 2008); Detlef Siegfried, *Time Is on My Side: Konsum und Politik in der westdeutschen Jugendkultur der 60er Jahre* (Göttingen, 2006). Detlef Siegfried, "Protest am Markt. Gegenkultur in der Konsumgesellschaft um 1968," in: Christina von Hodenberg und Detlef Siegfried (eds.), *Wo 1968 liegt. Reform und Revolte in der Geschichte der Bundesrepublik* (Göttingen, 2006); Jens Gehret, *Gegenkultur: von Woodstock bis Tunix 1969–1981* (Asslar, 1985).

6   See, for example, Dick Hebdige, *Subculture: The Meaning of Style* (London, 1979).

7   See, for example, Andy Bennett, *Cultures of Popular Music* (Buckingham/ Philadelphia, 2001); James Lull, *Media, Communication, Culture. A Global Approach* (Cambridge, 1995).

8   Dieter Kunzelmann, *Leisten Sie keinen Widerstand! Bilder aus meinem Leben* (Berlin, 1998), p. 49.

9   Ibid.

10   See Timothy S. Brown, "A Tale of two Communes: The Private and the Political in Divided Berlin, 1967–1973," in: Martin Klimke, Jacco Pekelder, and Joachim Scharloth (eds.), *Between Prague Spring and French May 1968: Opposition and Revolt in Europe, 1960–1980* (New York/ Oxford, 2011).

11   See Timothy S. Brown, "1968 in the German Democratic Republic," in Martin Klimke and Joachim Scharloth (eds.), *1968 in Europe: A Handbook on National Perspectives and Transnational Dimensions of 1960/70s European Protest Movements*. Transnational History Series (London, 2008).

12   On publics, see Thomas Olesen, "Transnational Publics: New Spaces of Social Movement Activism and the Problem of Global Long-Sightedness," *Current Sociology* 53 (May 2005), 419–40. See also Laila Abu-Er-Rub, Jennifer Altehenger, and Sebastian Gehrig, "The Transcultural Travels of Trends: An Introductory Essay," *Transcultural Studies* 2 (2011), https://heiup.uni-heidelberg.de/journals/index.php/transcultural/article/viewFile/9073/3112.

13   See Florian Havemann "68er Ost," *UTOPIE kreativ* 164 (June 2004), pp. 544–56, p. 546; Frank Havemann, in Rainer Land and Ralf Possekel, *Fremde Welten. Die gegensätzliche Deutung der DDR durch SED-Reformer und Bürgerbewegung in den 80er Jahren* (Berlin, 1998), p. 220; Paul Kaiser, "Kommune 'K1-Ost', Ostberlin," unpublished radio broadcast manuscript for Deutschlandfunk-Radio, copy in possession of the author, p. 28; Ulrich Enzensberger, *Die Jahre der Kommune I* (Cologne, 2004), p. 233; Kunzelmann, *Leisten Sie keinen Widerstand!*, p. 91.

14   See Ulrike Poppe, "'The Support We Needed': Petra Kelly and the East German Opposition," in Heinrich Böll Foundation (ed.), *Petra Kelly. A Remembrance* (Berlin, 2007), pp. 70–3, p. 73.

15   Alex Vasudevan, "Autonomous Urbanisms and the Right to the City: The Spatial Politics of Squatting in Berlin, 1968–2012," in Bart van der Steen et al. (eds.), *The City Is Ours. Squatting and Autonomous Movements in Europe from the 1970s to the Present* (Oakland, 2014), p. 131.

16   Rudi Dutschke, *Ausgewählte und kommentierte Bibliographie des revolutionären Sozialismus von Karl Marx bis in die Gegenwart Ausgewählte und kommentierte Bibliographie des revolutionären Sozialismus von K. Marx bis in die Gegenwart* (Heidelberg/Frankfurt/Hanover/Berlin, 1969).

17   See Michael Baumann, *How It All Began* (Vancouver, 1977).

18   See Markus Henning and Rolf Raasch, *Neoanarchismus in Deutschland. Enstehung. Verlauf. Konfliktlinien* (Berlin, 2005). See also Timothy Scott Brown, "The Sixties in the City: Avantgardes and Urban Rebels in New York, London, and West Berlin," *Journal of Social History* 46 (2013) 4, pp. 817–42.

19   Daniel Cohn-Bendit and Gabriel Cohn-Bendit, *Obsolete Communism. The Left-Wing Alternative* (London, 2000) (originally published 1968).

20   Rüddenklau, *Störenfried*.

21   Vasudevan, "Autonomous Urbanisms," p. 132.

22   *Hundert Blumen*, March 1973, APO Archiv Berlin.

23   Here, see Alissa Bellotti "Style Identities and Individualization in 1980s East and West Germany," in Carter, Palmowski, and Schreiter, *German Division as Shared Experience* (New York, 2019).

24   For a vivid depiction of this moment, see Ingo Hasselbach, *Führer-Ex: Memoirs of a Former Neo-Nazi* (New York, 1996).

25   Hartmut Sander and Ulrich Christians (eds.), *Subkultur Berlin. Kommunen Rocker subversiven Gruppen* (Darmstadt, 1969).

26   "Im Süden, im Osten, im Norden, im Westen, es sind überall dieselben, die uns erpressen"; "Reißen wir die Mauern ein, die uns trennen."

27   *telegraph*, December 21, 1990, Robert Havemann Gesellschaft, Opposition, UeG 1/1.

28   On this score, Timothy Scott Brown, "Subcultures, Pop Music and Politics: Skinheads and Nazi Rock in England and Germany," *Journal of Social History* 38 (2004) 1, pp. 157–78.

29   "Ausschreitungen von Nazis und Hooligans am 20.4.," *telegraph* 8, April 26, 1990, pp. 6–9.

30   Rolf Schwendter, "Zur Theorie der Subkultur," *Song. Deutsche Underground-Zeitschrift* 8 (1968).

31   Quoted in Richard Hinton Thomas and Keith Bullivant, *Literature in Upheaval. West German writers and the challenge of the 1960s* (Manchester, 1974), pp. 167–8.

32   See "Sind Hippies Kulturrevolutionäre?," *Agit 883*, 35, October 9, 1969.

33   Ibid.

34   Aktionszentrum Unabhängiger und Sozialistischer Schüler (Action Center for Independent and Socialist School Pupils—AUSS.

35   "Sexualität nach der Sexwelle," *konkret* 17, August 11, 1969, p. 20.

36   "Scheisst auf diese Gesellschaft," flier originally distributed in West Berlin the summer of 1969, reprinted in *Gefundene Fragmente, 1967–1980*, vol. 1 (Berlin, 2003), p. 9.

37   "Ist *Hair* Subkultur?," *Gefunde Fragmente 1967–1980*, p. 24.

38   Ibid.

39   Thomas Klein, *"Frieden und Gerechtigkeit!": die Politisierung der Unabhängigen Friedensbewegung in Ost-Berlin während der 80er Jahre* (Cologne/Weimar, 2007), p. 49.

40   See Michael Rauhut, *Beat in der Grauzone: DDR-Rock 1964 bis 1972. Politik und Alltag* (Berlin, 1993).

41   In Thomas Klein's words: "Measures to nip a 'cultural opposition' in the bud led instead precisely to its development." Klein, *"Frieden und Gerechtigkeit!,"* p. 53.

42   See Robert Gildea et al., *Europe's 1968: Voices of Revolt* (Oxford, 2013).

43   Paul Kaiser and Claudia Petzold, "Perlen vor die Säue: Eine Boheme im Niemandsland," in Paul Kaiser and Claudia Petzold, *Boheme und Diktatur in der DDR: Gruppen, Konflikte, Quartiere, 1970–1989* (Berlin, 1997), pp. 13–41, p. 33.

44   Uta Poiger, *Jazz, Rock, and Rebels. Cold War Politics and American Culture in a Divided Germany* (Berkeley, 2000); Mark Fenemore, *Sex, Thugs and Rock 'n; Roll. Teenage Rebels in Cold-War East Germany* (New York/ Oxford, 2007).

45   On the distinction between these two types of politicization, see Detlef Siegfried, "Unsere Woodstocks: Jugendkultur, Rockmusik und gesellschaftlicher Wandel um 1968," in *Rock!*, pp. 52–61.

46 Wolfgang Kraushaar, *Die Bombe im Jüdischen Gemeindehaus* (Hamburg, 2005).
47 See, for example, Anke Fesel and Chris Keller (eds.), *Berlin Wonderland. Wild Years Revisited 1990–1996* (Berlin, 2014).
48 See Felix Denk and Sven von Thülen, *Der Klang der Familie: Berlin, Techno and the Fall of the Wall* (Books on Demand, 2014).

8

Living in the Shadow of the Wall: Berlin's Turkish Community, 1961–89

Sarah Thomsen Vierra

When Sevim Özel decided she wanted to get her driver's license, she felt a little concerned. She had come to West Berlin in the mid-1960s, along with a train carriageful of her fellow countrywomen, to work for Siemens. Soon after, she married and started a family, living in the working-class district of Wedding. Between working for various German companies and taking care of her growing family, Özel had had little time for anything else. When she did decide to learn to drive, she felt unsure that she knew the city well enough to drive in it. A coworker tried to ease her anxiety, saying, "Özel, no worries. Wherever you go, the Wall comes to you. No, you shouldn't get lost."[1]

Much of the scholarship on the history of West Germany's *Gastarbeiterprogramm* recognizes the importance of Cold War politics and economics in the inception and course of the temporary foreign worker program.[2] Yet for Özel, the Wall—and, by extension, the Cold War—also played an especially critical role in shaping the lives of Turkish guest workers and their families in West Berlin. While labor shortages in the wake of World War Two prompted West Germany to embark on a series of bilateral labor contracts with southern and southeastern European countries, it was not until the construction of the Berlin Wall effectively halted immigration from the German Democratic Republic (GDR) that the Federal Republic (FRG) included Turkey in the guest worker program. Turks concentrated in Berlin in part due to their late entrance into the guest worker program. Furthermore, due to its location and in spite of the government's efforts to attract German residents, Berlin suffered from labor shortages that big businesses decided to address through the importation of foreign workers.

When Turkish workers started looking beyond the company-run dormitories for housing, they ran up against Berlin's housing shortage, and struggled to find apartments that were both affordable and available, which led them to the areas of the city least attractive to most Berliners: those bordering the Wall. Kreuzberg, Wedding, Neukölln, and, to a somewhat lesser extent, Tiergarten came to be characterized by their "foreign" populations, which, in turn, contributed to a broader struggle over the identity of the city.

In this chapter, I examine how the Wall affected the lives and experiences of Turkish Berliners. How did the Wall create the environment that prompted their "invitation" to the city? How did it shape their settlement, and what influence did it exert on their daily lives as Berliners? Finally, I reflect on how the fall of the Wall impacted the identity and rootedness of Berlin's Turkish community. Ultimately, by putting the Wall—both as a physical site and a symbol of the broader Cold War—at the center, we see that, although the Wall initially cast its long shadow over Berlin's Turkish community, over time that community itself began to overshadow the Wall.

The Cold War, West Berlin, and Guest Worker Recruitment

At the close of World War Two, the tensions between the Allies that had been growing in part due to disagreements as to what was to be done with postwar Germany found a physical outlet in the occupation of its capital city. The four zones of occupation in Berlin increasingly merged into two: those administered by Great Britain, France, and the United States and the territory under the control of the Soviet Union. With the signing of separate constitutions in 1949, Germany officially split into two states, and the boundaries of the occupation zones between East and West became international borders. The capital city, as well, divided into East and West, but constituted a special case, as West Berlin lay deep within the GDR. Its status as an outpost of West Germany, and of the "West" in the broader Cold War context, lent to West Berlin a geopolitical significance and symbolism that would be a central part of its identity for the decades that followed.

West Berlin's location also meant that it continued to serve as a point of entry for the many Germans on the eastern side of the border who sought to flee to the Federal Republic. The closing of the inner German border in 1952 and the GDR's institution of a new passport control system at the end of 1957 further channeled East German emigration through the Berlin loophole. Over the course of the 1950s, some 3 million people used the unique status and location of the city to escape life in the GDR for the political freedoms and career prospects the West offered.[3] The damage that such large-scale emigration inflicted on the economy as well as the political image of the new East German state prompted its government to construct an imposing physical barrier along the border with West Berlin. The "Anti-Fascist Protective Rampart," which the GDR argued was defensive rather than restrictive, effectively halted the East–West emigration and isolated West Berlin still further—cutting off West Germany and particularly West Berlin from a much-needed source of labor.

Labor shortages in West Germany had been only partially answered by the inpouring of Germans from the east. While women could have been recruited to address the shortages, as in wartime, West German politicians wanted to avoid the large-scale employment of women into fulltime positions. Keeping women out of the workforce would, they argued, maintain the traditional gender roles necessary to a healthy society—in contrast to the labor practices across their eastern border.[4] The answer West German officials and industrialists arrived at was a temporary labor program, euphemistically termed a *Gastarbeiter* program, that would recruit and employ foreign workers on a limited-term basis.[5] Through the "guest worker" program, the Federal Republic sought to address manpower shortages with cheap migrant workers who then could be sent back to their countries of origin should their employment no longer benefit the West German economy. The FRG could also avoid the recruitment of German women as well as paying out much social welfare support to these guest workers, who would return home before they would be eligible for retirement benefits. Finally, participants in the program would develop skills in agriculture, mining, industry, and construction, which they would in turn use to the benefit of their sending countries' economies.

The *Gastarbeiter* program officially began with a bilateral labor contract between the Federal Republic and Italy in 1955, and was extended five years later to include Spain and Greece. And then, in the late summer of 1961, the East German government erected the Berlin Wall, removing a critical source of manpower from the West German economy. West Berlin felt the effects of this development keenly. While people across the Federal Republic and the Western world considered West Berlin as an outpost of political and economic freedom, few, given its physical location, wanted to live there. Government support for businesses and individuals only went so far in attracting in-migration from the Federal Republic, and the construction of the Wall cut off both the influx of migrants as well as East Berlin commuters. Thus, in October 1961, the FRG extended the *Gastarbeiter* program to the Republic of Turkey.[6]

While Turkey was the first non-European country to participate in the *Gastarbeiter* program, its status as a Cold War ally and its recent evolution into a multiparty democracy demonstrated its existing and significant political connections to the FRG and the broader Western world. The United States and Great Britain saw the Soviet Union's efforts to extend its borders into eastern Anatolia and assume control of the Turkish Straits in 1945 as evidence of its dangerous expansionism, recognized the county's strategic importance, and began to draw it into a Cold War alliance. In 1947, the United States codified this growing relationship in the Truman Doctrine, which promised foreign aid to strengthen Turkey against the looming Soviet threat and insure it was not the first of the Middle Eastern states to fall to communism. Five years later, Turkey became a full-fledged member of the North Atlantic Treaty Organization (NATO). During this time, Turkey underwent significant internal political reform, resulting in the formation of an opposition party and the peaceful election and transfer of power from the longtime ruling Republican People's Party to the Democratic Party.[7] In 1960, a military coup d'état that sought to reassert the secularist and statist policies of the Republic's founder, Mustafa Kemal Atatürk, interrupted this experiment in a more open, democratic system. From a foreign policy perspective, inviting Turkey to be a part of this until-then exclusively European community could both reinforce those Cold War ties as well as influence the state's internal political and economic developments.[8]

Once the papers of the bilateral labor agreement were signed, German businesses had to persuade Turkish workers to come to West Germany, and to West Berlin in particular. Siemens' efforts demonstrate how recruitment reflected both perceptions about what would appeal to prospective workers from developing countries as well as representations of West Berlin's Cold War identity. In promotional literature from the mid-1960s, Siemens stressed the character of the city at least as much as of the company itself. One brochure describes a stroll down Kurfüstendamm, where "a thousand illuminated advertisements glow," and one could see how so many of their landsmen "have found a well-paying workplace in this capital city of the free western world." The brochure goes on to list the many opportunities for enjoyment in the city: large department stores, modern squares and transportation, rivers, parks, restaurants, cafes, churches, theater, movies, dance halls, and so on.[9] The images of the brochure similarly convey an image of West Berlin as an exciting, urban, and progressive place to make (and spend) money. Photographs show city streets at night illuminated by streetlights, advertisements, headlights, and light pouring out of restaurant and club windows. The streets are crowded with people on foot, in cars and busses, sitting down at cafes. Modern architectures—apartment buildings, theaters, and Siemens' own factories—dominate the images.[10]

In selling the city, Siemens found that those same attributes recruiters felt would appeal to prospective guest workers were also those central to West Berlin's identity as a Cold War capital. The twin messages of prosperity and freedom echo throughout the text and the images of the brochure. The stress on modernity, consumption, and enjoyment reinforces the Cold War perception of what anyone could find in West Berlin, not on the other side of the Wall. West Berlin was a "capital city of the free western world"; East Berlin was not. The Wall then proved central to Siemens' recruitment strategy; it helped to create the economic conditions for implementing the guest worker program, and strengthened the West Berlin identity that helped to sell it.

Siemens' and other companies' appeals to the economically motivated and adventure-seeking prospective guest worker resonated with many in Turkey, both in terms of what they were looking for in their own working goals and in what (little) they already knew about West Germany in general and West Berlin in particular. Information about the city came back to potential workers through business and governmental literature, but also word-of-mouth from family and friends already working there and in the form of consumer goods.[11] Leyla Sezer knew slightly more about the city when she and her friend traveled to Istanbul to sign up for the program, as her husband was already working in West Germany at the time. When asked by their taxi driver why they would go to Berlin, Sezer answered: "Because in Berlin's there's the Wall, there's a lot of money."[12] Mehmet Korkmaz was working in construction in Düsseldorf when he happened to meet a Turkish engineer who ran a construction firm in West Berlin. "The Germans themselves weren't interested in going to Berlin," Korkmaz recalled, "but for us, it didn't matter. We wanted to make money." When the engineer confirmed that Korkmaz and his friend could earn almost double their current wage in West Berlin, and offered them the train fare for the journey, the decision was easily made. He and his friend became two of the first fifty Turkish guest workers to officially enter the city.[13]

People like Sezer and Korkmaz were getting the message: West Berlin was a city rife with money-making opportunities, and that somehow those opportunities were linked to the Wall. For Korkmaz, his experiences in West Germany had begun to give him insight into the attitudes of his German coworkers, and he saw their reluctance to go to West Berlin as a chance for him to earn a substantially higher wage. Sezer's perception of the city, possibly influenced by her husband's knowledge of West Berlin, was less developed, but no less accurate. "There's a Wall," and somehow that Wall created an opportunity for young people like herself to earn some good money and even have an adventure in the process. And so, by train and later by plane, Turks came by the tens, the hundreds, and ultimately, the thousands to live and work in the city with the Wall.

Living in Cold War West Berlin

Once in West Berlin, Turkish guest workers soon encountered the ideological contexts and physical consequences of the city's Cold War status. The governments of both West Germany and Turkey feared that the new and unsettling experiences associated with migration would render the workers susceptible to communist propaganda and agitators from the East. In response, they set out to ensure their workers' anti-communism. In 1961, the *Presse- und Informationsamt der Bundesregierung* (Press and Information Ministry, BPA) convened a meeting of various involved West German ministries to develop ways to, as a representative from the *Deutsche Gewerkschaftsbund* (German Trade Union Federation, DGB) put it, "protect guest workers from the communist temptation."[14] Ultimately, those present decided to produce newspapers for the different national groups represented in the *Gastarbeiter* program, which would be published in their native languages and work to "immunize" workers against the threat of communism. While the initial focus was on producing newspapers for the Italian and Spanish guest workers, who constituted the largest populations in the program, the BPA soon saw the benefit of a Turkish-language periodical. In November 1962, Dr. Johannes Sobotta of the BPA wrote an internal memo in which he advocated his agency's financial support for a Turkish-language newspaper with a monthly publication of 10,000 copies. That paper, named *Anadolu Gazette*, would be headed up by Erdoğan Olcayto, a Turkish journalist and entrepreneur living in Darmstadt. Although Olcayto had wanted total control over the paper, the BPA instead hired him as managing editor and gave final responsibility for the paper to the International Committee for Information and Social Activity (CIAS), a coalition of European anti-communist groups.[15]

The story of *Anadolu Gazette* is important, because it demonstrates the concern of both the West German and Turkish governments over the susceptibility of guest workers to communist influence and provides a concrete example of how the FRG sought to battle the Cold War on its domestic front. Its first issue appeared in June of 1963 across the Federal Republic, available at German businesses, Turkish firms, guest worker organizations, and governmental offices. Initially, relatively few copies of the newspaper were sent to West Berlin, but as the Turkish guest worker population there grew, so, too, did the stack of *Anadolu Gazette* that the CIAS shipped off from Bonn each month. In September 1963, fewer than three dozen issues were sent to West Berlin, while just two years later that number had reached just over 1,000.[16] But newspapers were not just making it to West Berlin; the city itself was making it into the pages of the newspaper. The inaugural issue, for example, featured a photograph of a brother and sister attempting to play through a barbed-wire fence, accompanied by the phrase "the Berlin Catastrophe."[17] In an article presenting a general history and introduction to

Germany in the January 1964 edition, Olcayto highlighted the existence of the Berlin Wall. Referring to it as "the Wall of Shame," the editor described how "thousands of refugees [had chosen] freedom" from East Germany through the city of Berlin.[18] Later articles would continue this focus on the Wall as a mark of shame and East Berliners as suffering under their ruling communist regime. Although participants in the endeavor later felt that they had overreacted to the communist threat to guest workers, their efforts to shape the mindset of those workers, particularly in regard to the situation of Berlin, reveal how the Cold War permeated the ideological and symbolic contexts in which the Turkish guest workers, newly arrived to West Berlin, found themselves.

Yet, the consequences of the Cold War that Turkish guest workers encountered were in no way limited to the symbolic. Rather, the Cold War shaped their experiences with the city in very real, physical ways. The situation of housing is particularly instructive. When guest workers first moved to West Berlin, most found housing in a company-run *Wohnheim* (dormitory). An extension of the workplace, the *Wohnheim* offered foreign workers basic amenities (shared bedrooms, bathrooms, kitchens, and some areas for recreation), but were highly regulated spaces and did not allow spouses or families to live together. As Turkish guest workers found their stay in West Berlin stretching on longer than initially anticipated, many chose to start families or to bring their families from Turkey to live with them. That decision to establish a family-centered household necessitated a move out of the company *Wohnheim* and into German neighborhoods. Finding decent housing, however, proved quite difficult.

Guest workers were not alone in their struggle for adequate housing. The city of West Berlin, from the immediate postwar period until well into the 1970s and even into the early 1980s, faced a significant housing shortage. Many of the city's apartment buildings were in poor condition, whether as a result of the war, neglect, or both, and housing in districts that abutted the Wall was even worse. And, while finding adequate housing provided a challenge to any Berliner, for Turks securing a decent apartment that was available *to them* proved that much more difficult. Their exhausting and fruitless search for housing often met with discrimination. One man described his efforts to find an apartment for his family to an interview in 1980: checking the *Berliner Zeitung* each morning for listings, having a German-speaking friend make the telephone inquiries, visiting the *Wohnungsamt* (housing office). After all these efforts, he, his wife, and his four children who joined him in 1974 were still living in a single-room apartment with no rental contract. In other cases, landlords made the discrimination much more blatant by simply specifying "no foreigners" in their advertisements.[19]

City officials were not blind to the housing problem; indeed large-scale renovation projects were a central focus of city government in the postwar decades. The motivation behind postwar renovation in West Berlin lay in two separate, yet related factors. First, the idea of creating a more balanced social space in the city had been a political value in urban planning since the early nineteenth century. In the context of postwar West Berlin, the city government saw *Sanierung* (redevelopment or renovation) as part of the project of "rehabilitating the moral character of West German society within the family/domestic sphere."[20] Connected to this goal was the drive to make West Berlin— as a "capital city of the free Western world"—a showpiece of the West. Deep inside the communist East, "Berlin (west)" needed to reflect its identity as a member of the progressive and successful western world. Crumbling tenements did not project this image. And so, the city embarked on a massive *Sanierung* project. While much of the focus was on the districts on the outskirts of the city and resulted in large-scale building projects like Gropiusstadt in Neukölln and Märkisches Viertel in Reinickendorf, city planners also turned their attention to the degraded nineteenth-century *Mietskasernen* (tenements) in the inner city districts of Kreuzberg and Wedding. Here, however, they met with considerable resistance.

Part of the resistance encountered by the government in its efforts to refashion the city sprung from on the economic ramifications of *Sanierung*. Rather than ease the housing shortage, *Sanierung* exacerbated it. The new buildings had fewer apartments than the ones they replaced, and the rents increased. Additionally, the older housing was being torn down more quickly than it was being replaced. The choice to pursue such broad-scale renovation projects was influenced partly by the ideological goals for the new housing, but also by the financial considerations of the companies in charge of the project—profit margins were higher for complete destruction and rebuilding than they were for the renovation of existing housing stock.[21] Throughout the 1960s and 1970s, neighborhood organizations and individual activists began to organize and try to change the course of the city's renovation strategies. In 1979, frustrated by their lack of success and by the West Berlin Senate's continued forced evictions, activist groups in Kreuzberg, beginning with Citizens' Initiative SO 36, began occupying buildings slated for demolition. The movement spread rapidly, so that, by the early 1980s, "only two of West Berlin's neighborhoods did *not* contain illegally occupied buildings," and nearly half of the 122 attempts at squatting a building had taken place in Kreuzberg.[22]

While a diverse group, participants in the squatters' movement considered "the prevailing world order and particularly U.S. hegemony in the West" a root cause of their struggles in West Berlin.[23] For some, this meant a continued focus on local politics and housing issues. Others adopted a more national and international perspective, seeing their activities as a rejection of West Germany's capitalism and militarism, which they saw as being nurtured by their country's close relationship with the United States. In the 1970s, this took the form of anti-Vietnam war protest, and in the 1980s, demonstrations against US intervention in El Salvador and Nicaragua.[24] Yet, the leftist activists' focus on multiethnic solidarity and anti-imperialism appears to have been stronger on the level of international discourse than it was on the ground in Kreuzberg, where their relationship with their Turkish neighbors was more ambivalent. While the most inclusive efforts of German Berliners included advocacy for both housing and political rights for "foreigners," these still "relied on a familiar conceptual framework of two homogeneous and culturally distinct groups."[25] More often leftist activists failed to take into account migrants' unequal and uncertain political footing and cast Turks squarely in the role as victims.[26] Further, the few references to the Turkish population in the squatters' scene literature employed common stereotypes, including the ever-popular "flood" metaphor. In one article, the writer cast Turkish guest workers as allies of the West German state, and therefore an enemy to fight against for the continued existence of Kreuzberg.[27]

Not all reactions to the city's renovation plans were as politically charged and adversarial as in Kreuzberg. Quieter forms of resistance also formed in Wedding, another of the city's districts that abutted the Wall and whose residents—including a large population of Turks—suffered from degraded and dilapidated housing. The example of *Sanierung* in the Sparrplatz neighborhood of Wedding demonstrates how city officials' ideas about the identity and aesthetic of the city were influenced and redirected, in part, by Turkish residents. While not directly bordered by the Wall, the Sparrplatz neighborhood experienced similar consequences after its construction. Many of the younger, more upwardly mobile German residents moved out, the elderly and *Sozialschwache* remained behind and were joined in increasing numbers in the 1970s by Turkish guest workers and their families. The city and companies involved in the *Sanierung* efforts made the decision in 1979/1980 to demolish and rebuild the apartment buildings around Sparrplatz, but did not immediately inform the neighborhood's residents of this decision. The residents garnered their first information about the extent of the city's plans when a friend (and a fellow member of an antinuclear power organization) tipped off a local resident. While the city initially resisted efforts at further information, the residents of Sparrplatz eventually learned the extent to which their neighborhood would be affected.[28]

Dissatisfied with the city's plans for their neighborhood, residents formed a tenants' initiative (*Mieter-Initiative-Sparrplatz*) through which they worked to educate their neighbors of the consequences of *Sanierung* and petition various city offices involved in the process. Eventually, their efforts resulted in the city's creation of a new office, the *Büro für stadtteilnahe* Sozialplanung (Office for District-Level Social Planning, BfsS), which would act as a liaison between residents and the government in matters dealing with the social implications of infrastructure. Turkish residents comprised a significant percentage of the neighborhood's population, were disproportionally affected by the *Sanierung*, and faced state-led eviction with the "opportunity" to relocate to more expensive apartments in Märkisches Viertel.[29] The tenants' initiative and the BfsS were aware of their situation and considered the inclusion and participation of the neighborhood's Turkish residents a critical part of the process. One of the tenants' initiative founders recalled: "[W]e wanted to achieve a better situation for the residents […], we couldn't care less, which nationality they were."[30] The BfsS representative, himself of Turkish background, saw the need to establish trust with the Turkish residents, and visited many personally to talk with them about an alternate plan for the *Sanierung*, and help them move past their skepticism.[31] Flyers announcing community meetings and containing updates related to the *Sanierung* were published in German and Turkish, including one that invited all those interested to attend the monthly meetings.[32] Ultimately, the residents and the city came to a compromise solution that allowed for the demolition of some buildings and the renovation of others, and the community organization and BfsS continued to work on developing the neighborhood to meet the needs of all of its residents.

Turkish Berliners' daily lives, therefore, continued to be influenced by the broader Cold War and the physical reality of the Wall after their initial recruitment to work in the city. They congregated in the neighborhoods available to them—those bordering the Wall and therefore no longer appealing to many German Berliners. The city's plans to renovate these neighborhoods, to create spaces more in line with their social goals and with West Berlin's Cold War status, brought Turkish residents into more contact with their German neighbors and with the state, encouraging the cross-cultural cooperation and the beginnings of West Berlin's multiculturalism. And, in part because so many of the apartments slated for demolition were inhabited (and many of those by Turks), the city was forced to reassess its plans and renovate existing buildings rather than replace them, preserving a part of the city's architectural history. Yet, even as Turkish Berliners were causing the city to preserve part of its traditional identity, they were also challenging Germans to consider West Berlin in a new way and grapple with its internal divisions rather than its international importance.

International Identity, Internal Divisions

The division of Berlin prompted the West to invest heavily in the Western sector in order to secure it and to create it as a showpiece of Western democracy, progress, and capitalism. West Berlin's identity, then, was in large part defined by its Cold War position and symbolic significance. It was a German city, but also an international one—a "capital city of the free western world." President John F. Kennedy's identification with Berliners in the famous speech during his visit to the city in 1963 exemplifies the significance of Cold War Berlin; symbolically, the fate of its citizens and the fate of the West were linked. For West Germans and the rest of the Western world, West Berlin was important because of where it was and what it stood for. And for West Berliners, that internationally recognized symbolic identity informed how they saw their own city and themselves.[33]

During the 1970s, and then especially in the 1980s, this image of West Berlin as a city defined by its international symbolism and relationships began to be augmented by fissures and challenges within the city itself. As we have seen, the issue of housing, for example, prompted considerable internal conflict when the government's vision of housing as a way to improve the city's infrastructure, population, and reputation met with the resistance of local residents, who considered *Sanierung* an example of the state's militarism and materialism. The clashes between leftist activists and the city— both verbal and violent—challenged the external identity of a unified West Berlin.[34] However, the influx and settlement of thousands of guest workers, and the majority of those from Turkey, provoked a new and more fundamental fear: that Berlin would lose its German identity.

Anxiety about the numbers of Turks living in Berlin began cropping up as the West German economy slowed in the early 1970s, and this anxiety became especially sharp in response to the 1973 Oil Crisis. Districts bordering the Wall, and particularly Kreuzberg, drew the keen and increasing attention of West German politicians, the public, and the media. In a 1973 article in *Der Spiegel* entitled "*Die Türken kommen— rette sich, wer kann*," the author emphasizes the shift in identity from "*echt Kreuzberg*" [true Kreuzberg] to a place where "*unübersehbar Kundschaft aus dem Morgenland*" [highly visible customers from the Orient] frequents the Turkish-operated businesses that make up the landscape. The article is rife with statistics that call attention to the large numbers of Turkish in relation to German residents, likening the previous year's growth of the "Turkish colony" to the size of a brigade.[35] In addition to use of the word "colony" to describe Turkish settlement, the article describes the development as a "ghetto," and compares Turkish Kreuzberg to Harlem. The city government attempted to counter "ghettoization" by implementing a ban [*Zuzugssperre*] in 1975 that restricted "foreigners" from moving into parts of the city deemed to have already exceeded their capacity for non-German residents.

Concerns about the "*Ausländerstrom*" [torrent of foreigners], however, continued and prompted Senator of the Interior Heinrich Lummer (CDU) to issue an order in November 1981 that markedly restricted teenaged Turks from joining their families living in Berlin. An article covering the decision in *Die Welt* echoed the worrying statistics related to immigration and births, cited fears of criminality and leftist extremism among Turks, and reported that both the CDU and SPD agreed something needed to be done to halt the development of Turkish ghettos in the German city.[36] A related article published the following week in the *Rheinischer Merkur* provocatively asked whether Berlin was even "still a German city." The reporter refers to areas of the city densely populated by Turks as slums, ghettos, and colonies, and baldly states that "integration is not occurring."[37] Turkish families were taking over German neighborhoods, Turkish children were overflowing German schools, and German Berliners, this article and others point out, were ageing. The identity of West Berlin as a German city, politicians and the media agreed, was imperiled. The "negative symbols" of "the foreigner problem," the squatters' scene, housing issues, and "the threatening collapse of city culture" damaged West Berlin's identity and required an "improved image for Berlin."[38]

To what extent were the fears expressed by politicians and print media reflecting developments on the ground? To be sure, Turkish immigrants and their children had moved into those districts bordering the Wall in significant numbers, largely due to the fact that those apartments were the only ones available to them to rent. And those who placed the blame for the poor conditions of those apartments conveniently forgot that, for those buildings in *Sanierungsgebieten* [redevelopment zones], companies often deliberately allowed them to fall into disrepair as a way to justify their demolition, and then rented them out to guest workers, whose residence was assumed to be temporary. In any case, Turkish immigrants and their families settled, and began to adapt their everyday landscapes to address their own needs and expectations. Entrepreneurs opened a range of businesses that served both Turkish Berliners and the broader community,[39] adults and youth adopted various neighborhood spaces for socializing in,[40] and the second generation attended local schools, prompting educators to devise new ways to deal with the increasing multicultural nature of their classrooms.[41] The increasing public presence and the daily activities of Turkish Berliners did result in changes for West Berlin, although the discourse heralding the loss of its German identity oversimplified the complex and not uncommon interactions between immigrants and host societies. In an ironic twist, even as the Wall played such a significant role in the recruitment of Turkish guest workers and the resulting immigrant community, it is clear that Turkish Berliners challenged the city's Cold War identity and prompted a reevaluation of West Berlin's self-conception and external image.

Conclusion

While the direct influence of the Wall in the lives of Turkish Berliners had receded in the later 1980s, the significance of the Cold War division of the city reasserted itself in 1989 when the Berlin Wall fell. Many Turkish Berliners, like their German neighbors, reacted with surprise and joy, followed the events on television, and went themselves to chip away pieces of the "scuzzy Wall."[42] Elation, however, soon turned to apprehension as businesses began to fold or move out of the city and Turkish Berliners found themselves facing higher rates of unemployment than their German coworkers. By the mid-1990s, German Berliners were grappling with a 16.4 percent unemployment, but Berliners from an immigrant background were experiencing almost 27 percent unemployment.[43] During an interview several years after reunification, the Turkish-Berliner owner of a small *Kneipe* in Wedding expressed a common frustration among former West Berliners that people from the East worked for cheap, making the poor job market even more difficult. Moments after positioning himself as a West Berliner, however, he dismissed the idea that becoming a German citizen would improve his or his community's situations: "Ha! We have black heads, and everyone knows that we're not Germans. You know?"[44] Belonging in reunified Germany took on an increasing ethnically based character, which excluded those Turkish Berliners—some of whom had been born and lived their entire lives in the city—from being a part of the "new" national community.[45] With the Wall gone and Germans from both sides struggling to forge a new national identity, "Turk" became a synonym for "outsider."[46]

The Berlin Wall, seen primarily as a symbol of the division of the German people and a tangible demarcation of Cold War alliances, also played a critical role in the origins and development of Berlin's Turkish community. Brought to the city to solve a manpower shortage caused by the construction of the Wall and settled into neighborhoods made less desirable by its presence, Turkish Berliners' relationship to the Wall was highly ambivalent, creating both opportunity for economic improvement as well as the conditions for a marginalized position relative to German society. Yet, even as the Wall exerted such influence in the lives of Turkish Berliners, the Turkish community, in turn, played a significant role in challenging Germans' perceptions of the city. Once an island of the democratic West surrounded by the communist East, West Berlin instead became defined by its internal divisions and its increasingly "non-German" character. With the Wall's demise and the reunification of the city, Turkish Berliners were left without its orienting influence, and had to deal with the repercussions of life in reunified Berlin. That the Wall played such a vital role and that, in its absence, Turkish Berliners had to make a new place for themselves in the uncertain social and economic landscape of the new city makes their story a profoundly German one.

Notes

1   Sevim Özel (pseudonym), interview by author, June 30, 2009, transcription by Perrin Saylan, Berlin, Germany, p. 26.

2   For example, see Klaus Bade (ed.), *Auswanderer- Wanderarbeiter- Gastarbeiter: Bevölkerung, Arbeitsmarkt und Wanderung in Deutschland seit der Mitte* des 19. Jahrhunderts (Ostfildren, 1984) and *Europa in Bewegung: Migration vom späten 18. Jahrhundert bis zur Gegenwart* (Munich, 2000); Jochen Blaschke and Ahmet Ersöz, *Herkunft und Geschäftsaufnahme türkischer Kleingewerbetreibender in Berlin* (Berlin, 1987); Ulrich Herbert, *A History of Foreign Labor in Germany, 1880–1980: Seasonal Workers, Forced Laborers, Guest Workers*, trans. William Templer (Ann Arbor, 1990); David Horrocks and Eva Kolinsky (eds.), *Turkish Culture in Germany Today* (Providence, 1996); Ayse S. Çağlar, "Constraining Metaphors and the Transnationalisation of Spaces in Berlin," *Journal of Ethnic and Migration Studies* 27, 4 (October 2001), pp. 601–13; Karen Schönwälder, *Einwanderung und ethnische Pluralität: Politische Entscheidungen und öffentliche Debatten in Grossbritannien und der Bundesrepublik von den 1950er bis zu den 1970er Jahren* (Essen, 2001); Andreas Goldberg, Dirk Halm, and Faruk Şen, *Die Deutschen Türken* (Münster, 2004); Karin Hunn, *"Nächstes Jahr kehren wir zurück ...": Die Geschichte der türkischen "Gastarbeiter" in der Bundesrepublik* (Göttingen, 2005); Monika Mattes, *"Gastarbeiterinnen" in der Bundesrepublik: Anwerbepolitik, Migration, und Geschlecht in den 50er bis 70er Jahren* (Frankfurt am Main, 2005); Rita Chin, *The Guest Worker Question in Postwar Germany* (Cambridge, 2007).

3   Mary Fullbrook, *The Divided Nation: A History of Germany, 1918–1990* (New York, 1991), p. 184.

4   Mattes, *"Gastarbeiterinnen" in der Bundesrepublik.*

5   For a history of the Gastarbeiter program, see Bade, *Auswanderer-Wanderarbeiter-Gastarbeiter*; Herbert, *A History of Foreign Labor in Germany*; Klaus Bade, *Europa in Bewegung: Migration vom späten 18. Jahrhundert bis zur Gegenwart* (Munich, 2000).

6   For the history of Turkish participation in the guest worker program, see Karin Hunn, *"Nächstes Jahr kehren wir zurück ...."*

7   William Cleveland and Martin Bunton, *A History of the Modern Middle East* (Boulder, 2009), pp. 275–8.

8   Heike Knortz, *Diplomatische Tauschgeschäfte: "Gastarbeiter" in der westdeutschen Diplomatie und Beschäftigungspolitik 1953–1973* (Cologne, 2008).

9   "In Berlin bummeln," in: "Deutscher Text für Broschüre zum Anwerben von Arbeitskräften aus Griechenland und der Türkei," p. 2, Rundschreiben zur Beschäftigung von Ausländischen Arbeitnehmern, Sig. 10585–1, Schlüssel 04610585, Siemens Corporate Archives (SCA), Munich, Germany. While the document is not dated, the content, language, and placement in the file suggest publication in the mid-1960s.

10   "Έναν περίπατο στήν λεωφόρο Κονρφίρστενταμ του Βερολίνου" in "Deutscher Text für Broschüre zum Anwerben von Arbeitskräften aus Griechenland und der Türkei," p. 2, Rundschreiben zur Beschäftigung von Ausländischen Arbeitnehmern, Sig. 10585–1, Schlüssel 04610585, SCA. The brochure is the Greek-language version of a brochure designed for recruitment in Greece and Turkey.

11   Özel, 31. Özel's first introduction to Berlin came in the form of a sewing machine her father brought home shortly before he decided that she and her mother should sign up for the guest worker program. Özel remembered that, on the side of the machine, "there stood 'Berlin.' And I thought, 'Well, what's that then?'"

12   Leyla Sezer (pseudonym), interview by Ursula Trüper and Hatice Renc, January 28, 1993, transcript, "Die Leute vom Sparrplatz" Ausstellung, Mitte Museum Archiv, Berlin, Germany, p. 1.

13 Mehmet Korkmaz (pseudonym), interview by Rita Klages, June 25, 1998, transcript, "Projekt Migrantenbiographien," Heimatmuseum Neukölln, Berlin, Germany, p. 6.

14 "Protokoll dem am 17.10.1961, 15.00 h im Presse- und Informationsamt der Bundesregierung abgehaltenen Arbeitsbesprechung über die publizistische Betreuung der ausländischen Gastarbeiter in der Bundsrepublik," Bonn, November 4, 1961 Authored: BPA—IV/4. *Auswärtige Amt, Bestand B85, Bestell-Nr.: 618, Raum: U2.0.25, Regal: 263, Karton: 27405*, as cited in Brian J.K. Miller, "Reshaping the Turkish Nation-State: The Turkish-German Guest Working Program and Planned Development, 1961–1985," (PhD dissertation, University of Iowa, 2015), p. 128. I am greatly indebted to Brian J.K. Miller for sharing his expertise and sources related to *Anadolu Gazette*. For a more in-depth examination of West German and Turkish governmental efforts to shape the perspectives and purposes of Turkish guest workers, see his above-referenced dissertation.

15 Miller, "Reshaping the Turkish Nation-State," pp. 130–7.

16 Zeitung für die türkischen Gastarbeiter in der Bundesrepublik "ANADOLU," H. Alseher, CIAS to BPA September 4, 1963. *Bundesarchiv Koblenz Bestandssignatur: B/145, Archivsignatur: 2405, Standort: 10, Magazin: II 2A. U.2.05, Reihe: 230, Karton: Original*, "Vertriebslisten für das Bundespressamt, ANADOLU; Stand per 15.8.1965." Letter from Verlag der Wertag to Fritz Cramer, August 15, 1965 CIAS. *Bundesarchiv Koblenz, Bunderarchiv Signatur 6643, Bestandssignatur B/145/, Archivsignatur: 6643, Standdort: 10, Magazin: II 2A U.2.05, Reihe: 227*.

17 "Berlin Faciası," *Anadolu Gazetesi*, June 1963, p. 4; as referenced in Miller, p. 147.

18 "*Türk işçisi ile ilgili bildiriler*," *Anadolu Gazetesi*, January 1964, p. 2; as cited in Miller, p. 144.

19 Kemal Kurt and Erika Meyer (eds.), … *weil wir Türken sind/ … Türk oldugumuz için: Bilder und Texte von Türken/Türklerin resim ve öyküleri* (Berlin, 1981), pp. 23–9.

20 Carla Elizabeth MacDougall, *Cold War Capital: Contested Urbanity in West Berlin, 1963–1989* (PhD Dissertation, Rutgers, State University of New Jersey, 2011), p. 66. See also Stephan Lanz, "Inclusion and Segregation in Berlin, The 'Social City,'" in: Jeffry M. Diefendorf and Janet Ward (eds.), *Transnationalism and the German City* (New York, 2014), pp. 55–71.

21 Emily Pugh, *Architecture, Politics, and Identity in Divided Berlin* (Pittsburgh, 2014), pp. 205–6.

22 Ibid., p. 209.

23 MacDougall, *Cold War Capital*, p. 209.

24 Ibid., pp. 224–6.

25 Ibid., p. 213.

26 Ibid., pp. 208–20.

27 Ibid., pp. 221–3.

28 Klaus Wolfermann, interview by author, June 10, 2009, transcription by Perrin Saylan, Berlin, Germany, 18.

29 See "Sanierungsskandal im Wedding," *taz*, February 9, 1983; "Sparrstrasse 24," *Berliner Morgenpost*, February 10, 1982.

30 Wolfermann, p. 18.

31 Zafer Turan (pseudonym), interview by Ursula Trüper, October 11, 1993, audio cassette, DLSA, MMA.

32 Mieter-Initiative-Sparrplatz, "Stadterneuerung: Untersuchungsbereich Sparrplatz," Der Senator für Bau- und Wohnungswesen, April 1981, Presse Inhalte: Sozial—Spi W, MMA.

33 See Pugh, *Architecture, Politics, and Identity in Divided Berlin*.

34 MacDougall, *Cold War Capital*.

35 "Die Türken kommen—rette sich, wer kann," *Spiegel*, Nr. 31/1973, p. 24.

36 Hans R. Karutz, "Ausländerstrom schwillt immer bedrohlicher an," *Die Welt*, November 28, 1981, p. 5.

37 Jürgen Engert, "Ist Berlin noch eine deutsche Stadt?," *Rheinischer Merkur*, December 4, 1981, p. 3.

38 Friedhelm Kemna, "Das neue Berlin-Gefühl: Chancen für den Aufstieg mit Weizäcker," *Die Welt*, May 27, 1982, 9.

39 For example, see Jochen Blaschke and Ahmet Ersöz, *Herkunft und Geschäftsaufnahme türkischer Kleingewerbetreibender in Berlin* (Berlin, 1987).

40 Sarah Thomsen Vierra, *Turkish Germans in the Federal Republic of Germany: Immigration, Space, and Belonging, 1961–1990* (Cambridge, 2018). Newspapers often referred to local parks full of Turkish-background children as resembling scenes from "rural Anatolia." For an example of this from the 1990s, see "Kinder können den Sparrplatz malen," *Berliner Morgenpost*, July 20, 1994, "Presse Inhalte: Sozial— Spi. W," MMA.

41 For example, Ray C. Rist, *Guestworkers in Germany: The Prospects for Pluralism* (New York, 1978); Joyce Marie Mushaben, "A Crisis of Culture: Isolation and Integration among Turkish Guestworkers in the German Federal Republic," in: İlhan Basgöz and Norman Furniss (eds.), *Turkish Workers in Europe: An Interdisciplinary Study* (Bloomington, 1985), pp. 125–50; Ursula Boos-Nünning and Manfred Hohmann, "The Educational Situation of Migrant Workers' Children in the Federal Republic of Germany," in Lotty van den Berg-eldering and Jo Kloprogge (eds.), *Different Cultures, Same School: Ethnic Minority Children in Europe* (Berwyn, 1989); M. Alamdar-Niemann, D. Bergs-Winkels, and H. Merkens, "Educational Conditions of Turkish Migrant Children in German Schools," *Anthropology and Education Quarterly* 22 (June 1991) 2, pp. 154–61; Sarah Thomsen Vierra, "At Home in Almanya? Turkish-German Spaces of Belonging in West Germany, 1961–1990," *Bulletin of the GHI* 52 (Spring 2013), pp. 55–73.

42 Bilge Yılmaz (pseudonym), interview by author, June 2, 2009, transcription by Perrin Saylan, Berlin, Germany, 20. Also, Özel, 27.

43 Hedwig Rudolph and Felicitas Hillmann, "Döner contra Boulette—Döner und Boulette: Berliner türkischer Herkunft als Arbeitskräfte und Unternehmer im Nahrungsgütersektor," in: Hartmut Häußermann and Ingrid Oswald (eds.), *Zuwanderung und Stadtentwicklung* (Opladen/Wiesbaden, 1997), p. 93.

44 Eren Keskin (pseudonym), Wirt einer Kneipe am Sparrplatz, interview with Ursula Trüper, 1993, audio cassette, side A, "Die Leute vom Sparrplatz" Ausstellung (DLSA), Mitte Museum Archiv (MMA), Berlin, Germany.

45 Nevim Çil, *Topographie des Außenseiters: Türkische Generationen und der deutsch-deutsche Wiedervereinigungsprozess* (Berlin, 2007).

46 Nevim Çil, "Türkische Migranten und der Mauerfall," *APuZ* 59 (May 2009), pp. 40–6.

9

Experimental Art and Cultural Exchange in Late Cold War Berlin

Briana Smith

In May 1986, representatives of the two German states signed a long-deliberated cultural treaty. The diplomatic agreement immediately eased the exchange of travelling arts and cultural exhibitions between the FRG and GDR, fostering stronger cultural connections among Germans across the Iron Curtain.[1] Although exhibitions of East German art in the West were already quite common, the FRG welcomed the opportunity for more West German art to be seen by East German viewers.[2] In East Germany, the SED sought the influx of valuable foreign currencies through art sales abroad and the greater legitimization of homegrown Socialist Realist art. Later that year, an exhibition featuring West German painters Sigmar Polke, Anselm Kiefer, and Gerhard Richter was already making its way from Dresden to East Berlin's Altes Museum as a result of the treaty. Numerous exhibitions followed, including the debut of many East German artists in West German galleries and museums. Ongoing party control over culture in the GDR, however, ensured most of those artists were proper representatives of socialist culture.

In Cold War Berlin, the 1986 cultural treaty was in many ways superfluous for the city's experimental artists and their audiences, who had participated in an unofficial network of cultural exchange since the early 1970s. Although working in a variety of mediums and forms, these artists were united by an interest in breaking down the barriers between art and everyday life. Their work was often interactive or collaborative and focused more on the social processes initiated through art than the final product. Because of the great value placed on social interaction, the desire to connect with other artists, including those from the "other" Germany, was high.

Experimental artists in other Eastern bloc nations such as Poland and Hungary were forging even more robust networks with the West at the same time.[3] Unlike East German artists, they enjoyed greater freedom to travel to Western Europe to participate in exhibitions. Conversely, Western European artists were invited to join official exhibitions behind the Iron Curtain, which further supported the growth of these networks. This was less common in the GDR. East German artists were largely prohibited from traveling to the West in the 1970s and cultural officials rarely invited Western artists to exhibit their work in the GDR. Instead, after the construction of the

Wall in 1961, exchanges between experimental artists in divided Berlin took place in small neighborhood galleries and private art spaces in East Berlin. Once this network was established, however, artists and gallerists worked to sustain these connections via return trips, correspondence, contributions to publications, and, by the end of the 1980s, joint exhibitions.

Despite the city's division into rival halves, artists in East and West Berlin embraced a similar set of experimental practices and a philosophy of art that transcended the city's political division. But it was also precisely because of the city's extraordinary partition and West Berlin's geographical isolation that many of these artists were in the city in the first place. Artists migrated to West Berlin in the late 1960s and 1970s from hometowns across the FRG to consciously distance themselves from the tradition-bound, capitalist art world. With access to generous art grants and other subsidies, they avoided pressures to create work for the purpose of selling on the market. The scarcity of high-end galleries and wealthy collectors further encouraged their experimentation with social functions for art outside the commercial frame.

In East Berlin, all art was officially serving a social function. Party cultural officials rejected the "decadent imperialist" orientation of art in the capitalist West. Instead, art in the GDR was Socialist Realist—made by and for the workers and farmers. But many artists and gallerists also chafed at this official policy, which insisted art be didactic, easily legible, and serve the greater purpose of forging a distinctive socialist culture. Under Socialist Realism, artists were limited to the production of traditional art forms such as painting, sculpture, and drawing. A brief cultural thaw in the early 1970s enabled artists to engage with a broader set of themes in their work, including real world issues and concerns that parted from the former insistence on projecting a positive and aspirational view of socialist society.[4] But art forms including performance, installation, and video art, associated by the Ministry for Culture with contemporary Western art, continued to be banned until 1988.[5] In spite of these restrictions, many experimental artists remained committed to the socialist system. They participated in conferences run by the official Union of Visual Artists (VBK) and created traditional work to show in regional exhibitions. But many also envisioned the GDR moving toward a pluralist concept of art in socialism that welcomed experimental forms. Encounters with artists from West Berlin and the FRG in the 1970s and 1980s helped East German artists situate their work within a longer tradition of critical, socially engaged art dating back to Weimar Germany. For some, these exchanges also confirmed their belief that the socialist system offered the most favorable conditions for uniting art and life and sustaining a noncommercial art practice.

This chapter begins in the early 1970s, as a series of cultural and political reforms in East Germany led to the creation of more spaces for viewing and engaging with visual art. With the passage of the German-German Transit Treaty in May 1972, following the signing of the four-power agreement the previous year, West Germans and West Berliners could more easily attend events, present their work, and exchange ideas in East Berlin galleries. A second section examines three significant moments of artistic exchange and collaboration in East Berlin in the early 1980s. During these meetings and performances, artists from the two German states gathered to view and participate in projects exploring themes that transcended the Cold War division. In so doing, they contributed to a shared German tradition of critical, experimental, and socially engaged art. A final section examines other forms of exchange among Berlin-based artists in the mid-to-late-1980s, including the appearance of the arts and culture journal *No Man's Land* in 1987, which featured contributors from both sides of the Wall. During this time, East Berlin artists were also being issued short-term visas to travel to the West to view exhibitions and meet with artists and gallerists. This late era of unofficial cultural exchange culminated in a month-long performance art festival hosted in East Berlin in June 1989 featuring East Berlin artists at an official gallery and a parallel series at a private gallery with artists from West Berlin. The festival marked the culmination of over a decade of exchange among artists that increasingly conveyed what a pluralist socialist culture—with unimpeded channels of communication with Western artists—might look like. But rather than further pursuing this vision in the coming years, local artists instead called on these Cold War-era networks to organize protests against a series of unwelcome changes resulting from the city's reunification.

Contact Art: Cultural Exchange in East Berlin after Détente

In the aftermath of the early 1970s Cold War détente, artists and gallerists in Berlin enjoyed greater opportunities for exchange in the divided city. Residents of West Berlin could now pay a fee to travel to the GDR capital on day visas to meet artists in official and private galleries. The new cultural political orientation within the SED in the early 1970s had directly contributed to the presence of these gallery spaces. Soon after Erich Honecker became the new Party Secretary in 1971, the GDR's Ministry for Culture and Culture Association (*Kulturbund*) began efforts to make art more accessible to East Germans and increase participation in arts and cultural activities during leisure time. They oversaw the establishment of a chain of small art galleries in urban neighborhoods and rural areas. These galleries were intended to bring art closer to people in their daily lives, while also providing people the chance to purchase inexpensive art for their homes. East Germans were also encouraged to participate in the production of art by joining amateur art "circles" led by professional artists in neighborhood cultural houses or clubs.[6]

The impulse to promote broad participation in the arts was a longstanding goal among the GDR's cultural leaders dating back to the first of two Bitterfeld Conferences in 1959. The resulting "Bitterfeld Way" called for the organization of art and writing groups within the factories and collective farms to be led by professional artists.[7] The Bitterfeld Way caught the attention of artists across the Wall associated with West Berlin's New Society for Visual Arts (NGBK), who sought a similar democratization of art in the early 1970s. Founded during the height of the city's anti-authoritarian protests and cultural revolt in 1969, the NGBK was soon plotting its own Bitterfeld-inspired initiatives for removing art from the museum temples and integrating it into prisons, schools, factories, and nursing homes.[8] Although the overtly Marxist orientations of the NGBK had dampened by the late 1970s, subsequent projects maintained a focus on art as a source of social and political transformation.

In the early 1970s, the SED was already taking leave of the Bitterfeld Way and shifting the sites of amateur art making and consumption from the factory to residential areas such as regional cultural houses and neighborhood art galleries. For the artist Robert Rehfeldt, whose art practice already focused on increasing the presence of art in daily life, this change created new possibilities for engaging with city residents and for encountering visitors from the West. Rehfeldt was an all-round artist. His work included traditional prints and drawings that earned him invitations to show work in large exhibitions and galleries. He also made unconventional collages, super-8 films, and installations, while energetically circulating self-made postcards within the international mail art network. Mail artists sent hand-made prints, photographs, and other work through the postal service to artists affiliated with the network across the world, transcending the barriers of ideology and geography.[9] Rehfeldt's prolific contributions to this network reflect his interest in shaping his local community, while seeking connections with artists far beyond the GDR. His postcards typically featured his own stamped phrases about art including "art in contact is life in art" and "art is when it originates in spite of it all."[10] Beyond his personal art practice, Rehfeldt was deeply devoted to promoting art making as a social and collaborative endeavor. In the 1970s and 1980s, he led a popular amateur art circle, collaborated with other artists on public art projects in new housing developments and factories and helped operate small galleries in East Berlin's northern Pankow district. At the same time, Rehfeldt was in contact with West German artists cut from a similar cloth as him, including happening and video artist Wolf Vostell in West Berlin and the Düsseldorf-based artist Joseph Beuys. Exhibition catalogs and art magazines smuggled from the West also kept Rehfeldt informed of contemporary debates and artistic trends outside the GDR.[11]

Through his indirect engagement with the Western art world, Rehfeldt established an appreciation for the possibilities for art in socialism. He articulated this position in a 1977 letter published in the West German journal *Kunst Magazin*. His letter was a response to a feature article on experimental art in Hungary and Poland by a West German curator and art historian. In the letter, Rehfeldt argued that the desire "to remove the distance between artistic processes and society" had originated with artists in the East, dating back to Russian Constructivism. He conceded that artists in the West, namely Joseph Beuys, helped spread this aesthetic philosophy in the postwar period.[12] Rehfeldt also underscored the advantages of making art outside the capitalist system, explaining how "in the places where art is neither investment capital or commodity, one experiences it as essential to societal development and change. And through this process, artists are also changed."[13] As West German artists met Rehfeldt and other artists harboring these views during their visits to galleries in East Berlin, they, too, were changed.

Rehfeldt was among a collective of East Berlin artists who organized the Galerie Arkade in the late 1960s, which became a hub of experimental and contemporary art in the 1970s under the direction of Klaus Werner. Although the Galerie Arkade was incorporated into the gallery network of the newly created State Art Trade in 1975, it continued to function as a space for audiences to encounter art that challenged the traditional definition of Socialist Realism.[14] But this was no peripheral or underground gallery. Located on the prominent Strausberger Platz, just off Karl Marx Allee—East Berlin's grand socialist boulevard—gallery events were well-publicized and highly visible to passersby. Until its abrupt closing in 1981, Galerie Arkade hosted dozens of exhibitions from iconoclastic artists including Rehfeldt, action artist Erhard Monden and members of experimental artist group Clara Mosch from Karl-Marx-Stadt (Chemnitz). Werner also used the gallery to introduce audiences to West German artists through exhibitions and slide lectures and the sale of inexpensive prints and posters from collage artist Klaus Staeck and Joseph Beuys.[15]

The large crowds attending events at Arkade also inspired the organization of unofficial art spaces in East Berlin. These illegal, private art galleries, often constructed within apartments and studios, offered gallerists and artists the freedom to operate beyond state regulations and censorship. Although rare, private art spaces had existed since the GDR's inception, creating what Yvonne Fiedler characterizes as a partial public sphere for East Germans seeking independence from the "collective we."[16] In East Berlin, painters Heidrun Hegewald and Rudi Ebeling ran the private Galerie Konkret from 1960 to 1961. Art historian Lothar Lang also organized an independent *Kunstkabinett* in Berlin-Weissensee and Pankow in the 1960s.[17] The most prolific and enduring of East Berlin's private galleries was Jürgen Schweinebraden's EP Galerie, located in a back courtyard apartment on Duncker Strasse in Prenzlauer Berg. Schweinebraden was interested in the gallery providing a space for locals in which to encounter work from international artists and to keep GDR artists up to date on trends outside East Germany. Gallery events also provided a valuable opportunity for artists and local arts enthusiasts to socialize with international visitors. West Berlin artists attending events at EP Galerie included Wolf Vostell, artist, gallerist, and environmental activist Ben Wa(r)gin and sound artist and founder of the nonprofit Galerie Giannozzo, Rolf Langebartels.[18] The EP Galerie also featured work from American performance artists Bill Caglione and Anna Banana, Italian *arte povera* artist Michaelangelo Picoletto, and Eastern bloc action artists Marek Konieczny and Vladislav Novak.[19] West Berlin gallerists were also regular visitors, including representatives of the city's few commercial galleries like Lothar Poll and Michael Werner, and those pursuing nonprofit gallery work like Langebartels.

Due to the popularity of events at the EP Galerie and the nature of the art on display, Schweinebraden was the target of extensive measures by the Ministry for State Security (MfS) to intimidate, threaten, and tarnish his reputation.[20] Yet security operatives never moved to shut down the illegal gallery, preferring to observe the social networks convening in private spaces such as the EP Galerie.[21] But the invasive measures levied against Schweinebraden eventually led to his dismissal from his day job as a military psychologist and sex therapist, motivating his application for an exit permit in 1980. The gallery closed on his departure. Yet connections forged at the EP Galerie in the 1970s lived on between artists and gallerists in East and West Berlin, even after the gallery disappeared. For example, Rolf Langebartels continued traveling to East Berlin long after Schweinebraden's gallery closed. After presenting a lecture on photography at the Galerie Arkade, Langebartels became acquainted with additional East German artists and art historians and planned future opportunities for expanding this network. He and Arkade director Klaus Werner developed a traveling exhibition of GDR photography. He smuggled prints from West German photographers into the East and he worked with East Berlin's Evangelical Art Service to arrange a weekend art retreat for East and West Berlin artists within the sanctuary of a Prenzlauer Berg church.[22] Not only did exchanges like these help expand the network between experimental artists from East and West, they also fostered the development of friendships. Many years later, Langebartels still recalls joining an auto excursion to the Spreewald with a group of artists and art historians from East Berlin.[23]

Exchange in Action: East–West Performance Art in East Berlin

Months before leaving the GDR, Schweinebraden hosted West Berlin-based artist Wolf Kahlen at the EP Galerie for the first and only video performance art piece in the GDR. On the evening of the performance, both Kahlen and Schweinebraden delivered opening remarks noting the singularity of the event and its significance for German-German exchange.[24] Indeed, Kahlen's collaborative video performance at the EP Galerie represented an extraordinary example of the type of exchange and collaboration made possible by the Cold War thaw in the 1970s. The unofficial conduit for cultural exchange in East Berlin galleries allowed artists like Kahlen to establish social networks that transcended German division. Through their interactions across the Wall, West German artists also discovered the existence of artists seeking to expand the boundaries of Socialist Realism through the staging of more experimental forms. This information was not readily available in the Western press.

During the performance, titled *Camera Rolling*, Kahlen moved about the gallery with a closed-circuit video camera, a model used in scientific experiments that Kahlen had carried across the border without incident.[25] There was no viewfinder, rather a simple lens transmitting captured images to a monitor across the gallery. As Kahlen spun the camera around he shouted the phrase "camera rolling" and froze the lens on an object or person in the room. Schweinebraden then held a piece of plexiglass in front of the monitor. Dresden-based painter A.R. Penck was playing drums as Kahlen swept the camera around the room. Whenever Kahlen froze the camera, Penck dropped his drum sticks, picked up a paintbrush and rapidly painted over the small piece of glass covering the screen. On some occasions, Penck accentuated the lines and shapes of the images; other times he painted over the glass to efface any resemblance of the frozen image. Penck then returned to drumming and Kahlen resumed spinning the camera around the room before stopping to announce again "camera rolling." The artists continued this process for sixteen rounds.[26]

Kahlen intended the closed-circuit camera to incite collective reflection on the role of media technology in surveillance and security procedures in modern life. Resonating with the audience members' personal experiences with MfS observation, the camera's West German origins reminded viewers that video surveillance was not limited to state socialist contexts. At the same time, Penck's translation of the images on the monitor into abstract paintings suggested the limitations of video technology to transmit, represent, and control reality. Although Kahlen intended the video performance to be light-hearted, he also sensed the awareness of the MfS presence simmering just below the surface among the audience. As Kahlen describes, the audience members knew that "everything was at the same time surveyed by the secret police, since the place ... was of course a delicate space."[27] Reports detailing the performance from unofficial collaborators (IMs) working for MfS confirm Kahlen's assumption. One report suggested Kahlen's appearance at the gallery was proof of Schweinebraden's subversive support for "consciously intellectual and elitist content" that defied the requirement that socialist art be easily legible.[28] Despite Kahlen's hyper-awareness of the MfS presence at the gallery, the large crowd packed into the space, estimated around fifty in one report, reveals a surprising indifference among some East Berliners toward the presence of security operatives.[29] The general understanding that the event would be under surveillance did not prevent the gallery from being filled. Neither did it deter Schweinebraden from extending personal invitations to his large friend circle, including one individual who later turned out to be working for the MfS.[30]

Beyond Schweinebraden's informal cultural diplomacy at the EP Galerie, the Federal Republic's diplomatic station in East Berlin, known as the Permanent Mission of the Federal Republic in the GDR, also became a valuable space for artists from East and West to intersect. The existence of the Permanent Mission near the Invaliden Strasse border crossing on East Berlin's Western edge was another outcome of the early 1970s' Cold War détente. Although the West Germans refused to officially recognize the GDR as a foreign nation, which would have necessitated an embassy, the treaties prompted the opening of this quasi-diplomatic space in 1974. The East Germans set up a parallel institution in Bonn. In East Berlin, the Permanent Mission's team of cultural attachés sought to open broad lines of communication in an effort to unite all corners of the East Berlin art scene with artists and critics from the West.[31] Most importantly, the Mission sponsored art exhibitions from Western artists and hosted private receptions and concerts in the courtyard. These events connected East and West Berlin visual artists, writers, journalists, and cultural functionaries, while offering East Germans the chance to personally view art otherwise inaccessible to them. Beyond hosting events at the mission, the cultural attachés made "house calls" around the city—attending private parties, exhibitions at the Galerie Arkade and the EP Galerie, and meeting artists in their studios. They also sought to cultivate cordial relationships with official cultural functionaries, and invited VBK leaders to attend "breakfast talks" at the Permanent Mission.[32] GDR cultural officials were generally quite suspicious of these efforts.

In October 1981, the Permanent Mission sponsored an exhibition of work from Joseph Beuys that was of particular significance to local experimental artists. Although the exhibition focused on his early drawings and object art, the main event was the artist's appearance at the opening reception. Beuys' mere physical presence in the space, with his trademark fishing vest and felt hat, was itself performance art.[33] He was a sensation. With half his face coated in white as part of the treatment for a kidney infection, Beuys embodied the figure of a "mystical shaman," a label often applied to the artist by supporters and critics.[34] In the spirit of uniting artists from East and West Germany in the same room, the Permanent Mission had also extended invitations to the Beuys reception to the GDR's top cultural intelligentsia and party cultural functionaries in addition to nontraditional artists. Members of the Western press and artists from West Germany and West Berlin also accepted invitations, including Klaus Staeck and conceptual artist Fritz Rahmann from the West Berlin collective Büro Berlin.[35]

Beuys' aesthetic concepts of the "social sculpture" and "progressive concept of art" famously posited that all forms of human production, even the mundane, were creative acts.[36] According to Beuys, when people recognized the creativity inherent in their work, they would understand themselves as a "participant in shaping and defining the world." This realization would contribute to a more democratic society.[37] Due to the emphasis on art's effect on society, certain East German artists and art historians viewed Beuys' ideas as complementary with Socialist Realist tenets. For Robert Rehfeldt as well as East Berlin action artist Erhard Monden, the pursuit of the Beuysian "social sculpture" was already intrinsic to their artistic process. But due to the implicit call for social change at their core, art historian and curator Eugen Blume has argued that Beuys' ideas were "absolutely subversive" and "dangerous to the East and West."[38] As a result, the Beuys reception at the Permanent Mission caused great concern among security operatives and VBK leaders.[39] The VBK's aging functionaries were unwilling to reconcile Beuys' esoteric art actions and performances, often involving felt, margarine, and the occasional animal cadaver, with the concrete and inspiring messages they expected from socialist art. As VBK President and painter Willi Sitte explained in response to an inquiry from an East Berlin art teacher regarding the VBK's position on Beuys:

> The work or non-work of Joseph Beuys hardly corresponds to GDR art and its goals: to reach the majority of working people with its humanitarian awareness for the thoughts and feelings of man and to convey to them, through works of art, intellectual and aesthetic enrichment and pleasure. Therefore, we have no use for engaging with Beuys' work.[40]

Despite the VBK's rejection of Beuys, visitors crowded into the Permanent Mission to view the exhibition and meet the artist, whose work and ideas reinforced a socialist-inflected belief in the power of art to change the world. Personal encounters with Beuys likely emboldened many artists in the GDR to continue pursuing artistic practices at the quotidian level and exploring the unique possibilities for achieving the "social sculpture" in the East. During their brief meeting, Beuys had even advised Erhard Monden to remain in the East, where his socially engaged art could be more effective.[41] The exchange with Beuys helped connect experimental artists in East Berlin such as Monden with a body of ideas about the relationship between art and society that were relevant under capitalist and socialist systems. Furthermore, Beuys' interest in East German artists helped validate the meaningful art making taking place in the GDR, in spite of the party's top-down control of culture.

The Permanent Mission also supported the realization of a performance art piece that straddled West and East Berlin to draw attention to the shared past uniting the divided city. In 1985, Bavarian artist Nikolaus Lang strapped a deer skeleton to his back and began a two-day art action across West and East Berlin. His starting point was the Artist House Bethanien at Mariannenplatz near the path of the Wall in Berlin-

Kreuzberg. Lang and the skeleton walked the streets of Kreuzberg: from the brush-covered site of the former Gestapo headquarters at Prinz-Albrecht Strasse and along the path of the Berlin Wall to the Checkpoint Charlie border crossing. The next day, Lang crossed into East Berlin, with permission secured by the Permanent Mission workers. He immediately made his way to Prenzlauer Berg, to continue his sojourn among the residents in the performance he titled *Showing the Deer to Prenzlauer Berg*.

Although Lang's previous work focused on the collection of objects connected to the past lives of individuals, in this action, Lang used his peripatetic body to confront the ghosts of Berlin's traumatic past that haunted both sides of the Wall. Art critic Walter Aue identified the deer skeleton in Lang's action as a "symbol of rebirth and awakening life" and a "guide through the realm of the dead."[42] By uniting East and West Berlin in this border-crossing action, Lang highlighted the shared experience of division among Berliners and the need for a collective confrontation with the past. East Berlin artists in contact with the Permanent Mission employees were notified of Lang's action ahead of time. They followed the artist as he walked through their neighborhood. In a documentary photograph from Lang's walk, you can just make out the face of action artist Erhard Monden trailing Lang with a camera in hand.[43] The artist and his entourage later stopped at a corner pub, where Lang took the opportunity to rest and remove the skeleton.[44]

East Berliners in the West and the Alternative Public Sphere of *No Man's Land*

In the 1980s, the network between experimental artists, gallerists, and viewers that formed in the small art galleries or at Permanent Mission receptions was further maintained through personal visits, correspondence, contributions to publications, and joint exhibitions. Although the Galerie Arkade and EP Galerie were both closed by 1981, a new constellation of private and official art spaces appeared in their absence. In June 1983, a group of artists, critics, and gallerists including Erhard Monden, Eugen Blume, and Klaus Werner founded the private *rot-grün* gallery collective in a back courtyard apartment at Sredzki Strasse 64 in Prenzlauer Berg. Although this was another private gallery operating outside the GDR's official gallery network, artists from the West were made aware of the *rot-grün* space through their existing GDR contacts. Visitors from West Berlin included Wolf Vostell and members of West Berlin's Büro Berlin collective, who had all previously attended events at the Permanent Mission and EP Galerie. The space was also visited by Hans Haacke, the West German-born conceptual artist based in New York City.[45] From the perspective of gallery organizer Erhard Monden, artists visiting the *rot-grün* space from the West observed how experimental artists in the GDR operated "without compromises."[46] Echoing Rehfeldt's 1977 letter to *Kunst Magazin*, this comment suggests an understanding among certain artists in East Berlin that creating experimental and noncommercial work was more feasible under state socialism. Yet the hundreds of East German artists applying for exit permits to leave the GDR throughout the 1980s indicates many also felt quite differently.

At the same time, the increase in exit permits had also led the VBK to begin granting more short-term visas to the West to prevent artists from seeking to leave permanently. Although artists had long had the chance to participate in study visits throughout the Eastern bloc, permission to travel to West Berlin and the Federal Republic was quite rare until the 1980s. Nevertheless, the VBK still used travel visas as a tool for rewarding compliance and readily revoked these privileges to punish a variety of infractions. Many emotional pleas were sent to local VBK officials when travel applications were denied.[47] In 1982, a group of artists, including Robert Rehfeldt, sent a letter to the local VBK requesting greater flexibility regarding the approval of travel visas to West Berlin.[48] In 1987, former Galerie Arkade leader Klaus Werner threatened to boycott a VBK conference in protest of the repeated rejection of his applications, explaining, "eventually, one gets to the point where they begin to feel resigned."[49] Yet an affiliation with underground galleries and experimental art forms did not automatically restrict their ability to travel West and many artists and art historians with ties to private galleries had travel applications approved in the late 1980s. In October 1988, East Berlin performance artist and conceptual photographer Kurt Buchwald was allowed a six-day trip to the FRG. During the trip, Buchwald attended a photography exhibition at the Museum Ludwig in Cologne and a series of private galleries in the city. He also met with artists in their studios, participated in a gallery discussion on performance art, and viewed a performance art piece from Swiss artist Roman Signer.[50]

In 1987, the publication of a new arts and culture journal titled *No Man's Land: Journal Between the Cultures*, aimed at a joint Berlin readership, helped to further normalize the cultural network connecting artists across the city, while inviting a broader community of readers into the circle. The journal's subtitle underscored the existence of a space for like-minded artists in East and West Berlin who rejected the rhetoric of cultural competition between the two German states. Divided Berlin was the geographical hub of this otherwise abstract space "between the cultures." Appearing shortly after the signing of the 1986 cultural treaty, *No Man's Land* also reflected how the postwar divisions were breaking down at multiple levels of society. *No Man's Land* was published by West Berlin's Nishen Verlag, with support from the Paul Löbe Institute and the *Ästhetik und Kommunikation* press. The journal's editors, art historian Eckhart Gillen, historian and museum curator Wolfgang Dreßen, and literary scholar Siegfried Radlach, understood the journal as providing a "forum" for individuals in Berlin operating "between and next to established culture" and outside national contexts.[51] The Permanent Mission employees had a hand in enabling this border-blurring publication to reach its desired readers, distributing complimentary copies among contacts in East Berlin, and keeping free copies on hand at the Mission. Articles in *No Man's Land* included reviews of contemporary art, interviews with writers, artists and curators, and essays on local cultural political debates. In-depth articles on experimental artists and photographers from East Berlin and across the Eastern bloc introduced West Berlin readers to artists and artistic practices largely unknown to the Western art world. The journal also kept East Berlin readers informed of upcoming art exhibitions and publications through advertisements from local publishers and art institutions. Through its joint Berlin readership, the publication created a form of imagined community among readers on either side of the Wall as a supplement or replacement for face-to-face exchange. By denying the ongoing divisions, the journal acted as if the city were no longer split in two. That would soon be the case.

In June 1989, the "31-day Permanent Art Conference" (PAC), a month-long performance art festival, exposed even broader audiences to the experimental art of East Berlin, while highlighting the engagement with performance art on both sides of the Wall. The PAC was by far the most significant exhibition of performance, action, and installation art in the GDR's history. A supplemental program to the annual regional art exhibition, the festival was hosted at the city-run Galerie Weisser Elefant on Almstadt Strasse, not far from the central hub of Alexanderplatz.[52] The month-long festival included experimental theater, installation art, an urban art action, and panel discussions on art and politics. A series of visceral and shocking performances from the Auto-Perforation Artists, a young artist collective originally from Dresden, had a particularly profound effect on audiences.

Festival organizers Christoph Tannert and Eugen Blume wanted to include artists from West Berlin in the official program at the Galerie Weisser Elefant. City authorities rejected this plan. Instead a parallel program of performances titled the "World-Language Action 1989" took place at the *rot-grün* gallery in Prenzlauer Berg. Tannert and Blume's insistence on a performance art festival featuring artists from both East and West reveals the importance placed on highlighting the personal and artistic connections uniting artists in the divided city. Visitors to the official program were notified through verbal announcements and fliers of the additional programming featuring West Berlin artists including Wolfgang Mueller and Käthe Kruse of the art punk band *Tödliche Doris*, and action artists Kain Karawahn, Marc Brandenburg, and Käthe B.[53] Having sworn off appearances at official exhibitions, Erhard Monden elected to perform with his daughter Kathleen alongside the Westerners at *rot-grün*, making it an integrated East–West event. Johannes Stüttgen, a former assistant to Joseph Beuys and representative of Beuys' Free International University, was also invited to participate in the series. The decision to invite Stüttgen reflected the ongoing importance of the late Joseph Beuys. Although Beuys had died in 1986, his ideas continued to deeply shape the artists presenting at the parallel festivals in June 1989 and their work after the city's reunification the next year.

Conclusion

The many nodes of exchange connecting experimental artists in late Cold War Berlin reinforce what we already know: the Berlin Wall was porous and failed to stop the flow of ideas, art, and people between the two city halves.[54] But there is also much to be gained by studying these artists and the relationships they independently established long before the signing of the 1986 cultural treaty. West Berlin's isolation from the Western art market and the foundations of Socialist Realism in the East led experimental artists in both city halves to explore functions for art outside the market. The shared experience of living in Cold War Berlin contributed to their embrace of a set of ideas and practices that prioritized the artistic process over product. These artists drew on a tradition of critical and socially engaged art extending back to the Dadaists in Weimar Germany—forms that took on new meaning in postwar society. Furthermore, East and West Berlin artists created work that sidestepped the rhetoric of division and Cold War polarization. Instead, they engaged with issues and concerns affecting individuals on both sides of the Iron Curtain such as surveillance, social isolation, and the shared Nazi past. After the city's reunification in 1990, experimental artists from both former Berlins drew on their Cold War-era networks to organize in response to a new set of concerns.[55] The sudden arrival of real estate speculators in early 1990 led to the immediate rise in rent prices on artist studios, threatening the livelihoods of experimental artists and their ability to create noncommercial work. But because Berlin's artists had a longer history to draw on, they were prepared to unite in a series of performance-infused protests to insist that experimentation and affordability went hand in hand. They continue to do so in the contemporary city.

Notes

1   Sebastian Lindner, "Ein Verhandlungsmarathon. Das deutsch-deutsche Kulturabkommen," in: Bernd Lindner and Rainer Eckert (eds.), *Mauersprünge/Klopfzeichen: Kunst und Kultur der 80er Jahre in Deutschland* (Leipzig, 2002), pp. 55–71.

2   Lindner, "Ein Verhandlungsmarathon," p. 57; April A. Eisman, "East German Art and the Permeability of the Berlin Wall," *German Studies Review* 38 (October 2015) 3, p. 599.

3   Klara Kemp-Welch, *Networking the Bloc: Experimental Art in Eastern Europe, 1965–1981* (Cambridge, 2019).

4   Bernd Lindner, *Verstellter, offener Blick: eine Rezeptionsgeschichte bildender Kunst im Osten Deutschlands 1945–1995* (Cologne, 1998), pp. 156–7.

5   See Ulrike Goeschen, *Vom sozialistischen Realismus zur Kunst im Sozialismus: Die Rezeption der Moderne in Kunst und Kunstwissenschaft der DDR* (Berlin, 2001).

6   Anke Scharnhorst, "Trojanische Pferde im sozialistischen Kulturbetrieb? Die Zirkel als private 'Akademien neben den Akademien,'" in Günter Feist, Eckhart Gillen, and Beatrice Vierneisel (eds.), *Kunstdokumentation SBZ/DDR 1945–1990: Aufsätze, Berichte, Materialien* (Berlin/Cologne, 1996), pp. 616–24.

7   Manfred Jäger, *Kultur und Politik in der DDR: 1945–1990* (Cologne, 1995), pp. 103–5.

8   Gisela Weimann in discussion with the author, April 20, 2015.

9   Franziska Dittert, *Mail-Art in der DDR: eine intermediale Subkultur im Kontext der Avantgarde* (Berlin, 2010); Rosa von Schulenburg et al., *Arte Postale: Bilderbriefe, Künstlerpostkarten, Mail Art aus der Akademie der Künste und der Sammlung Staeck* (Berlin, 2013).

10   SAdK, Berlin, VBK-Künstlerbiographien Nr. 2228, Robert Rehfeldt. See also Lutz Wohlrab (ed.), *Robert Rehfeldt: Kunst im Kontakt* (Berlin, 2009).

11   Eugen Blume, "In freier Luft—Die Künstlergruppe Clara Mosch und ihre Pleinairs," in "Die Künstlergruppe Clara Mosch and ihre Pleinairs," in: Günter Feist, Eckhart Gillen, and Beatrice Vierneisel (eds.), *Kunstdokumentation SBZ/DDR 1945–1990: Aufsätze, Berichte, Materialien* (Berlin/Cologne, 1996), p. 738; Kemp-Welch, *Networking the Bloc*, pp. 298–9.

12 Robert Rehfeldt, "Kunst zwischen Hammer und Pinsel," *Kunst Magazin* 17 (1977) 3, p. 8.

13 Ibid.

14 Barbara Barsch, "Freiräume Betreten," in: Gabriele Muschter (ed.), *Klaus Werner: Für die Kunst* (Cologne, 2009), pp. 79–80.

15 Eugen Blume, "Joseph Beuys and the GDR: The Individual as Political," in: Claudia Mesch and Viola Maria Michely (eds.), *Joseph Beuys: The Reader* (Cambridge, 2007), p. 309.

16 Yvonne Fiedler, *Kunst im Korridor: Private Galerien in der DDR zwischen Autonomie und Illegalität* (Berlin, 2013), p. 11.

17 Günter Feist and Eckhart Gillen (eds.), *Kunstkombinat DDR. Daten und Zitate zur Kunst und Kunstpolitik der DDR 1945–1990* (Berlin, 1990), p. 47.

18 BStU Berlin, MfS HA XX/9 575, "Abschlußbericht zum OV, 'Arkade,'" March 8, 1982, folio 67; BStU Berlin, MfS AOP 7030/82 Bd. 9, November 4, 1980, folio 107–8, 222–3. Berlin artist Ben Wagin was formerly Ben Wargin, but has dropped the "r" to remove the word "war" from his last name.

19 BStU Berlin, MfS AOP 7030/82 Bd. 4, Quelle IM "Andre," April 30, 1976, folio 22–5; August 18, 1976, folio 211–13; BStU Berlin, MfS AOP 7030/82 Bd. 7, October 25, 1978, folio 129. According to one IM report, Anna Banana planned to walk around the city in a banana costume and introduce herself to the East Berlin mayor, but was convinced by Schweinebraden not to follow through on the plan.

20 BStU Berlin, MfS AOP 7030/82 Bd. 1, March 30, 1981 Sachstandsbericht im OV "Arkade" folio 125–30.

21 Jürgen Schweinebraden, *Die Gegenwart der Vergangenheit Bd. 1: Blick zurück im Zorn?* (Niedenstein, 1998), p. 108.

22 Rolf Langebartels in discussion with the author, November 27, 2014.

23 Ibid.

24 BStU Berlin, MfS AOP 7030/82 Bd. 9, Information über Jürgen Schweinebraden, February 28, 1980, folio 108–9. Kahlen was not the only Westerner in the gallery that night. Also in attendance were the West Berlin sculptor Josef Erben, Swiss art historian Toni Stooss, and West Berlin-based arts publisher Rainer Pretzell and his wife.

25 Wolf Kahlen, email correspondence with the author, February 22, 2017.

26 Video documentation of *Camera Rolling* can be found on *40 Jahre Videokunst.de,* DVD, eds. Christoph Blase and Peter Weibel (1980; Karlsruhe, 2000).

27 Wolf Kahlen (ed.), *Wolf Kahlen: VideoTapes 1960–2010: Werkverzeichnis* (Berlin, 2010), pp. 236–7.

28 BStU, MfS AOP 7030/82 Bd. 1, 6 Sachstandsbericht zum Operativvorgang "Arkade" February 18, 1980, folio 108.

29 BStU Berlin, MfS AOP 7030/82 Bd. 9, Information über Jürgen Schweinebraden, February 28, 1980, folio 108–9.

30 Ibid.

31 Simone Hain, "Schwebende über einer Grenze: Kulturelle Begegnungen in der Ständigen Vertretung der Bundesrepublik," in: Lindner and Eckert (eds.) *Mauersprünge/Klopfzeichen* (Leipzig, 2002), p. 73.

32 BStU Berlin, MfS AOP 14485/82 Bd. 1 "Eröffnungsbericht zum 'OV Galerie,'" November 29, 1980, folio 14.

33 Andreas Kaps, "Der Hirte und das geteilte Land: Joseph Beuys in der Ständige Vertretung," *Der Tagesspiegel*, October 27, 1981, p. 5.

34 Benjamin Buchloch, "Beuys: The Twilight of the Idol. Preliminary Notes for a Critique," in: Gene Ray, Lukas Beckmann, and Peter Nisbeth (eds.), *Joseph Beuys: Mapping the Legacy* (Michigan, 2001), pp. 199–211.

35 Kaps, "Der Hirte und das geteilte Land," p. 5.

36 Heiner Stachelhaus, *Joseph Beuys*, trans. David Britt (New York, 1991), p. 61.

37 Stachelhaus, *Joseph Beuys*, p. 64.

38 Eugen Blume, "Laborismus gegen Kapitalismus und Kommunismus im Dunkeln: Joseph Beuys," in: Lindner and Eckert (eds.), *Wahnzimmer/Klopfzeichen* (Leipzig, 2002), pp. 48–9.

39 BStU Berlin, MfS HA XX/AKG 119, folio 268–9; BStU Berlin, MfS BV Berlin, AIM 3477/88, folio 116–21.

40 SAdK, Berlin, VBK-ZV, Nr. 54, Willi Sitte response to Carmen Maier, December 6, 1985.

41 Erhard Monden in discussion with the author, April 13, 2015.

42 Walter Aue (ed.), *Umfeld Bethanien: Karina Raeck, Fritz Gilow, Raffael Rheinsberg, Wolf Kahlen, Anna Oppermann, Dieter Appelt, Dorothee von Windheim, Nikolaus Lang, Lili Fischer* (Berlin, 1985), p. 132.

43 Aue (ed.), *Umfeld Bethanien*, p. 143.

44 Daniela Dahn, *Prenzlauer Berg-Tour* (Leipzig, 1987), p. 195.

45 Eugen Blume, "Raum r-g, Sredzistraße 64," in: Bernd Lindner and Rainer Eckert (eds.), *Wahnzimmer/Klopfzeichen: Kunst und Kultur der 80er Jahre in Deutschland* (Leipzig, 2002), p. 55.

46 Ibid.

47 See BStU MfS HA XX 12851 folio 255–6, "Schreiben der Sektion Bildhauer des VBK/DDR Bezirk Berlin zu Problemen der Genehmigung von Studienreisen für Künstler in das kapitalistische Ausland."

48 AdK, VBK-BZ-Berlin, Nr. 43/2, December 13, 1982, "Vorschläge und Gedanken zum Thema Studienreisen in das nichtsozialistische und das sozialistische Ausland."

49 AdK, Berlin, Klaus-Werner-Archive, Nr. 265, April 13, 1986, Klaus Werner to Klaus Weidner.

50 SAdK, Berlin, VBK-ZV, Nr 1713/1, November 11, 1988, Reiseberichte, Kurt Buchwald.

51 BStU Berlin, MfS HA XX 12176, "Niemandsland: Zwischen deutschen Kulturen, " May 1985, folio 179; Editorial Board, "Niemandsland und Utopie," *Niemandsland: Zeitschrift zwischen den Kulturen* 1 (1987) 1, pp. 2–4.

52 Ralf Bartholomäus (ed.), *Permanente Kunstkonferenz: Installation—Performance— Performance Art 30.5.—30. 6.1989* (Berlin, 1990).

53 AdK, Berlin, VBK-BZ-Berlin, Nr. 33/1, Wolfram Seyfert to Christian Hartenhauer, June 15, 1989.

54 See April A. Eisman, "East German Art and the Permeability of the Berlin Wall," *German Studies Review* 38 (October 2015) 3, 597–616; Patrick Major, *Behind the Berlin Wall: East Germany and the Frontiers of Power* (Oxford, 2009).

55 Manfred Butzmann, "Ohne Atelier, Keine Kunst!," *Kultur Politik* 20 (1991) 2, p. 69; Eugen Blume and Manfred Butzmann (eds.), *Butzmanns Heimatkunde in 24 Abteilungen* (Berlin, 1992), pp. 178–9.

10

Behind the Wall, Across the Wall: Gay Activism in East Berlin

Teresa Tammer
Translated by Scott H. Krause

Young Michael Eggert[1] occasionally met West Berlin men at the Mocca Bar in the former Hotel Sophia, just off the Friedrichstraße transit hub that served as entry point into East Berlin. One of these men once brought him a copy of *Him*[2] magazine, which Eggert had seen featured on Western TV channels. Eggert recalls how the magazine blended photo spreads of naked men with reports on newly established groups in the Federal Republic and West Berlin, whose members referred to themselves as gay and lesbian and advocated rights for homosexuals. Now and again young gay activists came to East Berlin, and brought along their advocacy papers, talking about their campaign for public visibility in West Germany.[3] Shortly afterwards, Eggert and Peter Rausch,[4] together with other men and women, founded the first and for the time being only gay and lesbian group in the GDR, the Homosexual Interest Group Berlin (HIB). State authorities tolerated the group for a time, yet never recognized it outright as such. Over the course of the 1980s, a new gay and lesbian rights movement developed in East Berlin and across the GDR at large. Lutheran parishes opened their doors for so-called *Arbeitskreise Homosexualität*, where these working groups could gather legally under the protection of the Protestant Church.

This chapter examines the history of East Berlin gay rights activism during the Cold War and probes if and how this social movement was Western oriented or even dependent on encounters and transfers across the Wall. Did the activists on Berlin's Eastside see themselves as part of a transnational movement or as groups rooted in the GDR? How did these activists interact with GDR authorities and what strategies did they pursue to assert themselves? The chapter closely examines the role of divided Berlin. How far did this urban space marked by a not fully impermeable Wall provide the environment for gay rights activism on both sides and on the Eastern side in particular? Finally, this chapter explores what kind of caesura and/or fresh start the fall of the Wall and German reunification constituted for the East Berlin activists. Answers to these questions can be gleaned from a host of sources: the legacies of East Berlin gay rights movements, their samizdat publications, West German gay and lesbian magazines, the files of the Ministry for State Security (MfS, of *Stasi* notoriety) and other state agencies, as well as through personal conversations with protagonists of that era. The terms "gay" and "lesbian" are contemporary and have been used by the actors to describe themselves. "Homosexual" has been used both as self-description and as designation in official parlance for all those individuals who felt attracted to people of the same sex.

This chapter focuses on the East German gay rights movement, and its actors in East Berlin in particular. Jens Dobler and Harald Rimmle have defined the *Schwulenbewegung*, the gay rights movement in German-speaking contexts, as a new social movement that formed in the early 1970s. As it proclaimed a discrete gay identity, it distinguished itself from the homophile movement of the 1950s and 1960s. The actors of the new social movement reinterpreted the derogatory term *schwul* positively as a self-designation.[5] But Dobler and Rimmle have tailored this definition for the West German gay rights movement. Hence it is only partially applicable to the East German case, as that was also significantly different, a topic that will be discussed in more detail here. Nonetheless, the East German case has been referred to as a gay rights movement, even if it has been consistently characterized in relationship to the West German one.

Dobler and Rimmle, for instance, have concluded that gays and lesbians cooperated differently in East and West. According to them, the West German lesbian rights movement has to be distinguished from the gay rights movement as it operated under different circumstances and pursued unique strategies. In contrast, the authors maintain that a shared movement of gay men and lesbians formed within the GDR.[6] Yet a more nuanced picture emerges on closer examination of activism within the realities of state socialism. Mixed groups existed, which were predominantly attended and led by men, such as the HIB. But separate working groups such as Lesbians in the Church and Gays in the Church also operated in the East Berlin of the 1980s. This chapter concentrates on the activities of male actors within the HIB and Gays in the Church, but without negating lesbian commitment or dimensions of shared history. What were the conditions that both gay and lesbian activists encountered during the 1970s and 1980s in East and West and what courses of action did both German states take regarding homosexuality?

Homosexuality in Divided Germany

On its introduction in 1871, Paragraph 175 of the German criminal code (RStGB) criminalized the *widernatürliche Unzucht* between men, or "unnatural fornication." In 1935, the Nazis expanded this paragraph to include "lusty intent" and threatened to send men to jail or concentration camps.[7] The GDR reverted to the more liberal version of 1871 on its founding in 1949, until abolishing Paragraph 175 outright in 1968. But equality between homo- and heterosexuality did not constitute an aim of this reform. Instead, the new Paragraph 151 now also penalized female homosexuality, defining the age of consent as eighteen years, while setting the age of consent at sixteen years for heterosexual relationships.[8] Apart from continuing discrimination in legal codes, homosexuals within the GDR still faced prejudice, common defamation, marginalization, and discrimination in the workplace. On top of that, the state limited places for homosexuals to meet into parks and individual bars. Tightly controlled public discourse formed another obstacle. While the state initially stifled conversations on homosexuality outright, even later official acknowledgment of the phenomenon entailed monopolizing discourse.[9] Unsurprisingly, the self-assertion and public visibility of gays and lesbians that swept Western countries during this period failed to emerge in the GDR.

The Federal Republic, which had adopted Paragraph 175 in its national socialist version, reformed its criminal code in 1969 and introduced an age of consent for male–male sexual contacts at twenty-one years of age. Even as this age of consent was lowered to eighteen years in 1973, West German women remained exempted from it until the paragraph was finally abolished in 1994.[10] Following the liberalization of the criminal code, new gay and lesbian liberation movements developed. Predominantly leftist groups formed, which publically championed the rights of homosexuals. A new homosexual culture flourished in West German metropolitan areas with West Berlin leading the way, offering space for intellectual debates and alternative lifestyles, but also commercial offers.[11]

Starting in the 1980s, new avenues for self-organization opened for gays and lesbians in the GDR, since Lutheran parishes agreed to host alternative groups and thus shield them from state intrusion. At least fourteen homosexual working groups developed under the umbrella of the Lutheran Church until 1989.[12] The state and party leadership perceived all these grassroots initiatives as a threat, particularly those associated with the Church. Hence the Ministry for State Security placed them under close surveillance. But they were not outlawed outright.[13] Starting in the mid-1980s, the state's attitude toward homosexuality shifted gradually. While the grassroots groups monitoring continued, the state and party leadership made tentative overtures to better "integrate" gays and lesbians into socialist society, particularly to curtail the influence of the churches.[14] In 1988, the *Volkskammer*, the GDR's toothless parliament, rubber-stamped changes to the criminal code, that mandated a uniform age of consent of sixteen years for both homo- and heterosexual contacts.[15] In the meantime, Paragraph 175 remained on the statutes in the Federal Republic, until it was deleted in 1994 during the process of legal harmonization following German reunification.[16] A fundamental shift in attitudes toward homosexuality failed to materialize in the GDR before the fall of the Wall since the SED state monopolized public conversations on the topic and denied self-organized homosexual groups any kind of access to the public sphere due to state's paranoia. These grassroots initiatives still could not form independent associations and publish on their own, with the exception of newsletters designated as "for internal Church use only."[17] At the same time, interest groups of homosexuals had already formed in trade unions, parties, churches of the Federal Republic, including the *Bundesverband Homosexualität*, an umbrella organization on the federal level. Meanwhile, the diversification and professionalization of interest groups, publically subsidized projects, and commercial enterprises further accelerated.[18]

The developments just outlined have been closely linked with the city of Berlin. Magnus Hirschfeld and others founded the Scientific Humanitarian Committee here in 1897. This constituted the first organization that denounced the criminal persecution of gay men and sought to educate society on homosexuality. By the turn of the century, first venues had established themselves in particular neighborhoods and Berlin started to develop into the European capital of homosexual life.[19] The anonymity of European metropolises wrought by rapid urbanization formed a prerequisite for communities of sexual minorities to form. Robert Beachy has argued that collaboration between Berliner medical scientists such as Hirschfeld and individual expressions of sexual identity created the homosexual "species" that has formed the basis for the modern conception of sexual orientation. The term *schwul* ("gay") derives from the Berlin vernacular as well, according to Beachy, and women as well as men in the homosexual subculture had claimed this term for themselves during the 1920s.[20] But the eradication of this community and research on it also had its origins in Berlin, when after 1936 the Reich Central Office for Combating Abortion and Homosexuality coordinated the persecution. After 1945 a homosexual subculture developed again, but slowly. While located primarily in West Berlin, many East Berliners participated until the construction of the Wall in 1961.[21] Visits across the divide were only possible again starting in the early 1970s, but now exclusively from West to East. Gay rights movements on both sides of the Wall shared a common history when they encountered one another during the 1970s and 1980s. While one learned from the other, both were forced to pursue differing paths.

Michael Sontheimer and Peter Wensierski have characterized Berlin as a "city of revolt," in which uprisings have taken place since the nineteenth century and after the 1960s in increasing succession. The "urge to resist" has been inscribed in "Berlin's DNA," according to the authors. During the Cold War, West Berlin formed an island without draft or closing hour, in which leftwing radicals, autonomists, and punks eluded state authority. East Berlin also constituted a hotbed for opposition in the GDR. While state surveillance and restrictive legal frameworks made the situation on the eastside considerably more difficult, the "revolt gene" connected both sides.[22] This link explains why both West and East Berlin emerged as centers of gay rights movements in both German states, respectively. Not only shared traditions proved formative. It can be argued that during the 1970s and 1980s, close proximity defined the gay rights movement in East Berlin. While it remained rooted in the East and acted locally, it still has to be understood as part of a transnational activism.

Gay Self-Assertion in the Homosexual Interest Group Berlin (HIB)

The HIB can be regarded as the beginning of a gay and lesbian rights movement in the GDR, even if it never reached the same size and audiences as similar initiatives in the West. Up to 200 persons attended its events, yet the group itself only had about fifteen permanent members.[23] They tirelessly wrote to ministries, the *Volkskammer*, and other state agencies and forced these to at least acknowledge the HIB's existence and its demands.[24]

Scholarship has ascribed the almost simultaneous formation of the HIB and West German movement in the early 1970s to personal contacts across the Wall. From this perspective, transfers between gay activists in East and West Berlin established a feeling of community and created the conditions for adopting ideas of the Western gay rights movement[25] also in the East.[26] The 1971 Quadripartite Agreement on Berlin formed a prerequisite, as it enabled West Berliners and West Germans to enter East Berlin and the GDR starting October 3, 1972.[27] Contacts developed between East Germans and already organized gay men from West Berlin due to geographic proximity, shared language, the same sexual orientation, but also socialist ideals proclaimed on both sides of the Wall.[28] Media events such as broadcasting Rosa von Praunheim and Martin Dannecker's movie *It Is Not the Homosexual Who Is Perverse, But the Society in Which He Lives* (FRG, 1971) on January 15, 1973, on West German public television, galvanized a political consciousness in East Berlin, according to Josie McLellan. The HIB later traced its inception back to this day and consciously emulated mostly gay groups in West Berlin and the Federal Republic that had formed following screenings of the movie at select theaters.[29] The World Festival of Youth and Students in July and August 1973 also sparked activism among East Berliners. On this occasion, West Berliner and British gay activists distributed pamphlets in East Berlin and called attention to the homosexual participants with banners during the closing ceremony.[30]

The HIB therefore has to be placed in the contexts of both the political optimism within the GDR in the early 1970s and the development of new social movements in West Germany, Western Europe, and the United States since the late 1960s. The name Homosexual Interest Group Berlin referred to both: on the one hand, it referenced the Homosexual Action West Berlin (HAW) or Homosexual Action Hamburg (HAH), and other West German groups.[31] The sense of belonging also manifested itself in the positive appropriation of the terms *schwul* and *lesbisch*. On the other hand, the designation "interest group," or *Interessengemeinschaft*[32] stemmed from GDR's civil code and illustrated how the HIB, as any such initiative, planned to voice its concern within East Germany's legal framework. Moreover, the HIB's self-representation differed significantly from that of its Western counterparts. East Berliners never viewed themselves as political entities, as Magdalena Beljan has concluded for the West German gay rights movement, which understood "being gay" as inherently political and staged comings out in opposition to mainstream society.[33] The HIB activists did not aim to attack the GDR's political system, but to explain to its officials that "homosexual emancipation [...] was part of a successful socialism," as Peter Rausch recalled in 1991.[34] Following the pattern that Alf Lüdtke has defined as *eigensinnig*,[35] the activists expressed their views, but within the boundaries of what was permissible in public as defined by the state. For instance, they championed the education of homosexuals as "socialist personalities" or branded the "capitalist system" as the common enemy. In 1975, as the HIB approached the (East) Berlin Magistrate for the "opening of a homosexual communication center," it assured the state authorities to affect both the world view and sexual behavior of its audience:

> In particular, we are anxious not only for openness and trust within the community, but also for social commitment, our development to socialist personalities, as well as implementing moral practice within our sexual relations.[36]

But apart from professions of loyalty toward socialism, the HIB also drew comparisons between both German states and concluded that the GDR failed in its claims of superiority over the Federal Republic. In a letter to the *Junge Welt*, the party's youth magazine, HIB member Bodo Ameland hailed *It Is Not the Homosexual Who Is Perverse* on the West German ARD channel as the "best program" he had ever seen. Yet it surprised him that "a capitalist state (and not the GDR)" had debated "this problem."[37] By presenting the Federal Republic as setting a low bar, Amelang pursued two goals in one stroke: he rhetorically invoked the state-mandated policy of dissociation (*Abgrenzung*) from the West and took aim at the state and party leadership for failing to realize socialist ideals.

HIB members did not limit themselves to petitioning state agencies, but also wrote contributions for the publication of the Homosexual Action West Berlin, to which they had maintained personal contacts from its inception. Four reports appeared since mid-1973 under pseudonyms. A certain F.-P. reviewed in *HAW-Info* the sex education book[38] by GDR pedagogue and sexologist Kurt Bach under the headline "Is this Socialist Sex Education?"[39] and concluded that it could not be classified as socialist. As three other East German contributions to *HAW-Info* did, the review drew a connection between HIB and HAW, as both expected socialism to champion homosexuals. The HAW appropriated the East German criticism of GDR sexual science texts, as it accompanied no statement that the author remained responsible for his own views. Moreover, these publications gave East German activists the opportunity to weigh in on a public debate on homosexuality in sexual scholarship in the first place.

The HIB members maintained close contacts in West Berlin and the Federal Republic until the mid-1970s. Yet when they learned that GDR authorities attempted to prevent any kind of exchanges, the HIB duly complied by breaking off all visible Western contacts on its own.[40] When official recognition as the desired reward for this obedience failed to materialize, the HIB felt compelled to stop its work altogether in 1979. Hence the HIB's struggle for self-assertion, even if ultimately futile, seems to have been a balancing act: these activists had to navigate between affirmations of socialism and criticism of the GDR regime, on the one hand, and between skepticism of the West and participation in a transnational social movement centered in West Berlin, on the other.

The Working Group Gays in the Church as Mediators between East and West

The Working Group Gays in the Church—Homosexual Self-Help Berlin, under the roof of the Bekenntniskirche in southeastern Treptow—formed one of three church-affiliated groups of homosexuals in East Berlin of the 1980s. According to main organizer Christian Pulz, it was particularly important that those responsible for the working group "had debated the topic of homosexuality in some way, [...] so that they learned to accept themselves and to represent the cause vigorously."[41] Few scholarly insights were accessible in the GDR that could have supported the emancipatory work of these groups. Until 1989, only two sex education books[42] devoted to homosexuality were published, whereas already at the end of the 1970s entire book stores existed in the West that specialized in gay and lesbian literature.

Hence it was not far-fetched to seek reading material from these sources. McLellan has underscored the importance of books smuggled into East Germany by Western visitors in *Love in the Time of Communism*. Through these channels, homosexuals in the GDR could not only glean insights on Western gay/lesbian subculture and political developments within the Federal Republic, but also found a source for information on their own country.[43]

These books, magazines, and clippings mostly found their way illegally through West Berliner or West German visitors to the GDR. This literature was read, collected, and circulated. It also formed the basis for putting one's own perspectives in writing. In 1983, Ulrich Zieger authored "On Gay Reality in the GDR: Eight Remarks and One Attempt Against," which was intended as the Treptow Working Group's foundational text. Zieger first critiqued the heterosexual norms that shaped the upbringing of gays, to then criticize the lack of mingling spaces for gays as well as the tabooing of the topic in the GDR. The author did not comment on the situation of homosexual women. According to Zieger, fostering the solidarity between gays and enabling its members to represent their interests vis-à-vis church and state constituted the Working Group's priorities.[44] This article chiefly cited the 1974 book *Der gewöhnliche Homosexuelle*, or *The Ordinary Homosexual*, by Frankfurt sociologist and gay rights activist Martin Dannecker and psychoanalyst Reimut Reiche.[45]

Wolfgang Rüddenklau, member of Gays in the Church as well, adopted from this source his argumentation against so-called *Klappen*, the German term for cottaging practices in which men sought other men for sexual contacts in public restrooms, parks, or other spaces. For Rüddenklau, "patriarchic repression marked" these meeting places, since "interest in one's counterpart" was "reduced to narcissist self-referentiality and hurried courting of sexual partners." While the manuscript reads like a synopsis of *The Ordinary Homosexual* for many passages, it has remarks on uniquely East German circumstances interspersed. For instance, Rüddenklau points out that "besides the 3–4 larger cities no asylum in form of special venues exist," consequently gays remained "dependent on the cottage as the only place to meet."[46] Hence Dannecker and Reiche's book that, in conjunction with the aforementioned Rosa von Praunheim movie, played a decisive role in galvanizing the gay rights movement in West Germany and also provided some of the most important theoretical underpinnings for the East Berlin activists. West German literature found wide reception without reservations. Conversely the working groups acted as mediators of West German emancipation strategies, in which they tailored these texts to fit their perspective and subsequently made them accessible to a GDR audience.

The *Info-Brief*[47] of the Working Group provided another avenue for publishing commentary on emancipation and topical debates as well as excerpts of books and magazines that were not available in the GDR. For instance, two West German reviews of *Homosexuality: Challenge to Knowledge and Toleration* (East Berlin, 1987) by Reiner Werner[48] found an East German audience as reprints.[49] Debates on East German publications nominally took place in West German magazines, but the editors of the *Info-Brief* brought them to the GDR. Thus they made a critical engagement with Reiner Werner's work possible. Simultaneously, East German readers became attuned to a West German perspective, which can be classified as a diffident cross-border exchange.

The Working Group Gays in the Church furthermore attempted to reach an audience in the West itself. The East Berliners called attention to their situation through the article "Coming Out in a Vacuum: Why Gays in the GDR Turn to the Lutheran Churches" that was printed in multiple West German magazines.[50] The working group was known to non-organized homosexuals in West Berlin at least since the mid-1980s, because the guide book *Berlin from Behind*[51] first mentioned the group in 1985 and *Eldoradio*, West Berlin's first gay and lesbian radio broadcast, publicized the group's regular meetings starting in 1987. As a consequence, the number of attendants of the biweekly meetings from West Berlin increased.[52] The Working Group thus had become a meeting point for gays from both parts of Berlin, even if West Berliners surely frequented the Treptow congregation out of curiosity rather than a lack of alternatives. Christian Pulz hoped that name recognition in the West would give him and the Working Group some safety, even though activists had to pay close attention not to appear as enemies of the socialist state.[53] Just like the HIB had during the 1970s, the Working Group had to perform multiple balancing acts simultaneously: on the hand, to exist in the GDR in the first place, and, on the other, to attain the resources to conduct substantive work. Hence the East Berlin groups were constantly torn between distancing themselves from the West and making the most of the opportunities that contacts to West Berlin or the Federal Republic offered. But this web of constraints and chances prompted the Working Group to assert itself as an actor that shaped proximity and distance between East and West Berlin under the paradigm of the Cold War.

Coming Out During German Reunification

On November 9, 1989, *Coming Out*, the first and only GDR movie on a gay romance, premiered in East Berlin's *Kino International*. The fact that the film could be produced and screened in the GDR was a sensation, since it first depicted everyday life of gay men under state socialism and East Berlin's gay scene. The filmmakers succeeded in creating a remarkably frank and thus critical piece, but a political groundswell threatened to displace discussions on the movie's relevance. The state's dominance in the public sphere collapsed with the Berlin Wall on the very night of its first screening. In an instant, the GDR citizenry gained unfettered access to movies, magazines, and books from Western sources. In this moment, the leadership of the East German gay rights movement feared losing everything that they had built up in the preceding years.[54] Yet the gay and lesbian rights movement initially experienced an unexpected upturn, as many of the prior restrictions fell by the wayside.[55] By midyear 1990, thirty associations and initiatives had either been founded or developed from the circa eighteen church-based or non-affiliated groups that preceded the fall of the Wall.[56] In February, the Gay Association in the GDR (SVD) founded itself in Leipzig as an umbrella organization that aimed for "equal rights and equal treatment for gays in all areas of GDR society."

But many working groups also disbanded once restrictions had ended. Continuing one's activities under the Church's purview was no longer necessary, according to

Pulz.[57] As soon as the state's heavy hand had been lifted, those circles that had been kept intact by external pressure mostly fragmented. Conversely, Pulz entered Berlin's reunited city parliament in 1990 and served as Alliance 90/The Greens' spokesperson for gay and youth affairs until 1995.[58] East Berlin's gay rights activism accordingly shifted to other arenas and took new forms. The Working Group Gays in the Church disbanded, as did the *Arbeitsgemeinschaft Courage* that had formed out of the non-church-affiliated Sonntags-Club, as well as the *Magnus-Hirschfeld-Arbeitskreis* that had been connected with the state-recognized cultural association *Klub der Kulturschaffenden Johannes R. Becher*.[59] This last association wanted to rebrand itself as the Magnus Hirschfeld Gesellschaft and establish itself as its own association. But these plans failed since a historians' association by the same name had existed in West Berlin since 1982. Such duplication would have not been an issue in the days of the Wall, but in the reunited city East and West German associations now faced one another as competitors. During the 1980s, Ralf Dose of West Berlin's *Magnus Hirschfeld Gesellschaft* had maintained a host of contacts to East Berlin and other GDR cities, such as Rainer Herrn, who had been active in Leipzig's Working Group Homosexuality and had been instrumental in establishing the crisis intervention service *AIDS-Hilfe DDR* based in East Berlin since late 1989. Following reunification, West Berlin job centers made funds available to employ East Germans through public works programs. The *Magnus Hirschfeld Gesellschaft* could now make recourse to these earlier connections and establish together with Herrn a research center for the history of sexual scholarship in Eastern Berlin and recruit a number of GDR acquaintances in 1992.[60] Gay rights activities in East Berlin cannot have disappeared altogether, as some had feared; not even in the Lutheran congregations. One of the earliest church-affiliated groups in the GDR, the Conversation Circle Homosexuality, carries on to this day in Berlin's Advent Parish. The persistence of the Sonntags-Club that could meet in various state-controlled and private spaces since 1986 as the first non-affiliated gay and lesbian group also points to a degree of continuity of homosexual activism in East Berlin after German reunification.

The specter of expanding Paragraph 175 to former GDR territories provided the strongest incentive for the East and West German gay rights movements to close ranks. While the GDR decriminalized homosexual intercourse in 1988, the process of harmonizing the legal codes after German reunification galvanized hopes of striking the infamous paragraph from the books altogether. One of the high-profile events organized together was the demonstration against Paragraph 175 in Berlin on October 27, 1990. The organizers called for "German-German days of action against Paragraph 175" and hence highlighted both history and present of the shared struggle against the legal discrimination against gay men and stigmatization of same-sex couples.[61] Eventually, lawmakers backed off from extending Paragraph 175 to the *neue Bundesländer*, the Federal Republic's new constituent states. Instead, a principle of location would determine if the criminal code could become applicable, depending on which side of the former divide intercourse had taken place in. The legal disparity raised the pressure to reform the criminal code of the Federal Republic, until Paragraph 175 was struck from the books completely in 1994.[62]

Gay Cross-Border Entanglements

The actors presented here always operated within the context of divided Germany and within a divided city, in which encounters and transfers were as crucial as dangerous for East Berliners. Both the HIB in the 1970s and the Working Group Gays in the Church in the 1980s developed specific strategies to secure their own existence and expand their courses of action. On the one hand, these groups drew on terms, slogans, and ideas of West German and West European gay and lesbian rights movements. On the other hand, they were constantly concerned to not come across as being "run" by the West. McLellan has argued that the HIB has to be viewed as part of the social, political, and cultural change that had been sweeping Western Europe and the United States since the end of the 1960s.[63] In this regard, the HIB can be placed in the context of a transnational gay and lesbian rights movement of the 1970s, even if the group's members themselves never did so. It is no coincidence that the HIB formed in East Berlin. The self-styled socialist metropolis and "capital of the GDR" possessed the closest geographic proximity to the West. Moreover, it shared a long history of homosexual subcultural life with West Berlin.

The Working Group Gays in the Church also possessed contacts to West Berlin and the Federal Republic, engaged with West German texts on homosexual emancipation, and tried to draw attention through West German gay and lesbian media. At one and the same time, the Working Group prioritized reading on the West German debate on gay liberation and subsequently ignored the divide between East and West to an extent. But this was also impossible. The Working Group, too, had to walk a thin line between closeness to and distancing from the German neighboring country. No other East German gay rights enjoyed the same recognition in the West as the Working Group Gays in the Church, both because it actively drew attention, but also because West Berlin gay and lesbian media increasingly saw homosexuals in both Berlins as their audience and regularly reported on the East Berlin scene. The encounters, transfers, and reciprocal perceptions hence highlight how gay activism in divided Berlin inherently entailed communicating across walls and undermined the division, whether wittingly or unwittingly.

The Wall's collapse brought no end to East Berlin's gay rights activism, but demanded from the activists to part not only from the GDR, but also from tactics tailored to a dictatorial environment. Encounters between the movements in East and West that had developed in parallel entailed further challenges. At the same time, Berlin offered the best opportunities for planning together and organizing through old and new initiatives. Gay rights activists on both sides of the breached Wall now had the advantage of sharing contacts and an agenda that had developed in prior years through cross-border entanglements.

Notes

1   Michael Eggert was born in East Berlin in 1953. As a co-founder of the HIB, he was active in the city's gay rights movement. Today, he lives in Berlin.

2   *him* first appeared in April 1970 and after *DON* was the second commercial gay magazine to be published in the Federal Republic after the 1969 revision of Paragraph 175.

3   Interview Michael Eggert, March 21, 2013.

4   Peter Rausch was born in 1953. He was co-founder of the HIB and remains active to this day, e.g., in the *Sonntags-Club*, among others.

5   Jens Dobler and Harald Rimmele, "Schwulenbewegung," in: Roland Roth and Dieter Rucht (eds.), *Die sozialen Bewegungen in Deutschland seit 1945. Ein Handbuch* (Frankfurt/New York 2008), pp. 541–56, p. 542.

6   Ibid.

7   Christian Schäfer, "Widernatürliche Unzucht" (175, 175a, 175b, 182 a.F. StGB). Reformdiskussion und Gesetzgebung seit 1945 (Berlin, 2006), pp. 41–2.

8   Ibid., p. 209.

9   Josie McLellan, *Love in the Time of Communism* (Cambridge, 2011), p. 118.

10 Schäfer, "Widernatürliche Unzucht," p. 198.

11 Andreas Pretzel and Volker Weiß, "'Die westdeutsche Schwulenbewegung der 1970er Jahre. Annäherungen an ein legendäres Jahrzehnt," in: idem (eds.), *Rosa Radikale. Die Schwulenbewegung der 1970er Jahre* (Hamburg, 2012), pp. 9–26.

12 Kristine Schmidt, "Lesben und Schwule in der Kirche," in: Jens Dobler (ed.), *Verzaubert in Nord-Ost. Die Geschichte der Berliner Lesben und Schwulen in Prenzlauer Berg, Pankow und Weißensee* (Berlin,2009), pp. 198–220, p. 212. Further individual groups existed outside the church, once allowed in 1987. Anonymous, "Beratungsmöglichkeiten in den Bezirken der DDR," in: Friedrich-Schiller-Universität Jena and Hans Schmigalla (eds.), *Psychosoziale Aspekte der Homosexualität* (Jena, 1989), pp. 232–5.

13 Eduard Stapel, *Warme Brüder gegen Kalte Krieger. Schwulenbewegung in der DDR im Visier der Staatssicherheit* (Magdeburg, 1999); Günther Grau, "Erpressbar und tendenziell konspirativ. Die 'Bearbeitung' von Lesben und Schwulen durch das MfS," *Weibblick* 16 (1994), 21–5; Dominik Heck, *Homosexualität in der DDR* (Erfurt, 2012), p. 42.

14 Bundesarchiv, DO 4/821, Staatssekretär für Kirchenfragen, Abteilung II (Evangelische Kirchen und Religionsgemeinschaften), "Zu Aktivitäten in den evangelischen Kirchen in der DDR gegenüber homosexuellen Bürgern sowie weitergehenden Überlegungen für eine organisierte staatliche und gesellschaftliche Einflußnahme in diesem Bereich," October 1, 1986.

15 Gesetzesblatt der Deutschen Demokratischen Republik, Bekanntmachung der Neufassung des Strafgesetzbuches der DDR, January 31, 1989.

16 Schäfer, "Widernatürliche Unzucht," p. 282.

17 Bert Thinius, *Aufbruch aus dem grauen Versteck. Ankunft im bunten Ghetto? Randglossen zu Erfahrungen schwuler Männer in der DDR und in Deutschland Ost* (Berlin, 1994), p. 48.

18 Andreas Pretzel and Volker Weiss, "Bewegung zwischen Autonomie und Integration," in: idem (eds.), *Zwischen Autonomie und Integration. Schwule Politik und Schwulenbewegung in den 1980er und 1990er Jahren* (Hamburg, 2013), pp. 9–20.

19 Jens Dobler, *Von anderen Ufern. Geschichte der Berliner Lesben und Schwulen in Kreuzberg und Friedrichshain* (Berlin, 2003), p. 10.

20 Robert Beachy, *Das andere Berlin. Die Erfindung der Homosexualität. Eine deutsche Geschichte 1867–1933* (Munich, 2015), pp. 12–16.

21 Rainer Herrn, *Anders bewegt. 100 Jahre Schwulenbewegung in Deutschland* (Hamburg, 1999), p. 50.

22 Michael Sontheimer and Peter Wensierski, *Berlin. Stadt der Revolte*, Sonderausgabe für die Bundeszentrale für politische Bildung (Bonn, 2018), pp. 13–14.

23 Josie McLellan, "Glad to Be Gay behind the Wall: Gay and Lesbian Activism in 1970s East Germany," *History Workshop Journal*74 (2012) 1, pp. 105–30, p. 105.

24 Archiv Schwules Museum, DDR, HIB, Nr. 4, Korrespondenz, Schreiben an das Berliner Bezirkssekretariat des Kulturbundes der DDR, October 23, 1978; Schreiben an den Rechtsausschuss der Volkskammer der DDR, October 22, 1978; ibid., Bestand Bodo Amelang, Nr. 1 Korrespondenz, Brief Siegfried Spremberg an das Ministerium des Inneren der DDR, June 18, 1976.

25 It explicitly refers to a Western gay rights movement, as only connections to activists in West Berlin and Federal Republic can be substantiated.

26 McLellan, "Glad to Be Gay," p. 126; Jochen Kleres, "Gleiche Rechte im Sozialismus. Die Schwulen und Lesbenbewegung der DDR," *Forschungsjournal Neue Soziale Bewegungen* 4 (2000), pp. 52–63, p. 53; Thinius, *Aufbruch aus dem grauen Versteck*, p. 14; Günter Grau, 'Sozialistische Moral und Homosexualität. Die Politik der SED und das Homosexuellenstrafrecht. 1945 bis 1989—ein Rückblick', in Detlef Grumbach (ed.), *Die Linke und das Laster. Schwule Emanzipation und linke Vorurteile* (Hamburg, 1995), pp. 85–141, p. 125; Heck, *Homosexualität*, p. 33; Kay Nellißen and Kristine Schmidt, "Homosexuelle Interessengemeinschaft Berlin," in Dobler, *Verzaubert in Nord-Ost* (Berlin, 2009), pp. 178–85.

27 Hans-Hermann Hertle, Konrad Jarausch et al. (eds.), *Mauerbau und Mauerfall. Ursachen, Verlauf, Auswirkungen* (Berlin, 2002), pp. 296–7. Western visitors had to have departed through the border crossing by midnight. Starting in July 1982, the visits for the day could be extended until 2:00 am. Citizens of the Federal Republic received a valid visa directly at the border check and could thus enter as often as they wished, www.verfassungen.de/de/ddr/einreisenbrd72.htm (accessed May 4, 2018).

28 McLellan, "Glad to Be Gay," p. 126.

29 Ibid., pp. 109–10.

30 Ibid., p. 111.

31 Ibid., pp. 111–15.

32 According to Paragraph 266 of the GDR's 1975 civil code, citizens "could form associations through contract to create and maintain through labor and material resources institutions and facilities for collective and individual uses that improve working and living conditions." Zivilgesetzbuch der Deutschen Demokratischen Republik, June 19, 1975, www.verfassungen.de/ddr/zivilgesetzbuch75.htm (accessed February 2, 2020).

33 Magdalena Beljan, *Rosa Zeiten? Eine Geschichte der Subjektivierung männlicher Homosexualität in den 1970er und 1980er Jahren der BRD* (Bielefeld, 2014), pp. 85–6.

34 Peter Rausch, "Die vergessene Lesben- und Schwulengeschichte in Berlin-Ost (70er Jahre)," in: Ilse Kokula and Referat für gleichgeschlechtliche Lebensweise (eds.), *Geschichte und Perspektiven von Lesben und Schwulen in den neuen Bundesländern* (Berlin, 1991), pp. 21–6, p. 22.

35 Alf Lüdtke, "Lohn, Pausen, Neckareien: Eigensinn und Politik bei Fabrikarbeitern in Deutschland um 1900," in idem (eds.), *Eigen-Sinn. Fabrikalltag, Arbeitererfahrungen und Politik vom Kaiserreich bis in den Faschismus* (Hamburg, 1993). For an English language introduction of the concept, see https://docupedia.de/zg/Lindenberger_eigensinn_v1_en_2015.

36 Bundesbeauftragter für die Unterlagen des Staatssicherheitsdienstes der ehemaligen DDR (BStU), MfS, HA VII, Nr. 2743, Abschrift "Konzept für die Errichtung eines

homosexuellen Kommunikationszentrums," 1974, pp. 15–22, p. 19. The petition to East Berlin's Magistrate demanding an official counseling and communication center was sent only in April 1975. The reply was negative. Nellißen and Schmidt, "Homosexuelle Interessengemeinschaft Berlin," p. 180.

37 Archiv Schwules Museum, DDR, Bestand Bodo Amelang, Nr. 2 Korrespondenz Junge Welt, Brief Bodo Amelang an die Junge Welt, 1974.

38 Kurt R. Bach, *Geschlechtererziehung in der sozialistischen Oberschule* (Berlin/DDR, 1973).

39 F.-P., "Ist das 'sozialistische Geschlechtererziehung'? Bemerkungen zu einer Veröffentlichung aus der DDR," *HAW-Info* 12 (1973), pp. 38–41.

40 Interviews Michael Eggert, March 21, 2013, Peter Rausch February 19, 2013.

41 Interview Christian Pulz, August 12, 2013.

42 Reiner Werner, *Homosexualität. Herausforderung an Wissen und Toleranz* (Berlin/DDR, 1987); Günter Grau, *Und diese Liebe auch. Theologische und sexualwissenschaftliche Einsichten zur Homosexualität* (Berlin/DDR, 1989).

43 McLellan, *Love in the Time of Communism*, p. 120.

44 BStU, MfS, HA XX/AKG, Nr. 723, Ulrich Zieger, "Zur Schwulen Realität in der DDR. 8 Bemerkungen und ein Versuch dagegen," pp. 54–64.

45 Martin Dannecker and Reimut Reiche, *Der gewöhnliche Homosexuelle. Eine soziologische Untersuchung über männliche Homosexuelle in der Bundesrepublik* (Frankfurt am Main, 1974).

46 Robert Havemann Gesellschaft, Archiv der DDR-Opposition, Sammlung Wolfgang Rüddenklau, WR 03, "Schwule in der Kirche," Manuskript "Klappenabend—Kontraposition," without date, without page numbers. The manuscript must have been written between 1983 and 1985, since Wolfgang Rüddenklau left the Working Group in 1985. Ibid., Brief Wolfgang Rüddenklau an den Vorbereitungskreis Schwule in der Kirche, November 3, 1985.

47 The *Info-Brief* appeared bi-annually between January 1985 and February 1988. During this period, it developed from a two-page calendar of events into typewritten magazine with up to thirty pages and without pictures. Each issue was accompanied with the notice "for internal Church use only."

48 Reiner Werner (1932–2003) was Professor for forensic psychology at East Berlin's Humboldt University and director of an interdisciplinary work group homosexuality since 1984 that had been tasked by the SED leadership Berlin to study the everyday life of homosexuals in the GDR.

49 The reviews stem from the gay and lesbian magazine *Rosa Flieder* 10–11 (1987) and the magazine *Konkret* 9 (1987). Archiv Schwules Museum, DDR, Kirchliche Arbeitskreise Homosexualität, Nr. 3b, Schwule in der Kirche (Plesserstraße, Berlin-Treptow), Schwule in der Kirche, Info-Brief Nr. 4, February 1988, pp. 8–11.

50 Anonymous, "Wir leben in einem Vakuum," *Torso* 11 (1983), pp. 16–17; Kopie desselben Artikels in *HuK-Info* 43 (1983), pp. 29–30; Anonymous, "Coming out im Vakuum. Schwulbewegtes aus der DDR," *Rosa Flieder* 33 (1984), pp. 42–43; Anonymous, "Coming out im Vakuum," *aha info* 10 (1983), pp. 5–8.

51 Bruno Gmünder and Christian Maltzahn (eds.), *Berlin von hinten. Lese- und Reisebuch für Schwule, Gays und andere Freunde. 1985* (Berlin, 1985), pp. 227.

52 BStU, MfS, HA XX, ZMA, Nr. 10050/3, Bd. 5, p. 23; BStU, MfS, HA XX, Nr. 5192, p. 110.

53 Interview Christian Pulz, August 12, 2013.

54 Ibid.; Günter Grau, "Kehrtwende. Auch als Vorwort zu lesen," in: Günter Grau (ed.), *Lesben und Schwule, was nun?* (Berlin, 1990), pp. 9–23, p. 22.

55 Ibid.

56 Heck, *Homosexualität in der DDR*, p. 61.

57 Interview Christian Pulz, August 12, 2013.

58 Christoph Links, "Biographie Christian Pulz," in: Helmut Müller-Enbergs et al. (eds.), *Wer war wer in der DDR? Ein Lexikon ostdeutscher Biographien* (Berlin, 2010), www.bundesstiftung-aufarbeitung.de/wer-war-wer-in-der-ddr-%2363%3B-1424.html?ID=2734 (accessed February 2, 2020).

59 Archiv Schwules Museum, DDR, Teilnachlass Dieter Berner, Nr. 6, Gruppen und Vereine, Magnus-Hirschfeld-Arbeitskreis beim Kulturbund der DDR, Einladung an Dieter Berner zur Gründung Magnus-Hirschfeld-Arbeitskreis 1988, July 4, 1988.

60 Ibid.; Interview Rainer Herrn, October 16, 2015.

61 Archiv Grünes Gedächtnis, B.II.1, 6092, 1–2, Schwulenverband in Deutschland, Bundesverband Homosexualität et al., Aufruf zur Demo gegen § 175 StGB in Berlin am 27 Oktober 1990.

62 Schäfer, "Widernatürliche Unzucht," p. 278.

63 McLellan, "Glad to Be Gay," p. 105.

11

Exhibiting Berlin: Local History in Berlin's Museums

Andreas Ludwig
Translated by Torben Brown

Cold War Berlin sells. An exhibition on West Berlin shown in Berlin's City Museum in 2014/15[1] was a big hit with visitors. The same holds true for other sites that represent the divided city. The architecture of East and West Berlin garner wide public interest and determine how people orient themselves in the city, in particular tourists. The latter cite "history" as the third most important reason to visit Berlin.[2]

Only now that the Cold War is history has it gained cultural recognition in museums,[3] exhibitions, and memorial sites. Until 1989, Cold War Berlin—with the exception of the museum at Checkpoint Charlie that opened as early as 1963—was largely absent from this landscape of cultural representations. In fact, none of the existing local history museums took into account Berlin's more recent past in spite of the fact that postwar developments had such a significant impact on the city. In this chapter, I would like to take a closer look at how local history museums in both parts of divided Berlin reacted to the Cold War.[4]

"Old Berlin" in the Undivided City

Berlin's venerable local history museum, the Märkisches Museum, founded in 1874, was intended to represent not only Berlin but also the surrounding areas, and when the museum building opened in 1908, both the architecture and the collections on display paid tribute to the margraviate of Brandenburg. Nevertheless, the museum was founded under the impression of urbanization and the consequent vanishing of much of Berlin's traditional character, and so visitors to the newly opened museum were to be treated to an experience of the "old Berlin." This dual character was a manifestation of the desire to see the "good old days" preserved and remembered.

Much of Berlin's relationship to history can be explained by the effects World War Two had on the city. The Märkisches Museum had been destroyed, one ruin among others in the southeastern city center. In 1946, however, it became the first museum to be reopened in Berlin and, as before, it presented artifacts of Berlin's cultural history in its provisional rooms: porcelain, drawings by Heinrich Zille, interiors of

Gerhart Hauptmann's study, the traditional Christmas presentation of toys, a display on Berlin in Goethe's time in 1949 to celebrate the author's 200th birthday, but also contemporary works of art. Walter Stengel, the museum's director since 1925, seemed to be rather ignorant of the changing political situation in the city, but when he lost his position in 1952 for reasons that remain obscure, things began to change. The following year, 1953, was declared "'Karl Marx Year" and the museum contributed to the official celebrations with an exhibition called *Berlin wie Karl Marx es sah* ("Berlin as Karl Marx Saw It").

A few years later, in 1958, Erik Hühns was appointed as director and transformed the institution into a "socialist" museum, meaning that the history of the working class became a focus both of acquisitions and exhibits.[5] The programmatic first exhibition under Hühns was dedicated to the revolution of November 1918 and more presentations on political events were to follow. Another emphasis was placed on contemporary art with frequent exhibitions tracing postwar developments in particular. However, the core of the "socialist museum" was its permanent presentation. It was developed over time and provided a chronological survey of Berlin's history up to the present. Since 1958, the museum struggled to develop a *kulturpolitisch richtige Einstellung* (the "right" approach to cultural politics), and Hühns was said to have helped implement a Marxist-Leninist model for the museum's activities.[6]

However, neither the acquisitions policy nor the exhibitions were entirely colored in red. Traditional museum work continued, as published overviews of new acquisitions and the themes of many exhibitions show.[7] Toys at Christmas time, Berlin porcelain, medieval archaeology, historic city maps, and depictions of the town, mechanical instruments, arts and crafts, rooms commemorating Gerhart Hauptmann and Theodor Fontane, memorabilia of famous Berliners—all these exhibits represent the strengths of the collection and the traditional character of a local history museum. The press continued to call the Märkisches Museum "*Unser Heimatmuseum*"[8] and visitors seem to have remained critical toward "modern" themes such as contemporary art.[9]

The Märkisches Museum upheld the cultural legacy of the "old Berlin" but it was located on the eastern side of a divided city. We don't know how many West Berliners visited the museum before 1961, but on the occasion of an exhibition on Charlottenburg—the only instance where a West Berlin district was the subject of an exhibit—the newspaper *Neues Deutschland* pointed out that many West Berliners came to see the show, that it displayed a richer collection of original objects than could be found in West Berlin, and that the exhibit was suited to strengthening the ties between all Berliners.[10]

The Construction of the Wall and West Berlin's New History Museum

On August 13, 1961, the Berlin Wall was erected. This affected the city's museum landscape with regard to the presentation of local history. Now closed off from East Berlin's Märkisches Museum, an initiative was organized to found a comparable museum in West Berlin.

As early as the 1950s, plans were mooted to establish an *Auffangstelle für Berolinensien*[11] or a local history museum in West Berlin, in reaction to the turn toward a Marxist interpretation of history in East Berlin. These plans were blocked on the political level; before 1961, official recognition of the division of the city was to be avoided. However, these early discussions laid the groundwork for the notion that West Berlin, now walled-in, needed a local history museum, an idea that suddenly found support among cultural elites and the press. Art historian Edwin Redslob in particular promoted the project and came up with an appealing description of what this new "Berlin Museum" should look like. It should not be another Märkisches Museum but a *Heimatmuseum von weltstädtischem Gepräge*.[12] This goal combined Berliners' feelings of loss ("*Heimat*") with the role West Berlin was hoping to play in a global context. The founders of the new museum managed to win the support of donors to facilitate the acquisition of significant objects for the collection and to help find a provisional venue where they could be put on display. Exhibitions were organized from 1964 on and the museum officially opened in a Baroque palais in Kreuzberg, the so-called Collegienhaus, in 1969.[13] It remained there until 1993.

What the Berlin Museum collected and presented in public was neither *Heimat* nor *weltstädtisches Gepräge*, but a fine selection of art and arts and craft related to Berlin. The first exhibition, opened by West Berlin mayor Willy Brandt in 1964, presented views of Berlin by the nineteenth-century artist Eduard Gaertner and, over the years, all the prominent names of the local art world, from the eighteenth to the early twentieth century, would follow.

Without the space to go into details, I would like to stress two points here: one is the obvious similarity in the interpretation of what aspects of Berlin's history should be represented that prevailed on both sides of the city. Well into the 1960s, and on both sides of the Berlin Wall, representations of Berlin's history remained traditional in style, material, and visual evidence. It is the traditional town of Berlin before the expansion caused by urbanization and industrialization and before the destruction in war—and the postwar destructions, I might add. There is a general tone of mourning over these losses that seems to accompany the construction of the historical narrative which was, especially in West Berlin, additionally fired by a sentimental feeling of displacement, as can be found in Marlene Dietrich's song *Ich hab noch einen Koffer in Berlin* ("I still have a suitcase in Berlin") of 1951/3 or Hildegard Knef's *Ich hab so Heimweh nach dem Kurfürstendamm* ("I am longing for home on Kurfürstendamm") of 1963. Second, contrary to its East Berlin counterpart, the Berlin Museum did not make the side of the city in which it was located the subject of its presentations. For one thing, most of Berlin's historical sites were to be found in the city center, now located in the East. The Berlin Museum itself was housed in the only building in West Berlin remaining from the eighteenth century. For another, postwar history was not dealt with in the museum. West Berlin really seemed a *geschichtsarmer Ort* ("a history-deprived place"), an expression used during the debate over the need to establish a local history museum in West Berlin in the 1950s.[14]

Representations of local history, acquisition policies, and the overall appearance of both the Märkisches Museum and the Berlin Museum remained antiquarian. Neither had the museum in East Berlin being transformed into a *sozialistisches*

Heimatmuseum ("socialist heritage musem") as it has been demanded by the SED, nor had it taken up the emerging field of modern urban history. This was yet to come in the course of the 1980s.

More Local History Museums—an Overview of the Situation in the 1970s

A competing but not a conflicting history as it was presented in the local history museums of East and West Berlin was the norm for the top level of urban historiography in the divided city. Other museums existed that dealt with the history of the formerly independent towns that now comprise the boroughs of Berlin.

These museums tended to be founded in four time periods: around 1900, the 1920s, the 1950s, and the 1980s. At the turn from the nineteenth to the twentieth century, the independent towns of Charlottenburg, Rixdorf (later Neukölln), Spandau, and Schöneberg founded city archives that included collections of historic objects. The Neukölln Emil-Fischer-Museum of 1897, however, was the only true *Heimatmuseum* before World War One. The year 1920 marked the loss of the independence of these towns. As they were swallowed up in the urban agglomeration, a commensurate loss of local identity was felt here as well as in other residential areas that were incorporated into Greater Berlin. This prompted a series of efforts to establish local history collections during the 1920s and early 1930s such as—in what would become East Berlin—in the formerly independent town of Köpenick (1929) and in Lichtenberg, which already belonged to Berlin (1932), and in what would become West Berlin in Reinickendorf (1932), Steglitz (1923), Zehlendorf (1924), and the former town of Wilmersdorf (1931).[15] Most of these collection were destroyed during the war or looted during the postwar period and rebuilt in the course of the 1950s. At that time, other local history museums were opened in districts such as Tempelhof, Tiergarten, and Wedding—all in West Berlin, and in Pankow in the East. All these projects were of a private nature when individuals or small groups of citizens took the initiative but, especially in the 1950s, they began to receive public funding as they proved of interest to primary schools and their *Heimatkunde* curriculum. There is no indication that these museums ever took notice of the other part of Berlin or that they ever went beyond the local. In West Berlin, the responsibility for local history was assumed by the individual borough administrations and this reinforced a narrative focus on reconstruction and self-assertion. A publication accompanying the 250th anniversary celebrations of Charlottenburg stated: "In der seit 1948 politisch, wenn auch nicht gesinnungsmäßig geteilten Stadt [Berlin, A.L.] sind Charlottenburg die Aufgaben einer kristallisationsbildenden City zugefallen."[16] Mayor Willy Brandt's preface to a publication on the 700th anniversary of Schöneberg's founding makes the same point: "In der 700jährigen Geschichte Schönebergs haben die letzten sechzehn Jahre diesen erst 1920 in Groß-Berlin eingemeindeten Bezirk in besonderem Maße in das Blickfeld der Weltöffentlichkeit gerückt."[17]

All of the local history museums mentioned in this chapter underwent a decline during the 1970s. The number of visitors to the Berlin Museum, for example, rose from its opening year until 1975 and then fell slightly until 1980. Some of the local institutions even closed temporarily and were only reopened during the 1980s. Both the cultural history of the old Berlin and *Heimatgeschichte* seemed to hold less interest at a time when the postwar reconstruction period had ended, school curricula had changed, and Berlin's role in world politics had become less dramatic.

The Grassroots and Challenging History in the 1980s

Ideas regarding the uses and presentation of history began to change in the early 1980s in West Berlin. Local history became a part of larger grassroots initiatives in West Germany to foster a greater awareness of the city as a place to live. The notion of a car-friendly city and the neglect of turn-of-the-century housing were just two issues that were viewed increasingly critically. Later, a focus was placed on the effects of national socialism on the local level. The consequences for the local history museums in the West were manifold. Some of them developed a new approach, urban micro-history, in the course of the 1980s. The local history museums in West Berlin developed exhibitions that dealt with late nineteenth- and twentieth-century issues, for example local urban planning, sites in transition, the industrial heritage, immigrants, and, most prominently, the Nazi past on the occasion of the fiftieth anniversary of 1933. These exhibitions were strictly local and did not mention the Eastern part of the city. Only in the Wedding district were the postwar period, the Berlin Wall, and the borough's leftwing proletarian past subjects of exhibits.

Changing perspectives on history also left their mark on West Berlin's Berlin Museum. In 1980, Dieter Sauberzweig, West Berlin's social democratic senator for cultural affairs, quite brusquely criticized the museum's stance on history, stating, "that predominantly an idyllic Berlin was presented here whereas political and social struggles are missing." As the new director Rolf Bothe put it, the museum should aspire to meet the expectations of the public in light of a new political situation and before the backdrop of a changing consciousness of the city (*Stadtbewußtsein*).[18] It was said that the museum had in the past created the image of a city that no longer existed and that it should address issues of contemporary history. In the years that followed, in addition to its traditional program devoted to themes of cultural history, the museum organized exhibitions on the life of homosexuals in Berlin (1984) and Jewish history (1983). In the latter exhibit, the Berlin Museum took note of sites in the East and also encouraged East Berlin historian Hermann Simon to publish in the West.[19]

Another example of the increasing recognition of the Eastern part of the city is in the realm of photography. West Berlin's museum of modern art, the Berlinische Galerie, which had been founded as a result of a private initiative in 1975, devoted its attention to the postwar demolition in Berlin as early as 1981 when it exhibited photographs of Potsdamer Platz under the curatorship of Janos Frecot, showing how this former center square in Berlin became a wasteland trapped between the two halves of the city.[20] The exhibition is an early example of the rediscovery of central Berlin's historic legacy in the still neglected area along the Berlin Wall, a part of the city that would later garner attention through research conducted in the context of the *Internationale Bauausstellung* (IBA) of 1984/7. Here, East Berlin's urban reconstruction policy was also taken into account.[21]

1987—History Omnipresent

As Krijn Thijs has shown in detail,[22] the 750th anniversary of Berlin's first mention in 1987 became an issue of national importance on both sides of the Wall. Here, I would like to concentrate on the world of museums and exhibitions, starting with West Berlin.

Let us look first to institutions with a broader focus. In West Berlin, the foundations of the German Historical Museum were laid only a few hundred yards from Potsdamer Platz and the Brandenburg Gate in recognition of the new found prominence of the former central areas of the city close to the Berlin Wall. As a present of the Federal Republic to Berlin on the occasion of the city's anniversary, the museum was supposed to sum up 2,000 years of German history. It was heavily criticized in Berlin where there was a strong preference for the more open concept of negotiating history in a forum.[23]

For the celebrations, the West Berlin Senate had installed a commissioner to organize the various festivities, including concerts, festivals, a boat parade, fireworks, as well as exhibitions.[24] The Berlin Museum presented paintings showing cityscapes from the seventeenth century to the present[25] and the Berlinische Galerie arranged an exhibit on the big city in twentieth-century German painting.[26] Both exhibitions sought to show off pieces that had been collected in West Berlin since the 1960s. They succeeded in demonstrating West Berlin's importance as a cultural center, confirming claims that had been made in the years after 1961. Although focusing on the "Old Berlin," the metropolis of the 1920s, and West Berlin in the arts, a few paintings also showed East Berlin. The other part of the city thus was not completely left out, but appeared rather marginal in West Berlin's discussions about history. The same can be said about the official exhibition on Berlin's history presented at the Gropius Bau Exhibition Center that had opened its doors in 1981 and was situated directly at the Berlin Wall: *Berlin, Berlin. Die Ausstellung zur Geschichte der Stadt.* The title suggests that the exhibit was to be seen as the culmination of all historical debate and the presentation did provide a modern interpretation of the role of Berlin throughout history. It also did not shy away from a rather political interpretation of Berlin, of a metropolis of the twentieth century that, in spite of fascism, destruction in war, and political division, was going to continue to be important as an example of the city of the future—the judgment of Reinhard Rürup as stated in the exhibition catalog.[27]

Exhibitions were a new and modern medium at the time that could serve to attract the public to history; both the objects on display and the venues in which they were presented carried meaning. In 1987, West Berlin was no longer seen as a place without much history, as had been claimed in the 1960s. On the margins of the urban development efforts conducted after the construction of the Berlin Wall, the city's history was uncovered, the "rediscovery of the historic center" proclaimed. Also, the method of *Spurensuche*—a search for traces of the past—received official recognition in the context of the Senate's celebrations program.[28] The program (and the funding, of course) comprised a distinct number of exhibits, such as "Myth of Berlin" (*Mythos Berlin*) at the ruins of the former Anhalter Bahnhof, Berlin as a center of railroad and travel (*Reise nach Berlin*, Museum für Verkehr und Technik), "Half of a Lifetime" on labor in Berlin (organized by the DGB labor union), the local history of the working-class districts of Wedding and Schöneberg (presented by the Berlin history workshop), medieval Berlin (presented by the Museum für Ur- und Frühgeschichte), "Out of the Rubble" on postwar Berlin (organized by the city archives), *Ich und die Stadt*, an arts exhibition (organized by Berlinische Galerie), and *Stadtbilder* ("Cityscapes") from the seventeenth century to the present (organized by the Berlin Museum). The very broad base of participation of institutions, organizations, and civil society was programmatic and a reaction to the turmoil in the city in the 1980s. Mayor Eberhard Diepgen, in his foreword to the official celebrations program, even stated that the APO, the Alternative Liste, and squatters were part of the pluralistic community of Berlin.[29]

The historic center was the focal point of East Berlin's museum exhibitions as well. The Märkisches Museum presented exhibitions on *Die mittelalterliche Handelsstadt Berlin/Kölln*, Berlin's history up to 1648 (presented at the newly reconstructed Nikolaikirche), on the post-1945 cityscape in the arts and "Berlin from 1648 to 1871," both at the Märkisches Museum. The national history museum Museum für deutsche Geschichte presented *Berlin 1871–1945* at the Zeughaus and an open-air exhibition at the Franziskaner-Klosterkirche showed the reconstruction of Berlin from 1945 to the present in photographs. Other exhibits focused on medals and coins, arts and crafts, theater, and much more—in total there were 120 exhibits in East Berlin over the year. And despite the fact that in the official East German interpretation of Berlin's history,[30] the so-called *Thesen*, four out of nine chapters were dedicated to post-1945 developments, most of what was presented was pre-1933 history. Even in the exhibition showing the modern cityscape in drawings and paintings, the nineteenth-century city still dominated over representations of modern socialist Berlin.[31] East German officials had pointed out that the years after 1945 were the most important in Berlin's history,[32] but as far as we can tell from the exhibition catalogs, this was not the main message of the presentations. Rather, it seems that the significance of the cultural heritage of the nation's capital was stressed. Traditional local history and an image of Old Berlin prevailed.

From today's point of view, the Eastern presentations appear traditional in comparison to the new recognition of urban developments in West Berlin. The topics were the same as in the 1950s and 1960s, relying on collections that were considered appropriate for representing cultural history in a traditional manner—and artifacts that were quite similar to what West Berlin's Berlin Museum had collected during the 1960s and 1970s.

In a comparative view of the 1987 celebrations, another remarkable similarity between East and West becomes clear: the founding or expansion of local history museums in all of Berlin's then twenty-three boroughs. West Berlin's Senate made it clear that all West Berlin boroughs were expected to have a local history museum[33] and all eleven East Berlin boroughs had to have at least a *heimatgeschichtliches Kabinett* as a first step toward a local *Heimatmuseum*.

Summary

While these initiatives were strictly local, one has to ask whether a Cold War rivalry nevertheless existed in the field of museums and exhibition in 1980s Berlin. While in the 1960s the founding of the Berlin Museum was a clear reaction to the division of the city, the exhibition and acquisition policy seems to support the notion that certain topics and museum artifacts were considered relevant in both East and West. But the postwar mourning about the loss of the old Berlin disappeared with a new generation and a younger public newly appropriated the city's history, focusing instead on urban renewal and Berlin's history over the course of the twentieth century. At the same time (that is, in the 1980s), the conception of history clearly drifted apart in the two halves of the city. In the East, Berlin's history and cultural tradition was viewed through the prism of the official narrative that emphasized the Eastern part of the city as the capital of the GDR and its representational role. In West Berlin, the focus was placed on the metropolis of the late nineteenth and early twentieth centuries, which gave the neglected areas close to the wall their due, but also allowed room for alternate interpretations of Berlin in the twentieth century. The 750th anniversary of Berlin's founding reflected a general new interest in history that could be found in both parts of the country. But the stories told had to be adapted to the contemporary political situation, meaning that both parts of the city concentrated on what they had, not on dreams of "one Berlin."

Notes

1   Franziska Nentwig and Dominik Bartmann (eds.), *West: Berlin. Eine Insel auf der Suche nach Festland* (Berlin, 2014).

2   Senatsverwaltung für Wirtschaft, Technologie und Frauen (ed.), *Tourismuskonzept Berlin. Handlungsrahmen 2011+* (Berlin 2011), p. 12, www.berlin.de/sen/kultur/_assets/kulturpolitik/kulturelle-teilhabe/tourismuskonzept.pdf (accessed February 2, 2020).

3   A detailed overview provide Hans Georg and Katrin Hiller von Gaertingen, *Eine Geschichte der Berliner Museen in 227 Häusern* (Berlin/Munich, 2014).

4   Berlin since 1920 is a rather new construction. It is composed of twenty boroughs as an agglomeration of various formerly independent towns, villages, and estates administratively subsumed under the term "Greater Berlin." The later development of local history museums should be understood in part as a consequence of this specific circumstance.

5   Hans-Joachim Beeskow and Herbert Hampe, "Dr. Erik Hühns—Direktor des Märkischen Museums von 1958 bis 1973," *Jahrbuch des Märkischen Museums* I (1975), pp. 44–7.

6   Ibid., p. 46.

7   See Jahrbücher des Märkischen Museums I (1975) to X (1984).

8   See *Berliner Zeitung*, September 22,1953, and other evidence.

9   Statement of Erik Hühns, *Neues Deutschland*, April 23, 1960.

10   *Neues Deutschland*, July 27, 1955, on the occasion of Charlottenburg's 250th anniversary.

11 Kai Michel, "Edwin Redslob und die Gründung des Berlin Museums—eine Staffette seines Lebens," in: Stiftung Stadtmuseum Berlin (ed.), *Jahrbuch Stadtmuseum Berlin* V/1999 (Berlin, 2000), pp. 86–120, p. 100.

12 *Der Tagesspiegel*, August 26, 1962.

13 For further details on early history, see Irmgard Wirth, "Gründungsgeschichte des Berlin Museums (1964–1980)," in *Jahrbuch Stadtmuseum Berlin* V/1999, pp. 121–41. Wirth was the founding director of the museum.

14 Michel, "Edwin Redslob," p. 101.

15 All information of local history museums on the Bezirks level in Oliver Bätz and Michael Haben, *Bericht zur Aktuellen Situation der Heimatmuseen und -archive in Berlin (West)*. Erstellt im Auftrag des Senators für Kulturelle Angelegenheiten vom Museumspädagogischen Dienst Berlin (Ms., Berlin, 1988); Arbeitskreis der Regionalmuseen Berlins (ed.), *Neue Wege in die Stadtgeschichte. Ostberliner Heimatmuseen und Sammlungen* (Berlin, 1991).

16 Konrad Haemmerling, *Charlottenburg 1905–1955. Lebensbilder einer Stadt* (Berlin, 1955), p. 144.

17 Helmut Winz, *Es war in Schöneberg. Aus 700 Jahren Schöneberger Geschichte* (Berlin, 1964), p. 7.

18 *Erwerbungen des Berlin Museums 1964–1981. Festgabe für Irmgard Wirth* (Berlin, 1981), p. 8 f, cit. in Dominik Bartmann, "Zur Geschichte des Berlin Museums 1981–1995," *Jahrbuch Stadtmuseum Berlin* V/1999 (Berlin, 2000), p. 143.

19 Hermann Simon, *Das Berliner Jüdische Museum in der Oranienburger Straße* (West Berlin, 1983; East Berlin, 1988). The museum was formerly located in Berlin-Mitte, part of East Berlin until 1990. It had been closed and looted in 1938.

20 Janos Frecot, *Berlin im Abriß. Beispiel Potsdamer Platz* (Berlin, 1981).

21 Josef Paul Kleihues (ed.), *750 Jahre Architektur und Städtebau in Berlin. Die Internationale Bauausstellung im Kontext der Baugeschichte Berlins* (Stuttgart, 1987); Hans Stimman, *Stadterneuerung in Ost-Berlin vom "sozialistischen Neuaufbau" zur "komplexen Rekonstruktion." Überblick und Materialien* (Berlin, 1985).

22 Krijn Thijs, *Drei Geschichten, eine Stadt. Die Berliner Stadtjubiläen von 1937 und 1987* (Cologne/Weimar/Vienna, 2008). See also Thijs' contribution to this volume.

23 Der Senator für Kulturelle Angelegenheiten Berlin (ed.), *Forum für Geschichte und Gegenwart. Protokolle der Anhörungen vom 18. November 1983 und 13. Januar 1984*, 2 vols. (Berlin, 1983/4).

24 Der Beauftragte des Senats für die 750-Jahr-Feier 1987 (ed.), *750 Jahre Berlin. Das Programm* (Berlin, 1987).

25 Berlin Museum (ed.), *Stadtbilder. Berlin in der Malerei vom 17. Jahrhundert bis zur Gegenwart* (Berlin, 1987).

26 Berlinische Galerie (ed.), *Ich und die Stadt. Mensch und Großstadt in der deutschen Kunst des 20. Jahrhunderts* (Berlin, 1987).

27 Reinhard Rürup, "Stadt der Widersprüche," in: R. Rürup and G. Korff (eds.), *Berlin, Berlin. Die Ausstellung zur Geschichte der Stadt* (Berlin, 1987), p. 622.

28 Ulrich Eckhardt, "Das doppelte Fest. Berliner Geschichte(n) in West und Ost," in: U. Eckardt (ed.), *750 Jahre Berlin. Stadt der Gegenwart. Lese- und Programmbuch zum Stadtjubiläum* (Frankfurt am Main/ Berlin, 1987), p. 18.

29 Eberhard Diepgen, "Vorwort," in: U. Eckardt (ed.), *750 Jahre Berlin. Stadt der Gegenwart. Lese- und Programmbuch zum Stadtjubiläum* (Frankfurt am Main/ Berlin, 1987), p. 13.

30 Komitee der Deutschen Demokratischen Republik zum 750jährigen Bestehen von Berlin, *750 Jahre Berlin. Thesen* (Berlin/DDR, 1986).

31 Märkisches Museum (ed.), *Das Bild der Stadt Berlin von 1945 bis zur Gegenwart* (Berlin/DDR, 1987).

32 *750 Jahre Berlin. Thesen*, p. 9.

33 Abgeordnetenhaus von Berlin, *Mitteilung zur Kenntnisnahme über ein erstes Entwurfskonzept zur Vorbereitung und Durchführung der 750-Jahr-Feier Berlins 1987*, Drs. 9/1283, September 13, 1983.

12

Performing Berlin: The Rivaling 750th Anniversaries of 1987

Krijn Thijs
Translated by Torben Brown

In the twentieth century, Berlin was one of the most hotly contested cities in the world. In Germany and far beyond, the political history of the last century can be told as a battle between three distinct social orders: fascism, communism, and liberal democracy.[1] Each one of these created its own Berlin, and each also happened to stage its own Berlin anniversary celebrations. The first birthday party took place in 1937, celebrating the 700th anniversary of the founding of what was then the Nazi capital of Germany. In 1987, there followed the 750th anniversary, with celebrations both in East Berlin, the capital of the GDR, and in the walled-in island city of West Berlin. Thus, Berlin experienced three big birthday parties in the last century, each informed by a different ideology.

Of course the anniversary celebrations in 1937 and 1987 comprised more than just street fairs, bear mascots, and general pageantry. In each case, the city authorities recognized, rightly, that the event was highly political. The guise of a birthday party, ostensibly apolitical in nature, was particularly well-suited to communicating political values by reinforcing emotional ties, identifying friend and foe, creating a sense of community, and by establishing one's place in the arc of history.[2] In performing the past, the anniversary celebrations of 1937 and 1987 created three historical narratives, each composed of its own collection of communal memories, providing its own historical evidence and its own storyline, featuring heroes, villains, and golden ages.[3] Thus, it is hard to imagine how the city of Berlin could have been presented more differently than in the capital of the Third Reich, the metropolis of the GDR, or insular West Berlin. And because of this, potential similarities between the three always were highly controversial.

The festivities and events of 1987 with all their pomp pose a challenge for historians. The extensive anniversary programs in both East and West Berlin took place during the "late" Cold War, just two years before the fall of the Wall and more or less at the very end of the period of division lasting from 1948 to 1989. Thus, there is a significant temptation to see them as a prelude of what was to come, as a foreshadowing of the collapse of the GDR, the opening of the borders, even of the reunification of the two halves of the city. However, when we reconstruct the lived experience of the population of mid- to late 1980s' Cold War Berlin, then the 750th anniversary celebrations hold a fascination for an entirely different, even polar opposite reason: 1987 marks what was perhaps the last year of the old order. East and West Berlin celebrated the city's birthday separately; they created narratives that, at least in part, stood in intentional contrast with each other. After forty years of division, the two rival parts of Berlin marshaled all the splendor they could muster to stage one last altercation before the old order, which had literally been etched in stone, would in two years' time crumble with incredible speed.

This chapter will look at the staging of the 750th anniversary celebrations in order to reconstruct the range of experience prevailing in 1980s' Berlin on both sides of the Wall. Because both halves of the city had to confront the legacy of the preceding regime, a short discussion of the 700th anniversary celebrations of 1937 is necessary. After reviewing the festivities of 1987, the essay will conclude by illuminating the numerous ways in which these three politicized presentations of Berlin in the twentieth century are interconnected while they in turn sought to differentiate themselves from one another.

The 700th Anniversary Celebrations of the Nazi Capital in 1937

Before the twentieth century, Berlin did not have any tradition of marking the city's founding or anniversaries. We do not know the date the medieval twin settlement of Berlin and Cölln was founded or when it received its town charter. Since the age of industrialization, Berlin had been perceived as a city without history, perhaps even as a place antagonistic to history, always pushing forward and striving to be a metropolis. The notion of Berlin having a birthday was first discussed in the 1920s, a time when many German towns organized anniversary festivities, notably Brandenburg, which celebrated its 1,000th birthday. In 1928, the municipal administration was asked if Berlin might not also have a birthday it could celebrate. The city archivist confirmed that Berlin was "probably" founded in "1230 or 1231." (He missed the mark, we now know—the city is a little older).[4] The suggested date would have allowed for anniversary celebrations in 1930 or 1931, but Lord Mayor Gustav Böß rejected the idea. He maintained that the precise date of the founding was not known and, moreover, that "the current climate [*Zeitverhältnisse*] is not conducive to ostentatious celebrations." He also noted that "political considerations do not warrant such festivities, either."[5] In the crisis-rattled capital of the Weimar Republic, an expensive party did not seem appropriate and so Berlin, still democratic, decided to forego this opportunity.

The situation, however, had completely changed eight years later. In 1936, after three years of national socialist rule, Julius Lippert, a local politician and early member of the Nazi party, was finally able to establish the authority over the municipal administration he had long aspired to. As the new "city president and lord mayor," Lippert now had many reasons to organize a splendid party that would elevate him and his office. Lippert revived the old idea of a 700th anniversary celebration and decided on the summer of 1937 as the date, predicating it on the earliest mention of Cölln in 1237. In doing so,

Berlin's Nazis began a tradition that is still adhered to today: thus the celebrations in 1987 and—much more modest—those of 2012.[6]

Berlin's national socialists were the first to celebrate Berlin's birthday. Their 700th anniversary festivities in 1937 were a local event. They were designed to bolster a sense of community and the attachment of Berliners to their hometown, and to anchor the city more firmly in the Third Reich. The program lasted for one week in August and included a pageant and a festival performance in the Olympic Stadium, an open air exhibition, and a flower parade. All of this was loaded with Nazi pathos, but it remained within the realm of a typical town festival at the time. No Albert Speer and no plans for "Germania"—the 700th anniversary celebrations were no more and no less than a local town fair. City President Lippert congratulated himself and ostentatiously subordinated his city and its people to the Third Reich. "I am convinced," he announced, "that all of Berlin's citizens [*Volksgenossen*] are proud of their hometown today and, in the spirit of the 700th anniversary celebration, will support me in creating a community of the people [*Volksgemeinschaft*] that will stand in the front lines in the battle for Germany's greatness."[7] And Berliners indeed proved eager to participate in the festivities: they came out in force to watch the pageant, decorated their windows, and took part in the flower parade.

Nazi big shots showed little interest in the local event. Hitler did not make an appearance and Berlin's popular Gauleiter Goebbels took part as a guest of honor only on one day. In his speech, he looked back on the "time of struggle [*Kampfzeit*]" after 1926, differentiated the Third Reich from the hated Republic and claimed, "In just under ten years we have succeeded in turning what was the reddest city in the world after Moscow back into a truly German city."[8] Afterward, he attended the big pageant. His diary entry, however, was scathing: Lippert was "not up to his task in Berlin [*gar kein Format für Berlin*]" and his 700th anniversary celebration was "a real joke." Goebbels continued: "Berlin decorated itself for its 700th year festival. Lots of pomp, but little taste. Typical Lippert."[9]

Traditionally, the historical parade was the highlight of town anniversary celebrations, and the 1937 event was no different. The birthday party began on Sunday, 15 August, with the historical pageant that included 4,300 actors, seventy wagons, and ten music bands. According to the program, the theme of the 130 parade presentations was "the development and growth of our home, the city that went from a small town founded on East German colonial soil to the capital of the Third Reich."[10] The content and political message of the parade was carefully prepared by the organizing committee that sought, in the pageant's first part, to illustrate the city's history in representative scenes. The second part was devoted to the boroughs of Berlin that had become a part of the city only seventeen years earlier and that, in part, had their own strong sense of identity. The last, somewhat shorter part presented contemporary Nazi Berlin: Hitler Youth and soldiers marched amid floats dedicated to industry. The size of the parade was informed to a large degree by traditional German rivalries, in this case, competition with Munich where a month earlier the "Day of German Art [*Tag der deutschen Kunst*]" had included an impressive parade. The Lippert-controlled organizing committee immediately decided that "no matter the cost, the Berlin parade should not be inferior to the Munich parade" and that the "staging of the Berlin parade be as pompous as possible."[11] In the end, a glamorous historical parade marched over twenty kilometers, and, in spite of occasional rain showers, attracted thousands of spectators from all over Berlin.

Unlike the parade, the historical performance in the Olympic Stadium was a perfect example of Nazi mass choreography. Here, the city's history was staged in a manner that made use of trumpet fanfare, the ringing of bells, and the beams of searchlights in a dark stadium. The medieval idyll and modern military altercations were the focus. Berliners in the sold-out Olympic Stadium were spellbound by a varied theater of the masses. This was the wish of the director of the performance, Hanns Niedecken-Gebhard, who wrote in the program: "The festival is a performance by the people for the people, tens of thousands are performing for hundreds of thousands. May it bring us all together in a community [*Gemeinschaft*] truly moved by joy and in a festive spirit."[12] The festival was such a success that three additional performances were added to the originally scheduled three.

Thus, anniversary celebrations like those of 1937 could reify a Berlin identity through parades and exhibitions, could in a sense make the contours of the city more visible, and could illuminate its history. Whether and to what extent the population bought into these attempts to create a common meaning and a shared identity is open to question. It is harder to identify dissent and protest when it comes to the relatively modest and short-lived anniversary celebrations of 1937 than for 1987.

The East Berlin 750th Anniversary Celebrations in 1987

Fifty years later, Berlin was a divided city and the end of that division could not yet be predicted. East Berlin, which had long stood in the shadow of the much more resonant West Berlin and whose government had completed the division of the city with the construction of the Wall, had been experiencing something of a boom since the 1970s. The GDR was receiving increasing international recognition, and the Quadripartite Agreement on Berlin of 1971 had bolstered East Berlin's reputation. Under Honecker it took to its role as the "capital of the GDR," although the Western powers rejected the claim. This legal ambiguity caused the authorities to be hypersensitive when it came to questions of East Berlin's status. Thus, East Berlin's official name underlined its role in East Germany: "Berlin, capital of the GDR."

In the East, discussions about the coming anniversary began in 1980 and it was immediately understood that this was an event that demanded the involvement of the East German government. Kurt Hager, a member of the politburo, declared in 1981 that the anniversary could serve, first, to "make a significant contribution to consolidating a sense of socialist belonging and a national consciousness among the citizens of the GDR"; second, to "strengthen the international prestige of Berlin as a socialist metropolis"; and, finally, to "help to effectively destroy imperialist concepts of a 'common history' or of 'keeping open the German question.'"[13] Unlike in the Third Reich, in the GDR, the festival became a state affair. That made one thing clear from the outset: in 1987, East and West Berlin would definitely *not* be celebrating the anniversary together.

In the following years, however, the GDR entered a period of stagnation, economically in the first place, but also politically and socially. The necessary generational shift did not occur, the number of people seeking to leave the country rose, and, particularly in the capital and under the auspices of the church, opposition and "independent" groups were formed. The country of "real socialism," of all places, had no credible ideas for the future. And yet in 1987 Honecker celebrated his greatest diplomatic triumph, traveling to Bonn on an official visit—the head of the GDR was now considered a statesman, some even saw him as an ambassador of peace.

Meanwhile, the plans for the 750th anniversary celebrations had reached new heights, driven by a battle for legitimacy with West Berlin. The head of state and party leader himself chaired the preparations committee, which had been set up in February 1985 and whose membership counted no fewer than "169 personalities from all branches of the social life of our republic."[14]

The Socialist Unity Party (SED) and the politburo signed off on the important decisions behind the scenes, while Berlin's municipal administration was mainly tasked with putting the decisions into effect. The significance of the celebrations becomes especially clear when looking at the residential construction projects that were pursued and at changes in the perception of the city's cultural heritage. After decades in which a modernist approach to city planning had been ascendant, the GDR now began to realize several prominent reconstruction projects. On the Platz der Akademie (today's Gendarmenmarkt), long an impressive collection of ruins, the concert hall as well as the French and German cathedrals were rebuilt from 1978 to 1987. Equally surprising was the resurrection of the Nikolaiviertel, Berlin's birthplace. As an historical stage set constructed in real socialist East Berlin, it was rather spectacular.[15] And it served to underline the fact that the roots of the city were to be found here and not on the other side of the Wall in West Berlin. Detractors joked that the Nikolaiviertel, closed off as it was with its pretty façades to its surroundings and which, in stark contrast to the drab GDR reality, was well-supplied, was "Honni's Disney World."

In competing with West Berlin, the 750th anniversary celebrations had been extended to include the full year. There were international conferences, carnivals, books, fine consumer goods, rock concerts, and street fairs.[16] The birthday itself was celebrated in an official event in the Palace of the Republic. Here Honecker gave proud voice to his city of dreams, contrasting the brutal reality of the closed border and the Wall:

> This official ceremony marks the high point of the 750th anniversary celebrations for Berlin. [...] During the last months we have had an impressive demonstration of how vibrant the pulse of life is in our land. Berlin, the city of peace, has proven to be a cosmopolitan setting for a meeting of minds, for dialogue and cooperation, a magnet for prominent artists and ensembles representing international culture.[17]

Unquestionably, the highlight of the festivities was the great historical pageant that paraded down the main boulevards of the capital on July 4, 1987 in brilliant sunshine. Compared with 1937, the parade route from Unter den Linden to Karl Marx Allee was fairly short, but with 40,000 people it boasted almost ten times the number of participants. The pageant comprised 291 scenes and lasted a full five hours. However, the struggling GDR had to expend tremendous energy to ensure that the parade went off "without incident." A wide security perimeter kept people from the square surrounding the grandstand on Karl Liebknecht Straße. *Stasi* officers were out in force.[18] But the day was a great success. The parade impressed friend and foe alike with its imaginative scenes. *Stasi* informants and Western journalists could agree that, unlike with the usual socialist marches, the atmosphere was both relaxed and festive.

Content-wise, the parade hewed to the "750 Years Berlin Theses," a short history of Berlin published by party officials that served as a guide for all anniversary events with an historical theme.[19] This ensured that a uniform history of Berlin was presented, predicated on the idea of class struggle and the ineluctable progression toward socialism. In this view, the years after 1949 were as important for East Berlin as the 700 years that preceded them: officially, the GDR was considered the climax of Berlin's history, a promise fulfilled.

The pageant did not ignore the sensitive aspects of East Berlin's history. The city's "liberation" by the Red Army in 1945 was featured, for instance, despite the fact that this had been a terrible experience for many older Berliners. Even the Berlin Wall made an appearance. One float, "August 13—we reliably protect the borders of the Republic and peace," displayed the Brandenburg Gate, walled-in and guarded by veterans. However, one aspect of postwar history went entirely without mention in the East: West Berlin. Neither the historical narratives nor the festival events acknowledged the Western half of the city. As a matter of course, the presentation of the city's history after 1949, the year the GDR was founded, narrowed to comprise only East Berlin.

All in all, East Berlin's birthday celebrations were pretty spectacular. The carefully maintained façade, however, already showed a number of cracks, especially in retrospect. Mikhail Gorbachev came to Berlin and was particularly loudly cheered, while his relationship with the SED leadership had already become markedly more strained. In April, Kurt Hager decried *perestroika* as nothing more than "a change of wallpaper" and demonstrators sported Gorbachev pictures during the official Labor Day rallies on May 1.[20]

The opposition was also visible at some of the anniversary events. During Pentecost, rock concerts held in West Berlin near the Wall led to unrest in East Berlin. At the end of June, a "church congress from below" was held, and *glasnost* and *perestroika* were openly debated. The alternative scene responded to state propaganda by offering its own images of Berlin. The photographer Harald Hauswald and the writer Lutz Rathenow presented their photography exhibition "East Berlin—the Other Side of a City" for the first time in the Umweltbibliothek. Their project, in part designed as a reaction to the anniversary, documented those considered "misfits" by the regime as well as everyday life and youth culture in the capital, garnering interest beyond the borders of the GDR. Hauswald's pictures became famous in the West, as well; the magazine *GEO*, for instance, published a special edition on the alternative scene in West and East Berlin that featured his photographs.[21]

Thus, the fact that the festival was freighted with political importance by the government was also a burden for the anniversary. There was little space provided to emphasize a local Berlin identity. In addition, resentment of the capital increased all over the country as it became clear that, for the 1987 event, East Berlin would be even more privileged than usual. To complain about Berlin was almost considered a patriotic duty in 1987. Snarky slogans and jokes abounded: "For Berlin the best, for the Republic the rest"; "Can you count to 1,000 without being disgusted? No, you have to get past 750"; "The problem with shortages under socialism has been solved: We'll send everything to Berlin and everyone can pick up what they need from there." Construction workers from all over the Republic were sent to Berlin to spruce up the capital while at home the town centers continued to fall apart. As a response, cement trucks arrived in Berlin featuring slogans like, "1,026 Years Halle." Bumper stickers and signets boasting "781 Years Dresden" and "821 Years Leipzig" were cynically interpreted by the government as expressions of socialist patriotism.[22] Sometimes the hatred for Berlin led to acts of vandalism: in numerous instances in the suburbs, cars bearing Berlin license plates were damaged or covered with paint ("Asses 750"). Western media greedily pounced on these images. Thus, the Berlin anniversary was conflated with a host of issues affecting the late socialist GDR. In this respect at least, things were not all that different in the West.

The West Berlin 750th Anniversary Celebrations in 1987

In the mid-1980s, West Berlin was one of the strangest places in Europe. It had survived for almost forty years as half a metropolis, walled-in and yet free, an enclave in enemy territory. The Berlin Agreement of 1971 had mitigated the vulnerability caused by its geographic location, but that led in essence to the question: why does West Berlin still exist? As an island it was entirely dependent on subsidies from the Federal Republic and in 1981 it was veritably thrown into crisis as it confronted construction and corruption scandals, squatters, and street fights under three different governing mayors. Increasingly, it seemed that Berlin's new role within the Federal Republic was to integrate new, alternative movements. As a fascinating (but no longer dangerous) borderland, the half-city attracted not only conscientious objectors from West Germany, but also artists, students, and adventure seekers from all over the Western world. On their island they somewhat arrogantly claimed an autonomous position in divided Germany. On the one hand, they were familiar with faraway West Germany, peopled by small-minded Berlin tourists and led by a provincial chancellor. The uninspiring GDR, on the other hand, they mostly got to know through the moody border agents they met on the ghostly transit routes. Berlin, in short, was its own world. National identity, reunification, and capital aspirations were notions completely unknown to large segments of the younger generation. Politically, however, the conservative Berlin was in charge, first in the person of Richard von Weizsäcker, then, from 1984, of Eberhard Diepgen.[23]

The 750th anniversary posed a challenge for the island. The 1980s did not provide much impetus for showing off. The historic old town was located behind the Wall. And in the House of Representatives, the contrast with the East was emphasized: "We do not want a celebration issued by decree like the one currently being planned with military pomp in East Berlin."[24] Originally, the hope had been to stage an event together with East Berlin to underline the common bond. The representatives were right in thinking that a separate/double anniversary would make Berlin "more or less the laughingstock" of the world.[25] But by the end of 1985, all hopes had been dashed. East Berlin was staging its own state-run festival and utterly ignoring its so-called "suburbs in the West." Thus, it was left to West Berlin to demonstrate the city's unity. "The historical festival is being staged twice, but is being seen together," the program announced; it pointedly included East Berlin events.[26] West Berlin chose the area "in front of the city gates" as the main venue. Historically, this ambiguous term had referred to the strip of land along the former city boundary between the Brandenburg Gate, the Potsdam Gate, the Halle Gate, etc. This is where the Berlin Wall now ran, and thus the festival choreography "in front of the gates" in 1987 also had a political dimension, as expressed by the Senate's guidelines: "The Wall shall not and should not turn the center of Berlin into a periphery. The Senate will consciously celebrate the year 1987 by looking to the Reichstag and the Wall—but also beyond it."[27]

In the 1980s, West Berlin was already in the process of rediscovering the long neglected urban centers of former metropolis.[28] In 1987, a series of renovation projects was underway to restore, for instance, the Hamburger Bahnhof, the Martin Gropius Bau, and the Kongresshalle. A first exhibition had been set up in the film museum planned for the Hotel Esplanade; Wim Wenders' movie *Wings of Desire*, an homage to the old Potsdamer Platz, was in theaters. At the Kulturforum, a chamber music hall was added to the Philharmonic and a test track for a futuristic magnetic rail line was set up. The founding of the German Historical Museum was part of the strategy to revive the old city center. The new museum was to be located across from the Reichstag and Chancellor Helmut Kohl symbolically unveiled the foundation stone as part of the birthday celebrations.

Berlin's empty center was also the site, at the Gropiusbau, of the anniversary exhibit *Berlin, Berlin*, in which West Berlin celebrated its proud history as a metropolis. For visitors, the dynamic history of the big city was to be presented as a sensual experience. Illustrative of this is the exhibition in the large atrium titled "The Fastest City in the World," which sought to recreate the lost metropolis of the Weimar Republic. The dark sides of Berlin's past were not excluded from the historical narrative and would have been hard to ignore at the Gropiusbau in any case. Its main entrance was blocked by the Berlin Wall. Next door was the wasteland that had once been the site of the headquarters of SS and Gestapo. As a result of grassroots efforts, in 1987 an accompanying exhibit, the forerunner of the "Topography of Terror," dealt with the history of the premises for the first time. Thus, West Berlin presented what can fairly be described as a thoughtful exhibition program that reflected the—in the Western view—unsatisfactory current political situation marked by division. Unlike the capital of the GDR, contemporary West Berlin could not see itself as experiencing a "golden age" in the city's history. Thus, it attempted to channel the mythological power of the 1920s.

Like Gorbachev and the leading lights of the Warsaw Pact in the East, the Western allies made an appearance at the birthday celebrations in West Berlin. François Mitterrand, Queen Elizabeth II, and President Ronald Reagan visited the city still under their protection. The American birthday party took place on June 12 in a hangar at Tempelhof Airport. Afterwards, Ronald Reagan gave his famous speech in front of the Brandenburg Gate. In it, he addressed Mikhail Gorbachev, his opponent in the Cold War, directly: "Mr. Gorbachev, tear down this wall."[29]

The construction projects, exhibitions, and state visits outlined above made for a decent party. But the main festival events demanded careful attention and creativity from the Organizing Agency. The Nazi 700th anniversary celebrations had discredited a number of traditional events, notably among them the parade. The earliest brainstorming sessions led the organizers to emphasize that "all embarrassment involving historical parades and the accompanying mass choreography" were to be avoided.[30] Historical pageants in the Olympic Stadium were also out of bounds. There was not a willingness to forego folk festivals, however, and so West Berliners had to be innovative. They succeeded first and foremost with the "Water Procession," in which historical ships were invited to Berlin from all over Western Europe. This way, the dreaded goosestepping could be avoided and the city could present itself as cosmopolitan. "No anniversary without a parade!," the organizers announced: "But this time no one has to march, because the parade will take place on the water, on the canals, the Havel lakes, and of course on the Spree, which has been flowing on its course for 750 years, indifferent to the city's borders."[31]

Another highlight was the multimedia show at the Victory Column. The *SternStunden* presented a theater and music variety show on the history of Berlin in August. This, too, was designed as a democratic version of a folk festival. Instead of using the Olympic Stadium as a venue, West Berlin chose a public park, the Tiergarten, and organized a show that was based not on mass choreography, but on individual performances and technical projections. Looking back, the senator responsible for cultural affairs emphatically declared that the *SternStunden* had "erased the 700th anniversary celebrations" of 1937. The Victory Column now had been transformed into a "column of peace."[32]

And yet in West Berlin, too, there was a lot of criticism and, in the end, violence. In the course of the year, the never-ending succession of festival events, speeches, receptions, and exhibitions were subject to growing ridicule and cynicism, especially in light of riots in Kreuzberg in May and June that had been exacerbated by the ongoing, self-indulgent political pageantry. In the rush to respond, senators even suggested that the rioting radicals were not real Berliners, but rather "anti-Berliners," which was soon adopted as a proud designation in Kreuzberg. In October, the "anti-Berliners" took over the Kurfürstendamm on a satirical-carnivalesque B750 antiparade.[33] Slogans such as "750 Years—We've Had Enough" began to appear on walls and façades. In addition, some avant-garde public art projects did not go over well with locals, thereby calling into question West Berlin's view of itself as liberal-minded and tolerant. By the fall, then, the mood was rather sober: the anniversary had gotten a little out of hand and had not, as had been the hope, led to clear progress in improving relations within the city. Or had it?

Interaction, Knocking Signs, and Echoes

This review of the Berlin anniversaries shows that, in forging and defining their identities, urban communities seek to relate to and differentiate themselves from each other. City rivalries play an important role, as in 1937 when Berlin was motivated to stage a grander parade than Munich had managed earlier. In the GDR, competing identities played an important role in the anger felt by those who saw the capital city as being unfairly privileged: At least Dresden at 781, Leipzig at 821, and Halle at 1,026 could boast that they were older than the mighty East Berlin. The rivalry between East and West in 1987 over which was the "true" Berlin is, of course, a special case brought on by the Cold War and the division of the city.

But it wasn't just such "synchronous" rivalries that informed the different, politically loaded city identities in the twentieth century. Berlin was hotly contested as a result of "diachronic" factors, the rapid succession of different political systems, and developed its identity in a constant effort to distinguish itself from its past. Berlin's birthday celebrations reflect this. West Berlin made what can be described as a conscious attempt to come to terms with its past by introducing the "Water Procession" and by eschewing the Olympic Stadium as a venue for the festival. The Senate and the organizing agency explicitly confronted the 700th anniversary as celebrated by the Nazis and sought to differentiate itself from that event. They concluded that their own programs had proved "that an open, democratic society can also appropriate large areas and that it doesn't have to give them up to the memory of the goose-stepping columns of a wretched past."[34] This sort of differentiation produced democratic legitimacy.

In the East, the diachronic connections were of an entirely different nature. According to its general stance on the Nazi past, the SED regime chose to ignore the 1937 anniversary celebrations entirely.[35] The party leadership itself had excised the reference to them in the manuscript of the "750 Years Berlin Theses" and the GDR media otherwise did not make specific mention of it. Thus the party leadership did not have to justify its decision to hold a parade. Because the issue was a taboo, it turned into subaltern knowledge only discussed in opposition circles. Thus, samizdat magazine *grenzfall* described the anniversary as an invention of Joseph Goebbels: "Thus the 50th anniversary of the 700th anniversary is celebrated in both parts of Berlin. We cannot comment on potential similarities between the two or, rather, three festivals, since we know too little about the events of the 700th anniversary."[36] These lines document alternative connections between the Berlin anniversaries of 1937 and 1987. Both East and West referenced the preceding anniversary and, even more so, each other, by competing with, adopting the ideas of, but also by aggressively distinguishing themselves from, one another. This became especially clear in July 1987. In light of the Nazi festival, West Berlin had rejected the idea of a parade and, after much debate, decided on the "Water Procession." East Berlin liked the idea and did not want to see the West steal its thunder, so it arranged its own "Water Festival" as well, on the same day. On July 25 and 26 1987, both halves of the city celebrated the same birthday on the same Berlin river in direct rivalry.

The careful planning and preparation that went into the anniversary celebrations notwithstanding, there were, of course, always unexpected and spontaneous events taking place in 1987. The direct exchange between East and West Berlin proved especially unpredictable. Interactions of this kind occurred via myriad channels; they were often described as "knocking signs at the Wall." Of course it was usually West Berlin that took the initiative, since it wanted to underscore what the two sides had in common. But signals also came from the East, both from the government and the people—and sometimes even from abroad.[37]

A well-known example of this are the rock concerts at the Reichstag and their violent echoes in East Berlin mentioned earlier.[38] Concerts had taken place at the Wall on numerous occasions before and the West Berlin organizers quite intentionally arranged for the music to be audible in East Berlin. This was certainly the case on Pentecost weekend in June 1987 when the three-day "Concert for Berlin" was held, featuring— among others—David Bowie, New Model Army, Neil Young, the Eurythmics, and Genesis. The event, however, proved extraordinary. While 60,000 paying attendees in West Berlin were looking forward to a relaxed concert, across the Wall on Unter den Linden tensions were rising. The youth in the GDR were well-informed about the festival, and so a few hundred fans congregated as close to the Wall as possible on Saturday night to hear David Bowie. The rock star even greeted his friends "on the other side of the Wall" in German. The police (*Volkspolizei*) were not prepared for this and pushed the crowds back. Angry, they responded with chants.

News of this made the rounds and the next Sunday the crowd of East Berlin fans had grown to over 2,000. The GDR security services deployed undercover agents to mix with the fans in order to discover the "ringleaders" and to keep the masses in check. They did not quite succeed. There was severe unrest during the Eurythmics' performance. The rock fans chanted, "We want Gorbachev," and later even, "The Wall must go!"

The following Monday considerably more people turned out. However, the area around the Brandenburg Gate had been cordoned off at such a distance on the Eastern side that the Genesis concert could hardly be heard. Now the situation escalated. Youth called out, "Cops out!"; "The Wall must go!"; but also "Kreuzberg is everywhere!", and "Nights in Kreuzberg are long!"—the last a reference to events in the West Berlin district where, in May, as the East Berliners were well aware, there had been substantial unrest. Bottles were thrown and nightsticks wielded, the authorities applied brute force and arrested approximately 120 people. An altercation between police and youth of this kind was highly unusual in the GDR. Western media covered the events closely, not least because some Western journalists, eager for a story, had mingled among the demonstrators and had themselves been provoked by *Stasi* officers. West Berlin television came close to covering the demonstration live so that Germany also got to see the ugly side of East Berlin during the 750th anniversary celebrations.

The East Berlin "Brawl at the Wall" during the West Berlin rock concerts was still an important topic of discussion a few days later when Ronald Reagan arrived.[39] His great speech on June 12 was one of the carefully planned and choreographed "knocking signs" at the Wall. The choice of venue, the telegenic backdrop with a view toward East Berlin, proved particularly ingenious. This time, the area around the Western side of the Brandenburg Gate was cordoned off; there had been unrest in West Berlin for days. Demonstrations took place in the Western city center, road blocks cut off radical demonstrators in Kreuzberg, and a select audience was assembled in front of the stage, including numerous Americans and so-called "stabilizers" who could surround and drown out would-be hecklers. The leftwing *taz* newspaper sarcastically contrasted the "Stabis" on one side of the Wall with the "Stasis" on the other. With the president turning his back to East Berlin, it looked as if the archenemy was actually considered the slightest threat. The GDR authorities carefully monitored the goings-on in front of "their" Brandenburg Gate. In his speech, Reagan, as expected, repeatedly addressed the East Berliners behind him: "There is only *one* Berlin," he said in German. And directing his sights beyond East Berlin he issued his famous appeal to Moscow: "Mr. Gorbachev, tear down this wall."

Reagan's visit garnered approval, but also a lot of criticism. The president was considered to be a hard cold warrior. Thus, demonstrators on both sides of the Wall called the current order into question by calling, "Gorbi, Gorbi," even though the situation in East and West Berlin could not have been more different. The stages of demonstration, confrontation, and escalation that could be observed during the anti-Reagan protests on June 11 and 12 were familiar. And so the call from across the Wall had its echo in the West: demonstrators who for hours were surrounded by vast police cordons near the Kaufhaus des Westens department store began chanting at the officers: "The Wall must go."

Approaching 1989

The anniversary rivalry of 1987 thus ended in exhaustion. In retrospect, many links to the monumental events of 1989 seem clear. Gorbachev's name was all over the place and East and West Berlin had found numerous communication channels by which to relate to one another, both in a diplomatically reserved and in an unrestrained, subversive fashion. In the East, the *Stasi* tried to turn back the clock after the jubilee year had seen a loosening of the reins and opposition successes. In November, the *Stasi* raided the Zionskirche where the independent Umweltbibliothek was housed. The raid proved a failure as Western media quickly descended on the scene, reported on the events, and caused an unusual degree of public pressure to be brought to bear. The so-called "Battle of Zion" in late 1987 was the first significant defeat the Ministry for State Security had incurred. Today it is understood to have been the *first* defeat, as those that would follow in 1988 and 1989 are known to us. Berliners at the time did not know. And yet, for those who were politically engaged, the signs of change were becoming more numerous, although what they would portend, the direction, and pace of change, could not be anticipated.

Thus, one can hardly overemphasize the fact that, in 1987, a lot was imaginable, just not the impending fall of the Berlin Wall. Although they could not agree on much, East and West were on the same page when it came to a belief that Germany's division would not end for a long, long time to come—if at all. This has to be taken into account if the actions, tensions, and hopes in late Cold War Berlin are to be understood. And this also informed the meaning of speech and wording. Reagan's appeal to Gorbachev to tear the Wall down is one example; it was resonant and daring because it appeared entirely unrealistic. Another is the insistence of the Berlin Senate, that Berlin was and would remain *one* city. This was neither a tired trope nor a clairvoyant prognosis of what was to be. It was instead a political decision to, against all odds, hold fast to an idea of Berlin that many contemporaries felt was anachronistic. The very fact that the pathos of this rhetoric with its emphasis on unity ran counter to the everyday experience of West Berliners made it so piercing and, for some, so controversial. Nevertheless, the government did not anticipate any substantive changes to the status of Berlin, as it for example made clear in 1986 that the coming anniversary was a big deal, "probably the biggest event for Berlin for the rest of the century."[40] One could hope, but it was hard to believe. And yet, but a few years later, Berliners were dancing on the "torn-down" Wall.

And thus the mood in the city remained muted after the tense period of the twice-celebrated anniversary. In spite of all the excitement, the prospects for the future had hardly improved. To the contrary, at the end of 1987 fatigue and skepticism abounded—people were tired of all the self-congratulation, not only the East, but also in the West. There was some nervousness about the new year, as in 1988 West Berlin was to become Europe's capital of culture (locals called it the "751 year anniversary"). Was the island city trying to camouflage its identity crisis by staging series of big parties? The newspaper *Volksblatt Berlin* thought so, and in late 1987 commented on future plans: 1987 Berlin anniversary, 1988 capital of culture, "for 1989 we are still trying to come up with a reason to celebrate."[41]

Notes

1   Konrad Jarausch, *Out of Ashes. A New History of Europe in the 20th Century* (Princeton, 2015).

2   Adelheid von Saldern (ed.), *Inszenierter Stolz. Stadtrepräsentationen in drei deutschen Gesellschaften (1935–1975)* (Stuttgart, 2005).

3   Karen Tillmans, Frank van Vree and Jay Winter (eds.), *Performing the Past. Memory, History and Identity in Modern Europe* (Amsterdam, 2010). More on Berlin narratives: Krijn Thijs, *Drei Geschichten, eine Stadt. Die Berliner Stadtjubiläen von 1937 und 1987* (Cologne, 2008). An early comparison can be found in Peter Jelavich, "Kulturgeschichtliche Bemerkungen zur Berlin-Historiographie," in: Konrad H. Jarausch (ed.), *Zwischen Parteilichkeit und Professionalität. Bilanz der Geschichtswissenschaft der DDR* (Berlin, 1991) pp. 107–21.

4   Landesarchiv Berlin [LAB], A Rep 021–2, 49: Ernst Kaeber an das Nachrichtenamt, January 19, 1928. Cf. Norbert Meier, *Berlin im Mittelalter. Berlin/Cölln unter den Akaniern* (Berlin, 2012); Wolfgang Fritze, *Gründungsstadt Berlin. Die Anfänge von Berlin-Cölln als Forschungsproblem* (Berlin, 2000).

5   LAB, A-Rep 021–2, Aktennotiz February 6, 1928.

6   Krijn Thijs, *Party, Pomp und Propaganda. Die Berliner Stadtjubiläen von 1937 und 1987* (Berlin, 2012).

7   Lippert, quoted in: *Berliner Morgenpost*, August 15, 1938. Vgl. Christoph Kreuzmüller and Michael Wildt (eds.), *Berlin 1933–1945* (Berlin, 2013); Gianluca Falanga, *Berlin 1937. Die Ruhe vor dem Sturm* (Munich, 2007).

8   Goebbels, quoted in: *Völkischer Beobachter*, August 17, 1937.

9   Entries from August 13 and 14, 1937, in: Elke Fröhlich (ed.), *Die Tagebücher von Joseph Goebbels*, Bd I/4 (Munich, 2000), pp. 263f.

10   LAB 001–2, 428: Programmheft, p. 1.

11   Ibid., 431: Vermerk zum Festzug, July 17, 1937.

12   Hanns Niedecken-Gebhard, "Zum Ausklang," in: *700-Jahr-Feier der Reichshauptstadt. Folge der Feier vom 14. bis 22. August 1937* (Berlin, 1937).

13   Kurt Hager to Konrad Naumann, July 9, 1981, in: Bundesarchiv Berlin SAPMO [BA], DY30/vorl SED 38791.

14   *750 Jahre Berlin. Konstituierung des Komitees der DDR* (Berlin, 1985).

15   Florian Urban, *Berlin/DDR, neohistorisch. Geschichte aus Fertigteilen* (Berlin, 2007).

16   *750 Jahre Berlin. Das Buch zum Fest* (Berlin, 1986).

17   *750 Jahre Berlin. Staatsakt der DDR am 23. Oktober 1987* (Berlin, 1988).

18   Berlin-Information, *Das Bilderbuch vom Festumzug* (Berlin, 1987); Jens Schöne, *Stabilität und Niedergang. Ost-Berlin im Jahr 1987* (Berlin, 2006).

19   *750 Jahre Berlin. Thesen* (Berlin, 1986).

20   On protest culture: Schöne: *Stabilität*; Ilko-Sascha Kowalczuk: *Endspiel. Die Revolution von 1989 in der DDR* (Munich, 2009).

21   Harald Hauswald and Lutz Rathenow, *Ost-Berlin. Die andere Seite der Stadt* (Berlin, 1990). Cf. *GEO Special* No. 6, December 3, 1986 (Themenheft Berlin).

22   Wolfgang Oschlies,"'Man nennt uns manchmal Fischkopf ... Zum DDR-Regionalismus und seinen subkulturellen Reflexen," *Deutschland Archiv* 21 (1988), pp. 778–86.

23   Wilfried Rott, *Die Insel. Eine Geschichte West-Berlins 1948–1990* (Munich, 2009). Spezifisch zu den späten 1980er-Jahren: Stefanie Eisenhuth, *West-Berlin und der Umbruch in der DDR. Grenzübergreifende Wahrnehmungen und Verhandlungen 1989* (Berlin, 2012); Krijn Thijs, "Enfernter Erfahrungsraum. Überlegungen zu West-Berlin und 1989," *Eurostudia* 7 (2011) 1–2, pp. 29–46, http://www.cceae.umontreal.ca/IMG/pdf/Eurostudia_vol.7_-_K._Thijs.pdf.

24   Abgeordnetenhaus von Berlin, *Plenardebatte 9/28*, September 23, 1982, p. 1737B (Biewald, CDU).

25   Abgeordnetenhaus von Berlin, *Plenardebatte 9/41*, March 10, 1983, p. 2445A (Kollat, SPD).

26   Ulrich Eckhardt (ed.), *750 Jahre Berlin. Stadt der Gegenwart* (Berlin, 1987) (Klappentext).

27   Abgeordnetenhaus Drucksache 9/2292, November 30, 1984, p. 3.

28   Krijn Thijs, "West-Berliner Visionen für eine neue Mitte. Die Internationale Bauausstellung, der 'Zentrale Bereich' und die 'Geschichtslandschaft' an der Mauer (1981–1985)," *Zeithistorische Forschungen* 11 (2014) 2, pp. 235–61, https://zeithistorische-forschungen.de/2-2014/id%3D5097.

29   For background information, see Helmut von Trotnow and Florian Weiß (eds.), *Tear down this Wall. US-Präsident Ronald Reagan vor dem Brandenburger Tor, 12. Juni 1987* (Berlin, 2007).

30   LAB, B Rep 150, 54: Ideenskizze September 19, 1983.

31   LAB, B Rep 150, 54: Pressematerialien September 3, 1984.

32   Torsten Maß (ed.), *750 Jahre Berlin. Sternstunden. Eine Dokumentation* (Berlin, 1987), p. 3.

33   Cornelia Kühn, "Trachtenumzug, Skulpturenboulevard oder B-750 Parade? Aushandlungsprozesse um die politische Repräsentation und ästhetische Gestaltung der 750-Jahr-Feier in West-Berlin," in: Kaspar Maase et al. (eds.), *Macher—Medien—Publika. Beiträge der europäischen Ethnologie zu Geschmack und Vergnügen* (Würzburg, 2014).

34   Maß, *750 Jahre Berlin. Sternstunden*, p. 3.

35   Jürgen Danyel, "Der vergangenheitspolitische Diskurs in der SBZ/DDR 1945–1989,"
     in: Christoph Cornelißen (ed.), *Krieg—Diktatur—Vertreibung. Erinnerungskulturen
     in Tschechien, der Slowakei und Deutschland seit 1945* (Essen, 2005), pp. 173–96.

36   *Grenzfall* 6/87.

37   For some chaotic Dutch sailing experiences in the "Water Battle" of 1987, see Krijn
     Thijs, "Niederländer auf dem Müggelsee. Wie eine Flotte historischer Seegelschiffe
     die 750-Jahr-Feier sprengte," in: Jürgen Danyel (ed.), *Ost-Berlin. 30 Erkundungen*
     (Berlin, 2018).

38   On the following: Schöne, *Stabilität*; Kowalczuk, *Endspiel*.

39   On the following: Trotnow/Weiß, *Tear down this Wall*.

40   Winfried Fest, in: Presse- und Informationsamt, *Informationen zur 750-Jahr-Feier*
     (Berlin, 1986).

41   Volksblatt Berlin, November 22, 1987.

Part Three

Berlin's Memory Culture

13

Divided Memory in United Berlin

Stefanie Eisenhuth
Translated by David Burnett

Berlin is a difficult place, whose history can hardly be condensed into a simple slogan let alone a single word. An unambiguous moniker the likes of "Lutherstadt Wittenberg" (Wittenberg, City of Luther), "Rattenfängerstadt Hameln" (Pied-Piper's Town Hamelin), or "Eulenspiegelstadt Mölln" (Till Eulenspiegel's Mölln) would be hard to find. One look at the city's official internet portal confirms the suspicion that Berlin has no clear master narrative. Instead, curious visitors are presented with nine different versions of the city: the "medieval trading center," the "electoral residence," the "royal capital," the "imperial capital," the "Weimar metropolis," "Berlin under Nazism," "Berlin after 1945," "from the Berlin Agreement to the Fall of the Wall," and the "new Berlin."[1] A conspicuous feature of these categories is the lack of any clear attribution after 1933. The history of the city is no longer reduced to a common denominator but is merely divided chronologically. This is why Andreas Huyssen concluded that Berlin is a "palimpsest," "a disparate city-text that is being rewritten while previous text is preserved, traces are restored, erasures documented." The result is a "complex web of historical markers that point to the continuing heterogeneous life of a vital city that is as ambivalent of its built past as it is of its urban future."[2]

Yet Greater Berlin, an entity created in 1920 through the incorporation of numerous surrounding areas, was always extremely heterogeneous. It has almost been forgotten nowadays that the distinction between East and West Berlin was not a product of the Cold War but existed much earlier, from just after the turn of the twentieth century in fact, in the form of an old historical center at Alexanderplatz and a new one at Bahnhof Zoo. Plans were made in the German Empire, and later under Albert Speer, to link the Western and Eastern halves of the city, none of which was implemented.[3] Starting in the 1950s, the two centers grew apart even more as each was developed with the intent of demonstrating the attractiveness and superiority of its respective system.[4] Administrative division was followed by a physical split in 1961 with the erection of the Wall. The "Cold War Berlin" in the title of this book was therefore a double Berlin, and should actually be thought of in the plural. Until the demise of the GDR in 1989–90 and the reunification of these two halves, there existed two different realms of experience that are linked to different memories today. Thus, this chapter will begin by exploring the memory of these two respective halves followed by a discussion of the memory of the nearly fifty-year presence of the victorious Allied powers in World War Two, a key feature of Cold War Berlin.

Remembering West Berlin

"West Berlin is back!," crowed the entertainment guide *tip Berlin* in January 2013.[5] This flashback was occasioned by a new David Bowie song reminiscing with a certain wistfulness on his Schöneberg years. Hagen Liebing, former bassist of the Berlin punk band *Die Ärzte*, and now a senior music editor, informed the readers of his magazine that several recent publications had revived memories of the "Wild West," of the "wild clubs, the shabby buildings, the bleak Wall, the sometimes hysterical, sometimes apathetic avant-garde in the arts and music scene."[6] He recommended that curious readers pay a visit to "West Berlin classics that are still a lot of fun": Slumberland bar, Cafe M, and Schwarze Café as well as the Paris Bar. It was all still there, everything just like it was in the old days.

The conservative daily *B.Z.* had quite a different take on things, however, and just a few months later declared that West Berlin was dead. In November 2013, its title page proclaimed in giant letters that West Berlin had passed away "after leading a full life" and that "we" should now say goodbye to it with "love and gratitude"—to the police motorcycle stunt team, the *Wasserklops* or "water meatball" fountain, to Café Möhring, the Schöneberg boys' choir, and many other icons of the Western half of the city. The paper's former lead columnist complained in the inside pages:

> One symbol after another is being demolished. […] How utterly perverse! We should in fact be doing the opposite, remembering the 40 years in which people persevered, surrounded by a hostile power, 28 years of it behind a wall. It was in this despairing situation that the western part of the city became a symbol of hope. West Berlin was truly the showcase of freedom, not in name only.[7]

Ansgar Hocke, a native West Berliner and long-time editor at Radio Free Berlin (SFB), also challenged the narrative of West Berlin as a happy-go-lucky biotope behind the Wall, calling on other "natives" to take action at the website Berlin-Brandenburg Broadcasting (RBB): "We finally have to reclaim our biography, for life in a walled-in city included experiences that were downright frightening […]. From childhood on, West Berliners had to endure the political moods of the Soviet Union as well as the East German Politbüro and East German border troops. It was not hard to sense how vulnerable this West Berlin was."[8] The West Berlin of *tip* magazine seemed to be wholly different from the one recalled by the *B.Z.* and *RBB*. The disparity of these experiences has turned West Berlin into an ambivalent place of memory.[9] In retrospect, an increasing social divide is evident in this half-city, oscillating between memories of a stuffy province and a hedonistic metropolis, between the lifeworlds of "Wilmersdorf widows,"[10] the "Kreuzberg Communards," and "children of Bahnhof Zoo,"[11] between Café Kranzler and Dschungel discoteque.

Yet, without being ascribed a concrete meaning, a place is nothing but a collection of "scattered fragments of a lost or destroyed nexus of life." Only when the existing relics and stories are condensed into a coherent narrative does a place become a place of memory, where "something of that remains which no longer exists but can be reflected in the memories of it."[12] There is no lack of material remains in Berlin, but many of them refer to diverging experiences, and therefore no master narrative has been established for West Berlin.[13] But the sources quoted do show that it is possible to identify recurrent narratives: the memory of a frontline city, the memory of normality, and the memory of a biotope.

The memory of a frontline or outpost city propagated by *B.Z.* and *RBB* was skillfully captured, if somewhat exaggerated, by sociologist and crime-fiction writer Horst Bosetzky:

> WE became the pivotal force in world history after the Second World War, and the nations of the world were watching us. WE were the showcase of the Free World, WE defied the Communist East. Neither its blockade nor the wall they built around us managed to bring us, the island children, to our knees. WE were canonized by John F. Kennedy.[14]

This heroic and self-confident memory focuses on the height of the Cold War, the stoic anticommunism of West Berlin, and the key role of the Allied "protecting powers," especially the United States.[15]

The same characteristics are also referenced by the memory of normality of those born in West Berlin after 1961. This narrative, however, insists on the idea of a normal life lived under abnormal circumstances and rejects any kind of heroism. The city's special status, its division and the presence of the Allied powers was entirely self-evident and only seems strange in retrospect, according to this version, which endeavors to explain this situation to subsequent generations lest West Berlin should be forgotten. The authors of numerous autobiographically inspired books have described in minute detail their childhood and youth in this lost world, recalling many things that have long since vanished—temporary IDs, waiting for hours every summer at the Dreilinden border crossing, taking part in military parades or public festivals put on by the Allies, etc.[16] They are strangely reminiscent of similar works written by their East German counterparts: the so-called Children of the Zone or Third Generation East.[17]

The memory of a biotope, in contrast, as described by *tip* magazine pays scant attention to the Cold War, concentrating instead on the 1970s and 1980s, and mostly on the neighborhoods of Kreuzberg and Schöneberg. It knows its own heroes, and has even spawned its own dictionary, nostalgically reminiscing on the curiosities of this half-city while repeatedly mocking the narrative of the frontline city.[18] Its literary tributes are frequently the stories of men who moved to Berlin from elsewhere in West Germany, drawn by the city's demilitarized status and/or the reputation of its local alternative scene.[19] These stories are having an increasingly formative influence on the present-day perception of West Berlin, as they easily lend themselves to the city's current image as a cosmopolitan party metropolis hosting a diverse expat community. Films such as *Herr Lehmann, B-Movie: Lust & Sound in West Berlin* or *My Wonderful West Berlin* offer viewers a seemingly coherent prologue to the new Berlin they know today. But the frontline city narrative, too, has been the subject of recent feature films and TV series. *The Airlift, Ku'damm '56, Deutschland '83,* and *Berlin: Divided Heaven* are more historical films, however, addressing a bygone era and having little to do with the world of modern-day viewers. Berlin, in this case, provides the "authentic" backdrop for gripping spy thrillers, love stories, and heroic tales. Unlike the biotope and frontline city narratives, the memory of normality of the younger generation has not yet received cinematic treatment. Its insistence on perceived normality apparently offers little material for an exciting movie script.

Remembering East Berlin

While the mention of West Berlin quickly conjures up a "photo album of memory,"[20] as shown already, the East Berlin "album" contains two predominant and competing images: the officially sanctioned version propagated by the Socialist Unity Party (SED) of Berlin as the capital of the GDR and the bohemian life of artists living in Prenzlauer Berg.[21] The capital motif is a colorful one, showing newly constructed buildings and cheerful people; the other captures in black and white the melancholy dreariness of older, prewar neighborhoods, whose gray façades merely hint at the colorful life that went on behind them.[22] The capital images were usually created on behalf of the state with the aim of documenting the achievements of socialism. But nowadays only connoisseurs of Eastern modernist architecture are enthused by these old color photographs of Alexanderplatz or the newly built neighborhoods of Marzahn and Hohenschönhausen. These pictures are "textualized," according to Stefan Wolle: the "content of these images is strictly canonized, more dogma than a reflection of any earthly reality."[23] The gray-scale counter-photos of dilapidated prewar neighborhoods, by the same token, are generally the work of critical artists such as Harald Hauswald. His photos, published and presented at an exhibit in West Berlin in 1987, were bemoaned by the East German authorities: "The intention of showing an image contrary to the real depiction of Berlin as the capital of the GDR is unmistakable."[24] This verdict was true enough, but opinion was certainly divided as to what in fact was "real." Harald Hauswald's photos are nowadays visual icons of cultural memory. They appear "authentic" in retrospect and from an outside perspective.[25] *Spiegel* magazine understood them to be an "undistorted impression of the GDR,"[26] *Der Tagesspiegel* described them as "the genuine East,"[27] and *Die Zeit* proclaimed: "This is what the GDR looked like."[28] These publications were referring, of course, to the dismal grayness, and less to the diversity and individuality that Hauswald likewise captured with his lens. His pictures, in this discourse, are often representative of the entire republic, of scarcity and surveillance. The makers of the movie *Sonnenallee* may have been guided by an idea like this in switching from color to black and white when the camera, in the film's final sequence, leaves the Eastern end of the street and crosses the line of demarcation into West Berlin, looking back at the receding East, which has suddenly lost its color. In the background, East German singer Nina Hagen croons: "You forgot the color film, dear Michael, no one will believe us now when we tell them how nice it was here."[29]

At the visual level, it seems that the "memory of dictatorship" (Sabrow) and the narrative of the economy of scarcity have prevailed. Thus, the writer Jan Eik, born in Berlin in 1940, recently bemoaned that the Eastern half of the city was much more than just drab, depressing streets, smelly "cardboard cars" and crumbling old buildings.[30] And yet what he recounts in his programmatically titled "East Berlin the Way It Really Was" could have just as well applied to Dresden or Rostock. So what made East Berlin unique? Officially it was never called "East Berlin" at all, of course, but was initially referred to as the "democratic sector of Greater Berlin" and later as the "capital of the GDR," or just plain Berlin. The other half behind the Wall was now called "Westberlin"—not hyphenated in the usual way as "West-Berlin," but written as a compound word with a lowercase "b" as if it were not Berlin at all—and disappeared altogether from city maps once the Wall was erected.[31] Alexanderplatz and its environs (Karl-Marx-Allee and Marx-Engels-Platz) were developed into a modern city center. The International cinema, the Moskau and Lindencorso restaurants as well as the Operncafé soon opened their doors, along with a number of government buildings and two luxury Interhotels (primarily for foreign tourists paying in Western currency). In addition, a number of historical buildings were restored on Unter den Linden, transforming it into a promenade as in the days of yore. The TV tower, completed in 1969, became the new city landmark. Residential highrises on Leipziger Strasse and the Ahornblatt restaurant soon followed. The number of inhabitants steadily increased as of 1970, whereas the average age decreased[32]—which could not be said of West Berlin. With a population of around 1.2 million, it was the largest city in the GDR, as well as the seat of its government and its cultural center. Jürgen Rostock, a former East German city planner, points out that the city had a lot to offer its visitors: "[T]he remnants of representative architecture, the romance of decaying older neighborhoods, major museums and libraries, low prices," but also an "interesting glimpse of the arts scene" and a touch of "big-city flair."[33] Apart from theaters and concert halls, its high-end dining facilities such as Restaurant Moskau or Tele-Café in the TV tower drew visitors to the "socialist cultural metropolis."[34]

Most memories, especially the literary kind, seem to contradict this view, however: "East Berlin was any number of things back then, but it wasn't a metropolis. A cosmopolitan city much less—not even by half. The entire East was provincial, East Berlin included."[35] This is the conclusion of historian Ilko-Sascha Kowalczuk, born in 1967 in the Berlin neighborhood of Friedrichshagen. But compared to other cities (with the exception of Leipzig with its international trade fairs), East Berlin was the closest thing the GDR had to a "socialist metropolis." It, too, like its Western counterpart, was intended as a showcase for the success of the system it represented.[36] With the 1976 Politbüro resolution on "tasks for the development of the capital of the GDR, Berlin," East Berlin was slated to become the "political, economic and cultural center of the GDR" by 1990.[37] Alongside a massive housing program, this included an expansion of retail trade. "Berlin Party orders" called for the creation of sixty-eight new supermarkets, two fresh food markets selling fruit and vegetables, and forty-three restaurants with seating for 11,000 diners. Moreover, stores in the capital were to be given priority in the distribution of goods.[38] West and East Berlin soon had something in common: being eyed with suspicion by the rest of the country for being subsidy guzzlers. West Berlin had long been known as a "bottomless pit." In response to the question of whether the high financial cost of maintaining West Berlin was worth it, Finance Senator Heinz Striek suggested with caustic humor in the summer of 1969 that the Kurfürstendamm might well be renamed "Berlin Aid Act Boulevard."[39] And rumor had it in the GDR that East Berlin was located in a very deep valley, since everything seemed to flow in that direction.

Resentment toward this subsidized showcase of the socialist republic may help explain why the term "capital" was often used ironically, lending expression to the perceived disparity between Berlin in the eyes of its rulers and the day-to-day life of East Germans. This enmity reached its peak in 1987 with the lavish 750-year-anniversary celebrations in East and West Berlin: "The celebrations were met with ridicule and hostility by people in the provinces. [...] Trabbis with Berlin plates were graffitied with the number 750, and in the south there were bumper stickers reading '781 years Dresden,' '821 years Leipzig' and even '1026 years Halle'."[40] These suspicions of the privileged capital were by no means unwarranted. Jan Eik recalls that "East Berliners felt superior to everyone else in the GDR. [...] What East Berliners felt towards the rest of the country was a little bit like how West Berliners felt towards them."[41] For Kowalczuk, too, it was the Western half of the city that made the Eastern half special: "The most important thing about East Berlin was that it bordered on the West, not just West Berlin but the West in general."[42] And yet this West Berlin was terra incognita, a mythical place of longing you could see from atop the TV tower but could hardly expect to visit before retirement age.

Remembering the Other Side

A look at the West Berlin literature of remembrance shows that here, too, the other half of the city was never out of mind. Horst Bosetzky, born in 1938, mainly recalls his fear of traveling to the other side of the Wall. Every excursion was akin to "flirting with death, or at least playing with fire." His fear of the *Stasi* always took center stage. At the same time, the Eastern half of the city had something "droll, if not to say silly" about it. Being seated in a restaurant (a custom utterly foreign to West Germans), eating with aluminum cutlery, drinking *Club Cola*, bizarre product names, *Klarofix* und *Kriepa*, for instance, unknown terms such as *Spartakiad* or forms of address such as *Jugendfreund* (friend of youth)—all of these were a regular source of amusement for West Berliners and were perceived "in equal measure as exotic and idiotic."[43] Olaf Leitner—of the same generation—admits, by way of contrast, that at some point he "didn't feel the Wall anymore." What's more, "from the Western perspective," it even had something "warm and cozy" about it: "You could make yourself comfortable on the lee side, shielded from adverse winds."[44] Claus Christian Malzahn, Berliner by choice since 1987, agrees with this assessment: "Not for a minute did we think about the Wall, landmines and barbed wire, even though it was all right there, staring us in the face. For us West Berliners, the 'protective wall' transformed over time into something like a piece of furniture, a chest of drawers, an unloved heirloom."[45]

The memories of Tanja Dückers, however, who was born in 1968, are marked by "contradictory feelings." On the one hand, "the colors were missing"; on the other hand, "the heart of Berlin" with its many historical buildings was located "in the East." The Eastern half of the city had "peculiar similarities with ours" and yet it seemed "completely alien." She concludes: "I never felt comfortable in the East. Being there was too complex emotionally" on account of the "constant back and forth between feelings of familiarity and foreignness."[46] Ulrike Sterblich, two years younger than Dückers, recalls a day trip to the East that was guided by the quest to spend the twenty-five marks she was forced to exchange at the border, summing up the experience as follows: "The East Berlin sky was gray and cloudy, but the sun was shining in the West."[47]

In many of these narratives, East Berlin figures as the exotic Other—familiar in many ways, but then completely different in others. Its otherness, perceived as being deficient or at the very least bizarre, usually confirmed the superiority of West Berliners' own half of the city, portrayed in turn as being more free, colorful, diverse, and prosperous.

Remembering the Allied Military Presence

A key feature of Cold War Berlin is the nearly fifty-year presence of the victors of World War Two. Andreas W. Daum called the Western half of the city "America's Berlin" because of its strong "cultural, spiritual and emotional ties" to the United States.[48] The list of German-American sites of remembrance in Berlin is correspondingly long, and includes material places such as the Free University, the American Memorial Library, and the Airlift Memorial, as well as immaterial ones such as John F. Kennedy's famous words *Ich bin ein Berliner* or Ronald Reagan's challenge: "Mr. Gorbachev, tear down this wall." The French army may have "left traces" in Berlin, "but their representatives seldom played a pivotal role there."[49] The British armed forces likewise didn't manage to inscribe themselves in the city's collective memory the way the Americans did.[50] And a Soviet counterpart to "America's Berlin" never really existed. The entire GDR was dubbed "Stalin's unloved child."[51] His successor, Nikita Khrushchev, considered West Berlin a thorn in his side, its only advantage being the leverage it gave him over the Western powers.[52] When people in the GDR spoke of the Russians as their "friends," it was hardly an expression of affection and solidarity but an ironic twist on state propaganda.[53] The separate ceremonies to mark the withdrawal of Allied troops in 1994 showed quite clearly where the city's sympathies lay. When asked about this event, 77 percent of Berliners described the Western Allies as "friends" and 49 percent said the Soviet Union were "occupiers."[54]

Two museums devote themselves nowadays to the memory of the victorious Allied powers or—as they were called in West Berlin—the "protecting powers." On the Westside in leafy Dahlem, a special exhibit entitled "More than a Suitcase in Berlin: The Western Powers and Berlin, 1944–94" opened to visitors as early as September 3, 1994, at the former American "Outpost" movie theater on Clayallee. Four years later, on the fiftieth anniversary of the Airlift, the new Allied Museum—made up largely of the previous exhibit—officially opened its doors as a "museum of gratitude."[55] The committee responsible for the museum decided on this name in spite of the objection that the use of the word "Allied" "would automatically [include] the Soviet Union," citing the fact that "since the 1960s Berliners only used the term in reference to the Western powers," and also that it "meant the same thing in all three languages."[56] The East Berlin perspective was apparently not taken into consideration. The permanent exhibit "How Enemies Became Friends" still tells the history of the three Western Allied powers in Berlin as a rather linear success story.[57]

As often in post-Wall Berlin, makeshift solutions have to endure at the Allied Museum. The museum remains at the pragmatically chosen former theater for the time being, while the desired Tempelhof Airport location remains elusive. Prolonged debate over relocation has effectively put the museum's development on hold. In spite of selected updates, the permanent exhibition has never been redesigned from ground up since. Temporary special exhibits and various events have tried to offset this shortcoming. In 2012, the Bundestag decided to bring the Allied Museum to the former Tempelhof airport and create a new "Museum of Freedom."[58] But again and again something comes up: First, the 2015 decision to house refugees at the airport site temporarily stalled plans for the "New Allied Museum."[59] Most recently, preconstruction examination confirmed that Tempelhof's terminal is in a worse structural condition than had initially been assumed. At the time of writing, the museum and federal authorities plan details for bringing the New Allied Museum into fruition during this decade.[60]

No comparable museum exists to honor the Soviet armed forces. The permanent exhibit at the German-Russian Museum in Karlshorst is focused (as it was before 1989–90) on World War Two and its aftermath.[61] An exhibit at the privately run Garrison Museum in Wünsdorf is devoted to the daily life of Soviet soldiers in the GDR.[62]

"Amateur" or "wild museums"[63] of this sort in Berlin exist for the history of the Western powers as well. Gundula Bavendamm talks about a "grassroots movement" consisting of "interested people in the general public, collectors, technology buffs, contemporary witnesses of the Airlift, former civilian employees or military service members and diplomats living in Berlin" who "strongly [identify] with the history of the Western Allies."[64] These initiatives usually emerged "in the moment of loss," which is why they tend to be highly nostalgic.[65] They are "insider museums," serving more as meeting places for former colleagues than as places to inform or educate the public.[66] Operated by contemporary witnesses and relying on donations for their survival, their existence is precarious.

It therefore seems that the historical role of the Allies in unified Berlin has been reduced to little more than the memories nurtured by small social niches. This might be due in part to competing narratives of the Cold War, which, in spite of leaving countless political, social, economic, and cultural traces across the world,[67] has been unable to secure a place for itself in global cultural memory: "[T]here is no Europe-wide holiday, no central memorial location, no systematic reflection on its legacy."[68] Added to this is the fact that the presence of the Western powers is only relevant for the cultural remembrance of a dwindling share of Berliners. Those socialized in the Eastern part of the city, those born after the withdrawal of Allied troops, and those who have moved to Berlin more recently have a no personal connection to the once so important narrative of West Berlin's "protecting powers."[69] Accordingly, the legacy of the Allies is usually only celebrated on the occasion of anniversaries (the blockade and airlift), or it becomes a source of controversy when plans are made to close or repurpose key urban places.[70]

The Allies do play a marginal role in a number of Berlin museums, such as the Palace of Tears or the Marienfelde Refugee Center Museum.[71] In general, however, the focus of these museums tends to be divided Germany, told as a narrative of national tragedy, and rarely put into a global context. Divided Berlin continues to serve here as a symbol and a warning example of divided Germany as a whole. The many specific features of Berlin on account of its special status are rarely addressed. Advocates at the Cold War Center, an initiative to establish a new museum at Checkpoint Charlie, have suggested telling the story of the Cold War as urban and global history, as well as from the perspectives of its varied protagonists. The reactions to this proposal, however, running the gamut from enthusiasm to demonization, once again underline in an explicit way the continued schism in the city's collective memory. Gunnar Schupelius, in an article in the *B.Z.*, gave vent to his fears of a supposed "museum of trivialization": "Checkpoint Charlie has to show who was the aggressor after 1945: the Soviet Union under Josef Stalin. [...] It also has to show who fortified the inner-German border in 1952 and who built the Wall in 1961: the SED under Walter Ulbricht. It was as simple and brutal as that. Why should history be relativized?"[72] This quotation makes clear to what extent recent history can still be an identity-shaping force in Berlin as well as how controversial it can be.

Conclusion

This brief panorama has shown that the memory of West Berlin is alive and varied, whereas the particularities of East Berlin are slowly sinking into oblivion. Certain facets of the Western half of the city have been rediscovered in recent years and celebrated in popular culture, while the Eastern half of the city is increasingly becoming a symbol for the drabness of the GDR in general. The edited anthology *Erinnerungsorte der DDR* ("Places of Memory in the GDR") contains no contribution at all on the former capital East Berlin that would offer a counter-perspective to the one on "West Berlin."[73] In the culture of memory as well as in historiography, East Berlin oftentimes merely serves to typify the GDR nowadays, in spite of the fact that in its day it was never considered "typical" of the rest of the GDR.[74]

A coherent Berlin narrative in which both halves of the city are given their due is only to be found when the history of this divided city is presented as a tragedy, one that was caused by external forces and ultimately overcome. But this master narrative comes at a price, in that any experience or memory contradicting it is immediately discounted. Hence Cold War Berlin is in danger of becoming a cipher, "an essentially empty space in which by chance, as it were, a Cold War battle took place."[75] More complex memories such as the countless international tourists who traveled to East Berlin for pleasure[76] have no place in such a narrative.

And yet there is one topos that the disparate Berlin memories do seem to agree on, and it is probably this that will have the most lasting formative influence on what Martina Löw calls the "intrinsic logic" of the city: Berlin as the "capital of freedom." This, at any rate, was the name of a new city advertising campaign launched in

February 2017, promoting the city with quotes from prominent individuals both past and present. The idea was based on the results of a survey, according to which almost three-quarters of all Berliners associated the city with the notion of "freedom"—a term that is also strongly linked to the city's reputation abroad (even though outside the city it is probably the events of 1989 that come to mind first, rather than, say, the Freedom Bell, the Free University, or the Radio Free Berlin).[77] Much like an earlier billboard with the slogan "Berlin has been through a lot—every weekend," the current campaign links vague hints to the city's history with its present-day reputation as a multicultural and tolerant metropolis, while also appealing to the city's supposed "anything goes" attitude (emphasized by the advertisement's fine print: "Because it's possible [*es geht*] in Berlin").[78] The campaign thus combines several narratives: (I) the narrative of a militant "outpost of freedom" concentrating on the political and symbolic role of West Berlin during the Cold War; (II) the narrative of individual freedom experienced in the alternative spaces of Kreuzberg and Schöneberg, as well as in Prenzlauer Berg; and (III) the narrative of 1989, the year in which East Germans fought for their freedom, ultimately enabling the city's reunification. The very vagueness of the concept of "freedom" allows the inclusion of conflicting memories and disparate identities, as well as building a bridge to the present.

Notes

1 See "Berlin im Überblick," www.berlin.de/berlin-im-ueberblick/geschichte/index. de.html (accessed February 2, 2020).

2 Andreas Huyssen, *Present Pasts: Urban Palimpsests and the Politics of Memory* (Stanford, 2003), p. 81. See also, idem, "'The Voids of Berlin," *Critical Inquiry* 24 (1997) 1, pp. 57–81.

3 See Bruno Flierl, "Stadtzentrum Berlin-Ost," in: Günter Schlusche, Verena Pfeiffer-Kloss, Gabi Dolff-Bonekämper and Axel Klausmeier (eds.), *Stadtentwicklung im doppelten Berlin. Zeitgenossenschaften und Erinnerungsorte* (Berlin, 2014), pp. 42–51.

4 Kerstin Wittmann-Englert, "'More than a Showcase of Liberty'. Zur Rolle der City-West im Kalten Krieg," in: Schlusche et al. (eds.), *Stadtentwicklung im doppelten Berlin*, pp. 52–61.

5 "West-Berlin ist zurück," *tip Berlin* 3/2013, Title page.

6 Hagen Liebing, "Das war der wilde Westen," *tip berlin* 3/2013, pp. 25–6.

7 Gunnar Schupelius, "War dafür wirklich kein Platz mehr in unserem neuen Berlin?," *B.Z.*, November 29, 2013, p. 1, pp. 4–5.

8 Ansgar Hocke, "Wird Zeit für eine Renaissance von West-Berlin," *RBB Online*, www. rbb-online.de/kultur/hintergrund/West-Berlin.html (accessed April 7, 2017).

9 This is the conclusion of Janet Ward: "Berlin's various geographical meanderings—its delayed jump-start into the world-city ranks of Imperial and Weimar modernity, and its subsequent near-fatal marring by Nazi planning, wartime bombing, Cold War division, and now post-Wall reclamation and reinvention—are the reasons why the identity of this city remains so disjointed." Janet Ward, *Post-Wall Berlin: Borders, Space and Identity* (New York, 2011), p. 5. See also Godela Weiss-Sussex, "Berlin: Myth and Memorialization," in idem/Katia Pizzi (eds.), *The Cultural Identities of European Cities* (Bern, 2011), pp. 145–64.

10   In the popular musical *Linie 1*, the "Wilmersdorf Widows" are the affluent wives of former Nazis who are still very proud of their staunch anticommunism.

11   The movie *Christiane F.—We Children from Bahnhof Zoo* from 1981 portrays the West Berlin drug scene in the 1970s. The story is based on interviews with Christiane Felscherinow.

12   Aleida Assmann, *Erinnerungsräume. Formen und Wandlungen des kulturellen Gedächtnisses*, 5th ed. (Munich, 2010), p. 309.

13   "Berlin is unique because a multitude of objects, places and practices have symbolic character and don't just refer 'to something else' but are in a complex referential relationship with each other, one which in turn can be viewed as the symbol of Berlin." Simone Derix, "Der Symbolkomplex Berlin. Berlin-Diskurs und Berlin-Praktiken nach 1945," in: Michael C. Bienert, Uwe Schaper, and Hermann Wentker (eds.), *Hauptstadtanspruch und symbolische Politik. Die Bundespräsenz im geteilten Berlin 1949–1990* (Berlin, 2012), pp. 183–220, quote on p. 185.

14   Horst Bosetzky, "Wir Einzigartigen," *Berliner Zeitung*, May 19, 2010. See also idem, *Erinnerungen eines Inselkindes* (Berlin, 2006).

15   Reinhard von Bronewski, *Aufgewachsen mit amerikanischen Soldaten. Wie im Berliner Grunewald Freundschaften entstanden* (Berlin, 2001).

16   For example, Tanja Dückers, *Mein altes West-Berlin* (Berlin, 2016); Ulrike Sterblich, *Die halbe Stadt, die es nicht mehr gibt: Eine Kindheit in Berlin (West)* (Reinbek, 2012); Andreas von Klewitz, "Dahlemer Erinnerungen," in: D. Holland-Moritz and Gabriela Wachter (eds.), *war jewesen. West-Berlin 1961–89* (Berlin, 2009), pp. 169–79; Kerstin Schilling, "Die Generation West-Berlin und die Freiheit," in: ibid., pp. 185–94; Kerstin Schilling, *Insel der Glücklichen. Generation West-Berlin* (Berlin, 2004).

17   For example, Jana Hensel, *Zonenkinder* (Reinbek, 2002); Michael Hacker, Stephanie Maiwald, Johannes Staemmler et al. (eds.), *Dritte Generation Ost. Wer wir sind, was wir wollen* (Berlin, 2012).

18   Ulf Mailänder and Ulrich Zander (eds.), *Das kleine Westberlin-Lexikon. Von "Autonome" bis "Zapf"—die alternative Szene der siebziger und achtziger Jahre* (Berlin, 2003).

19   One example are the novels of Sven Regener about the life of "Herr Lehmann." See also Claus Christian Malzahn, *Über Mauern. Warum das Leben im Schatten des Schutzwalls eine sonnige Sache war* (Berlin, 2009); Günter Brus, *Das gute alte West-Berlin* (Salzburg, 2010).

20   Stefanie Eisenhuth and Martin Sabrow, "'West-Berlin'. Eine historiographische Herausforderung," *Zeithistorische Forschungen/Studies in Contemporary History*, 11 (2014) 2, pp. 165–87, quote on p. 1, www.zeithistorische-forschungen.de/2-2014/ id=5090.

21   See Jürgen Danyel, "Ost-Berlin erkunden," in: idem (ed.), *Ost-Berlin. 30 Erkundungen* (Berlin, 2019), pp. 11–29; Stefan Wolle, *Ost-Berlin. Biografie einer Hauptstadt* (Berlin, 2020).

22   See Annette Vowinckel, *Agenten der Bilder. Fotografisches Handeln im 20. Jahrhundert* (Göttingen, 2016), pp. 255–60, pp. 340–57.

23   Stefan Wolle, "Die Welt der verlorenen Bilder. Die DDR im visuellen Gedächtnis," in: Gerhard Paul (ed.), *Visual History. Ein Studienbuch* (Göttingen, 2006), pp. 33–52, here p. 337.

24   Ilko-Sascha Kowalczuk, "Ein Buch und seine Geschichte. Erinnerungen und Akteneinsichten," in: Harald Hauswald and Lutz Rathenow, *Ost-Berlin. Leben vor dem Mauerfall* (Berlin, 2005), p. 25.

25 See also Karin Harteweig, "Einleitung," in: idem/Alf Lüdtke (eds.), *Die DDR im Bild. Zum Gebrauch der Fotografie im anderen deutschen Staat* (Göttingen, 2004), pp. 7–12.

26 Peter Wensierski, "Die Dunkelkammer in der Kastanienallee," *Spiegel Online*, June 6, 2014, www.spiegel.de/einestages/ost-berlin-fotograf-harald-hauswald-zeigt-unverfaelschtes-bild-der-ddr-a-974961.html.

27 "Fotograf Harald Hauswald: Der echte Osten," *Der Tagesspiegel*, May 7, 2014, www.tagesspiegel.de/kultur/fotograf-harald-hauswald-der-echte-osten/9852722.html (accessed April 2, 2020).

28 "DDR-Fotografie: So sah es im Osten aus," *Zeit Online*, April 21, 2013, www.zeit.de/wissen/geschichte/2013-04/fs-harald-hauswald-ferner-osten-lehmstedt (accessed April 2, 2020).

29 On the use of color as a stylistic device in *Sonnenallee*, see also Thomas Lindenberger, "Zeitgeschichte am Schneidetisch. Zur Historisierung der DDR in deutschen Spielfilmen," in: Paul, *Visual History*, pp. 353–72.

30 Jan Eik, *Ost-Berlin wie es wirklich war* (Berlin, 2016), pp. 9f.

31 The label "Berlin, capital of the GDR" took hold in the mid-1950s, but not until 1976 did the "Municipality of Greater Berlin" become the "Municipality of Berlin, capital of the GDR." See Michael Lemke, *Vor der Mauer. Berlin in der Ost-West-Konkurrenz 1948 bis 1961* (Cologne/Weimar/Vienna, 2011), pp. 33–7.

32 See Gerhard Keiderling, *Berlin 1945–1986* (Berlin, 1987), p. 859.

33 Jürgen Rostock, "Ostberlin—die Hauptstadt der DDR," in: Werner Süß and Ralf Rytlewski (eds.), *Berlin. Die deutsche Hauptstadt*, Bundeszentrale für politische Bildung (Berlin, 1999), pp. 33f.

34 See Stephanie Warnke, *Stein gegen Stein. Architektur und Medien im geteilten Berlin 1950–1970* (Frankfurt am Main, 2009), pp. 305–16.

35 Kowalczuk, "Ein Buch und seine Geschichte," p. 5.

36 See the various contributions in Michael Lemke (ed.), *Schaufenster der Systemkonkurrenz. Die Region Berlin-Brandenburg im Kalten Krieg* (Cologne, 2006).

37 "Für Berlin ein großes Programm," *Berliner Zeitung*, September 6, 1979, p. 9.

38 See Juliane Schütterle, *Klassenkampf im Kaufhaus. Versorgung und Sonderversorgung in der DDR 1971–1989* (Erfurt, 2009), pp. 15–25.

39 Wolfgang Müller-Haeseler, "Berlin ist uns zu teuer," *Die Zeit*, July 25, 1969.

40 Krijn Thijs, *Drei Geschichten, eine Stadt. Die Berliner Stadtjubiläen von 1937 und 1987* (Cologne/Weimar/Vienna, 2008), p. 272.

41 Eik, *Ost-Berlin*, pp. 50f.

42 Kowalczuk, "Ein Buch und seine Geschichte," p. 5.

43 Horst Bosetzky, *West-Berlin. Erinnerungen eines Inselkindes* (Berlin, 2006), pp. 79–92.

44 Olaf Leitner, "Windbeutel, Mantras, Hugenotten und der König der Löwen. Eine einseitige Einführung ins Thema," in idem (ed.), *West-Berlin! Westberlin! Berlin (West)! Die Kultur—die Szene—die Politik. Erinnerungen an eine Teilstadt der 70er und 80er Jahre* (Berlin, 2002), pp. 12–25, here p. 16.

45 Malzahn, *Über Mauern*, p. 22.

46 Dückers, *Mein altes West-Berlin*, pp. 96–8.

47 Sterblich, *Die halbe Stadt*, pp. 227–31.

48 Andreas W. Daum, *Kennedy in Berlin. Politik, Kultur und Emotionen im Kalten Krieg* (Paderborn, 2003), p. 195.

49 Dorothea Führe, "Besatzungsmacht zweiter Ordnung. Die französische Besatzungspolitik in Berlin 1945–1949," in Michael Bienert, Uwe Schaper and Andreas Theissen (eds.), *Die Vier Mächte in Berlin. Beiträge zur Politik der*

Alliierten in der besetzten Stadt (Berlin, 2007), pp. 31–49; idem, *Die französische Besatzungspolitik in Berlin von 1945–1949. Déprussianisation und Décentralisation* (Berlin, 2001); Jérome Vaillant, "Frankreichs Beitrag zur Demokratisierung Deutschlands nach dem Zweiten Weltkrieg," in: Heinrich Oberreuter and Jürgen Weber (eds.), *Freundliche Feinde? Die Alliierten und die Demokratiegründung in Deutschland* (Munich, 1996), pp. 231–7. In Rhineland-Palatinate, too, where French and American soldiers were stationed, the perception of the occupying powers until the mid-1960s was usually focused on the GIs, according to a study by Maria Höhn. As far as the French were concerned, it was often in conjunction with the observation of "how miserable their life was in comparison." See Maria Höhn, *Amis, Cadillacs und „Negerliebchen": GIs im Nachkriegsdeutschland* (Berlin, 2008), p. 364.

50 On the British occupation, see Volker Koop, *Besetzt. Britische Besatzungspolitik in Deutschland* (Berlin, 2007), on Berlin, pp. 279–90.

51 Wilfried Loth, *Stalins ungeliebtes Kind: Warum Moskau die DDR nicht wollte* (Berlin, 1994).

52 For more detail, see Michael Lemke, "Die Berlinkrisen von 1948/49 und 1958 bis 1963," in: Bernd Greiner et al. (eds.), *Krisen im Kalten Krieg* (Bonn, 2009), pp. 204–43; idem, *Die Berlinkrise 1958 bis 1963. Interessen und Handlungsspielräume der SED im Ost-West-Konflikt* (Berlin, 1995); Gerhard Wettig, *Chruschtschows Berlin-Krise 1958 bis 1963. Drohpolitik und Mauerbau* (Munich, 2006).

53 See Silke Satjukow, "Die 'Freunde'," in: Martin Sabrow (ed.), *Erinnerungsorte der DDR* (Munich, 2009), pp. 55–67.

54 Estimates varied between East and West: "[R]esearchers found that 33 percent of the East Berliners and 10 percent of the West Berliners saw the Western forces as occupiers, whereas 53 percent of the westerners and (notably) 42 percent of the easterners felt this way about the Russian troops. [...] Among those favoring the ex-Communist Party of Democratic Socialism (PDS), 61 percent saw the Russians as friends, whereas 51 percent of Social Democratic Party (SPD) supporters and only 22 per cent of Christian Democratic Union (CDU) partisans felt this way." Dirk Verheyen, *United City, Divided Memories? Cold War Legacies in Contemporary Berlin* (Lanham, 2008), p. 73.

55 Hanno Hochmuth, "Contested Legacies: Cold War Memory Sites in Berlin," in: Konrad H. Jarausch, Christian F. Ostermann, and Andreas Etges (eds.), *The Cold War. Historiography, Memory, Representation* (Berlin/Boston, 2017), pp. 283–99, here pp. 290ff.

56 Helmut Trotnow, "'Mehr als ein Koffer bleibt'. Die Entstehung der Ausstellung und das künftige AlliiertenMuseum," in: AlliiertenMuseum (ed.), *Ein Alliierten-Museum für Berlin. Dokumentation zur Ausstellung „Mehr als ein Koffer bleibt. Die Westmächte und Berlin 1944–1994"* (Berlin, 1995), pp. 5–19, here p. 16.

57 "The Allied Museum creates an unmistakably binary atmosphere in which the Cold War lingers more than two decades after the fall of the Berlin Wall: communism may have vanished [...], but those pesky Russians remain the suspicious 'other.'" David Lowe and Tony Joel, *Remembering the Cold War. Global Contest and National Stories* (London/New York, 2013), p. 216.

58 See "Entscheidung: Alliiertenmuseum könnte 2017 in Tempelhof eröffnen," *Berliner Morgenpost*, May 8, 2012, www.morgenpost.de/berlin/article106273160/ Alliierten-Museum-koennte-2017-in-Tempelhof-eroeffnen.html (accessed February 2, 2020).

59   "Trotz Flüchtlingen: Alliiertenmuseum zieht nach Tempelhof," *Tagesspiegel Online*,
      November 14, 2015, www.tagesspiegel.de/berlin/alliiertenmuseum-in-berlin-trotz-
      fluechtlingen-alliiertenmuseum-zieht-nach-tempelhof/12586504.html (accessed
      February 2, 2020).

60   "Alliiertenmuseum kann vielleicht nicht in Hangar umziehen," *Tagesspiegel Online*,
      1 June 21, 2019, www.tagesspiegel.de/berlin/marodes-tempelhof-alliiertenmuseum-
      kann-vielleicht-nicht-in-hangar-umziehen/24479874.html; "Bezirkspolitiker wollen
      Alliiertenmuseum in Dahlem behalten," Berliner Morgenpost, January 13, 2020,
      www.morgenpost.de/bezirke/steglitz-zehlendorf/article228087055/Bezirkspolitiker-
      wollen-Alliiertenmuseum-in-Dahlem-behalten.html (both accessed February 2,
      2020).

61   The permanent exhibit is called "Germany and the Soviet Union during the Second
      World War, 1941–45." See the museum homepage: www.museum-karlshorst.de
      (accessed February 2, 2020).

62   The museum is run by friends of the museum association in collaboration with the
      city of Wünsdorf. See the museum homepage: www.garnisonsmuseum-wuensdorf.eu
      (accessed February 2, 2020).

63   See Angela Janelli, *Wilde Museen. Zur Museologie des Amateurmuseums* (Bielefeld,
      2012).

64   Gundula Bavendamm, "Zwischen Graswurzelbewegung und Bundeskulturpolitik:
      Wie man in Deutschland an die Alliierten erinnert," in: Philipp Gassert et al. (eds.),
      Augsburg und Amerika. Aneignung und globale Verflechtung in einer Stadt (Augsburg,
      2013), pp. 277–300, quote on p. 285.

65   Ibid., pp. 298–300.

66   See Janelli, *Wilde Museen*, pp. 127–70.

67   See Bernd Greiner, "Spurensuche: Zum Erbe des Kalten Krieges," in: Bernd Greiner,
      Tim B. Müller, and Klaas Voß (eds.), *Erbe des Kalten Krieges, Reihe: Studien zum
      Kalten Krieg*, vol. 6 (Hamburg, 2013), pp. 9–41 as well as the other contributions in
      this volume.

68   Konrad H. Jarausch, Christian F. Ostermann, and Andreas Etges, "Rethinking,
      Representing, and Remembering the Cold War: Some Cultural Perspectives," in:
      idem (eds.), *The Cold War. Historiography, Memory, Representation* (Berlin/Boston,
      2017), pp. 1–18, here pp. 11, 17. See also Jon Wiener, *How We Forgot the Cold War: A
      Historical Journey Across America* (Berkeley, 2012).

69   "The Wall and other monuments recall controversial deeds, mostly of the recent
      past, deeds that prevent any consensus about the sort of things that monuments are
      supposed to embody, such as national identity or a common ideal." Brian Ladd, *The
      Ghosts of Berlin. Confronting Germany History in the Urban Landscape* (Chicago/
      London, 1997), p. 11.

70   On the debate over Checkpoint Charlie, see Sybille Frank, *Wall Memorials and
      Heritage. The Heritage Industry of Berlin's Checkpoint Charlie* (London/New York,
      2016).

71   A brief overview can be found in Wayne D. Cocroft, "Protect and Survive: Preserving
      and Presenting the Built Cold War Heritage," in: Jarausch et al., *The Cold War*, pp.
      215–38.

72   Gunnar Schupelius, "Die CDU lehnt mit Recht ein Museum der Verharmlosung
      am Checkpoint Charlie ab," *B.Z.*, May 16, 2012, www.bz-berlin.de/artikel-archiv/
      die-cdu-lehnt-mit-recht-ein-museum-der-verharmlosung-am-checkpoint-charlie-ab
      (accessed February 2, 2020).

73 Sabrow, *Erinnerungsorte der DDR*.

74 E.g., the introduction to one anthology: "It would surely be wrong to equate (East) Berlin with the GDR. Yet this city, once demonstratively labelled the capital of the now defunct GDR, lends itself to investigation as a representative cross-section of the GDR." Bernd Wilczek, "Vorwort," in: idem (ed.), *Berlin—Hauptstadt der DDR 1949–1989. Utopie und Realität* (Zurich/Baden-Baden, 1995), pp. 7–9, here p. 8.

75 Paul Steege, "'Finding the There There: Local Space, Global Ritual, and Early Cold War Berlin," in: Gary Backhaus and John Murungi (eds.), *Earth Ways: Framing Geographical Meanings* (Lanham, 2004), pp. 155–12, quote on p. 160.

76 See Stefanie Eisenhuth, "Freizeit beim Feind. US-amerikanische Soldaten in Ost-Berlin," *Zeithistorische Forschungen/Studies in Contemporary History* 15 (2018) 1, pp. 11–39, www.zeithistorische-forschungen.de/1-2018/id=5555.

77 Berlin Partner, Presseinformation: "Berlin kann Freiheit," March 24, 2017, www.berlin-partner.de/nc/presse/presseinformationen/detailansicht/berlin-kann-freiheit/ (accessed February 2, 2020).

78 This was underscored by the managing director of *Partner für Berlin* in conversation with the advertising magazine *Horizont*: "This initiative allows the German capital to professes its self-understanding [as a place] of freedom, thereby setting an example of tolerance and open-mindedness. We want to show that many things are possible in Berlin. For the simple reason that anything goes in Berlin." Bärbel Unckrich, "Stadtmarketing: Wie die Hauptstadt mit #FreiheitBerlin ein starkes Zeichen an die Welt sendet," March 27, 2017, www.horizont.net/agenturen/nachrichten/ Stadtmarketing-Wie-die-Hauptstadt-unter-dem-Motto-FreiheitBerlin-ein-starkes-Zeichen-an-die-Welt-sendet-156849 (accessed February 2, 2020).

14

Border Fragments, Border Fantasies:
Cold War Berlin in Retrospect

Paul Steege

In the National Museum of American History, item no. 2011.0015.01 bears the title *Berlin Wall Fragment, Berlin, Germany, 1961*. This small chunk of concrete (9.525 cm × 10.16 cm × 2.54 cm) still contains traces of yellow, pink, and blue paint. According to the online catalog entry, this item was "made" in 1989 and is "associated with" that same year. This particular piece was apparently purchased by a Canadian student at a flea market in Berlin and eventually sold on an online auction site.[1] The *Smithsonian's History of America in 101 Objects* includes a different Wall fragment (although one that is not included in the online catalog), this one allegedly obtained by a former Reagan administration official who borrowed a hammer and chisel to extract his own piece of the Wall, later donating it to the National Museum of American History when he served on its board.[2] In this mass circulation book, the Wall fragment is one of five items from the Smithsonian's collection used to sum up the American experience of the Cold War, which the volume dates "1946 to 1991." The Smithsonian's deploys this fragment as a signifier of Cold War history, in part because it is broken, its fragmenting a mark of the Cold War's end or at least, the collapse of its most potent icon. Yet even before enthusiastic wallpeckers (*Mauerspechte*) chipped away at the Wall with their hammers and picks in 1989 and 1990, the Wall already comprised myriad fragments, even if they were seldom recognized as such.

In its cataloging of this singular object, the Smithsonian also displays how tricky it is to locate this piece of the Wall historically. The museum dates the object 1961—the year in which East German authorities first erected a Wall in Berlin—and explains that it was made, that is rendered a fragment, in 1989. But, of course, the Wall of 1989 was not the same Wall as in 1961, and those differences were visibly distinguishable. The Wall's fourth generation with the smooth surface beloved by graffiti artists arrived only in the mid-1970s, meaning that the multicolored visual markers that define most retrospective images of the Wall (and souvenir fragments) effectively exclude half the Wall's history. By undertaking a double process of image critique—critiquing images but also using images to engage (critically) the cultures that produce them[3]—it will be possible to undermine any certainty about what *the* Wall looked like, but even more importantly, to challenge any easy notions about how it worked. In explaining the appeal of coming to Berlin to paint a section of the Wall, the American artist Keith Haring described it as "the most famous Wall in the world."[4] While that statement might explain its appeal for someone who started out doing graffiti in New York City subway stations, it risks reducing the Wall to a single surface. Its multifaceted stories demand rather more historical context in order to be told effectively.

Rainer Hildebrandt, the anticommunist activist and director of Berlin's *Haus am Checkpoint Charlie* museum, published several editions of a book entitled *Die Mauer Spricht—The Wall Speaks*. Although the book briefly relates the history of the Wall, it primarily celebrates the graffiti that, as he notes in the preface, made the Wall "interesting and worth a visit and worth mulling over."[5] Walter Momper, West Berlin's mayor at the time the Wall opened in 1989, similarly emphasized what Berlin's Wall Art had contributed to the divided city's historical trajectory: "We have no regrets for the Wall but we will miss Wall Art. [...] It is important for the Wall to be remembered for being a concrete proof of political failure as well as for the way people got used to it and integrated it into everyday life by painting it. Art challenged concrete and art won."[6] More than a quarter of a century after the collapse of the East German state and the Wall that defined it, such glib celebrations of how (Western) art triumphed over (Eastern) dictatorship overlook the visual and rhetorical disappearing act on which the Wall depended.

Simple structures "disappear" complexities,[7] and the Berlin Wall's smooth veneer made the Cold War seem uncomplicated. Already in June 1963, not quite two years after the Wall was built, US President John F. Kennedy made explicit that sense of the Wall's explanatory power. Speaking to a massive crowd in front of West Berlin's Schöneberg Town Hall—a speech most famous for Kennedy's use of the German sentence, *Ich bin ein Berliner*—the American president suggested that anyone who wanted to understand "what is the great issue between the free world and the communist [world]" should "come to Berlin."[8] His assertion presumed that once a person arrived in the city, Berlin's Cold War significance would be visible, that it went without saying and needed no deciphering. The Cold War world, including Berlin, had been divided into two (in Kennedy's terms, into a free world and a communist world), and those two halves were split by an impermeable boundary. The Wall, then, was simply a physical manifestation of a global geopolitical reality. The stakes of that struggle, Kennedy suggested, were perhaps a matter for political dispute (whether the West could "work with the communists," for instance), but the fact of the divide remained uncontested.

Yet what did that divide really look like, and how did it impact the people of Berlin? According to the latest calculations by the Berlin Wall Memorial Site, between August 13, 1961 and November 9, 1989 at least 140 persons died at the Berlin Wall or in conjunction with the Wall's security apparatus. Of those, 101 were people attempting to flee across the border; thirty were people from East or West Berlin, as well as one Soviet soldier, who, although they were not attempting to flee across the border, were nonetheless shot by border guards or killed in some sort of accident; eight were East German border guards, killed by their colleagues, by escapees, by escape assistants, or West Berlin policemen.[9] This summing up of moments of violence represents one story of the Wall; and the Berlin Wall Memorial Site has done an admirable job of investigating these cases, of putting faces, names, and stories to the numbers. Still, if we reduce the Wall only to a series of violent crisis moments, we miss something significant.

By detaching the Berlin Wall from the experiences of *people* other than its victims and the handful of border guards who fired on would-be escapees or the East German leaders who ordered its construction and operation, we reduce it to a technology of violence, a border apparatus that surrounded West Berlin and threatened violent death to any person who sought to cross the border illicitly. But even though it was erected by the East German state to prevent its populace from fleeing to the West, it is better to understand the Wall as an East–West coproduction, a structure with two sides, embedded within everyday practices—in the West as well as in the East— that effectively naturalized Cold War power relationships and the cultures on which they depended.[10] By turning to a broad set of individual experiences within these everyday practices, it is possible to develop a "complex sense of the concrete" even when wrestling with broad historical constructs.[11]

Looking at the Wall in the 1980s

A visitor to Berlin in the 1980s encountered the fourth and final generation of the Wall, which was put into place after 1975. Each steel-reinforced concrete panel measured 3.2 by 1.2 meters and weighed three tons. They combined to extend for nearly 100 miles (164 kilometers), including just over twenty-seven miles (forty-five kilometers) on the inner-city border between East and West Berlin.[12] A "hinterland wall" behind the "real" wall created a no-man's land, filled with the border apparatus: walls, fences, tank traps, brushed sand strips, guard towers, lights, and trip wires; a supply road, and occasional dog runs. As Peter Schneider described the border strip in his 1982 novel, *The Wall Jumper*: "Lit up in the afternoon by the setting sun and lavishly illuminated by floodlights after dark, the wall seems more a civic monument than a border."[13] This impression was only underscored by the observation platforms set up along the western side of the Wall to allow West Berliners and especially tourists to gaze across the concrete barrier, to look into the "death strip" and to gaze into East Berlin or East Germany. At the Potsdamer Platz platform, visitors paid particular attention to the sandy mound that concealed the remains of Hitler's World War Two bunker. In a way that proved even more fascinating than the details of the no-man's land that occupied what had been one of Europe's busiest squares. As for the Wall, the tourists who clambered up the observation platform already know what was there (they'd very likely already looked across at Checkpoint Charlie). But if we challenge the "banality of [those] images"[14] they encountered, if we look more closely, we can recognize messier experiences of the wall that were both extraordinary and normal, that were violently threatening and porous in ways that were not so easily visible to those Cold War tourists.

By the 1980s, as the Wall stabilized into the final structural and visual form that would be frozen by its disassembly, its explicit violence receded. Only sixteen of the

139 Wall victims died in the Wall's final decade. In its new format, however, the Wall was physically even more imposing. It was taller, its concrete harder and smoother, which helped to explain the explosion of graffiti on the Wall's Western side. Too often, however, the multicolored image of a Wall covered in graffiti has been collapsed into a declaration of its underlying potential for violence. In one popular history of the Berlin Wall, a photo taken by the French artist Thierry Noir is captioned (without any further comment) "Everyday Terror—The Wall in the 1980s" even though it is not obvious from the image what constitutes either part of that description.[15]

The photo shows a section of the Wall that Noir had painted along the Bethaniendamm in West Berlin's Kreuzberg district. On the Western side, a man is enjoying a quiet (traffic-free) stroll with his dog. On the Eastern side, we see an East German work detail engaged in, as Noir recalled looking back, cleaning up the trash thrown over the Wall by West Berliners. Noir suggested that occasionally such acts were "political," accompanied by derogatory comments directed at the East German state (*scheiß DDR*, among others).[16] But what does it mean to retrospectively declare an act "political" simply because it was accompanied by an ambiguous curse? Noir and his retrospective storytelling offers a much more interesting point of entry into this time and place. He was an artist for whom the Wall offered a uniquely accessible public "canvas," and since the fall of the Wall he has recreated that canvas around the World, on the East Side Gallery in Berlin after 1989 and even in a facsimile Wall in Los Angeles.[17] What can looking at the 1980s' version of the Wall tell us, especially in its post-1975 fourth-generation form, with its smooth, Westward-facing concrete face?

On July 4, 1986, Thierry Noir along with Christophe Bouchet used a stencil to paint a series of Statue of Liberty images on the Wall adjacent to the Checkpoint Charlie crossing point.[18] He retrospectively claimed it as a "dangerous" and "heroic" act. Less than a month later, between two and three in the morning on July 28, a 4.5-pound bomb blew a whole through a nearby portion of the Wall, shattering car and apartment windows in a 200-yard radius. The East German Foreign Ministry denounced this "serious provocation" and described the explosion as an "attack on the East German state border." The hole in the Wall was repaired later that afternoon as American MPs and East German border guards looked on.[19] Not quite twenty-five years after its construction, it seemed to take a major "incident" to get the Wall into the newspapers. Whereas Noir contrasted an American image of liberty to the East German structure of oppression, the two sides' response to the violent assault on the Wall provides a small example of the ways in which they collaborated to avoid or at least to clean up after any border incidents.[20]

In this context, Rainer Hildebrandt contacted Keith Haring to invite him to paint a mural on the Berlin Wall. In a letter sent to Haring on September 29, 1986, Hildebrandt writes: "I have studied your paintings and am hopeful that your paintings will be full of understanding for people who are separated from each other."[21] In subsequent correspondence, Hildebrandt discussed the timing of various events on the day that Haring would be working; he made sure to have the Wall prepared with the proper base color for the 100-meter long mural, and reiterated his belief that this mural would represent a chance to speak on behalf of the people of East Germany. He took great care to plan and arrange press conferences and to invite media representatives in the hope it would generate attention for his museum and his campaign against the Wall. In an October 14 invitation to the mural painting, Hildebrandt noted that Haring had previously been in Berlin, but had not picked up a brush, since most of the Wall was already covered with graffiti, and he was hesitant to paint over somebody else's work. Nonetheless, Hildebrandt suggested that artworks are continuously being painted over, and the various "lay artists" will not complain about sacrificing 100 meters of the Wall for Haring's painting.[22]

On October 22, Keith Haring arrived in Berlin, and the next day painted a collection of black and red figures on the prepared gold background. In a *New York Times* interview, Haring called it a "humanistic gesture […] a political and subversive act—an attempt to psychologically destroy the wall by painting it."[23] The *Times* also quoted one young Berliner who watched Haring paint and proved skeptical of the mural's importance: "This is Valium, there's no provocation in it. In every third toilet in Kreuzberg you can see the same graffiti." But in transforming the concrete structure into something no different than the wall in a Kreuzberg toilet, Haring demonstrated how the Wall as a border regime depended on much more than the structures built since August 13, 1961. What was most subversive about Haring's act was that he made visible the Wall in the head, which remained a collaborative East-West product. The collective avoidance of incidents at the Wall depended at least in part on the disappearance of the multilayered structures of coercive violence behind the palimpsestic surface of Wall art.

In spite of Hildebrandt's preparatory work, Haring was not working on a blank "canvas." Thierry Noir recalls:

> On 23 October 1986, I heard on the radio that Keith Haring was in Berlin to paint the Wall at Checkpoint Charlie. I went there and saw that my Statues of Liberty had all been painted over with yellow paint. I talked to Keith and he was embarrassed and apologi[z]ed. He said: "In New York you can get killed for that." He was invited over and the section of Wall had been pre-prepared for him. The yellow was very transparent so you could see my statues through it. I was angry, but it was not his fault. Keith was a great guy and a great artist.[24]

Within days, Haring's mural also began to vanish behind new layers of paint.

A week after Haring painted his mural, five friends, all originally from East Germany, took up paint brushes in an effort to force people really to look at the Wall. Irritated by a sense that the Wall now served primarily as a tourist destination—whether for its graffiti or its fetish value as a site of Cold War terror—they painted a white stripe over whatever artwork they encountered, including Haring's mural. On November 4, 1986, the second day of their project, East German border guards opened an access door through the Wall and seized one of the five. He remained in an East German prison until June 1987, when the West German government paid for him to be released to the West.[25]

This incident, coming on the heels of Haring's highly publicized painting of the Wall, challenges any sense of the Wall as a stable element of late Cold War iconography. It also highlights the Wall's permeability. The five activists had all crossed the border into West Berlin, either as émigrés or as expellees from the GDR. The return of one of the five to East Germany was possible only because of a literal hole in the Wall, a door behind which border guards waited and through which they dragged the unlucky target of their control measures. The guards recognized the "threat" to the border as they observed and photographed the friends during their first day working on the western side of the Wall. In effect, the five friends' effort to disrupt the normal operation of the Wall, to make it visible, was foiled by the nonconcrete, human elements of the security regime that they, too, had overlooked.

Post-Wall Fantasies

According to the head of the association working to erect a Cold War museum at the location of the former Checkpoint Charlie border crossing in Berlin, 4.1 million visitors come to the site each year. Some of them, former occupation soldiers or Berlin families return to this spot to try to recall a vanished past and hope that they may find a way to explain there the city's "history of division."[26] Across the street the artist Yadegar Asisi has produced a panoramic painting to visually recreate the crossing point as it appeared in the 1980s. According to the artist's website, his installation transports the viewer back to Checkpoint Charlie on "a fictional fall day in the 1980s." The Wall is viewed from a Western perspective and, quite literally, as a (painted) backdrop to an imagined everyday life (*Alltag* is the German word used on the website) into which the viewer has been relocated. Housed in a building with the remarkably alluring but nonetheless fantastic declaration: "The Berlin Wall: See it here," the painting promises to collapse past and present.[27] As a website describing an earlier project reconstructing the city of Pergamon explains, Yadegar Asisi engages a "culture of illusions" in order to ask: "How do we perceive our environment? What does each individual actually see?"[28] These illusions, however, represent more than just a tourist experience offered up at ten euros a ticket; even earnest arguments in defense of historical authenticity depend on their own version of historical fantasy.

In the spring of 2013, a public effort to save the East Side Gallery, what the *New York Times* called the "longest remaining expanse"[29] of the Wall mobilized the public on behalf of a fiction. The East Side Gallery had become a popular tourist destination after 1989 when artists (including Thierry Noir) painted new artwork to celebrate the fall of the Wall. In 2013, the portion of the wall activists sought to save from the push of gentrifying development had been part of the hinterland wall, the secondary barrier on the Eastern side of the border exclusion zone and had been transformed into a recognizable piece of the Berlin Wall only after its demise. By marking the Eastern side of the barrier with politicized graffiti images, the artists who created the East Side Gallery inverted the Wall, transforming the view from the Eastern side to retroactively adhere to the hegemonic gaze at the Wall defined by the side that "won" the Cold War.

But the fantastic imagining of the Wall is not just a retrospective phenomenon. In July 1948, the editors at *Life* published an image with which they sought to explain the ongoing Soviet blockade of Berlin's Western sectors. The caption read: "Blockade of

Berlin is shown symbolically in this map, with American British and French sectors enclosed within *an imaginary wall*."[30] This image both misrepresented the very porous blockade and helped create for an American readership a totalizing sense of the airlift as the sole solution to that "first Berlin crisis." It also helped to lay the foundation for a parallel understanding of the Wall, thirteen years later, as similarly total and absolute.

Even after the Wall was built, Berlin's sector borders were not impassable. Before 1961, the so-called *Grenzgänger* or border crosser was a vital subset of the Berlin population, working, living, and consuming goods and culture on either side of the East–West divide.[31] In her history of two towns on either side of the German-German border, Edith Sheffer has extended the story of occasional border-crossing into the 1980s;[32] but that history has yet to be written for Berlin between 1961 and 1989. In Berlin, after all, it was not only the spectacular escape artists who made it over the Wall. Even after the 1971 Quadripartite Agreement "normalized" the status of divided Berlin, the city remained under four-power occupation; and their representatives were allowed access throughout the city. Buses of US military personnel traveled on "shopping tours" to East Berlin to take advantage of the beneficial exchange rate (despite an East German ban on importing its currency into the country, East German border guards were not permitted to board or inspect the US buses on these tours), and the planned economy in the East apparently managed to produce sufficiently desirable goods that the Americans kept coming back. West Berliners and West Germans could also travel back and forth, so could privileged East Germans including party officials, artists, and athletes; but in greatest number, East German senior citizens could spend up to thirty days in the West after having achieved their *Reisemündigkeit*, their travel "coming of age."[33]

Yet, in addition to this variety of officially sanctioned border crossings that, to varying degrees, constituted a real coming and going to and from East and West, a more liminal form of border crossing can shed light on the quotidian processes by which the Wall became normal. Two lines of the West Berlin subway system ran under East Berlin (the U6 and the U8). Aside from the Friedrichstrasse station, where one could get off, and proceed through the border checkpoint into East Berlin or even switch to the S-Bahn to travel back to West Berlin, the other stations were closed, "ghost stations," through which the trains slowly passed as border guards armed with automatic weapons manned the platforms. On the one hand, this "haunted" passage made visible the immanent violence of the border regime; but it also integrated that potential violence into a West Berlin commute. The transportation system map offers a visually powerful performance of Berlin's division, but it also helps to create a script that makes it safe for consumption. East Berlin transit maps did similar work, in most instances rendering West Berlin as a blank white space. But even if they never went to look across the Wall and into the West, East Berliners could feel the rumble of West Berlin subway cars as they passed underneath their feet.

From 1961 to 1985, the interplay between the border regime and the Berlin cityscape also played out in a rather more spectacular fashion, first as a Cold War curiosity and tourist destination, then as an explosive erasure of a church building originally constructed in the late nineteenth century. When the Wall was built in 1961, the ironically named Church of the Reconciliation was inaccessibly located in no-man's land, cut off from both East and West Berlin.[34] In order to "heighten security and cleanliness" along the border (by creating improved sightlines, for example), East German authorities ordered the Church demolished, and at 10 am on January 22, 1985, the neogothic structure came crashing down. Those authorities' actions also reflected the way that the Wall necessitated a reimagining of Berlin's urban geography. The church's destruction marked a decisive material intervention into the city's built space and an imposition of an aesthetic of control even if that vision of control was not realized in practice. (It is perhaps worth a mention that this site now sits at the center of the Wall Memorial, the dimensions of the former church marked out on the ground, and a smaller chapel of reconciliation built to tie together East and West, the once again neighboring districts of Wedding and Mitte.[35]) Even at the Wall Memorial Site, the Wall had to be recreated. The original Wall is almost entirely gone: first pecked apart by hammer-wielding souvenir hunters, the remaining panels were lifted up by crane and dispersed around the world.

It is thus perhaps unsurprising that since November 9, 1989, we generally presume to live in a post-Wall world, but we ought to be cautious in assuming that "post-wall condition" as given.[36] In fact there are more international borders walls in existence now than during the Cold War.[37] And of course, there was no "real" fall of the Wall. The phrase "fall of the Wall" knits together the breach of November 9 (the opening of the gates) and the subsequent removal of the physical structures and installations that comprised the border regime. Janet Ward suggests that, even in Berlin, disappearance has proved only partial. She posits an "*ex*-Wall (its remnants and consequences, its lines and projections, traces and stagings, in short: its inverse, imaginary status, like a photographic negative) that is still marking the city." These residual marks of "former geometries can be both positive and pathological," but to make that assessment and move beyond the presumption of a disappeared Wall, it is necessary to remain attentive to fragments within their historical context.[38]

Everyday Violence and Fragments of Cold War Hegemony

In a May 1990 letter, Rainer Hildebrandt wrote to the Friends of Keith Haring to try to solicit their support for fundraising efforts to preserve sections of the Wall—especially the section that Haring had painted—but also to help fund the renovation of his museum. Keith Haring had died of AIDS in February and just three days after his death, Hildebrandt had written an odd letter addressed to Keith, in which he explained: "With your mural from Checkpoint Charlie to Kochstrasse, you managed—more than any other artist—to make the WALL [in all caps as 'DIE MAUER' in the German original] interesting and thus to make it known in its reality and as a wonder of the world (*Weltwunder*)."[39] Perhaps because it has stayed so historically interesting, we too often remain in awe of the Berlin Wall. But that way of looking at the Wall extracts it from the scale of human action and denies the multiple layers of human complicity in its production and operation. By looking back at the Wall in the 1980s, it is possible to recognize how its destructive power depended not on pathological brutality but on everyday violence that only occasionally met the eye.

In his book on watching the Iraq War that began in 2003, the visual cultural theorist Nicholas Mirzoeff examines a wonder of the ancient world as a means to investigate how people process images of war. He describes Babylon as a metaphor and a location. "Babylon is, then, a frame within which differing methodologies and histories can be productively thought alongside each other to generate knowledges that might be in that way different to the received disciplinary information that surrounds us."[40] To help make his point, he references an inscription placed by Nebuchadnezzar alongside the Ishtar Gate (an artifact held in the Pergamon Museum on Berlin's Museum Island): "I magnificently adorned them with luxurious grandeur for all mankind to behold in awe."[41] Mirzoeff sees this action as being at the heart of imperial practice, the discrediting of looking closely, of interrogating what one sees.

At first glance, the very occasional moments of physical violence at the Wall may appear to have occurred as ruptures in the course of everyday life, taking place in circumscribed (physical and chronological) "spaces of violence" in which the regular rules of social communication are suspended.[42] Even if those instances of violence may represent moments when words and speech failed, when the command "Stop!" was supplanted by the bullet fired at a would-be escapee, for example, any assessment of violence at the Wall demands much more than tracing out lines of culpability from individual border guards to some singular and iconic shoot-to-kill order.[43] By investigating how stories and storytelling surround and facilitate those moments of violence, it becomes possible to move beyond a perspective that restricts violence to places in which words are no longer possible. Rather, the words we should recognize and decipher in the midst of these violent acts get disappeared into fantastic narratives.[44] By looking at the multilayered disappearance of the Berlin Wall, we can historically contextualize a process in which the hegemonic structures of the Cold War depended on the disappearance of Cold War violence.

The Wall (and ultimately its violence) could operate effectively only on the basis of becoming "normal";[45] and that process was never just an East German imposition. It depended on the ability of East and West Germans (both inside and outside Berlin) as well as Allied occupiers, and even tourists visiting the city to integrate the Wall into their everyday lives. For visitors to Berlin, the Wall formulated the "visual scenography of a state of emergency"[46] that justified the sustained violence of the Cold War. But beneath that surface, people—and not just in Berlin—learned how to live with the Wall.

Gyanendra Pandey has recently proposed a new category—the "trifling"—within a catalogue of "unarchived histories" to be sought out in an ongoing effort to challenge the destructive hegemony of the imperial archive.[47] On the one hand, that destructive authority disappeared the accounts it declared mad (irrational), operating in a classic Orientalizing mode to discount the human agency of anyone other than (Western) political actors. Pandey has adduced this new category in an effort to expand that postcolonial critique, in order to engage those persons and experience that, while acknowledged to have existed, are nonetheless still deemed historically insignificant. This "trifling" category of everyday life is, of course, hardly a new discovery. Since the 1980s, German and American practitioners of everyday life history (*Alltagsgeschichte*) have fought off challengers deriding the historical insignificance of their investigations into ordinary life, particularly in the "extraordinary" context of totalizing regimes.[48] Thinking about the Berlin Wall in these sorts of fragmentary everyday term may help us to notice how the impetus to build walls makes visible an underlying tolerance for violence that both comes before, and lingers after a wall is built.

Notes

1   Berlin Wall fragment, Berlin, Germany, 1961, Smithsonian: National Museum of American History, http://americanhistory.si.edu/collections/search/object/nmah_1398384 (accessed February 2, 2020).

2   Richard Kurin, *The Smithsonian's History of America in 101 Objects* (New York, 2013), pp. 500–5.

3   Sunil Manghani, *Image Critique and the Fall of the Berlin Wall* (Chicago, 2008).

4   "Ein Ami trieb es bunt: Mauer mit Männekens bemalt," *BZ* (clipping, n.d.), Keith Haring Foundation, 1986 Press, Box 53.

5   Rainer Hildebrandt, *Die Mauer spricht: The Wall Speaks*, 6th ed. (Berlin, 1990). The first edition was published in 1982.

6   In Sigrid Mayer, "The Graffiti of the Berlin Wall: A Semiotic Approach," in: Ernst Schürer, Manfred Keune, and Philip Jenkins (eds.), *The Berlin Wall: Representations and Perspectives* (New York, 1996), p. 227.

7   Marcello Di Cintio, *Walls: Travels Along the Barricades* (Berkeley, 2013), p. 270.

8   John F. Kennedy Speeches, Remarks of President John F. Kennedy at the Rudolph Wilde Platz, Berlin, June 26, 1963, *John F. Kennedy Presidential Museum and Library*, www.jfklibrary.org/Research/Research-Aids/JFK-Speeches/Berlin-W-Germany-Rudolph-Wilde-Platz_19630626.aspx; also www.presidency.ucsb.edu/documents/remarks-the-rudolph-wilde-platz-berlin (both accessed February 2, 2020).

9   "Die Todesopfer an der Berliner Mauer," *Gedenkstätte Berliner Mauer*,www.berliner-mauer-gedenkstaette.de/de/todesopfer-240.html (accessed February 2, 2020).

10   Wladimir Fischer-Nebmaier, "Introduction: Space, Narration, and the Everyday," in: idem, Matthew P. Berg and Anastasia Christou (eds.), *Narrating the City: Histories, Space, and the Everyday* (New York, 2015), p. 7.

11   Lutz Niethammer in collaboration with Dirk van Laak, *Posthistoire: Has History Come to an End?* trans. Patrick Camiller (New York, 1992), p. 150.

12   Mayer, "The Graffiti of the Berlin Wall: A Semiotic Approach," p. 216.

13   Peter Schneider, *The Wall Jumper: A Berlin Story*, trans. Leigh Hafrey (Chicago, 1998), p. 5.

14   Nicholas Mirzoeff, *Watching Babylon: The War in Iraq and Global Visual Culture* (New York, 2005), p. 14.

15   Frederick Taylor, *The Berlin Wall: A World Divided, 1961–1989* (New York, 2007), p. 268ff.

16   "Graffiti in the Death Strip: Berlin's First Street Artist Tells His Story," *The Guardian*, April 3, 2014, www.theguardian.com/artanddesign/gallery/2014/apr/03/thierry-noir-graffiti-berlin-wall (accessed February 2, 2020).

17   Adrian Bridge, "Thierry Noir and the Art of Revisiting the Berlin Wall," *The Telegraph*, April 8, 2014, www.telegraph.co.uk/travel/destinations/europe/germany/berlin/articles/Thierry-Noir-and-the-art-of-revisiting-the-Berlin-Wall/ (accessed February 2, 2020).

18 "Graffiti in the Death Strip."

19 "Blast Hits the Wall in Berlin," *New York Times*, July 29, 1986, p. A3.

20 On the desire to avoid "incidents" on the sector border as clear point of agreement between Eastern and Western officials, see Edith Sheffer, *Burned Bridge: How East and West Germans Made the Iron Curtain* (Oxford, 2011), p. 171.

21 Keith Haring Foundation, Keith's Files: Special Reports.

22 Invitation dated October 14, 1986, Keith Haring Foundation, Keith's Files: Special Projects.

23 "Keith Haring Paints Mural on Berlin Wall," *New York Times*, October 24, 1986, www.nytimes.com/1986/10/24/arts/keith-haring-paints-mural-on-berlin-wall.html (accessed February 2, 2020).

24 "Graffiti in the Death Strip."

25 Anne Hahn and Frank Willmann (eds.), *Der weiße Strich: Vorgeschichte und Folgen einer Kunstaktion an der Berliner Mauer* (Berlin, 2011).

26 Isabel Metzger, "Geht's hier zum Brandenburger Tor?," *Die Welt*, June 20, 2015, www. welt.de/print/die_welt/berlin/article142799215/Gehts-hier-zum-Brandenburger-Tor. html (accessed February 2, 2020); also www.taz.de/!5203476/; Black Box Checkpoint Charlie, www.visitberlin.de/en/spot/black-box-history-of-cold-war; ZZF review, www.zeithistorische-forschungen.de/2-2014/id=5110.

27 "Die Mauer: Die Asisi Panorama zum geteilten Berlin," *Yadegar Asisi 360° Panorama*, www.asisi.de/de/panoramen/the-wall/photo-gallery-de.html (accessed February 2, 2020).

28 "'Yadegar Asisi—Culture of Illusions," ww2.smb.museum/pergamon-panorama/ index.php?node_id=9. This is just one of a series of efforts to "virtually" make the Berlin Wall accessible. See, e.g., the "Virtuelle Mauer," www.virtuelle-mauer-berlin. de/english/, a version of the Twinity social networking site (www.twinity.com/ en/community/berlin-wall), as well as in the 1991 video game *Berlin no kabe*. A more recent game, *1378 km*, gave players the chance to assume the role of either Republikflüchtling or Grenztruppe along the German-German border. Press reports denounced it as "Berlin Wall" game. More generally on Wall commemoration, see www.berlin.de/mauer/index.en.html.

29 Chris Cottrell, "In Berlin, a Protest to Keep What Remains of the Wall," *New York Times*, March 5, 2013, p. A12.

30 Emmet Hughes, "Berlin under Siege," *Life*, July 19, 1948, pp. 72–3.

31 Frank Roggenbuch, *Das Berliner Grenzgängerproblem: Verflechtung und Systemkonkurrenz vor dem Mauerbau*, Veröffentlichungen der Historischen Kommission zu Berlin 107 (Berlin, 2008).

32 Edith Sheffer, *Burned Bridge*.

33 Patrick Major, *Behind the Berlin Wall: East Germany and the Frontiers of Power* (Oxford, 2010), p. 175.

34 "Explosion im Todesstreifen: Die Versöhnungskirche fiel vor 30 Jahren," www. tagesspiegel.de/berlin/mauergedenken-in-berlin-explosion-im-todesstreifen-die-versoehnungskirche-fiel-vor-30-jahren/11261820.html (accessed February 2, 2020).

35 "Kapelle der Versöhnung," www.versoehnungskapelle.de/texte/seite.php?id=109204 (accessed February 2, 2020).

36 Manghani, *Image Critique and the Fall of the Berlin Wall*, pp. 22, 35, 104, 115.

37 Tom Vanderbilt, "The Walls in Our Heads," *New York Times*, November 4, 2016, www.nytimes.com/2016/11/06/opinion/sunday/the-walls-in-our-heads.html?actio n=click&pgtype=Homepage&clickSource=story-heading&module=opinion-c-col-

right-region&region=opinion-c-col-right-region&WT.nav=opinion-c-col-right-region (accessed February 2, 2020).

38 Janet Ward, *Post-Wall Berlin: Borders, Space and Identity* (New York, 2011), p. 59.

39 Letter to Keith Haring, February 19, 1990, Keith Haring Foundation, Keith's Files: Special Reports.

40 Mirzoeff, *Watching Babylon*, p. 10.

41 Ibid., p. 9.

42 Jörg Baberowski, *Räume der Gewalt*, 3rd ed. (Frankfurt am Main, 2015), p. 27.

43 Ruth A. Miller, "Violence without Agency," in: Austin Sarat, Carleen R. Basler, and Thomas L. Dumm (eds.), *Performances of Violence* (Amherst, 2011), pp. 43–68. See also Baberowski, p. 27. On the iconic status of the East German *Schiessbefehl* as a singular declaration of violence, see Pertti Ahonen, *Death at the Berlin Wall* (Oxford, 2011), p. 250.

44 Jan Philipp Reemtsma, *Die Gewalt spricht nicht: Drei Reden* (Stuttgart, 2002). Carolin Emcke, *Stumme Gewalt: Nachdenken über die RAF*. Mit Beiträgen von Winfried Hassemer und Wolfgang Kraushaar (Frankfurt am Main, 2008).

45 Of course, the East German state argued that the Berlin border was both "normal," like any other border in the world, as well as pathological, that is, so dangerous that it demanded special security mechanisms. That contradiction lay at the heart of the regime's confusion. See Paul Steege, "Crisis, Normalcy, Fantasy: Berlin and Its Borders," *Contemporary European History* 23 (2014), pp. 469–84.

46 Wendy Brown, *Walled States, Waning Sovereignty* (New York, 2010), p. 77.

47 Gyanendra Pandey, "Unarchived Histories: the 'Mad' and the 'Trifling,'" in: Gyanendra Pandey (ed.), *Unarchived Histories: The "Mad" and the "Trifling" in the Colonial and Postcolonial World* (London, 2014), p. 3.

48 Alf Lüdtke (ed.), *The History of Everyday Life: Reconstructing Historical Experiences and Ways of Life*, trans. William Templer (Princeton, 1989); For the initial critiques, see Institut für Zeitgeschichte (ed.), *Alltagsgeschichte der NS-Zeit: Neue Perspektive oder Trivialisierung?* Kolloquien des Instituts für Zeitgeschichte (Munich, 1984). For more recent assessments, see Paul Steege, Andrew Stuart Bergerson, Maureen Healy, and Pamela E. Swett, "The History of Everyday Life: A Second Chapter," *Journal of Modern History* 80 (2008) 2, pp. 358–78; Andrew Stuart Bergerson, Elissa Mailänder Koslov, Gideon Reuveni, Paul Steege, and Dennis Sweeney, "Everyday Life in Nazi Germany: A Forum," *German History* 27 (2009) 4, pp. 560–79.

Selected Bibliography

Ahrens, Ralf, "Teure Gewohnheiten. Berlinförderung und Bundeshilfe für West-Berlin seit dem Mauerbau," *Vierteljahrschrift für Sozial- und Wirtschaftsgeschichte* 102 (2015), pp. 283–99.

Arndt, Melanie, *Gesundheitspolitik im geteilten Berlin 1948 bis 1961* (Cologne/Weimar/Vienna, 2009).

Barclay, David E., *Schaut auf diese Stadt: Der unbekannte Ernst Reuter* (Berlin, 2000).

Barclay, David E., "Westberlin," in: Martin Sabrow (ed.), *Erinnerungsorte der DDR* (München, 2009), pp. 431–40.

Barclay, David E., "Kein neuer Mythos. Das letzte Jahrzehnt West-Berlins," *Aus Politik und Zeitgeschichte* 65 (2015) 46, pp. 37–42.

Bauer, Karin/Hosek, Jennifer (eds.), *Cultural Topographies of the New Berlin* (Oxford, 2018).

Beachy, Robert, *Gay Berlin: Birthplace of a Modern Identity* (New York, 2014).

Bienert, Michael C./Schaper, Uwe/Theissen, Andrea (eds.), *Die Vier Mächte in Berlin. Beiträge zur Politik der Alliierten in der besetzten Stadt* (Berlin, 2007).

Bienert, Michael C./Schaper, Uwe/Wentker, Hermann (eds.), *Hauptstadtanspruch und symbolische Politik. Die Bundespräsenz im geteilten Berlin* (Berlin, 2012).

Biskup, Thomas/Schalenberg, Marc (eds.), *Selling Berlin. Imagebildung und Stadtmarketing von der preußischen Residenz bis zur Bundeshauptstadt* (Stuttgart, 2008).

Bisky, Jens, *Berlin: Biographie einer großen Stadt* (Berlin, 2019).

Brown, Timothy S., "A Tale of two Communes: The Private and the Political in Divided Berlin, 1967–1973," in: Martin Klimke, Jacco Pekelder, and Joachim Scharloth (eds.), *Between Prague Spring and French May 1968: Opposition and Revolt in Europe, 1960–1980* (New York, 2011).

Brown, Timothy S., "The Sixties in the City: Avantgardes and Urban Rebels in New York, London, and West Berlin," *Journal of Social History* 46 (2013) 4, pp. 817–42.

Ciesla, Burghard, *Als der Osten durch den Westen fuhr. Die Geschichte der Deutschen Reichsbahn in Westberlin* (Cologne, 2006).

Ciesla, Burghard/Lemke, Michael Lemke/Lindenberger, Thomas (eds.), *Sterben für Berlin? Die Berliner Krisen 1948: 1958* (Berlin, 2000).

Daum, Andreas W., *Kennedy in Berlin. Politics and Culture in the Cold War* (Buffalo, 2008).

Davis, Belinda, "The City as Theater of Protest. West Berlin and West Germany, 1962–1983," in: Gyan Prakash and Kevin M. Kruse (eds.), *The Spaces of the Modern City. Imaginaries, Politics, and Everyday Life* (Princeton, 2008), pp. 247–74.

Dobler, Jens, *Von anderen Ufern. Geschichte der Berliner Lesben und Schwulen in Kreuzberg und Friedrichshain* (Berlin, 2003).

Duara, Prasenjit, "The Cold War as a Historical Period. An Interpretive Essay," *Journal of Global History* 6 (2011) 3, pp. 457–80.

Eisenhuth, Stefanie, *West-Berlin und der Umbruch in der DDR. Grenzübergreifende Wahrnehmungen und Verhandlungen 1989* (Berlin, 2012).

Eisenhuth, Stefanie, *Die Schutzmacht. Die Amerikaner in Berlin, 1945–1994* (Gottingen, 2018).

Eisenhuth, Stefanie/Krause, Scott H., "Inventing the 'Outpost of Freedom'. Transatlantic Narratives and the Historical Actors Crafting West Berlin's Postwar Political Culture," *Zeithistorische Forschungen/Studies in Contemporary History* 11 (2014) 2, pp. 188–211, www.zeithistorische-forschungen.de/2-2014/id=5093.

Eisenhuth, Stefanie/Sabrow, Martin, "Westberlin. Eine historiographische Herausforderung," *Zeithistorische Forschungen/Studies in Contemporary History* 11 (2014) 2, 165–87, www.zeithistorische-forschungen.de/2-2014/id=5090.

Engel, Jeffrey A. (ed.), *Local Consequences of the Global Cold War* (Washington, 2008).

Evans, Jennifer V., *Life among the Ruins. Cityscape and Sexuality in Cold War Berlin* (Houndmills, 2011).

Frank, Sybille, *Wall Memorials and Heritage. The Heritage Industry of Berlin's Checkpoint Charlie* (London/New York, 2016).

Gaddis, John Lewis, *The Cold War. A New History* (New York, 2005).

Geppert, Dominik, "'Proclaim Liberty Throughout All the Land': Berlin and the Symbolism of the Cold War," in: idem (ed.), *The Postwar Challenge. Cultural, Social, and Political Change in Western Europe, 1945–1958* (Oxford, 2003), pp. 339–63.

Goedde, Petra/Immerman, Richard (eds.), *Oxford Handbook on the Cold War* (Oxford, 2013).

Greiner, Bernd/Müller, Tim B./Voß, Klaas (eds.), *Erbe des Kalten Krieges* (Hamburg, 2013).

Grötzner, Björn, *Outpost of Freedom. Ernst Reuters Amerikareisen 1949 bis 1953* (Berlin, 2014).

Harrington, Daniel F., *Berlin on the Brink: The Blockade, the Airlift, and the Early Cold War* (Lexington, 2012).

Hauswald, Harald/Rathenow, Lutz, *Ost-Berlin. Leben vor dem Mauerfall* (Berlin, 2005).

Heimann, Siegfried, "Politische Remigranten in Berlin," in: Claus-Dieter Krohn and Patrik von zur Mühlen (eds.), *Rückkehr und Aufbau nach 1945 : deutsche Remigranten im öffentlichen Leben Nachkriegsdeutschlands* (Marburg, 1997), pp. 189–210.

Henke, Klaus-Dietmar (ed.), *Die Mauer. Errichtung, Überwindung, Erinnerung* (Munich, 2011).

Hertle, Hans-Hermann/Jarausch, Konrad H./Kleßmann, Christoph (eds.), *Mauerbau und Mauerfall. Ursachen, Verlauf, Auswirkungen* (Berlin, 2002).

Hochmuth, Hanno, *Kiezgeschichte: Friedrichshain und Kreuzberg im geteilten Berlin* (Göttingen, 2017).

Hochmuth, Katharina (ed.), *Krieg der Welten: Zur Geschichte des Kalten Krieges* (Berlin, 2017).

Höhn, Maria/Klimke, Martin: *A Breath of Freedom: The Civil Rights Struggle, African American GIs, and Germany* (New York, 2010).

Huyssen, Andreas, *Present Pasts: Urban Palimpsests and the Politics of Memory* (Stanford, 2003).

Jarausch, Konrad H., "'Die Teile als Ganzes erkennen'. Zur Integration der beiden deutschen Nachkriegsgeschichten," *Zeithistorische Forschungen/Studies in Contemporary History* 1 (2004) 1, pp.10–30.

Jarausch, Konrad H., *Out of Ashes. A New History of Europe in the Twentieth Century* (Princeton, NJ, 2015).

Jarausch, Konrad H./Ostermann, Christian F./Etges, Andreas (eds.), *The Cold War: Historiography, Memory, Representation* (Berlin, 2017).

Jeschonnek, Friedrich/Riedel, Dieter/Durie, William, *Alliierte in Berlin 1945–1994. Ein Handbuch zur Geschichte der militärischen Präsenz der Westmächte*, 2nd ed. (Berlin, 2007).

Kleßmann, Christoph, "Konturen einer integrierten Nachkriegsgeschichte," *Aus Politik und Zeitgeschichte* 55 (2005) 18–19, pp. 3–11.

Krause, Scott H., "Neue Westpolitik: The Clandestine Campaign to Westernize the SPD in Cold War Berlin, 1948–1958," *Central European History*, 48 (March 2015) 1, pp. 79–99.

Krause, Scott H., *Bringing Cold War Democracy to West Berlin: A Shared German-American Project, 1940–1972* (Abingdon, 2018).

Kraushaar, Wolfgang, "Berliner Subkultur. Blues, Haschrebellen, Tupamaros und Bewegung 2. Juni," in: Martin Klimke and Joachim Scharloth (eds.), *1968. Handbuch zur Kultur- und Mediengeschichte der Studentenbewegung*, Lizenzausgabe (Bonn, 2008), pp. 261–75.

Kreutzmüller, Christoph, *Final Sale in Berlin: The Destruction of Jewish Commercial Activity, 1930–1945* (New York, 2015).

Kuhn, Armin, *Vom Häuserkampf zur neoliberalen Stadt. Besetzungsbewegungen und Stadterneuerung in Berlin und Barcelona* (Münster, 2014).

Ladd, Brian, *The Ghosts of Berlin: Confronting Germany History in the Urban Landscape* (Chicago, 1997).

Lanz, Stephan, "Inclusion and Segregation in Berlin, The 'Social City'," in: Jeffry M. Diefendorf and Janet Ward (eds.), *Transnationalism and the German City* (New York, 2014), pp. 55–71.

Large, David Clay, *Berlin* (New York, 2001).

Leffler, Melvyn P./Westad, Odd Arne (eds.), *The Cambridge History of the Cold War*, vol. 1, Origins, 1945–1962 (Cambridge, 2012).

Leitner, Olaf (ed.), *West-Berlin! Westberlin! Berlin (West)! Die Kultur – die Szene – die Politik. Erinnerungen an eine Teilstadt der 70er und 80er Jahre* (Berlin, 2002).

Lemke, Michael (ed.), *Schaufenster der Systemkonkurrenz. Die Region Berlin-Brandenburg im Kalten Krieg* (Cologne, 2006).

Lemke, Michael (ed.), *Konfrontation und Wettbewerb. Wissenschaft, Technik und Kultur im geteilten Berliner Alltag (1948–1973)* (Berlin, 2008).

Lemke, Michael, *Vor der Mauer. Berlin in der Ost-West Konkurrenz 1948 bis 1961* (Cologne, 2011).

Lindenberger, Thomas (ed.), *Massenmedien im Kalten Krieg. Akteure, Bilder, Resonanzen* (Cologne, 2006).

Lindenberger, Thomas/Payk, Marcus M./Vowinckel, Annette (eds.), *Cold War Cultures: Perspectives on Eastern and Western European Societies* (New York, 2012).

Ludwig, Andreas, "Gab es eine materielle Kultur West-Berlins?," *Zeithistorische Forschungen/Studies in Contemporary History* 11 (2014) 2, pp. 272–87.

MacDougall, Carla, "In the Shadow of the Wall. Urban Space and Everyday Life in Kreuzberg," in: Timothy Brown and Lorena Anton (eds.), *Between the Avantgarde and the Everyday. Subversive Politics in Europe from 1957 to the Present* (New York/Oxford, 2011), pp. 154–73.

MacDougall, Carla, *Cold War Capital: Contested Urbanity in West Berlin, 1963–1989* (PhD Dissertation, Rutgers University, 2011).

MacDougall, Carla, "'We Too Are Berliners'. Protest, Symbolism, and the City in Cold War Germany," in: Belinda Davis, Wilfried Mausbach, Martin Klimke, and Carla MacDougall (eds.), *Changing The World, Changing Oneself. Political Protest and Collective Identities in West Germany and the U.S. in the 1960s and 1970s* (New York/Oxford, 2012), pp. 83–101.

Mailänder, Ulf/Zander, Ulrich (eds.), *Das kleine Westberlin-Lexikon. Von „Autonome" bis „Zapf"—die alternative Szene der siebziger und achtziger Jahre* (Berlin, 2003).

Major, Patrick, *Behind the Berlin Wall: East Germany and the Frontiers of Power* (Oxford, 2010).

Miller, Jennifer A., *Turkish Guest Workers in Germany. Hidden Lives and Contested Borders, 1960s to 1980s* (Toronto, 2018).

Nehring, Holger, "Review Article: What was the Cold War?," *English Historical Review* 127 (2012) 527, pp. 920–49.

Pfeil, Ulrich/Defrance, Corine/Greiner, Bettina (eds.), *Die Berliner Luftbrücke: Erinnerungsort des Kalten Krieges* (Berlin, 2018).

Poiger, Uta G., *Jazz, Rock, and Rebels: Cold War Politics and American Culture in a Divided Germany* (Berkeley, 2000).

Pugh, Emily, *Architecture, Politics, and Identity in Divided Berlin* (Pittsburgh, 2014).

Schöne, Jens, *Ronald Reagan in Berlin. Der Präsident, die Staatssicherheit und die geteilte Stadt* (Berlin, 2016).

Schlegelmilch, Arthur, *Hauptstadt im Zonendeutschland: Die Entstehung der Berliner Nachkriegsdemokratie 1945–1949* (Berlin, 1993).

Steege, Paul, "Finding the There There: Local Space, Global Ritual, and Early Cold War Berlin," in: Gary Backhaus and John Murungi (eds.), *Earth Ways: Framing Geographical Meanings* (Lanham, 2004), pp. 155–72.

Steege, Paul, *Black Market, Cold War: Everyday Life in Berlin, 1946–1949* (New York, 2007).

Redding, Kimberly A., *Growing Up in Hitler's Shadow. Remembering Youth in Postwar Berlin* (Westport, 2004).

Roggenbuch, Frank, *Das Berliner Grenzgängerproblem: Verflechtung und Systemkonkurrenz vor dem Mauerbau* (Berlin, 2008).

Rotenberg, Dirk, *Berliner Demokratie zwischen Existenzsicherung und Machtwechsel. Die Transformation der Berlin-Problematik 1971–1981* (Berlin, 1995).

Rott, Wilfried, *Die Insel: Eine Geschichte West-Berlins, 1948–1990* (Munich, 2009).

Rubin, Eli, "Amnesiopolis: From Mietskaserne to Wohnungsbauserie 70 in East Berlin's Northeast," *Central European History* 47 (2014), pp. 334–75.

Sheffer, Edith, *Burned Bridge. How East and West Germans Made the Iron Curtain* (New York, 2011).

Schlegelmilch, Arthur, *Hauptstadt im Zonen-Deutschland. Die Entstehung der Berliner Nachkriegsdemokratie* (Berlin, 1993).

Schivelbusch, Wolfgang, *In a Cold Crater. Cultural and Intellectual Life in Berlin, 1945–1948* (Berkeley, 1996).

Schürer, Ernst/Keune, Manfred/Jenkins, Philip (eds.), *The Berlin Wall: Representations and Perspectives* (New York, 1996).

Standley, Michaelle A., "From Bulwark of Freedom to Cosmopolitan Cocktails. The Cold War, Mass Tourism and the Marketing of West Berlin as a Tourist Destination," in: Tobias Hochscherf, Christoph Laucht, and Andrew Plowman (eds.), *Divided, but Not Disconnected. German Experiences of the Cold War* (New York, 2013), pp. 105–18.

Stöver, Bernd, *Geschichte Berlins* (Munich, 2010).

Stöver, Bernd, *Der Kalte Krieg: 1947–1991* (Munich, 2017).

Schwane, Daniel, *Wider den Zeitgeist? Konflikt und Deeskalation in West-Berlin 1949–1965* (Stuttgart, 2005).

Taylor, Frederick, *The Berlin Wall. 13 august 1961–9 november 1989* (London, 1996).

Thijs, Krijn, *Drei Geschichten, eine Stadt: Die Berliner Stadtjubiläen von 1937 und 1987* (Cologne, 2008).

Thijs, Krijn, *Party, Pomp und Propaganda. Die Berliner Stadtjubiläen von 1937 und 1987* (Berlin, 2012).

Thijs, Krijn, "West-Berliner Visionen für eine neue Mitte. Die Internationale Bauausstellung, der 'Zentrale Bereich' und die 'Geschichtslandschaft' an der Mauer (1981–1985)," *Zeithistorische Forschungen* 11 (2014) 2, pp. 235–61, zeithistorische-forschungen.de/2-2014/id%3D5097.

Thomsen Vierra, Sarah, *Turkish Germans in the Federal Republic of Germany. Immigration, Space, and Belonging, 1961–1990* (Cambridge, 2018).

Trotnow, Helmut/von Kostka, Bernd (eds.), *Die Berliner Luftbrücke. Ereignis und Erinnerung* (Berlin, 2010).

Urban, Florian, *Neo-historical East Berlin. Architecture and Urban Design in the German Democratic Republic 1970–1990* (Farnham, 2009).

Vasudevan, Alex, "Autonomous Urbanism and the Right to the City: The Spatial Politics of Squatting in Berlin, 1968–2012," in: Bart van der Steen, Ask Katzeff, and Leendert van Hoogenhuijze (eds.), *The City Is Ours. Squatting and Autonomous Movements in Europe from the 1970s to the Present* (Oakland, 2014), pp. 131–52.

Verheyen, Dirk, *United City, Divided Memories? Cold War Legacies in Contemporary Berlin* (Lanham, 2008).

Ward, Janet, *Post-Wall Berlin. Borders, Space and Identity* (New York, 2011).

Ward, Simon, *Urban Memory and Visual Culture in Berlin. Framing the Asynchronous City 1957–2012* (Amsterdam, 2016).

Warnke, Stephanie, *Stein gegen Stein. Architektur und Medien im geteilten Berlin 1950–1970* (Frankfurt am Main, 2009).

Weiss-Sussex, Godela, "Berlin: Myth and Memorialization," in: idem/Katia Pizzi (eds.), *The Cultural Identities of European Cities* (Bern, 2011), pp. 145–64.

Westad, Odd Arne, *The Cold War: A World History* (New York, 2018).

Wildt, Michael/Kreutzmüller, Christoph, *Berlin 1933–1945* (Munich, 2013).

Zierenberg, Malte, *Stadt der Schieber. Der Berliner Schwarzmarkt 1939–1950* (Göttingen, 2008).

Index

* 9 7 8 0 7 5 5 6 3 9 2 3 6 *